GW00888755

Social Security and St

Benefits: A Practical Guide

Social Security and State Benefits: A Practical Guide

Sixth Edition

by Simon Ennals
Solicitor, Essential Rights Legal Practice, and
part-time Chair of Appeals Tribunals

Tottel Publishing Ltd, Maxwelton House, 41–43 Boltro Road, Haywards Heath, West Sussex, RH16 1BJ

A CIP Catalogue record for this book is available from the British Library.

ISBN 10   1 84592 311 1
ISBN 13   978 1 84592 311 2

Typeset by Kerrypress Ltd, Luton, Beds
Printed and bound in Great Britain by Antony Rowe Ltd, Chippenham, Wiltshire

Contents

Table of Cases   xi

Table of Statutes   xii

Table of Statutory Instruments   xiv

Abbreviations and References   xix

1   **Introductory Materials**   1
    1.1   Introduction   1
    1.7   Social Security and benefit rates: 2001 to 2007   4
    1.14   Guides for consideration   49

2   **Assessment of Means**   56
    2.1   Introduction   56
    2.2   General   56
    2.3   Assessment of means for means-tested benefits   56
    2.35   Assessment of means for tax credits   79

3   **Claiming for the Family**   82
    3.1   Introduction   82
    3.2   Assessment of the family unit   82
    3.16   Eligible childcare costs   92

4   **Claims, Decisions and Appeals**   94
    4.1   Introduction   94
    4.2   Claims   95
    4.12   Secretary of State decisions   102
    4.23   Rights of appeal   110

5   **Overpayments and Recovery**   123
    5.1   Introduction   123
    5.2   Overlapping benefits rule   124
    5.3   Payment continuing for too long   125
    5.13   Incorrect award of benefit   131

| | 5.14 | Overpayments of Housing Benefit | 132 |
| | 5.24 | Overpayments of tax credits | 136 |

6	**Income Support**		139
	6.1	Introduction	139
	6.2	Basic rules	139
	6.31	How to claim	153
	6.32	Challenging decisions	153
	6.33	Common problems	154
	6.34	Checklist	155

7	**Income-based Jobseekers Allowance**		158
	7.1	Introduction	158
	7.2	Basic rules	158
	7.23	How to claim	168
	7.24	Challenging decisions	170
	7.25	Common problems	170
	7.26	Checklist	172

8	**Tax Credits**		175
	8.1	Introduction	175
	8.2	Legislation	176
	8.3	Working Tax Credit	176
	8.11	Child Tax Credit	181
	8.14	Calculating the tax credits	183
	8.18	Changes of circumstances and end of year reconciliations	186
	8.19	Annual reviews and renewals	186
	8.23	Administration	188
	8.28	Checklist	190

9	**Housing Benefit, Council Tax Benefit and Discretionary Housing Payments**		192
	9.1	Introduction	192
	9.2	Housing Benefit	192
	9.3	When Housing Benefit cannot be claimed	192
	9.9	Basic rules	195
	9.32	Housing Benefit in special circumstances	205
	9.37	Backdated claims	208
	9.38	Extended payments	209
	9.39	How to claim	211

9.40   Challenging decisions   211
9.45   Common problems   213
9.46   Council Tax Benefit   214
9.47   Second adult rebates   216
9.48   Discretionary housing payments   218

10   Home Renovation Grants   223
10.1   Introduction   223
10.2   Grants available   223
10.3   Disabled facilities grants   224
10.11   Discretionary assistance with housing repairs,
          adaptations and improvements   228
10.12   Energy efficiency grants   229

11   Assessment of Means in Community Care   231
11.1   Introduction   231
11.2   Domiciliary care   231
11.4   Assessment of means in residential care   232
11.14   How residential care affects other benefit entitlement   236

12   National Health Service Benefits   240
12.1   Introduction   240
12.2   Who can claim?   240
12.3   NHS prescriptions   241
12.6   NHS dental treatment   242
12.9   NHS sight tests, glasses and contact lenses   243
12.11   NHS travel costs to and from hospital for treatment   244
12.13   Assessment of means for the low income scheme   246
12.14   Amount payable   247
12.15   How to claim   248
12.16   Common problems   248
12.17   Checklist   248

13   The Social Fund   250
13.1   Introduction   250
13.2   Discretionary Social Fund payments   250
13.11   Regulated Social Fund payments   256
13.15   Challenging decisions   258

14   Child Support Assessments   259
14.1   Introduction   259
14.2   New system from March 2003   259

	14.3	Previous system – a brief guide	260
	14.4	The Child Support maintenance calculation	262
	14.8	Self-employed cases	267

15	**Child Benefit**		268
	15.1	Introduction	268
	15.2	Who can claim?	268
	15.5	Basic rules	270
	15.11	How to claim	272
	15.12	Challenging decisions	273
	15.13	Checklist	273

16	**Contributory Jobseekers Allowance**		275
	16.1	Introduction	275
	16.2	Basic rules	275
	16.17	How to claim	283
	16.18	Challenging decisions	283
	16.19	Common problems	284
	16.20	Checklist	285

17	**Incapacity Benefit and Statutory Sick Pay**		287
	17.1	Incapacity Benefit	287
	17.4	Basic rules	289
	17.13	Disqualification	295
	17.14	How to claim	296
	17.15	Challenging decisions	296
	17.16	Common problems	296
	17.17	Statutory Sick Pay	297
	17.21	How to claim	299
	17.23	Checklist	300

18	**Industrial Disablement Benefit**		302
	18.1	Introduction	302
	18.2	Basic rules	302
	18.7	How to claim	305
	18.8	Length of award	306
	18.9	Disqualification	307
	18.10	Challenging decisions	307
	18.11	Common problems	307
	18.12	Checklist	308

19   Carer's Allowance   310
    19.1   Introduction   310
    19.2   Overlapping benefits rule   310
    19.3   Who can claim?   311
    19.5   Ceasing payment   313
    19.6   How to claim   313
    19.7   Challenging decisions   314
    19.8   Common problems   314
    19.9   Checklist   315

20   Parenthood Benefits   317
    20.1   Introduction   317
    20.2   Statutory Maternity Pay   317
    20.8   State Maternity Allowance   320
    20.15   Sure Start Maternity Grants   323
    20.19   New paternity and adoption benefits   324
    20.20   Statutory Adoption Pay   325
    20.22   Statutory Paternity Pay (adoption)   325
    20.24   Statutory Paternity Pay (birth)   326
    20.26   Dismissal and payment   327
    20.27   Challenging decisions   327
    20.28   Checklist   328

21   Retirement Pensions   330
    21.1   Introduction   330
    21.2   Overlapping benefits rule   330
    21.3   Basic rules   331
    21.10   How to claim   333
    21.11   Challenging decisions   334
    21.12   Common problems   334
    21.13   Checklist   335

22   Bereavement Benefits   336
    22.1   Introduction   336
    22.2   Basic rules affecting all bereavement benefits   336
    22.3   Bereavement payments   337
    22.4   Widowed Parent's Allowance   337
    22.5   Bereavement Allowance   337
    22.6   Rates   339
    22.9   Overlapping benefits rule   339

22.10	Additional help with other linked benefits	340
22.11	How to claim	340
22.12	Challenging decisions	341
22.13	Checklist	341

23 Disability Living Allowance   **343**

23.1	Introduction	343
23.2	Disability Living Allowance care component	343
23.9	Disability Living Allowance mobility component	347
23.17	How to claim	351
23.18	Challenging decisions	352
23.19	Common problems	353
23.20	Checklist	354

24 Attendance Allowance   **356**

24.1	Introduction	356
24.2	Lower rate	357
24.6	Higher rate	359
24.7	How to claim	360
24.8	Challenging decisions	361
24.9	Common problems	361
24.10	Checklist	363

25 Pension Credit   **364**

25.1	Introduction	364
25.2	Key changes	364
25.3	Who can claim?	364
25.6	Calculating the guarantee credit	365
25.11	Calculating income and capital	367
25.12	Calculating the savings credit	368
25.13	Claims and backdating	369
25.14	Challenging decisions	369
25.15	Assessed income periods	369
25.16	People in residential care or nursing homes and hospitals	370
25.17	Checklist	370

Index   **373**

Table of Cases

References at the right-hand side of the columns are to para number

CDLA/2879/2004 .... 23.12
CDLA/2899/2004 .... 23.12
CIB/14332/96 .... 17.12
CIB/15804/96 .... 17.12
CIB/16237/96 .... 17.12
CIB/3013/97 .... 17.12
CIS/159/90 .... 5.6
CIS/4348/2003 .... 5.6
CSIB/12/96 .... 17.12
CSIB/13/96 .... 17.12
CSIS/17/96 .... 17.12
CSIB/38/96 .... 17.12
Francis v Secretary of State for Work & Pensions [2005] EWCA Civ
    1303 .... 13.12
Page v Chief Adjudication Officer (1991) Times, 4 July 5.4
R v Penwith District Council Housing Benefit Review, ex p Burt
    (1990) 22 HLR 292 .... 9.36, 11.16
R v Sefton Metropolitan Borough Council, ex p Help the Aged and
    Blanchard (1997) 1 CCLR 57 .... 11.11
R(G)3/83 .... 9.37
R(M)1/88 .... 23.12
Robson v Secretary of State for Social Services (1981) 3 FLR 232 .... 3.6
R(S)3/79 .... 9.37
R(SB)21/82 .... 5.6
R(SB)28/83 .... 5.6
R(SB)8/85 .... 3.4
R(SB)19/85 .... 3.4

Table of Statutes

References at the right-hand side of the columns are to para number

Child Support Act 1991 .... 14.1
  s 46.. 14.3
Child Support Pensions and Social Security Act 2000 .... 4.11, 4.25,
                                                                14.1, 21.1
  s 69, 70.. 9.48
Children Act 1989
  s 17(10)... 6.26
Chronically Sick and Disabled Persons Act 1970
  s 2... 11.2
Civil Partnership Act 2004 .... 2.3, 3.1, 3.2, 3.5
Employment and Training Act 1973
  s 2.. 7.22, 16.16
Health and Social Care Act 2001
  s 49.. 11.2
    54... 11.13
Health and Social Services and Social Security Adjudications
   Act 1983
  s 17(3)... 11.2
Housing Grants, Construction and Regeneration Act 1996 ..... 10.2
Jobseekers Act 1995
  s 2.. 16.6
Mental Health Act 1983
  s 117.. 11.2
National Assistance Act 1948 .... 9.8
Pensions Act 1995 .... 21.1
Social Security Act 1986 .... 5.4, 21.1
Social Security Act 1998 .... 4.11, 4.18, 4.25
  s 12, 13.. 4.36
    15.. 4.37
Social Security Administration Act 1992 .... 4.11
  s 71(1)... 5.3
    (3).. 5.9
    74(1)(b)... 5.2
Social Security Contributions and Benefits Act 1992
  Pt V... 4.12
  s 1... 4.3
    21.. 16.6

Social Security Contributions and Benefits Act 1992 – *contd*
  s 64–66.. 13.15
    70.. 19.3
    126(3)... 6.28
    130(1)(a)... 9.5
    137.. 3.2
    142.. 15.5
    171ZL... 20.20
Social Security Administration (Fraud) Act 1997 .... 5.17
Social Security Fraud Act 2001
  s 16... 5.17, 5.21
Social Security (Recovery of Benefits) Act 1997 .... 4.11
Social Security (Transfer of Functions, etc) Act 1999 .... 4.11
Tax Credits Act 2002 .... 4.1, 8.2
  s 3... 3.2, 8.5, 8.6, 8.12
    (1)... 4.4
    6.. 2.35
    7.. 8.18
    14–20.. 4.10
    28.. 5.24
Welfare Reform and Pensions Act 1999 .... 14.1, 21.1, 22.1

Table of Statutory Instruments

References at the right-hand side of the columns are to para number

Child Benefit (General) Regulations 2003 (SI 2003 No 493)
reg 30, 31 .... 15.2
Child Support (Maintenance Assessments and Special Cases)
Regulations 1992 (SI 1992 No 1815) 14.4
Child Tax Credit Regulations (SI 2002 No 2007) 8.2, 8.5
reg 2–5 .... 3.2, 8.12
7(3), (4) 8.13
8 .... 8.13
Children (Leaving Care) (England) Regulations 2001 (SI 2001
No 2874) 6.26
Council Tax Benefit (General) Regulations 1992 (SI 1992
No 1814) 9.28
reg 1, 5–7 .... 3.2
8 .... 9.19, 9.20
12–37 .... 2.8
28 .... 9.27
Sch 1 .... 9.19, 9.20
Sch 3 .... 2.8, 9.22
Sch 4 .... 2.8, 9.25
Sch 5 .... 2.8, 9.27
Discretionary Financial Assistance Regulations 2001 (SI 2001
No 1167) 9.48
reg 6(3) 9.51
8(1) 9.54
(2) 9.52
Discretionary Housing Payments (Grants) Order 2001 (SI 2001
No 2340) 9.48
Housing Benefit and Council Tax Benefit (Decisions and
Appeals) Regulations 2001 (SI 2001 No 1002) 4.11
reg 5 .... 4.25
11 .... 4.13
(1) 4.14
12 .... 4.14
15 .... 4.25

Housing Benefit (General) Regulations 1987 (SI 1987 No 1971)
reg 5(5)(d), (e) 9.33
    (7)(a) 9.33
    (8) 9.34
    6 .... 9.5
    7 .... 9.4
    8 .... 9.8
    10 .... 9.12
    12–15 .... 3.2
    16 .... 9.19, 9.20
    37 .... 9.6, 9.27
    19–45 .... 2.7
    47 .... 9.7
    62A 9.38
    63 .... 9.31
    91 .... 9.39
Sch 1 .... 9.13, 9.16
Sch 2 .... 9.19, 9.20
Sch 3 .... 2.7, 9.22
Sch 4 .... 2.7, 9.25
Sch 5 .... 2.7, 9.27, 9.28
Sch 5A
    para (2) 9.38
**Income Support (General) Regulations 1987 (SI 1987
No 1967)** 6.1
reg 2 .... 3.2
    5(4) 6.28
    7(9) 11.8
    13 .... 6.25
    14–16 .... 3.2
    17 .... 6.5, 6.6, 6.18
    28–32, 35–39 .... 2.4
    40 .... 2.4
      (2) 6.19
    41–43 .... 2.4
    45 .... 2.4, 11.6
    46 .... 2.4, 6.20
    47–52 .... 2.4
    53 .... 2.4
      (1)–(6) 11.6
Sch 2 .... 6.5, 6.6

Income Support (General) Regulations 1987 (SI 1987 No 1967) – *contd*
  Sch 3 .... 6.18
  Sch 8 .... 2.4
  Sch 9 .... 2.4, 6.19
  Sch 10 .... 2.4, 6.20, 6.21
Jobseeker's Allowance Regulations 1996 (SI 1996 No 207) 2.33
  reg 1 .... 3.2
    16 .... 16.10
    53–55 .... 7.4, 16.10
    72(5A)(b) 16.10
    76–78 .... 3.2
    93–102 .... 2.5
    103 .... 2.5
      (2) 7.19
    104–116 .... 2.5
  Sch 6 .... 2.5
  Sch 7 .... 2.5
  Sch 8 .... 2.5
**Paternity and Adoption Leave Regulations 2002 (SI 2002
  No 2788)** 20.19
**Regulatory Reform (Housing Assistance) (England and Wales)
  Order 2002 (SI 2002 No 1860)** 10.11
**Security Benefits (Computation of Earnings)
  Regulations 1996 (SI 1996 No 2745)**
  Sch 3 .... 19.3
**Social Security Amendment (Discretionary Housing
  Payments) Regulations 2001 (SI 2001 No 2333)** 9.56
**Social Security and Child Support (Decisions and Appeals)
  Regulations 1999 (SI 1999 No 991)** 4.11
  reg 12 .... 4.12
    13(1) 4.14
      (2)(i)–(iii) 4.14
    16 .... 4.13
    17, 18 .... 4.14
    19 .... 4.21
    20 .... 4.22
    25 .... 4.23
    26, 27 .... 4.23
    32 .... 4.24
    33 .... 4.25
    36 .... 4.26

Social Security and Child Support (Decisions and Appeals) Regulations
1999 (SI 1999 No 991) – *contd*
reg 39 .... 4.30
41 .... 4.27
49 .... 4.30
51 .... 4.31
52 .... 4.28
54 .... 4.32
57 .... 4.34
Sch 2 .... 4.23
Social Security and Child Support (Decisions and Appeals)
(Amendment) Regulations 1999 (SI 1999 No 1466) 4.11
Social Security and Child Support (Decisions and Appeals)
Amendment (No 3) Regulations 1999 (SI 1999 No 1670) 4.11
Social Security Benefits (Dependency) Regulations 1977
(SI 1977 No 343)
Sch 2
para 2B 19.4
6 .... 19.4
Social Security (Claims and Payments) Regulations 1979
(SI 1979 No 628) 4.23
reg 24, 25 .... 18.7
Sch 4 .... 18.7
Social Security (Claims and Payments) Regulations 1987
(SI 1987 No 1968) 4.1, 4.3
reg 4(1) 4.41
9 .... 4.3
(1) 4.41
Sch 1 .... 4.3
Social Security Commissioners (Procedure) Regulations 1999
(SI 1999 No 1495) 4.11
reg 5 .... 4.36
9, 33 .... 4.35
Social Security Commissioners (Procedure) (Amendment)
Regulations 2001 (SI 2001 No 1095) 4.11, 4.35
Social Security (Contributions) Amendment (No 4)
Regulations 1991 (SI 1999 No 1632) 4.11
Social Security (General Benefit) Regulations 1982 (SI 1982
No 1408)
Sch 2 .... 18.4

Social Security (Industrial Injuries) (Prescribed Diseases)
  Regulations 1985 (SI 1985 No 967) 18.3
Social Security (Invalid Care Allowance) Regulations 1976
  (SI 1976 No 409)
  reg 3 .... 19.3
    4 .... 19.3, 19.5
    5, 8, 9, 11 .... 19.3
Social Security (Overlapping Benefits) Regulations 1979
  (SI 1979 No 597)
  Reg 6 .... 16.3, 17.16, 19.2, 20.12, 21.2, 22.9
  Sch 1 .... 16.3, 17.16, 19.2, 20.12, 21.2, 22.9
Social Security (Payments on Account, Overpayments and
  Recovery) Regulations 1988 (SI 1988 No 664) 5.10, 5.12
Social Security Uprating Order 2006 .... 1.8
State Pension Credit Regulations 2002 (SI 2002 No 1792)
  reg 14–24 .... 2.9
  Sch 5 .... 2.9
  Sch 6 .... 2.9
Tax Credits (Claims and Notifications) Regulations 2002
  (SI 2002 No 2014) 4.1, 8.2, 8.25
Tax Credits (Definition and Calculation of Income)
  Regulations 2002 (SI 2002 No 2006) 2.35, 8.2
Tax Credits (Income Thresholds and Determination of Rates)
  Regulations 2002 (SI 2002 No 2008) 8.2
Tax Credits (Payments by the Board) Regulations 2002
  (SI 2002 No 2173) 8.2
Working Tax Credit (Entitlement and Maximum Rate)
  Regulations 2002 (SI 2002 No 2005) 8.2, 8.6
  reg 4 .... 8.5, 8.10
    (1) 8.7
    9 .... 8.6, 8.10
    10–18 .... 8.10
  Sch 1 .... 8.6
Working Tax Credit (Payment by Employers)
  Regulations 2002 (SI 2002 No 2172) 8.2, 8.24

Abbreviations and References

CA	=	Carer's Allowance
CSA	=	Child Support Agency
CTB	=	Council Tax Benefit
CTC	=	Child Tax Credit
DEA	=	Disability Employment Adviser
DHP	=	Discretionary housing payment
DLA	=	Disability Living Allowance
HB	=	Housing Benefit
IB-JSA	=	Income-based Jobseekers Allowance
IS	=	Income Support
JSA	=	Jobseekers Allowance
LEL	=	Lower earnings limit
MIG	=	Minimum Income Guarantee
NHS	=	National Health Service
NI	=	National Insurance
NIC	=	National Insurance Contribution
ODPM	=	Office of the Deputy Prime Minister
PC	=	Pension Credit
SAP	=	Statutory Adoption Pay
SDA	=	Severe Disablement Allowance
SERPS	=	State Earnings Related Pension Scheme
SFO	=	Social Fund officer
SMA	=	State Maternity Allowance
SMP	=	Statutory Maternity Pay
SPP	=	Statutory Parternity Pay
SRP	=	State Retirement Pension
SSP	=	Statutory Sick Pay
UEL	=	Upper earnings limit
WTC	=	Working Tax Credit

1 Introductory Materials

Introduction 1.1

The aim of this book is to provide a practical guide to Social Security and State benefit entitlements in a manner that is clear and easy to understand for both claimants and advisers.

The Social Security and State benefit system exists to provide financial assistance to those who meet the entitlement rules laid down by Parliament.

A claim may arise where a claimant is unable to find work, or is unable to work because of ill health, disability, age, or family or caring responsibilities. Additionally, the system provides financial assistance for those claimants who can and do work, but whose income is insufficient to provide for the needs of their family.

Because entitlement to benefits and tax credits is dependent on coming within specified criteria the rules relating to entitlement are often quite complex, requiring claimants to provide a substantial amount of information and evidence to support a claim. This requirement is absolutely essential for the purpose of ensuring that the correct benefit is paid to the correct person, who has a genuine entitlement to claim from the State.

The benefit system is predominately claimant-led, i e it relies on the claimant to know what benefit he might be entitled to and to actually make a claim for that benefit.

Furthermore, there is no one central point from which a claimant can claim all the benefits to which he might be entitled. Claims need to be made to the benefit office authorised to deal with the specific benefit in question.

Most benefits are administered by an agency of the Department for Work and Pensions (DWP). For example, Income Support, Incapacity Benefit, Industrial Injuries Disablement Benefit and Social Fund payments are administered by the local Social Security office, known as Jobcentre Plus; and Disability Living Allowance and Attendance Allowance are administered by the Disability and Carer Benefits Service.

However, tax credits available for those in work and out of work are administered by the HM Revenue & Customs (HMRC) Tax Credits Office; benefits for help with rent and council tax are administered by the claimant's

1

local authority and benefits for those who are unemployed and looking for work are administered by Jobcentre Plus.

So, not only does a claimant need to know what benefit can be claimed, he also needs to know how to claim that benefit and from where it can be claimed.

The contents of this book are as follows.

Introductory materials (Chapter 1) 1.2

Social Security benefit and tax credit rates – These include the main Social Security and State benefit rates relevant to this book, and rates for five previous years.

Benefit guides – These are checklists of potential benefits that might be claimed in certain circumstances, and are included to assist the reader in ensuring that benefit entitlement for an individual is maximised wherever possible.

General matters (Chapters 2–5) 1.3

This section addresses common rules affecting benefit and tax credit entitlement in general and includes:

- assessments of means and capital;
- claiming for the family;
- how to make a claim, understanding the decision and challenging decisions; and
- what to do if too much benefit has been paid.

Means-tested benefits and tax credits (Chapters 6–14) 1.4

This section addresses benefit entitlement which is dependent on a means test – this means that entitlement will be subject to a claimant's income and capital being sufficiently low. This section includes:

- benefits and tax credits that can be claimed by those not working or only working part time;
- benefits and tax credits that can be claimed by those working full time;
- benefits that can be claimed for help with housing and council tax liabilities;

- help with NHS charges;

- help for disabled people who need care;

- access to or responsibility for paying Child Support payments.

Non means-tested benefits (Chapters 15–25)   1.5

This section addresses benefit entitlement that is not necessarily dependent on the income of the claimant, but in most cases will be dependent on either claimants having satisfied specified rules regarding National Insurance contributions (NICs) or being sufficiently disabled, or having the responsibility to care for someone. Any capital that a claimant has will be ignored completely when considering entitlement to these benefits. This section includes:

- benefits for those who cannot work because of illness or disability;

- benefits for those who cannot work because they are caring for a disabled person;

- additional benefit entitlement needed by those who are very disabled; and

- benefits for pensioners, widows and widowers.

Contents of chapters   1.6

Each chapter relating to a specific benefit entitlement contains guidance relating to:

- the basic rules and conditions of entitlement;

- how to claim and what can be expected once a claim has been registered;

- how to challenge a decision that the claimant is not happy with;

- common problems; and

- a claim specification checklist, which includes information concerning important rules and time limits specific to the benefit in question, how difficult or easy the claim form is to complete, details of any other linking benefits that might be claimed, and the effect that the benefit could have on other State benefits of which the claimant is already in receipt.

This book will provide you with the guidance you need to find your way with ease around the benefit maze.

3

Social Security and benefit rates: 2001 to 2007

1.7

Benefit rates 2006/07

1.8

Important note: At the time of going to press, the *Social Security Uprating Order 2006* is awaiting parliamentary approval.

The figures used in this update are those proposed to Parliament, and each relevant government department is working to them until the uprating order is published.

In light of this, readers are advised to check the benefit rates with the relevant government department. Tax rates are those current for 2005/06, since any changes from the Budget 2006 were not known at the time of writing, although rates for NICs and tax allowances for 2006/07 were announced in December 2005, and are included in this work.

Non means-tested benefits increased by RPI – 2.7%. Means-tested benefits increased by ROSSI – 2.2%. However, some benefits and tax credits have increased in excess of these standard rates. The child elements in the Child Tax Credit have increased in line with earnings, as has the State Pension Credit.

Note: Additional payments for dependants (partners/children) can be paid in respect of those benefits marked *. Dependent increases for children were substantially replaced for new claims from April 2003 by the Child Tax Credit. Benefits for those that are protected under the old scheme are marked **.

The additional amounts are set out below.

Weekly rates unless otherwise shown.	£
INCOME SUPPORT	
Personal allowances:	
Single person under 18:	
Higher rate	45.50
Normal rate	34.60
Single person 18–24	45.50
Single person 25+	57.45
Lone parent (LP) 18+	57.45
Lone parent under 18	34.60
Lone parent under 18 and disabled	45.50
Couple, one or both over 18	90.10

Couple both under 18	68.65
Child 15 or under	45.58
Child 16–18	45.58

Premiums:

Family	16.25
Family (LP) **	16.25
Disabled child	45.08
Carer	26.35
Enhanced disability (child)	18.13
Enhanced disability (adult):	
Single person	11.95
Couple	17.25
Disability:	
Single person	24.50
Couple	34.95
Severe disability:	
Single person	46.75
Couple (both qualify)	93.50
Bereavement premium	26.80

Housing costs – non-dependant deductions:

Adult earning £338 per week	47.75
Adult earning £271–£337.99	43.50
Adult earning £204–£270.99	38.20
Adult earning £157–£203.99	23.35
Adult earning £106–£156.99	17.00
Others 18+ and not working or 25+ and on Income Support	7.40

Earnings disregards:

Single person	5.00
Claimant and partner	10.00
Lone parent (LP) ** disabled or carer	20.00

Capital disregarded: £6,000, then tariff income of £1.00 per £250 up to MAXIMUM CAPITAL of £16,000 (for people in residential care, the lower disregard is £10,000, with the same upper limit of £16,000)

HOUSING AND COUNCIL TAX BENEFIT

Personal allowances: same as for Income Support except:

Single person:	
Under 25	45.50
Over 25	57.45
Lone parent under 18	45.50
Family (LP) **	22.20
Pensioners:	
Single – 60–64	114.05
Couple – one or both 60–64	174.05
Single – 65 or over	131.95
Couple – one or both 65 or over	197.65

Non-dependant deductions as for Income Support

Applicable amounts for hospital patients:

From April 2006, benefits are no longer reduced after a stay in
hospital of over 52 weeks

COUNCIL TAX BENEFIT

Non-dependent deduction:

Income below £157	2.30
Income between £157–£270.99	4.60
Income between £271–£337.99	5.80
Income £338 or over	6.95

Housing Benefit and Council Tax Benefit disregards: as for Income Support except:

Earnings disregards:

Lone parent earnings	25.00
Claimant on disability or carer premium	20.00

Other income disregards:

Maintenance	15.00
30-hour working (WTC)	14.90
War pension and war widow	10.00
Voluntary and charitable payments	20.00
Student loans	10.00
Student covenanted income	5.00

Income from boarders plus 50% of balance of charge	20.00
Income from childminding – two thirds	

Capital disregarded: £6,000, then tariff income up to MAXIMUM CAPITAL of £16,000.

Disregarded childminding fees	175.00
	(300.00 for 2 or more)
Fuel deductions:	
Heating	11.95
Hot water	1.40
Lighting	0.95
Cooking	1.40
All fuel	15.70
One room	7.15
Three meals:	
Each adult	20.50
Each child under 16	10.35
Less than three meals:	
Each adult	13.65
Each child under 16	6.85
Breakfast only:	
Each person	2.50
ATTENDANCE ALLOWANCE	
Higher rate	62.25
Lower rate	41.65
CHILD BENEFIT	
First child	17.45
Others	11.70
Child Benefit (LP) **	17.55
GUARDIAN'S ALLOWANCE	
Higher rate	12.50
DISABILITY LIVING ALLOWANCE	
Care component:	
Highest rate	62.65
Middle rate	41.65

Lowest rate	16.50
Mobility component:	
Higher rate	43.45
Lower rate	16.50
CARER'S ALLOWANCE*	
Basic fixed rate	46.95
MATERNITY BENEFITS	
Standard rate Maternity Allowance	108.85
Standard rate Statutory Maternity Pay	108.85
Standard rate Statutory Adoption Pay	108.85
Standard rate Statutory Paternity Pay	108.85
Sure Start Maternity Grant	500.00

WORKING TAX CREDIT

	Annual amounts	Weekly equivalents
Basic element	1,665.00	32.01
Second adult element/Lone parent element	1,640.00	31.53
30-hour element	680.00	13.07
Disability element	2,225.00	42.78
Severe disability element	945.00	18.17
50+ element 16–29 hrs	1,140.00	21.92
50+ element 30+ hrs	1,705.00	32.78
Childcare element (80% of max)		
2+ children	12,480.00	240.00
1 child	7,280.00	140.00
Threshold:		
Income threshold	5,220.00	100.38
Withdrawal rate – 37%		

CHILD TAX CREDIT

	Annual amounts	Weekly equivalents
Family element	545.00	10.45
Additional family element	545.00	10.45
Child element	1,765.00	33.94

Disabled child element	2,350.00	45.19
Severely disabled child element	945.00	18.17

Thresholds:

First income threshold	5,220.00	100.38
First withdrawal rate – 37%		
Second income threshold for family element	50,000.00	958.90
First threshold for those not on IS or IB-JSA and entitled to CTC only	14,155.00	272.21

INCAPACITY BENEFIT*

Long-term	78.50
Short-term under pension age:	
Higher	70.05
Lower	59.20
Over pension age short-term	75.35

Increase for age:

Higher	16.05
Lower	8.25

Transitional Invalidity Allowance:

Higher rate	16.50
Middle rate	10.60
Lower rate	5.30

STATUTORY SICK PAY

Standard rate	70.05

SEVERE DISABLEMENT ALLOWANCE*

Basic amount (claimed before 6/4/01)	47.45

Age related addition:

Age under 40	16.50
Age 40–49	10.60
Age 50–59	5.30

CONTRIBUTORY JOBSEEKERS ALLOWANCE

Age under 18	34.60
Age 18–24	45.50
Age over 25	57.45

BEREAVEMENT BENEFITS
Bereavement payment — 2,000.00
Bereavement Allowance (depends on age) — 25.28–84.25
Widowed Parent's Allowance — 84.25

RETIREMENT PENSION
Category A or B — 84.25
B (lower) spouses — 50.50
C or D — 50.50
C (lower) — 30.20

STATE PENSION CREDIT
Standard minimum guarantee:
Single — 114.05
Couple — 174.05

Additional amount for severe disability:
Single — 46.75
Couple (one qualifies) — 46.75
Couple (both qualify) — 93.50
Additional amount for carers — 26.35

Savings credit:
Threshold – single — 84.25
Threshold – couple — 134.75
Maximum – single — 17.88
Maximum – couple — 23.58

ADDITIONS FOR DEPENDANTS
(a) Addition for spouse/person looking after child if claimant receiving:

State Retirement Pension — 50.50
Incapacity Benefit and claimant over pension age — 46.95
Short-term incapacity and claimant over pension age — 45.15
Short-term incapacity — 35.65
Severe Disablement Allowance — 36.60
Carer's Allowance — 28.05

(b) Addition for children if claimant receiving Incapacity Benefit, Carer's Allowance, Widowed Mother's Allowance or Severe Disablement Allowance if claimed prior to April 2003:

For each child	11.35

(c) Addition for children if claimant over pension age and receiving short-term incapacity:

For each child	11.35

(£11.35 is reduced by £3.65 for eldest child (£7.70))

INDUSTRIAL DISABLEMENT PENSION

Percentage over 18:

100%	127.10
90%	114.39
80%	101.68
70%	88.97
60%	76.26
50%	63.55
40%	50.84
30%	38.13
20%	25.42

NATIONAL INSURANCE CONTRIBUTIONS

Lower earnings limit (LEL)	84.00
Upper earnings limit (UEL)	645.00
Class 2 self-employed	2.10
Small earning exception	4,465.00
Class 3 voluntary	7.55

Class 4 (8%):

Lower profits limit per annum	5,035.00
Upper profits limit per annum	33,540.00

INCOME TAX

Personal Allowances:

Basic	5,035.00
Age related 65–74	7,280.00
Age related 75 and over	7,420.00
Blind person	1,660.00

Income tax rates (see 'important note' above):

Lower band rate (10%)	0–2,090
Basic band rate (22%)	2,090–32,400
Higher band rate (40%)	32,400+

Benefit rates 2005/06   **1.9**

Non means-tested benefits increased by RPI – 3.1%. Means-tested benefits increased by ROSSI – 1.0%. However, some benefits and tax credits increased in excess of these standard rates. The child elements in the Child Tax Credit increased in line with earnings, as did the State Pension Credit.

Note: Additional payments for dependants (partners/children) can be paid in respect of those benefits marked *. Dependent increases for children were substantially replaced for new claims from April 2003 by the Child Tax Credit. Benefits for those that are protected under the old scheme are marked **.

The additional amounts are set out below.

Weekly rates unless otherwise shown.	£
INCOME SUPPORT	
Personal allowances:	
Single person under 18:	
Higher rate	44.50
Normal rate	33.85
Single person 18–24	44.50
Single person 25+	56.20
Lone parent (LP) 18+	56.20
Lone parent under 18	33.85
Lone parent under 18 and disabled	44.50
Couple, one or both over 18	88.15
Couple both under 18	67.15
Child 15 or under	43.88
Child 16–18	43.88
Premiums:	
Family	16.10
Family (LP) **	16.10
Disabled child	43.89
Carer	25.85
Enhanced disability (child)	17.71
Enhanced disability (adult):	
Single person	11.70
Couple	16.90

Disability:
    Single person   23.95
    Couple 34.20
Severe disability:
    Single person 45.50
    Couple (both qualify) 91.00
Bereavement premium 25.85

Housing costs – non-dependant deductions:

Adult earning £322 per week 47.75
Adult earning £258–£321.99 43.50
Adult earning £194–£257.99 38.20
Adult earning £150–£193.99 23.35
Adult earning £101–£149.99 17.00
Others 18+ and not working or 25+ and on Income Support 7.40

Earnings disregards:

Single person 5.00
Claimant and partner 10.00
Lone parent (LP) ** disabled or carer 20.00

Capital disregarded: £3,000, then tariff income of £1.00 per £250 up to MAXIMUM CAPITAL of £8,000 (£16,000 if residential care – £10,000 disregarded).

HOUSING AND COUNCIL TAX BENEFIT

Personal allowances: same as for Income Support except:

Single person:
    Under 25 44.50
    Over 25 56.20
Lone parent under 18 44.50
Family (LP) ** 22.20
Pensioners:
    Single – 60–64 109.45
    Couple – one or both 60–64 167.05
    Single – 65 or over 125.90
    Couple – one or both 65 or over 188.60
Non-dependant deductions as for Income Support

Applicable amounts for hospital patients:

Single claimant	20.50
Couple (both in hospital)	41.00
Couple (only one in hospital) applicable amount reduced by	16.40

COUNCIL TAX BENEFIT

Non-dependent deduction:

Income below £150	2.30
Income between £150–£257.99	4.60
Income between £258–£321.99	5.80
Income £322 or over	6.95

Housing Benefit and Council Tax Benefit disregards: as for Income Support except:

Earnings disregards:

Lone parent earnings	25.00
Claimant on disability or carer premium	20.00

Other income disregards:

Maintenance	15.00
30-hour working (WTC)	14.50
War pension and war widow	10.00
Voluntary and charitable payments	20.00
Student loans	10.00
Student covenanted income	5.00
Income from boarders plus 50% of balance of charge	20.00
Income from childminding – two thirds	

Capital disregarded: £3,000 (if age over 60 – £6,000 disregard) then tariff income up to MAXIMUM CAPITAL of £16,000.

Disregarded childminding fees 175.00
(300.00 for 2 or more)

Fuel deductions:

Heating	10.55
Hot water	1.25
Lighting	0.85
Cooking	1.25

All fuel	13.90
One room	6.32
Three meals:	
Each adult	20.05
Each child under 16	10.15
Less than three meals:	
Each adult	13.35
Each child under 16	6.70
Breakfast only:	
Each person	2.45
ATTENDANCE ALLOWANCE	
Higher rate	60.60
Lower rate	40.55
CHILD BENEFIT	
First child	17.00
Others	11.40
Child Benefit (LP) **	17.55
GUARDIAN'S ALLOWANCE	
Higher rate	12.20
DISABILITY LIVING ALLOWANCE	
Care component:	
Highest rate	60.60
Middle rate	40.55
Lowest rate	16.05
Mobility component:	
Higher rate	42.30
Lower rate	16.05
CARER'S ALLOWANCE*	
Basic fixed rate	45.70
MATERNITY BENEFITS	
Standard rate Maternity Allowance	106.00
Standard rate Statutory Maternity Pay	106.00
Standard rate Statutory Adoption Pay	106.00
Standard rate Statutory Paternity Pay	106.00
Sure Start Maternity Grant	500.00

WORKING TAX CREDIT

	Annual amounts	Weekly equivalents
Basic element	1,620.00	31.15
Second adult element/Lone parent element	1,595.00	30.67
30-hour element	660.00	12.69
Disability element	2,165.00	41.63
Severe disability element	920.00	17.69
50+ element 16–29 hrs	1,110.00	21.34
50+ element 30+ hrs	1,660.00	31.92
Childcare element (70% of max)		
2+ children	10,920.00	210.00
1 child	6,370.00	122.50
Threshold:		
Income threshold	5,220.00	100.38
Withdrawal rate – 37%		

CHILD TAX CREDIT

	Annual amounts	Weekly equivalents
Family element	545.00	10.45
Additional family element	545.00	10.45
Child element	1,690.00	32.50
Disabled child element	2,285.00	43.94
Severely disabled child element	920.00	17.69
Thresholds:		
First income threshold	5,220.00	100.38
First withdrawal rate – 37%		
Second income threshold for family element	50,000.00	958.90
First threshold for those not on IS or IB-JSA and entitled to CTC only	13,910.00	267.50

INCAPACITY BENEFIT*

Long-term	76.45
Short-term under pension age:	
Higher	68.20
Lower	57.65
Over pension age short-term	73.35

Increase for age:

Higher	16.05
Lower	8.05

Transitional Invalidity Allowance:

Higher rate	16.05
Middle rate	10.30
Lower rate	5.15

STATUTORY SICK PAY

Standard rate	68.20

SEVERE DISABLEMENT ALLOWANCE*

Basic amount (claimed before 6/4/01)	46.20

Age related addition:

Age under 40	16.05
Age 40–49	10.30
Age 50–59	5.15

CONTRIBUTORY JOBSEEKERS ALLOWANCE

Age under 18	33.85
Age 18–24	44.50
Age over 25	56.20

BEREAVEMENT BENEFITS

Bereavement payment	2,000.00
Bereavement Allowance (depends on age)	24.62–82.05
Widowed Parent's Allowance	82.05

RETIREMENT PENSION

Category A or B	82.05
B (lower) spouses	49.15
C or D	49.15

ADDITIONS FOR DEPENDANTS

(a) Addition for spouse/person looking after child if
claimant receiving:

	State Retirement Pension	49.15
	Incapacity Benefit and claimant over pension age	45.70
	Short-term incapacity and claimant over pension age	43.95
	Short-term incapacity	35.65
	Severe Disablement Allowance	27.50
	Carer's Allowance	27.30

(b) Addition for children if claimant receiving Incapacity Benefit, Carer's Allowance, Widowed Mother's Allowance or Severe Disablement Allowance if claimed prior to April 2003:

For each child	11.35

(c) Addition for children if claimant over pension age and receiving short-term incapacity:

For each child	11.35

(£11.35 is reduced by £1.70 for eldest child (£9.65))

INDUSTRIAL DISABLEMENT PENSION
Percentage over 18:

100%		123.80
90%		111.42
80%		99.04
70%		86.66
60%		74.28
50%		61.90
40%		49.52
30%		37.14
20%		24.76

NATIONAL INSURANCE CONTRIBUTIONS

Lower earnings limit (LEL)	82.00
Upper earnings limit (UEL)	630.00
Class 2 self-employed	2.10
Small earning exception	4,345.00
Class 3 voluntary	7.35
Class 4 (8%):	
Lower profits limit per annum	4,895.00
Upper profits limit per annum	32,760.00

INCOME TAX	
Personal Allowances:	
Basic	4,895.00
Age related 65–74	7,090.00
Age related 75 and over	7,220.00
Blind person	1,610.00
Income tax rates (see 'important note' above):	
Lower band rate (10%)	0–1,960
Basic band rate (22%)	1,961–30,500
Higher band rate (40%)	30,500+

Benefit rates 2004/05   1.10

Non means-tested benefits increased by RPI – 2.8%. Means-tested benefits increased by ROSSI – 1.8%. However, some benefits and tax credits increased in excess of these standard rates. Retirement pension and bereavement benefits were uprated by more than the RPI. Retirement pension increased by 2.58% for a single pension and 2.57% for a couple. The child elements in the Child Tax Credit increased by significantly more than the rate of inflation.

State Pension Credit increased in line with the rise in earnings.

Note: Additional payments for dependants (partners/children) can be paid in respect of those benefits marked *. Dependent increases for children were substantially replaced for new claims from April 2003 by the Child Tax Credit. Benefits for those that are protected under the old scheme are marked **.

The additional amounts are set out below.

Weekly rates unless otherwise shown.	£
INCOME SUPPORT	
Personal allowances:	
Single person under 18:	
Higher rate	44.05
Normal rate	33.50
Single person 18–24	44.05
Single person 25+	55.65
Lone parent (LP) 18+	55.65
Lone parent under 18	33.50

Lone parent under 18 and disabled	44.05
Couple, one or both over 18	87.30
Couple both under 18	66.50
Child 15 or under	42.27
Child 16–19	42.27

Premiums:

Family	15.95
Family (LP) **	15.95
Disabled child	42.49
Carer	25.55
Enhanced disability (child)	17.08
Enhanced disability (adult):	
Single person	11.60
Couple	16.75
Disability:	
Single person	23.70
Couple	33.85
Severe disability:	
Single person	44.15
Couple (both qualify)	88.30
Bereavement premium	23.95

Housing costs – non-dependant deductions:

Adult earning £293 per week	47.75
Adult earning £235–£292.99	43.50
Adult earning £177–£234.99	38.20
Adult earning £137–£176.99	23.35
Adult earning £92–£136.99	17.00
Others 18+ and not working or 25+ and on Income Support	7.40

Earnings disregards:

Single person	5.00
Claimant and partner	10.00
Lone parent (LP) ** disabled or carer	20.00

Capital disregarded: £3,000, then tariff income of £1.00 per £250 up to MAXIMUM CAPITAL of £8,000 (£16,000 if residential care – £10,000 disregarded).

HOUSING AND COUNCIL TAX BENEFIT

Personal allowances: same as for Income Support except:

Single person:	
Under 25	44.05
Over 25	55.65
Lone parent under 18	44.05
Family (LP) **	22.20
Pensioners:	
Single – 60–64	105.45
Couple – one or both 60–64	160.95
Single – 65 or over	121.00
Couple – one or both 65 or over	181.20
Non-dependant deductions as for Income Support	

Applicable amounts for hospital patients:

Single claimant	19.90
Couple (both in hospital)	39.80
Couple (only one in hospital) applicable amount reduced by	15.90

COUNCIL TAX BENEFIT

Non-dependent deduction:

Income below £144	2.30
Income between £144–£246.99	4.60
Income between £247–£307.99	5.80
Income £308 or over	6.95

Housing Benefit and Council Tax Benefit disregards: as for Income Support except:

Earnings disregards:

Lone parent earnings	25.00
Claimant on disability or carer premium	20.00

Other income disregards:

Maintenance	15.00
30-hour working (WTC)	12.32
War pension and war widow	10.00
Voluntary and charitable payments	20.00
Student loans	10.00

Student covenanted income	5.00
Income from boarders plus 50% of balance of charge	20.00
Income from childminding – two thirds	

Capital disregarded: £3,000 (if age over 60 – £6,000 disregard) then tariff income up to MAXIMUM CAPITAL of £16,000.

Disregarded childminding fees	135.00
	(200.00 for 2 or more)

Fuel deductions:

Heating	9.80
Hot water	1.20
Lighting	0.80
Cooking	1.20
All fuel	13.00
One room	5.90

Three meals:

Each adult	19.85
Each child under 16	10.05

Less than three meals:

Each adult	13.20
Each child under 16	6.65

Breakfast only:

Each person	2.45

ATTENDANCE ALLOWANCE

Higher rate	58.80
Lower rate	39.35

CHILD BENEFIT

First child	16.50
Others	11.05
Child Benefit (LP) **	17.55

GUARDIAN'S ALLOWANCE

Higher rate	11.85
Lower rate	10.15

DISABILITY LIVING ALLOWANCE
Care component:
Highest rate	58.80
Middle rate	39.95
Lowest rate	15.55

Mobility component:
Higher rate	41.05
Lower rate	15.55

CARER'S ALLOWANCE*
Basic fixed rate	44.35

MATERNITY BENEFITS
Standard rate Maternity Allowance	102.80
Standard rate Statutory Maternity Pay	102.80
Standard rate Statutory Adoption Pay	102.80
Standard rate Statutory Paternity Pay	102.80
Sure Start Maternity Grant	500.00

WORKING TAX CREDIT

	Annual amounts	Weekly equivalents
Basic element	1,570.00	30.19
Second adult element/Lone parent element	1,545.00	29.71
30-hour element	640.00	12.30
Disability element	2,100.00	40.38
Severe disability element	890.00	17.11
50+ element 16–29 hrs	1075.00	20.67
50+ element 30+ hrs	1,610.00	30.96
Childcare element (70% of max)		
2+ children	7,280.00	140.00
1 child	4,914.00	94.50
Threshold:		
Income threshold	5,060.00	97.00
Withdrawal rate – 37%		

CHILD TAX CREDIT

	Annual amounts	Weekly equivalents
Family element	545.00	10.45
Additional family element	545.00	10.45
Child element	1,625.00	31.25
Disabled child element	2,215.00	42.59
Severely disabled child element	890.00	17.11

Thresholds:

	Annual amounts	Weekly equivalents
First income threshold	5,060.00	97.00
First withdrawal rate – 37%		
Second income threshold for family element	50,000.00	958.90
First threshold for those not on IS or IB-JSA and entitled to CTC only	13,480.00	259.23

INCAPACITY BENEFIT*

Long-term	74.15
Short-term under pension age:	
Higher	65.15
Lower	55.90
Over pension age short-term	71.15

Increase for age:

Higher	15.55
Lower	7.80

Transitional Invalidity Allowance:

Higher rate	15.55
Middle rate	10.00
Lower rate	5.00

STATUTORY SICK PAY

Standard rate	66.15

SEVERE DISABLEMENT ALLOWANCE*

Basic amount (claimed before 6/4/01)	44.80

Age related addition:

Age under 40	15.55

Age 40–49	10.00
Age 50–59	5.00

CONTRIBUTORY JOBSEEKERS ALLOWANCE

Age under 18	33.50
Age 18–24	44.05
Age over 25	55.65

BEREAVEMENT BENEFITS

Bereavement payment	2,000.00
Bereavement Allowance (depends on age)	23.88–79.60
Widowed Parent's Allowance	79.60

RETIREMENT PENSION

Category A or B	79.60
B (lower) spouses	47.65
C or D	47.65

ADDITIONS FOR DEPENDANTS

(a) Addition for spouse/person looking after child if claimant receiving:

State Retirement Pension	47.65
Incapacity Benefit and claimant over pension age	44.35
Short-term incapacity and claimant over pension age	42.65
Short-term incapacity	34.60
Severe Disablement Allowance	26.65
Carer's Allowance	26.50

(b) Addition for children if claimant receiving Incapacity Benefit, Carer's Allowance, Widowed Mother's Allowance or Severe Disablement Allowance if claimed prior to April 2003:

For each child	11.35

(c) Addition for children if claimant over pension age and receiving short-term incapacity:

For each child	11.35

(£11.35 is reduced by £1.70 for eldest child (£9.65))

INDUSTRIAL DISABLEMENT PENSION

Percentage over 18:

100%	120.10

25

90%	108.09
80%	96.08
70%	84.07
60%	72.06
50%	60.05
40%	48.04
30%	36.03
20%	24.02

NATIONAL INSURANCE CONTRIBUTIONS

Lower earnings limit (LEL)	79.00
Upper earnings limit (UEL)	610.00
Class 2 self-employed	2.05
Small earning exception	4,215.00
Class 3 voluntary	7.15
Class 4 (8%):	
Lower earnings limit per annum	4,745.00
Upper earnings limit per annum	31,720.00

INCOME TAX

Personal Allowances:

Basic	4,745.00
Age related 65–74	6,830.00
Age related 75 and over	6,950.00
Blind person	1,560.00

Income tax rates:

Lower band rate (10%)	0–1,960
Basic band rate (22%)	1,961–30,500
Higher band rate (40%)	30,500+

Benefit rates 2003/04   1.11

Non means-tested benefits increased by RPI – 1.7%. Means-tested benefits increased by ROSSI – 1.7%. However, some benefits for those aged over 60 increased in excess of these standard rates. Retirement pension and bereavement benefits were uprated by more than the RPI. Retirement pension increased by 2.58% for a single pension and 2.57% for a couple.

Minimum Income Guarantee (Income Support to people over 60) is increased in line with earnings.

Note: Additional payments for dependants (partners/children) can be paid in respect of those benefits marked *. Dependent increases for children were substantially replaced for new claims from April 2003 by the Child Tax Credit. Benefits for those that are protected under the old scheme are marked **.

The additional amounts are set out below.

Weekly rates unless otherwise shown.	£
INCOME SUPPORT	
Personal allowances:	
Single person under 18:	
Higher rate	43.25
Normal rate	32.90
Single person 18–24	43.25
Single person 25+	54.65
Lone parent (LP) 18+	54.65
Lone parent under 18	32.90
Lone parent under 18 and disabled	43.25
Couple, one or both over 18	85.75
Couple both under 18	65.30
Child 15 or under	38.50
Child 16–19	38.30
Premiums:	
Family	15.75
Family (LP) **	15.90
Disabled child	41.30
Carer	25.10
Enhanced disability (child)	16.60
Enhanced disability (adult):	
Single person	11.40
Couple	16.45
Disability:	
Single person	23.30
Couple	33.25
Severe disability:	
Single person	42.25
Couple (both qualify)	85.90

Bereavement premium	22.80
Pensioner:	
Single person	47.45
Couple	70.05
Enhanced pensioner:	
Single person	47.45
Couple	70.05
Higher pensioner:	
Single person	47.45
Couple	70.05

Residential allowance:

Private Greater London	72.85
Private elsewhere	65.50
Local authority	77.45
Spending allowance	17.50

Housing costs – non-dependant deductions:

Adult earning £293 per week	47.75
Adult earning £235–£292.99	43.50
Adult earning £177–£234.99	38.20
Adult earning £137–£176.99	23.35
Adult earning £92–£136.99	17.00
Others 18+ and not working or 25+ and on Income Support	7.40

Earnings disregards:

Single person	5.00
Claimant and partner	10.00
Lone parent (LP) ** or disabled	20.00

Capital disregarded: £3,000, then tariff income of £1.00 per £250 up to MAXIMUM CAPITAL of £8,000 (if age over 60 – £6,000 disregard, tariff to £12,000 capital) (£16,000 if residential care – £10,000 disregarded).

HOUSING AND COUNCIL TAX BENEFIT

Personal allowances: same as for Income Support except:

Single person:	
Under 25	43.25
Over 25	54.65

Lone parent under 18	43.25
Family (LP) **	22.20
Non-dependant deductions as for Income Support	

Applicable amounts for hospital patients:

Single claimant	19.35
Couple (both in hospital)	38.70
Couple (only one in hospital) applicable amount reduced by	15.50

COUNCIL TAX BENEFIT

Non-dependent deduction:

Income below £137	2.30
Income between £137–£234.99	4.60
Income between £235–£292.99	5.80
Income £293 or over	6.95

Housing Benefit and Council Tax Benefit disregards: as for Income Support except:

Earnings disregards:

Lone parent earnings	25.00
Claimant on disability or carer premium	20.00

Other income disregards:

Maintenance	15.00
30-hour working (WTC)	11.90
War pension and war widow	10.00
Voluntary and charitable payments	20.00
Student loans	10.00
Student covenanted income	5.00
Income from boarders plus 50% of balance of charge	20.00
Income from childminding – two thirds	

Capital disregarded: £3,000 (if age over 60 – £6,000 disregard) then tariff income up to MAXIMUM CAPITAL of £16,000.

Disregarded childminding fees	94.50
	(140.00 for 2 or more)

Fuel deductions:

Heating	9.65

Hot water	1.20
Lighting	0.80
Cooking	1.20
All fuel	12.85
One room	5.83
Three meals:	
Each adult	19.50
Each child under 16	9.85
Less than three meals:	
Each adult	12.95
Each child under 16	6.55
Breakfast only:	
Each person	2.40
ATTENDANCE ALLOWANCE	
Higher rate	57.20
Lower rate	38.30
CHILD BENEFIT	
First child	16.05
Others	10.75
Child Benefit (LP) **	17.55
GUARDIAN'S ALLOWANCE	
Higher rate	11.55
Lower rate	9.85
DISABILITY LIVING ALLOWANCE	
Care component:	
Highest rate	57.20
Middle rate	38.30
Lowest rate	15.15
Mobility component:	
Higher rate	39.95
Lower rate	15.15
CARER'S ALLOWANCE*	
Basic fixed rate	43.15
MATERNITY BENEFITS	
Standard rate Maternity Allowance	100.00
Standard rate Statutory Maternity Pay	100.00

Sure Start Maternity Grant 500.00

WORKING TAX CREDIT

	Annual amounts	Weekly equivalents
Basic element	1,525.00	29.20
Second adult element/Lone parent element	1,500.00	28.80
30-hour element	620.00	11.90
Disability element	2,040.00	39.15
Severe disability element	865.00	16.60
50+ element 16–29 hrs	1045.00	20.00
50+ element 30+ hrs	1,565.00	30.00
Childcare element (70% of max)		
2+ children	7,301.00	140.00
1 child	4,928.00	94.50

Threshold:

Income threshold	5,060.00	97.00
Withdrawal rate – 37%		

CHILD TAX CREDIT

	Annual amounts	Weekly equivalents
Family element	545.00	10.45
Additional family element	545.00	10.45
Child element	1,445.00	27.75
Disabled child element	2,155.00	41.30
Severely disabled child element	865.00	16.60

Thresholds:

First income threshold	5,060.00	97.00
First withdrawal rate – 37%		
Second income threshold for family element	50,000.00	958.90
First threshold for those not on IS or IB-JSA and entitled to CTC only	13,230.00	253.76

INCAPACITY BENEFIT*

Long-term	72.15
Short-term under pension age:	
Higher	64.35
Lower	54.40
Over pension age short-term	69.20

Increase for age:

Higher	15.15
Lower	7.60

Transitional Invalidity Allowance:

Higher rate	15.15
Middle rate	9.70
Lower rate	4.85

STATUTORY SICK PAY

Standard rate	64.35*

SEVERE DISABLEMENT ALLOWANCE*

Basic amount (claimed before 6/4/01)	43.60

Age related addition:

Age under 40	15.15
Age 40–49	9.70
Age 50–59	4.85

CONTRIBUTORY JOBSEEKERS ALLOWANCE

Age under 18	32.90
Age 18–24	43.25
Age over 25	54.65

BEREAVEMENT BENEFITS

Bereavement payment	2,000.00
Bereavement Allowance (depends on age)	23.24–77.45
Widowed Parent's Allowance *	77.45

RETIREMENT PENSION

Category A or B	77.45
B (lower) spouses	46.35
C or D	46.35

ADDITIONS FOR DEPENDANTS

(a) Addition for spouse/person looking after child if claimant receiving:

State Retirement Pension	46.35
Incapacity Benefit and claimant over pension age	43.15
Short-term incapacity and claimant over pension age	41.50
Short-term incapacity	33.65
Carer's Allowance or Severe Disablement Allowance	25.90

(b) Addition for children if claimant receiving Incapacity Benefit, Carer's Allowance, Widowed Mother's Allowance or Severe Disablement Allowance if claimed prior to April 2003:

For each child	11.35

(c) Addition for children if claimant over pension age and receiving short-term incapacity:

For each child	11.35

(£11.35 is reduced by £1.70 for eldest child (£9.65))

INDUSTRIAL DISABLEMENT PENSION
Percentage over 18:

100%	116.80
90%	105.12
80%	93.44
70%	81.76
60%	70.08
50%	58.40
40%	46.72
30%	35.04
20%	23.36

NATIONAL INSURANCE CONTRIBUTIONS

Lower earnings limit (LEL)	77.00
Upper earnings limit (UEL)	595.00
Class 2 self-employed	2.00
Small earning exception	4,095.00
Class 3 voluntary	6.95
Class 4 (7%):	
Lower earnings limit per annum	4,615.00
Upper earnings limit per annum	30,940.00

INCOME TAX

Personal Allowances:

Basic	4,615.00
Age related 65–74	6,610.00
Age related 75 and over	6,720.00
Blind person	1,510.00

Income tax rates:

Lower band rate (10%)	0–1,960
Basic band rate (22%)	1,961–30,500
Higher band rate (40%)	30,500+

Benefit rates 2002/03   1.12

Non means-tested benefits increased by RPI – 1.7%.

Means-tested benefits increased by ROSSI – 1.7%.

Note: Additional payments for dependants (partners/children) can be claimed in respect of those benefits marked *. Benefits for those that are protected under the old scheme are marked **.

The additional amounts are set out below.

Weekly rates unless otherwise shown.	£
INCOME SUPPORT	
Personal allowances:	
Single person under 18:	
Higher rate	42.70
Normal rate	32.50
Single person 18–24	42.70
Single person 25+	53.95
Lone parent (LP) 18+	53.95
Lone parent under 18	32.50
Lone parent under 18 and disabled	42.70
Couple, one or both over 18	84.65
Couple both under 18	64.45
Child 15 or under	33.50
Child 16–19	34.30

Premiums:

Family	14.75
Family (LP) **	15.90
Disabled child	35.50
Carer	24.80
Enhanced disability (child)	11.25

Enhanced disability (adult):

Single person	11.25
Couple	16.25

Disability:

Single person	23.00
Couple	32.80

Severe disability:

Single person	42.25
Bereavement premium	21.55

Pensioner:

Single person	44.20
Couple	65.15

Enhanced pensioner:

Single person	44.20
Couple	65.15

Higher pensioner:

Single person	44.20
Couple	65.15

Residential allowance:

Private Greater London	71.65
Private elsewhere	64.40
Local authority	75.50
Spending allowance	16.30

Housing costs – non-dependant deductions:

Adult earning £281 per week	47.75
Adult earning £225–£280.99	43.50
Adult earning £170–£224.99	38.20
Adult earning £131–£169.99	23.35
Adult earning £88–£130.99	17.00

Others 18+ and not working or 25+ and on Income Support	7.40

Earnings disregards:

Single person	5.00
Claimant and partner	10.00
Lone parent (LP) ** or disabled	20.00
Maintenance disregard	10.00

Capital disregarded: £3,000, then tariff income of £1.00 per £250 up to MAXIMUM CAPITAL of £8,000 (if age over 60 – £6,000 disregard, tariff to £12,000 capital) (£16,000 if residential care – £10,000 disregarded).

HOUSING AND COUNCIL TAX BENEFIT

Personal allowances: same as for Income Support except:

Single person:	
Under 25	42.70
Over 25	53.95
Lone parent under 18	42.70
Family (LP) **	22.20

Non-dependant deductions as for Income Support

Applicable amounts for hospital patients:

Single claimant	18.90
Couple (both in hospital)	37.80
Couple (only one in hospital) applicable amount reduced by	15.10

COUNCIL TAX BENEFIT

Non-dependent deduction:

Income below £131	2.30
Income between £131–£224.99	4.60
Income between £225–£280.99	5.80
Income £281 or over	6.95

Housing Benefit and Council Tax Benefit disregards: as for Income Support except:

Earnings disregards:	
Lone parent earnings	25.00
Claimant on disability or carer premium	20.00

Other income disregards:

Maintenance	15.00
30-hour working (WFTC or DPTC)	11.65
War pension and war widow	10.00
Voluntary and charitable payments	20.00
Student loans	10.00
Student covenanted income	5.00
Income from boarders plus 50% of balance of charge	20.00
Income from childminding – two thirds	

Capital disregarded: £3,000 (if age over 60 – £6,000 disregard) then tariff income up to MAXIMUM CAPITAL of £16,000.

Disregarded childminding fees 94.50
(140.00 for 2)

Fuel deductions:

Heating	9.40
Hot water	1.15
Lighting	0.80
Cooking	1.15
All fuel	12.50
One room	5.68

Three meals:

Each adult	19.25
Each child under 16	9.70

Less than three meals:

Each adult	12.80
Each child under 16	6.45

Breakfast only:

Each person	2.35

ATTENDANCE ALLOWANCE

Higher rate	56.25
Lower rate	37.65

CHILD BENEFIT

First child	15.75
Others	10.55

Child Benefit (LP) **	17.55
GUARDIAN'S ALLOWANCE	
Higher rate	11.35
Lower rate	9.65
DISABILITY LIVING ALLOWANCE	
Care component:	
Highest rate	56.25
Middle rate	37.65
Lowest rate	14.90
Mobility component:	
Higher rate	39.30
Lower rate	14.90
INVALID CARE ALLOWANCE*	
Basic fixed rate	42.45
MATERNITY BENEFITS	
Lower rate Maternity Allowance	75.00
Higher rate and Statutory Maternity Pay	75.00
Sure Start Maternity Grant	300.00
	(500 from
	16 June 2002)
DISABLED PERSON'S TAX CREDIT	
Maximum adult	
Single claimant	62.10
Couple/lone parent	92.80
30-hour allowance	11.65
Child/young person:	
Age 15 and under	26.45
Age 16–19	27.20
Childcare cost (taper)	70%
Childminding fees	135.00
	(200 for 2 or
	more)
Applicable amount/threshold:	
Single claimant	73.50
Couple/lone parent	94.50
Disabled child allowance	35.50

Taper	55%

Capital disregarded: £3,000, then tariff income up to maximum capital of £16,000.

Child Benefit disregarded

Maintenance disregarded

WORKING FAMILIES TAX CREDIT

Maximum adult

Single claimant or couple	60.00
30-hour addition	11.65

Child/young person:

Age 15 and under	26.45
Age 16–19	27.20
Childcare cost (taper)	70%
Childminding fees	135.00
	(200 for 2 or more)

Applicable amount/threshold:	94.50
Taper	55%

Capital disregarded: £3,000, then tariff income up to MAXIMUM CAPITAL of £8,000.

Child benefit disregarded

Maintenance disregarded

INCAPACITY BENEFIT*

Long-term	70.95

Short-term under pension age:

Higher	63.25
Lower	53.50
Over pension age short-term	68.05

Increase for age:

Higher	14.90
Lower	7.45

Transitional Invalidity Allowance:

Higher rate	14.90
Middle rate	9.50
Lower rate	4.75

STATUTORY SICK PAY

Standard rate 63.25*

SEVERE DISABLEMENT ALLOWANCE* 42.85

Basic amount (claimed before 6/4/01)

Age related addition:

Age under 40	14.90
Age 40–49	9.50
Age 50–59	4.75

CONTRIBUTORY JOBSEEKERS ALLOWANCE

Age under 18	32.50
Age 18–24	42.70
Age over 25	53.95

BEREAVEMENT BENEFITS

Bereavement payment	2,000.00
Bereavement Allowance	75.50
Widowed Parent's Allowance *	75.50

RETIREMENT PENSION

Category A or B	75.50
B (lower) spouses	45.20
C or D	45.20

ADDITIONS FOR DEPENDANTS

(a) Addition for spouse/person looking after child if claimant receiving:

State Retirement Pension	44.14
Incapacity Benefit and claimant over pension age	42.45
Short-term incapacity and claimant over pension age	40.80
Short-term incapacity	33.10
Invalid Care Allowance or Severe Disablement Allowance	25.45

(b) Addition for children if claimant receiving Incapacity Benefit, Invalid Care Allowance, Widowed Mother's Allowance or Severe Disablement Allowance:

For each child	11.35

(c) Addition for children if claimant over pension age and receiving short-term incapacity:

For each child		11.35

(£11.35 is reduced by £1.70 for eldest child (£9.65))

INDUSTRIAL DISABLEMENT PENSION

Percentage over 18:

100%	114.80
90%	103.34
80%	91.86
70%	80.73
60%	68.89
50%	57.41
40%	45.93
30%	34.45
20%	22.96

NATIONAL INSURANCE CONTRIBUTIONS

Lower earnings limit (LEL)	75.00
Upper earnings limit (UEL)	585.00
Class 2 self-employed	2.65
Small earning exception	4,025.00
Class 3 voluntary	7.00
Class 4 (7%):	
Lower earnings limit per annum	4,615.00
Upper earnings limit per annum	30,420.00

INCOME TAX

Personal Allowances:

Basic	4,615.00
Age related 65–74	6,100.00
Age related 75 and over	6,370.00
Blind person	2,110.00

Income tax rates:

Lower band rate (10%)	0–1,880
Basic band rate (22%)	1,881–29,400
Higher band rate (40%)	29,401+

Benefit rates 2001/02 1.13

Non means-tested benefits increased by RPI – 1.1%.

Means-tested benefits increased by ROSSI – 1.6%.

Note: Additional payments for dependants (partners/children) can be claimed in respect of those benefits marked *. Benefits for those that are protected under the old scheme are marked **.

The additional amounts are set out below.

Weekly rates unless otherwise shown.	£
INCOME SUPPORT	
Personal allowances:	
Single person under 18:	
Higher rate	42.00
Normal rate	31.95
Single person 18–24	42.00
Single person 25+	53.05
Lone parent (LP) 18+	53.05
Lone parent under 18	31.95
Lone parent under 18 and disabled	42.00
Couple, one or both over 18	83.25
Couple both under 18	63.35
Child 15 or under	31.45
Child 16–19	32.25
Premiums:	
Family	14.50
Family (LP) **	15.90
Disabled child	30.00
Carer	24.40
Enhanced disability (child)	11.05
Enhanced disability (carer):	
Single carer	11.05
Couple carer	16.00
Disability:	
Single person	22.60
Couple	32.25

<table>
<tr><td>Severe disability:</td><td></td></tr>
<tr><td>   Single person</td><td>41.55</td></tr>
<tr><td>   Bereavement premium</td><td>19.45</td></tr>
<tr><td>Pensioner:</td><td></td></tr>
<tr><td>   Single person</td><td>39.10</td></tr>
<tr><td>   Couple</td><td>57.30</td></tr>
<tr><td>Enhanced pensioner:</td><td></td></tr>
<tr><td>   Single person</td><td>39.10</td></tr>
<tr><td>   Couple</td><td>57.30</td></tr>
<tr><td>Higher pensioner:</td><td></td></tr>
<tr><td>   Single person</td><td>39.10</td></tr>
<tr><td>   Couple</td><td>57.30</td></tr>
</table>

Residential allowance:

Private Greater London	70.45
Private elsewhere	63.30
Local authority	72.50
Spending allowance	16.05

Housing costs – non-dependant deductions:

Adult earning £269 per week	47.75
Adult earning £215–£268.99	43.50
Adult earning £163–£214.99	38.20
Adult earning £125–£162.99	23.35
Adult earning £84–£119.99	17.00
Others 18+ and working or 25+ and on Income Support	7.40

Earnings disregards

Single person	5.00
Claimant and partner	10.00
Lone parent (LP) ** or disabled	15.00

Capital disregarded: £3,000, then tariff income of £1.00 per £250 up to MAXIMUM CAPITAL of £8,000 (if age over 60 – £6,000 disregard, tariff to £12,000 capital) (£16,000 if residential care – £10,000 disregarded).

HOUSING AND COUNCIL TAX BENEFIT

Personal allowances: same as for Income Support except:

    Single person:

Under 25	42.00
Over 25	53.05
Lone parent under 18	42.00
Family (LP) **	22.20
Non-dependant deductions as for Income Support	

Applicable amounts for hospital patients:

Single claimant	18.15
Couple (both in hospital)	36.30
Couple (only one in hospital) applicable amount reduced by	14.50

COUNCIL TAX BENEFIT

Non-dependant deduction:

Income below £125	2.30
Income between £125–£214.99	4.60
Income between £215–£268.99	5.80
Income £269 or over	6.95

Housing Benefit and Council Tax Benefit disregards: as for Income Support except:

Earnings disregards:	
Lone parent earnings	25.00
Claimant on disability or carer premium	15.00
Other income disregards:	
Maintenance	15.00
30-hour working (WFTC or DPTC)	11.45
War pension and war widow	10.00
Voluntary and charitable payments	20.00
Student loans	10.00
Student covenanted income	5.00
Income from boarders plus 50% of balance of charge	20.00
Income from childminding – two thirds	

Capital disregarded: £3,000 (if age over 60 – £6,000 disregard) then tariff income up to MAXIMUM CAPITAL of £16,000.

Disregarded childminding fees	70.00
	(105.00 for 2)

Fuel deductions:

Heating	9.25
Hot water	1.15
Lighting	0.80
Cooking	1.15
All fuel	12.35
One room	5.60

Three meals:

Each adult	18.95
Each child under 16	9.55

Less than three meals:

Each adult	12.60
Each child under 16	6.35
Breakfast only:	
Each person	2.30

ATTENDANCE ALLOWANCE

Higher rate	55.30
Lower rate	37.00

CHILD BENEFIT

First child	15.50
Others	10.35
Child Benefit (LP) **	17.55

GUARDIAN'S ALLOWANCE

Higher rate	11.35
Lower rate	9.70

DISABILITY LIVING ALLOWANCE

Care component:

Highest rate	55.30
Middle rate	37.00
Lowest rate	14.65

Mobility component:

Higher rate	38.65
Lower rate	14.65

INVALID CARE ALLOWANCE*

Basic fixed rate	41.75

MATERNITY BENEFITS

Lower rate Maternity Allowance	53.95
Higher rate and Statutory Maternity Pay	62.20
Sure Start Maternity Grant	300.00

DISABLED PERSON'S TAX CREDIT

Maximum adult:

Single claimant	56.05
Couple/lone parent	86.25
30-hour allowance	11.45

Child/young person:

Age 15 and under	26.00
Age 16–19	26.75
Childcare cost (taper)	70%
Childminding fees	100.00
	(150 for 2 or more)

Applicable amount/threshold:

Single claimant	72.25
Couple/lone parent	92.90
Disabled child allowance	30.00
Taper	55%

Capital disregarded: £3,000, then tariff income up to maximum capital of £16,000.

Child Benefit disregarded

Maintenance disregarded

WORKING FAMILIES TAX CREDIT

Maximum adult:

Single claimant or couple	54.00
30-hour addition	11.45

Child/young person:

Age 15 and under	26.00
Age 16–19	26.75
Childcare cost (taper)	70%
Childminding fees	100.00
	(150 for 2 or more)

Applicable amount/threshold: 92.90

  Taper   55%

Capital disregarded: £3,000, then tariff income up to MAXIMUM CAPITAL of £8,000

Child Benefit disregarded

Maintenance disregarded

INCAPACITY BENEFIT*

  Long-term   69.75

  Short-term under pension age:

    Higher   62.20

    Lower   52.60

  Over pension age short-term   66.90

Increase for age:

  Higher   14.65

  Lower   7.35

Transitional Invalidity Allowance:

  Higher rate   14.65

  Middle rate   9.30

  Lower rate   4.65

STATUTORY SICK PAY

  Standard rate   62.20

SEVERE DISABLEMENT ALLOWANCE*

  Basic amount (claimed before 6/4/01)   42.15

Age related addition:

  Age under 40   14.65

  Age 40–49   9.30

  Age 50–59   4.65

CONTRIBUTORY JOBSEEKERS ALLOWANCE

  Age under 18   31.95

  Age 18–24   42.00

  Age over 25   53.05

BEREAVEMENT BENEFITS

  Bereavement payment   2,000.00

  Bereavement Allowance   72.50

  Widowed Parent's Allowance *   72.50

RETIREMENT PENSION

Category A or B	72.50
B (lower) spouses	43.40
C or D	43.40
C (lower)	25.95

ADDITIONS FOR DEPENDANTS

(a) Addition for spouse/person looking after child if claimant receiving:

State Retirement Pension	43.40
Incapacity Benefit and claimant over pension age	41.75
Short-term incapacity and claimant over pension age	40.10
Short-term incapacity	32.55
Invalid Care Allowance or Severe Disablement Allowance	24.95

(b) Addition for children if claimant receiving Incapacity Benefit, Invalid Care Allowance, Widowed Mother's Allowance or Severe Disablement Allowance:

For each child	11.35

(c) Addition for children if claimant over pension age and receiving short-term incapacity:

For each child	11.35

(£11.35 is reduced by £1.65 for eldest child (£9.70))

INDUSTRIAL DISABLEMENT PENSION

Percentage over 18:

100%	112.90
90%	101.61
80%	90.32
70%	79.03
60%	67.74
50%	56.45
40%	45.16
30%	33.87
20%	22.58

NATIONAL INSURANCE CONTRIBUTIONS

Lower earnings limit (LEL)	67.00

Upper earnings limit (UEL)	535.00
Class 2 self-employed	2.00
Small earning exception	3,955.00
Class 3 voluntary	6.75
Class 4 (7%):	
Lower earnings limit per annum	4,535.00
Upper earnings limit per annum	29,900.00
INCOME TAX	
Personal Allowances:	
Basic	4,535.00
Age related 65–74	5,790.00
Age related 75 and over	6,050.00
Blind person	1,400.00
Income tax rates:	
Lower band rate (10%)	0–1,520
Basic band rate (22%)	1,521–28,400
Higher band rate (40%)	28,401+

Guides for consideration   1.14

These guides are provided to assist in ensuring that claimants have a general awareness of potential benefit entitlement in specific circumstances. The qualifying conditions for entitlement to each specific benefit are contained in the relevant chapters of this book.

These lists are not exhaustive.

Claimant (single or with a partner) is not in work, is aged under 60 and is capable of and available for full-time work   1.15

Consider:

- If the claimant has previously worked and paid sufficient NICs:

  - Contributory Jobseekers Allowance (**CHAPTER 16 CONTRIBU-TORY JOBSEEKERS ALLOWANCE**);

- ○ Income-based Jobseekers Allowance* (**CHAPTER 7 INCOME–BASED JOBSEEKERS ALLOWANCE**) (if the claimant has dependants and/or housing costs);

- ○ Council Tax Benefit* (**CHAPTER 9 HOUSING BENEFIT, COUNCIL TAX BENEFIT AND DISCRETIONARY HOUSING PAYMENTS**); and

- ○ Housing Benefit* (**CHAPTER 9**) (if the claimant pays rent).

- ● If the claimant has *not* previously worked or has not paid sufficient NICs:

- ○ Income-based Jobseekers Allowance* (**CHAPTER 7**);

- ○ Council Tax Benefit** (**CHAPTER 9**); and

- ○ Housing Benefit** (**CHAPTER 9**) (if the claimant pays rent).

*   Income-based Jobseekers Allowance cannot be claimed if the claimant is working for 16 hours or more per week, or the claimant's partner is working for 24 hours or more per week; or the claimant and partner jointly have £16,000 or more in savings and capital.

** Housing Benefit and Council Tax Benefit cannot be claimed if the claimant and partner jointly have £16,000 or more in savings and capital.

Claimant incapable of work (single or with a partner)   1.16

Consider:

- ● If the claimant has previously worked and paid sufficient NICs:

- ○ Statutory Sick Pay or Incapacity Benefit (**CHAPTER 17 INCAPACITY BENEFIT AND STATUTORY SICK PAY**) (short-term lower rate for the first 28 weeks); followed by Incapacity Benefit (short-term higher rate for the next 24 weeks); followed by Incapacity Benefit (long-term rate);

- ○ Income Support* (**CHAPTER 6 INCOME SUPPORT**) (if the claimant is under 60 and has dependants and/or housing costs);

- ○ Pension Credit** (**CHAPTER 25 PENSION CREDIT**) (if the claimant or partner is aged 60 or over);

- ○ Council Tax Benefit*** (**CHAPTER 9 HOUSING BENEFIT, COUNCIL TAX BENEFIT AND DISCRETIONARY HOUSING PAYMENTS**);

- ○ Housing Benefit*** (**CHAPTER 9**) (if the claimant pays rent);

      ○   Disablement Benefit (**CHAPTER 18 INDUSTRIAL DISABLEMENT BENEFIT**) (if incapacity is caused by an industrial accident or disease);

      ○   Disability Living Allowance (**CHAPTER 23 DISABILITY LIVING ALLOWANCE**) (if the claimant needs attention, supervision, or has problems with mobility); and

      ○   (also consider Carer's Allowance (**CHAPTER 19 CARER'S ALLOW-ANCE**) for anyone looking after a disabled claimant).

• If the claimant has not previously worked or has not paid sufficient NICs:

      ○   Incapacity Benefit (see **CHAPTER 17**) *and* Income Support* or Pension Credit** (see **CHAPTERS 6** and **25**);

      ○   Disability Living Allowance (see **CHAPTER 23**) (if the claimant needs attention, supervision, or has problems with mobility);

      ○   Council Tax Benefit*** (see **CHAPTER 9**);

      ○   Housing Benefit*** (see **CHAPTER 9**) (if the claimant pays rent); and

      ○   (also consider Carer's Allowance (see **CHAPTER 19**) for anyone looking after a disabled claimant).

* Income Support cannot be claimed if the claimant is working for 16 hours or more per week; or the claimant's partner is working for 24 hours or more per week; or the claimant and partner jointly have £16,000 in savings and capital.

** Pension Credit can be claimed where the claimant or partner is aged at least 60. There is no limit on a partner's hours of work and no upper capital limit.

*** Housing Benefit and Council Tax Benefit cannot be claimed if the claimant and partner jointly have £16,000 or more in savings and capital.

Claimant working more than 16 hours per week (single or with a partner) 1.17

Consider:

• If the claimant has dependent child/ren:

      ○   Working Tax Credit and Child Tax Credit (**CHAPTER 8 TAX CREDITS**);

    ○   Council Tax Benefit* (**CHAPTER 9 HOUSING BENEFIT, COUNCIL TAX BENEFIT AND DISCRETIONARY HOUSING PAYMENTS**); and

    ○   Housing Benefit* (**CHAPTER 9**) (if the claimant pays rent).

●   If the claimant is disabled, with or without children:

    ○   Working Tax Credit (**CHAPTER 8**);

    ○   Disability Living Allowance (**CHAPTER 23 DISABILITY LIVING ALLOWANCE**) (if the claimant needs attention, supervision, or has problems with mobility);

    ○   Disablement Benefit (**CHAPTER 18 INDUSTRIAL DISABLEMENT BENEFIT**) (if incapacity is caused by an industrial accident or disease);

    ○   Council Tax Benefit* (**CHAPTER 9**); and

    ○   Housing Benefit* (**CHAPTER 9**) (if the claimant pays rent).

*   Housing Benefit and Council Tax Benefit cannot be claimed if the claimant and partner jointly have £16,000 or more in savings and capital.

Claimant is a widow or widower   1.18

Consider:

●   If the claimant has dependent child/ren:

    ○   Bereavement Payment (**CHAPTER 22 BEREAVEMENT BENEFITS**);

    ○   Widowed Parent's Allowance (**CHAPTER 22**);

    ○   Income Support* (under 60) (**CHAPTER 6 INCOME SUPPORT**);

    ○   Pension Credit** (over 60) (**CHAPTER 25 PENSION CREDIT**);

    ○   Social Fund Funeral Payment (**CHAPTER 13 THE SOCIAL FUND**);

    ○   Disability Living Allowance (**CHAPTER 23 DISABILITY LIVING ALLOWANCE**) (if the claimant needs attention, supervision, or has problems with mobility);

    ○   Council Tax Benefit*** (**CHAPTER 9 HOUSING BENEFIT, COUNCIL TAX BENEFIT AND DISCRETIONARY HOUSING PAYMENTS**); and

    ○   Housing Benefit*** (**CHAPTER 9**) (if the claimant pays rent).

●   If the claimant has no dependent child/ren but is aged 45 or over at the date of spouse's death:

○ Bereavement Payment (**CHAPTER 22**);

○ Bereavement Allowance (**CHAPTER 22**);

○ Income Support*(under 60) (**CHAPTER 6**);

○ Pension Credit** (over 60) (**CHAPTER 25**);

○ Social Fund Funeral Payment (**CHAPTER 13**);

○ Disability Living Allowance (**CHAPTER 23**) (if the claimant needs attention, supervision, or has problems with mobility);

○ Council Tax Benefit*** (**CHAPTER 9**); and

○ Housing Benefit*** (**CHAPTER 9**) (if the claimant pays rent).

* Income Support cannot be claimed if the claimant is working for 16 hours or more per week; or the claimant's partner is working for 24 hours or more per week; or the claimant and partner jointly have £16,000 or more (in savings and capital).

** Pension Credit can be claimed where the claimant or partner is aged at least 60. There is no limit on a partner's hours of work and no upper capital limit.

*** Housing Benefit and Council Tax Benefit cannot be claimed if the claimant and partner jointly have £16,000 or more in savings and capital.

Claimant is a pensioner 1.19

Consider:

• Retirement Pension (**CHAPTER 21 RETIREMENT PENSIONS**);

• Pension Credit* (**CHAPTER 25 PENSION CREDIT**);

• Disability Living Allowance (**CHAPTER 23 DISABILITY LIVING ALLOWANCE**) (if the claimant is aged under 65 and needs attention, supervision, or has problems with mobility); or Attendance Allowance (**CHAPTER 24 ATTENDANCE ALLOWANCE**) (if the claimant is aged 65 or over and needs attention or supervision);

• Council Tax Benefit** (**CHAPTER 9 HOUSING BENEFIT, COUNCIL TAX BENEFIT AND DISCRETIONARY HOUSING PAYMENTS**);

• Housing Benefit** (**CHAPTER 9**) (if the claimant pays rent); or

• (also consider Carer's Allowance (**CHAPTER 19 CARER'S ALLOWANCE**) for anyone looking after the claimant).

* Pension Credit can be claimed where the claimant or partner is aged at least 60. There is no limit on hours of work, and no upper capital limit.

** Housing Benefit and Council Tax Benefit cannot be claimed if the claimant and partner jointly have £16,000 or more in savings and capital.

Claimant unable to work because caring for a disabled person for more than 35 hours per week

1.20

Consider:

- Carer's Allowance (**CHAPTER 19 CARER'S ALLOWANCE**);

- Income Support*(under 60) (**CHAPTER 6 INCOME SUPPORT**);

- Pension Credit** (over 60) (**CHAPTER 25 PENSION CREDIT**);

- Council Tax Benefit*** (**CHAPTER 9 HOUSING BENEFIT, COUNCIL TAX BENEFIT AND DISCRETIONARY HOUSING PAYMENTS**); and

- Housing Benefit*** (**CHAPTER 9**) (if the claimant pays rent).

* Income Support cannot be claimed if the claimant is working for 16 hours or more per week; or the claimant's partner is working for 24 hours or more per week; or the claimant and partner jointly have £16,000 or more in savings and capital.

** Pension Credit can be claimed where the claimant or partner is aged at least 60. There is no limit on a partner's hours of work and no upper capital limit.

*** Housing Benefit and Council Tax Benefit cannot be claimed if the claimant and partner jointly have £16,000 or more in savings and capital.

Claimant is a single parent not working 16 hours or more, with dependent children who are under the age of 16

1.21

Consider:

- Income Support* (**CHAPTER 6 INCOME SUPPORT**);

- Child Benefit (**CHAPTER 15 CHILD BENEFIT**);

- Child Tax Credit (**CHAPTER 8 TAX CREDITS**);

- Disability Living Allowance (**CHAPTER 23 DISABILITY LIVING ALLOWANCE**) (if the claimant needs attention, supervision, or has problems with mobility);

- Council Tax Benefit** (**CHAPTER 9 HOUSING BENEFIT, COUNCIL TAX BENEFIT AND DISCRETIONARY HOUSING PAYMENTS**); and

- Housing Benefit** (**CHAPTER 9**) (if the claimant pays rent).

* Income Support cannot be claimed if the claimant is working for 16 hours or more per week or the claimant has £16,000 or more in savings and capital.

** Housing Benefit and Council Tax Benefit cannot be claimed if the claimant has £16,000 or more in savings and capital.

2   Assessment of Means

Introduction   2.1

The assessment of entitlement to Social Security benefits and tax credits will, in most cases, require an assessment of means of the claimant, his partner and any member of the claimant's family for whom he is claiming benefit. Claims for means-tested benefits and tax credits will require extensive detailed information and evidence of means. Some non means-tested benefits will require an assessment of means, but to a far lesser extent.

General   2.2

The assessment of means for the purpose of entitlement to means-tested benefits will address all the income and capital that belongs to, or is available to, a claimant, his partner (including same sex partners) and any dependent child who lives with the claimant and, where housing costs are being considered in the assessment of entitlement to benefit, the income of any other person living as a member of the claimant's household.

The assessment of means for the purpose of entitlement to tax credits will address the income of the claimant and, if appropriate, his partner. No account is taken of capital, although income derived from capital is included. The assessment of income for tax credits is significantly different from means-tested benefits, with the primary difference being that annual gross income is assessed, rather than weekly net income.

The assessment of means for the purpose of entitlement to non means-tested benefits will only address certain types of income that belongs to or is available to the claimant and, where any dependant addition is claimed, any income belonging or available to the dependent partner and/or child. There will be no assessment of capital.

Assessment of means for
means-tested benefits   2.3

All references to the assessment of means of a claimant shall extend to mean the assessment of means jointly applying to a claimant and any same or opposite sex partner or spouse residing with the claimant as a member of his family. Under the *Civil Partnership Act 2004*, in force from December 2005, civil partners are treated, for Social Security and tax credit purposes, in the same way as spouses. Even where no civil partnership has been entered into, where two people of the same sex are living together as if they were in a civil partnership, then in common with opposite sex couples, they will be treated as a couple for the purposes of means-tested benefits and tax credits.

The rules relating to the assessment of means are contained in the general regulations relating to the specific benefit in question. However, the provisions of each set of individual regulations are very similar, taking into account five elements and principles of income:

- *Capital* – Prescribing capital limits for claiming benefits, provisions for the assessment of capital, and provisions for the disregarding of capital in certain circumstances (this information is contained in the schedules to the regulations).

- *Income* – Prescribing the treatment of income for couples, how income should be calculated on a weekly basis, and the period over which income should be assessed.

- *Earned income from employment* – Prescribing details of how income from earned employment will be assessed and provisions for the disregarding of income in certain circumstances (this information is contained in the schedules to the regulations).

- *Income from self-employment* – Prescribing details of how income from self-employment will be assessed and provisions for the disregarding of income and expenses in certain circumstances (this information is contained in the schedules to the regulations).

- *Other income* – Prescribing details of how income which is not earned income will be assessed and provisions for the disregarding of certain types of income (this information is contained in the schedules to the regulations).

The regulations relevant to the assessment of income and capital are as follows.

Chapter 6 Income Support   2.4

(*Income Support (General) Regulations 1987 (SI 1987 No 1967)*).

- Capital – *Regulations 45–53, Sch 10*.

- Income – *Regulations 28–32*.

- Earned income from employment – *Regulations 35–36, Sch 8*.

- Income from self-employment – *Regulations 37–39, Sch 8*.

- Other income – *Regulations 40–43, Sch 9*.

Chapter 7 Income-based Jobseekers Allowance   2.5

(Jobseeker's Allowance Regulations 1996 (SI 1996 No 207)).

- Capital – *Regulations 107–116, Sch 8.*
- Income – *Regulations 93–97.*
- Earned income from employment – *Regulations 98–99, Sch 6.*
- Income from self-employment – *Regulations 100–102, Sch 6.*
- Other income – *Regulations 103–106, Sch 7.*

Chapter 9 Housing Benefit and Council Tax Benefit   2.6

Housing Benefit   2.7

(Housing Benefit (General) Regulations 1987 (SI 1987 No 1971)).

- Capital – *Regulations 37–45, Sch 5.*
- Income – *Regulations 19–27.*
- Earned income from employment – *Regulations 28–29, Sch 3.*
- Income from self-employment – *Regulations 30–32, Sch 3.*
- Other income – *Regulations 33–36, Sch 4.*

Council Tax Benefit   2.8

(Council Tax Benefit (General) Regulations 1992 (SI 1992 No 1814)).

- Capital – *Regulations 28–37, Sch 5.*
- Income – *Regulations 12–18.*
- Earned income from employment – *Regulations 19–20, Sch 3.*
- Income from self-employment – *Regulations 21–23, Sch 3.*
- Other income – *Regulations 24–27, Sch 4.*

Chapter 25 Pension Credit   2.9

(State Pension Credit Regulations 2002 (SI 2002 No 1792)).

- Capital – *Regulations 18–24, Sch 5.*

- Income – *Regulations 14–18, Sch 6*.

- For Pension Credit, many of the detailed rules relating to the assessment of income are found in the *State Pension Credit Act 2002* itself.

Capital   2.10

Where the aggregated capital of a claimant and any partner exceeds the capital limit for claiming any particular means-tested benefit, there will be no entitlement to that benefit, except for Pension Credit, which has no upper capital limit. The capital limit for claiming other means-tested benefits is:

- £16,000 for Income Support and income-based Jobseekers Allowance (increased from £8,000 from April 2006);

- £16,000 for Housing Benefit and Council Tax Benefit;

- £16,000 for claimants who are in permanent residential or nursing home care. This capital limit applies to all means-tested benefits.

The first £6,000 of any assessed capital belonging to a claimant and partner will be ignored in an assessment of entitlement to any means-tested benefit. This limit was increased from £3,000 in respect of Income Support and income-based Jobseekers Allowance from April 2006.

The first £10,000 of any assessed capital belonging to a claimant in permanent residential or nursing home care will be ignored.

From October 2003, the Pension Credit replaced the Minimum Income Guarantee as the way of paying means-tested support to people over 60. There is no upper capital limit for this credit, and the rate of assumed 'tariff income' from capital over the threshold of £6,000 is £1 for every £500.

Any capital a claimant and partner have or are treated as having which exceeds the amount disregarded (i e £6,000 or £10,000) will attract what is called a 'tariff income' for the purposes of any assessment of entitlement to means-tested benefits.

This tariff income will be assessed at £1 per week for every £250 (or part thereof) (£500 in the case of Pension Credit) by which the capital of the claimant and partner exceeds the disregarded amount, up to the capital limit. It is, however, important to point out that any income the claimant and partner receive from capital is entirely ignored.

For instance, a claimant and partner under the age of 60 have savings, capital and investments to the value of £8,530. The first £6,000 will be ignored and the remaining £2,530 will attract a tariff income of £11 per week. This amount will be added to the claimant's weekly income for the assessment of entitlement to a means-tested benefit.

Any capital belonging to a dependent child of the claimant or his partner will be completely ignored in the assessment of the claimant's capital. However, capital of more than £3,000 belonging to a child may affect the claimant's entitlement to benefit for that dependent child (see **CHAPTER 3 CLAIMING FOR THE FAMILY**).

Table of tariff income   2.11

If the claimant holds capital between the amounts shown, the tariff income will be taken into account up to the capital limit for the relevant means-tested benefit. Since October 2003, the rate of tariff income for the Pension Credit has been £1 per £500.

Capital	Aged under 60	Aged 60 and over	In permanent care
£	£	£	£
Nil–6,000	Nil	Nil	Nil
6,000.01–6,250	1	1	Nil
6,250.01–6,500	2	1	Nil
6,500.01–6,750	3	2	Nil
6,750.01–7,000	4	2	Nil
7,000.01–7,250	5	3	Nil
7,250.01–7,500	6	3	Nil
7,500.01–7,750	7	4	Nil
7,750.01–8,000	8	4	Nil
8,000.01–8,250	9	5	Nil
8,250.01–8,500	10	5	Nil
8,500.01–8,750	11	6	Nil
8,750.01–9,000	12	6	Nil
9,000.01–9,250	13	7	Nil
9,250.01–9,500	14	7	Nil
9,500.01–9,750	15	8	Nil
9,750.01–10,000	16	8	Nil
10,000.01–10,250	17	9	1
10,250.01–10,500	18	9	2

Capital	Aged under 60	Aged 60 and over	In permanent care
£	£	£	£
10,500.01–10,750	19	10	3
10,750.01–11,000	20	10	4
11,000.01–11,250	21	11	5
11,250.01–11,500	22	11	6
11,500.01–11,750	23	12	7
11,750.01–12,000	24	12	8
12,000.01–12,250	25	13	9
12,250.01–12,500	26	13	10
12,500.01–12,750	27	14	11
12,750.01–13,000	28	14	12
13,000.01–13,250	29	15	13
13,250.01–13,500	30	15	14
13,500.01–13,750	31	16	15
13,750.01–14,000	32	16	16
14,000.01–14,250	33	17	17
14,250.01–14,500	34	17	18
14,500.01–14,750	35	18	19
14,750.01–15,000	36	18	20
15,000.01–15,250	37	19	21
15,250.01–15,500	38	19	22
15,500.01–15,750	39	20	23
15,750.01–16,000*	40	20	24

*   Capital limit for claimants under 60 claiming Income Support or income-based Jobseekers Allowance, and all other claimants claiming Housing Benefit and Council Tax Benefit. For Pension Credit, tariff income continues to apply however much capital is held.

Disregarded capital   2.12

Certain types of capital can be totally disregarded so that they do not come into the calculation at all, and the fact that the claimant and/or his partner owns all or any of them will not affect entitlement to means-tested benefits. These are listed in full in the schedules to the regulations, but the most important of them are listed below:

- The main dwelling occupied as the claimant's home, regardless of its value.

- The value of premises purchased by the claimant, which he intends to occupy as his home within 26 weeks or such longer period as may be needed to obtain possession.

- The sale proceeds of any previous home of the claimant which he intends to use to buy a new home within 26 weeks or such longer period as may be needed to complete the purchase.

- Any property occupied by:

  o a partner or relative of the claimant or his family as his home, where that person is either over 60 or incapacitated; or

  o a former partner of the claimant from whom the claimant is neither estranged or divorced (this disregard would cover the situation where, for example, the claimant had to go into a home leaving his spouse living in the matrimonial home); or

  o a former partner who is living as a lone parent.

- The assets of any business owned wholly or partly by the claimant, so long as the claimant is engaged in that business as a self-employed earner (temporary periods of absence due to sickness or disability of the claimant will not affect this exemption). If the business ceases, the assets can continue to be disregarded for a reasonable period to allow for sale. However, if the proceeds of a sale are reinvested in a new business in which the claimant intends to be re-engaged as a self-employed person within 13 weeks of the sale, the exemption will still apply.

- Any payment of arrears of Social Security benefits, but only for 52 weeks from the date of receipt.

- Money received (for example under an insurance policy) for the purpose of replacing the loss of, or repairing damage to, the claimant's home or personal possessions, or any loan or other sum acquired for essential repairs or improvements to the home, for 26 weeks or such longer period as is reasonable.

- Any personal possessions of the claimant except those acquired by the claimant with the intention of reducing his capital for the purpose of obtaining benefit or increased benefit. So, if the claimant spends £10,000 on a diamond ring for his spouse and then claims benefit, the ring is unlikely to be disregarded under this heading.

- Damages recovered for personal injury to the claimant, which have been placed in trust (for Pension Credit there is no requirement that the damages are placed in trust in order for them to be disregarded). From

October 2006, it is intended to introduce a 12 month period of grace from receipt of a personal injury award, during which time it will be disregarded.

• The surrender value of a life insurance policy.

• Where payment of capital is being made by instalments, the right to receive any outstanding instalments. (This disregard apparently only covers the right to receive the payments, not the payments themselves. If the claimant has the right to receive £5,000 over the next two years that right could be assigned to a third party for a price. It is that price which is to be disregarded. So far as the payments themselves are concerned, regulations provide that if the total of any remaining instalments when added to the claimant's other capital would take him over the capital limit, any such instalments are to be treated as income and not capital.)

• Any Social Fund payment.

Capital taken into account   2.13

If the capital does not fall within any of the disregards contained in the regulations (see **2.12** above), the next question is whether it is of such a nature that it has to be taken into account.

Capital includes all assets of any kind owned by the claimant and will thus include money saved in the home, bank or building society accounts, premium bonds, stocks and shares, unit trusts, items of value such as paintings, stamp collections etc. Also included will be items such as debts or other assets which have a market value and can be sold, even though they may not be payable until some future date. For example, in Commissioner's decision *R(SB)31/83* the claimant sold a house and left £4,000 outstanding on a private mortgage, to be redeemed in six months' time. It was held that the mortgage had a value, which must be taken into account as a capital resource.

Personal possessions, such as wedding rings, clothes, ornaments etc, will be disregarded as stated in **2.12** above unless they have clearly been purchased in order to reduce capital.

Ownership   2.14

Only capital which is beneficially owned by the claimant will be taken into account as capital. If the claimant only holds property as a trustee, whether the trust is formal or informal, it should not be held to be part of his capital resources.

Money held by another for the account of, or for the benefit of, the claimant will be counted. So money held by a solicitor or any other third party would be capital owned by the claimant if the claimant can call for it to be transferred to him.

If a husband and wife own the matrimonial home jointly, and the wife stays in the property after divorce by agreement with the husband, the share owned by the husband may be treated as a capital resource. In this sort of situation, however, there may be some difficulty in establishing the present value of the husband's share.

If, as part of a divorce settlement, the claimant transfers a share in the matrimonial home to a child of the family, that again will be treated as a capital resource belonging to the child which, depending upon valuation, might bar a subsequent claim by that child for any means-tested benefit.

Valuation   2.15

Capital is to be valued at its current market or surrender value less:

- in the case where there would be sale expenses, a fixed amount of 10% of the value to cover such expenses; and

- the amount of any encumbrance secured upon it.

The value to be given to any property is that which a willing buyer would pay for the asset. This can mean, in the case of jointly owned property, that a share of an asset may have limited value. For example, where spouses have separated or divorced, leaving one in the jointly owned matrimonial home, with the children, the share of the partner who has left may be very difficult to dispose of. Any prospective buyer of the share would have to consider that he may have to apply to the court for an order for sale in order to gain access to his investment, unless the other joint owner is prepared to join in a sale. This is likely to have a significant effect on how much a buyer would be prepared to pay for the asset, and may even mean that the asset is currently valueless.

However, the value of any property owned but not occupied by the claimant will be ignored for up to six months if the claimant:

- has left the property following the breakdown of his marriage or relationship with his partner;

- is taking reasonable steps to dispose of the property. This could include taking legal steps to reach a financial settlement following divorce, that will include disposal of the matrimonial assets, including the home. If an arrangement is reached for the property to be sold once the youngest child is 17, for example, that is arguably still part of a process of taking steps to dispose of the property, and the six months should be extended to cover this period of time;

- is carrying out essential repairs or renovations in order to occupy the property as his home;

- has acquired the property for occupation but for some good reason cannot move in, for example because it must be adapted for a disabled person prior to his moving in, or because renovations or repairs need to be carried out which could cause harm or be detrimental to the health of a member of his family, for example, if a damp proof course was to be installed which might be harmful to young children and expectant mothers, or if a member of the family suffered from asthma and the work to be carried out was extremely dusty;

- has received a payment of compensation in respect of a damaged or destroyed property which he intends to use for repairs or to acquire another home for his own occupation;

- has sold his home and intends to use the proceeds to purchase another home which will be used for his occupation;

- has obtained money for the express purpose of essential repairs and improvements to his home;

- has deposited money with a housing association as a condition of occupying a home; or

- being a local authority tenant, has obtained a grant to buy the home or to carry out essential repairs or alterations to his home.

Although the above disregards are generally applied for only six months, there is discretion to extend them for longer periods if it is reasonable to do so, with the exception of the disregard following divorce or estrangement. At the end of the period they must be taken into account in full when assessing the claimant's capital.

Notional capital   2.16

Once the amount of the claimant's actual capital has been established, the question of whether he has any notional capital sometimes has to be considered as well.

Notional capital is capital which the claimant does not actually possess but which he is deemed to possess. Subject to certain exceptions, a claimant will be treated as possessing capital of which he has deprived himself for the purpose of securing entitlement to the benefit that he is claiming or increasing the amount of the benefit which he is in receipt of.

Two matters must be established. The first is that there has been an actual deprivation, and the second that such deprivation was for the purpose of securing entitlement or increased entitlement to benefit.

It follows that before the claimant can deprive himself of an asset it must be established that he owned it – if the claimant denies this, the burden of proof rests on the Secretary of State. If that burden is discharged, however, and it is established that the claimant owned the asset, it is then for the claimant to show what has happened to it. If he is unable to produce a satisfactory explanation then it is likely that he will be held still to own it, i e it will be decided that it is still part of his actual capital. So if, for example, it is shown that the claimant has recently received a payment of £10,000, and apart from £2,000 spent on a carpet which the claimant reasonably needed, he is unable to show where the rest went, he will be held still to have capital of £8,000.

If it is shown that there has in fact been deprivation (which includes not only giving away but also exchanging, for example, goods for a cash sum) the question then arises as to the claimant's purpose, and of course here there are obvious difficulties.

No claimant is likely to admit that his purpose in depriving himself of an asset was to be able to claim benefit and so the question must be considered in the light of all the surrounding circumstances, bearing in mind that the burden of proof is on the Secretary of State.

There is a formula for reducing notional capital over a period of time. It is considered unreasonable to treat the claimant as continuing to keep the capital while depriving him of benefit and therefore the theory is that he will spend part of his capital each week in order to live, and so his capital will steadily diminish.

For instance, where a claimant is paying more rent in consequence of his capital, then he should be treated as spending some of that capital on his rent, and thus diminishing his capital amount. Or where the claimant does not qualify for any other means-tested benefit because he has too much capital, then the amount of that means-tested benefit which he would have been awarded but for the capital will also diminish his capital, as in theory he would have to subsidise his living expenses from his capital.

An initial assessment of diminishing capital would not have to be carried out until the claimant makes a further claim for benefit at least 26 weeks after the initial assessment. However, after this point the diminishing capital rule should be applied at intervals of not less than 13 weeks, where so requested in writing by the claimant.

Income 2.17

Income belonging to the claimant and any spouse or partner living with the claimant will be assessed to establish the average weekly income belonging to the claimant for the purpose of establishing any entitlement to a means-tested benefit for the claimant and his family. Any assessment of a weekly income that results in a fraction of a penny will be rounded down to the nearest penny where the fraction is less than 0.5, and rounded up to the nearest penny where the fraction is 0.5 or over.

Where a claimant's income is paid weekly, fortnightly or four-weekly, the actual weekly payment will be established by dividing that payment by the number of weeks for which it is payable.

Where the claimant's income is paid monthly, the payment will be multiplied by twelve and divided by 52 weeks in order to establish an average weekly income.

Where the claimant's income is paid by any other period, the payment will be multiplied by seven and divided by the number of days which the payment period covers.

For example, a payment of £120 paid to a claimant for a specific job over 17 days would be assessed as follows:

£120 × 7 divided by 17 = £49.411. As the fraction is less than 0.5 this total will be rounded down to produce a weekly assessed income of £49.11.

A payment of £121.50 paid for a period of 17 days' work would be assessed as follows:

£121.50 × 7 divided by 17 = £50.029. As the fraction is more than 0.5 this total will be rounded up to produce a weekly assessed income of £50.03.

The period of assessment for employed earnings 2.18

For Housing Benefit and Council Tax Benefit, the assessment period for a claimant's average weekly income from employment will be five consecutive weeks in the six weeks prior to the date of claim or, where paid monthly, the two months falling immediately before the date of claim. Where payments fluctuate and the prescribed period of the assessment is not a true representation of the claimant's average weekly earnings, the assessment may be carried out over a period preceding the date of the claim which will enable the claimant's average weekly earnings to be determined more accurately.

Where the claimant has not worked for the number of weeks over which the average weekly earnings might be assessed, or where the claimant's hours of work have increased or decreased (excluding periods where the claimant's hours of work have fluctuated in consequence of a trade dispute or temporary (i e less than 13 weeks) short-time working), the claimant's employer will be asked to provide an estimate of the claimant's average likely weekly or monthly earnings.

For Income Support and income-based Jobseekers Allowance, the earnings to be taken into account will be the actual amount paid during any week in which entitlement to benefit is established. Where the claimant's income or hours of work fluctuate, his average weekly income may be taken over a period of five weeks or any other recognised cycle of work (over the period of that cycle) in order to establish a weekly income that is a fairer representative figure for the assessment of the claimant's average weekly earnings from employment.

The claimant's assessment of earned income will also include any bonuses or commission he has received during the 52-week period prior to the date of claim.

The period of assessment for self-employed income   2.19

For all benefits, the assessment period over which a claimant's average income (derived from assessed net profits) from self-employment is determined will be the last year's trading account or, where appropriate, a period which is more representative of the current trading position, or of fluctuations in business activity (e g the latest three months), can be used. In any case the period should not exceed a year.

Where a business has just been set up, there is scope for the assessment of projected self-employed income to be estimated in the short term as to the likely future level of earnings, so as to avoid causing hardship to the claimant by denying benefit solely on the grounds of uncertainty.

The period of assessment for other income   2.20

Income from other sources may include income from other State benefits, occupational pensions, maintenance payments, income from trust funds, charitable or voluntary payments etc. The assessment period for a claimant's average weekly income from sources other than earnings will be any period (following the date of application for the specific means-tested benefit) over which that income is due to be paid and may be estimated accurately.

So, for example, if a claimant is claiming Housing Benefit and is in receipt of a tax credit award which is due to expire in 20 weeks' time, the average weekly income from this credit can only be estimated over the 20 weeks' that it is actually due to be paid, but if a claimant is in receipt of Industrial Injuries Benefit and that benefit is not due to expire, the receipt of this benefit may be estimated over a period of 52 weeks.

Where a payment due to the claimant fluctuates, for instance, in the case of maintenance payments, the assessment of this income will take into account regular patterns of payments received by the claimant over a period of 13 weeks immediately prior to the date of claim, or any other period which is more representative to establish an average weekly income from such sources. For instance, if the claimant is due a periodical payment of maintenance of £40 per week, but is paid £420 in a lump sum payment, then the lump sum payment will be deemed to have been paid over a period of ten weeks at £40 per week and one week at £20. The commencement date for the assessment of the period of maintenance will be the week in which the payment is actually made.

If a lump sum payment of maintenance is paid, which does not specify the period in respect of which that payment is made, the period of the assessment of that income will be the actual payment received, divided by the claimant's 'relevant applicable amount' plus a fixed sum of £2 attributable to the assessment of the claimant's entitlement to Income Support or income-based Jobseekers Allowance. However, the 'relevant applicable amount' only includes personal allowances and premiums attributable to the person/s for whom the maintenance payment is made, i e the claimant and any child, including a family premium, any disabled child premium and any enhanced disability premium or carer premium paid in consequence of a disabled child (see **CHAPTER 6 INCOME SUPPORT** and **CHAPTER 7 INCOME-BASED JOBSEEKERS ALLOWANCE**).

For example, a lump sum payment of maintenance of £420 paid to a claimant (for no specified period) who is a single parent with one child aged six would be calculated from the date of actual payment as follows, prior to his transfer onto Child Tax Credit:

Applicable amount £119.28 (made up of an adult personal allowance of £57.45, child addition £45.58 and family premium £16.25).

£119.28 + £2.00 = £121.28.

£420 divided by £121.28 = 3 weeks @ 121.28 and 1 week at £56.16. Therefore, the period over which the non-periodical payment will be assessed will be four weeks from the date of receipt of the payment. In this example, for three weeks the claimant will be treated as having maintenance of £121.28 (and will not qualify for Income Support or income-based Jobseekers Allowance) and in the fourth week his applicable amount will be reduced by the excess, being £56.16.

Earned income from employment   2.21

It is the claimant's net income from employment that is taken into account in the assessment of earned income. A claimant's net income from employment is usually shown on the payslip from his employer. However, frequently the claimant's net income as shown on his payslip is not the income that will be used in the assessment of benefit. Travel and other 'out of pocket reimbursements' will be ignored:

- deductions for income tax and National Insurance (NI) will be allowed in full;

- only 50% of the claimant's contribution to a pension will be allowed in the assessment of net income;

- deductions from the claimant's gross income for items such as trade union subscriptions and car loan repayments will not be allowed at all in the assessment of net income.

EXAMPLE

If the claimant's gross income is £1,050, including £50 for travel reimbursements, but there are deductions of £152 for income tax, £127 for National Insurance contributions (NICs), £60 for pension contributions, £7 trade union subscriptions and £70 for the repayment of a car loan, the claimant's payslip will show a net income of £634.

However, the assessment of net income for means-tested benefit payments will ignore any payment of travel reimbursement. Therefore, the starting point of the gross income will be £1,000 and the net assessment will allow the deduction of £152 for income tax, plus £127 for NICs, £30 for pension contributions (i e only 50% allowed). This will produce a net assessable income from employment of £691.

Income from self-employed earnings   2.22

It is the net profit of a self-employed claimant's income that is taken into account in the assessment of entitlement to benefit, but the rules relating to the assessment of net profit are not necessarily what the claimant may have assessed his net profit for tax purposes to be.

The first stage in the assessment is to establish the gross profit of the business. If a self-employed claimant is employed in a partnership, his share of the net profit should be taken into account. This applies also to share fishermen.

Business Start-up Allowances are a form of gross income of the employment, but should not be treated as income until the payment has been made.

Business expenses   2.23

The next stage in establishing actual earnings is to make the following deductions (if they apply) from gross profit:

- the repayment of capital on any loan used for replacing existing business assets such as tools, plant, equipment or machinery or the repair of an existing business asset (but only if there is no insurance policy to cover the cost of repair);

- income spent on the repair of an existing business asset unless covered by an insurance policy;

- interest paid on loans including hire purchase agreements taken out for business purposes;

- VAT paid in excess of VAT received;

- expenses that have to be met in order to conduct the business, including employees' wages;

- bad debts proved to be such (i e where default has occurred);

- any banking or commission charges made on converting self-employed earnings from another currency into sterling.

The result is the chargeable income.

Deductions should not be made for the following expenditure:

- capital expenditure, i e expenditure on a capital item such as a taxi for a self-employed taxi driver;

- money used to set up or expand a business;

- depreciation or write-off of equipment etc;

- domestic or personal expenses ('drawings') that are not essential in running the business, e g personal use of a vehicle;

- money spent on business entertainment or meals, including promotional events;

- compensation for losses incurred before the beginning of the assessment period, or for other losses (other than proven bad debts);

- losses suffered in running other businesses.

Once net profit is established, further deductions in respect of tax, NI and 50% of the claimant's pension contributions need to be established:

- income tax, including personal reliefs;

- NICs (Class 2 and/or 4, as appropriate); and

- half of the qualifying premium for any pension scheme or retirement annuity if taken out prior to the self-employed pension scheme.

Drawings 2.24

Actual drawings from the business for personal use should not immediately be counted as income, but should be added back into the gross profit before deductions are taken for allowable items.

EXAMPLE 1

Gross profit declared (after deducting drawings of £1,000)	£6,500
Personal drawings	£1,000
Gross profit of the business	£7,500

EXAMPLE 2

Gross profit declared (no deduction for drawings)	£6,500
Personal drawings	£1,000
Gross profit of the business	£6,500

Where no proper accounts are kept but there is some indication of potential earnings (i e an excess of income over outgoings), the benefit authority will have to make an assessment of average weekly income, based on the best evidence to hand (i e sales ledgers, notebooks, bank statements, receipted invoices, chequebook stubs, etc). Payments of tips, gratuities, royalties etc will be included in the gross profit figure.

There may also be cases where the claimant is unable to explain adequately the source of the drawings. Where this is so, the only reasonable explanation may be that the drawings came from money coming into the business. In which case, they should be treated as earnings in the normal way.

Deductions of tax and NICs for self-employed earners 2.25

Class 2 contributions in 2006/07 are due and payable by the claimant at a fixed weekly rate of £2.10 per week if the claimant has a gross profit of more than £4,465 per year.

Class 4 contributions are earnings-related and are set at a percentage of profits or gains chargeable to tax under Cases I and II of Schedule D. Most claimants will not know how much Class 4 contributions they will have to pay until their tax assessment. The Inland Revenue calculates Class 4 contributions together with the assessment of income tax. In 2006/07, the claimant will not pay any Class 4 contributions in respect of the first £5,035 of his gross income, but will pay 8% of any excess gross income up to £33,530, and 1% above this upper threshold.

EXAMPLE

The claimant earns £10,000 – for Class 4 contributions the first £5,035 is ignored and his Class 4 contribution will be 8% of the excess: £4,965 × 8% = £397.20 divided by 52 weeks = £7.64 per week.

Because of the lapses of time which may occur between:

- the period during which earnings are generated;
- lodging a claim for a means-tested benefit; and
- the fixed dates when tax and Class 4 NICs are payable (generally at the end of the tax year),

benefit authorities will need to establish a notional figure for assessment of tax and NICs deductions for the purposes of a means-tested benefit entitlement. Since the figures are used as a basis for an estimate of the claimant's income during the period covered by the benefit award, the current year's tax and NI figures should be used to calculate notional tax and NI deductions.

Assessment of net profit for the self-employed 2.26

Expenses are allowed as long as they are wholly and exclusively incurred for the purpose of the business. No allowances can be made where the benefit authority, given the nature and amount, feel that the expense has not been reasonably incurred.

Business expenses	Deductible Other (for business purposes only)	Not deductible Other
Running costs – heating, lighting, stationery, telephone, advertising, cleaning, repairs, special clothing etc.	Mortgage loan interest.	Other capital expenditure.
Goods bought for resale.	Capital payments on loan to repair/replace business equipment (not covered by insurance).	Depreciation of capital.
Wages of employees and NICs.	Transport for business.	Assets.
Mortgage for business premises, or rent, rates for business premises.	Excess VAT in assessment period.	Purchase of business equipment.
Hire purchase and leasing fees.	Bank charges.	Cost of expansion or setting up business, other than interest.
Subscriptions to professional bodies.	Insurance premiums.	Debts not proven.
Accountancy and legal fees.	Repair costs (not covered by insurance).	Any losses before the business period.
Travel and business trips (not to and from work).	Proven bad debts.	Repayment of capital on loan taken out for business use which does not fall into column 2.
Tax.	Cost of recovery of proven bad debts.	Business entertainment.
NI Class 2 and 4.		Any sum for domestic or private use.
50% of pension contributions.		
Interest on business loans.		

Particular forms of self-employment   2.27

- *Childminders* – Childminders who work from their own home and often receive incidental or low earnings, and whose function allows others to work outside the home, will only have one third of their earnings taken into account in the calculation of benefit entitlement. To calculate net profit for this group, tax, NICs, and half of the qualifying premium for any pension scheme should be deducted from one third of earnings. The appropriate earnings disregard should also be applied (see **2.28** below).

- *Partnerships* – Partners are similar to sole traders, except that ownership and control of the business is shared between two or more people. If a deed of partnership exists it will contain details of how profits are calculated, shared etc. If there is no deed, profits are to be regarded as shared equally among the partners, unless there is any express or implied agreement between them to the contrary.

Disregarded earned income   2.28

In the assessment of entitlement to Income Support, income-based Jobseekers Allowance, Pension Credit, Housing Benefit and Council Tax Benefit all claimants will have a small amount of their earned income disregarded in the assessment of entitlement to benefit. The amount of the disregard will depend on the claimant's circumstances and provisions for the disregards are contained in the schedules to the regulations. There is only one earnings disregard per claim regardless of whether the claimant would qualify for a disregard under a number of headings. In such cases the highest possible disregard will be applied. Main weekly earnings disregards are as follows.

Qualifying conditions	*IS, PC and IB-JSA*	*HB and CTB*
Claimant attracts a disability premium	£20	£20
Claimant attracts the higher pensioner premium and would also qualify for a disability premium (i e because a partner is aged under 60)	£20	£20

Qualifying conditions	IS, PC and IB-JSA	HB and CTB
Claimant qualified for a higher pensioner premium and qualified for a disability premium in the eight weeks immediately before reaching the age of 60	£20	£20
Claimant is a single parent	£20	£25
Claimant attracts a carer premium (and it is the carer who is working)	£20	£20
Emergency services part-time relief workers	£20	£20
Claimant is a member of a couple	£10	£10
In any other case	£5	£5
Dependent child's earned income	£15	£15

Earned income of a child   2.29

Where a claimant's dependent child receives an earned income, and that child is receiving secondary education, his earnings will be disregarded in full.

Where the child is undertaking further education and a personal allowance and/or disabled child premium for that child is included in the claimant's assessment of his applicable amount, the earned income of the child will be treated as that of the claimant to the extent of the amount of the child's personal allowance and/or child disability premium.

Where the child has an income that is not an earned income, either employed or self-employed, the income of the child will be disregarded in full.

For Housing Benefit and Council Tax Benefit further disregards from earnings are provided where the claimant works for more than 30 hours per week and/or pays eligible childcare charges (see **CHAPTER 9 HOUSING BENEFIT, COUNCIL TAX BENEFIT AND DISCRETIONARY HOUSING PAYMENTS**).

Other income   2.30

Any other income that a claimant has will need to be assessed for the purpose of entitlement to means-tested benefits. In most cases the full amount of the claimant's 'other income' will be assessed in full. There is, however, some scope for disregarding some of the claimant's other income, in whole or in part – full details of these disregards are contained in the schedules to the regulations.

Prior to a parent on Income Support or Jobseekers Allowance being compulsorily transferred onto Child Tax Credit his Income Support assessment will still include allowances for dependent children. If he is receiving Child Tax Credit already, then the full amount is taken into account as income in the Income Support assessment. Once his case has been fully incorporated into the tax credit structure, then the amount of any tax credit award will no longer affect the amount of Income Support or Jobseekers Allowance, since these will no longer included allowances for children.

Notional income   2.31

A claimant will be treated as having an income that would be available to him upon application, and he will be deemed to have income to that value which will be included in his assessment of income. This might be, for example, where the claimant is working for a friend, and the work he is undertaking is work that in normal circumstances he would be paid for, or where a claimant has arranged for his former partner to make payments directly to a third party for the benefit of the claimant and his family (e g an estranged husband paying the utility bills for his wife etc).

Income treated as capital   2.32

There are certain prescribed payments of income which are treated as capital, but such payments are not usually regular periodical payments. Full details of these are given in schedules to the regulations, but the most common are as follows:

- tax refunds;

- holiday pay other than earnings;

- any loan from an employer or advance earnings;

- any payment or advance made to prisoners on discharge;

- any voluntary or charitable payment not made at regular intervals; and

- any compensation from employment which is not treated as earnings.

Disregards for income other than earnings   2.33

There are certain prescribed payments of income which are disregarded in full or in part in the assessment of entitlement to means-tested benefits – the most common are as follows:

77

- Disregarded in full for all benefits:

    o   reimbursement of expenses paid to a voluntary worker;

    o   payment of Housing Benefit;

    o   Disability Living Allowance;

    o   Attendance Allowance;

    o   any childcare expenses reimbursed to the claimant in respect of his participation in employment training provided for under the *Jobseeker's Allowance Regulations 1996 (SI 1996 No 207)*;

    o   any income from a non-dependant;

    o   any educational maintenance allowance payment, paid by an education authority in respect of a child in full-time further education;

    o   any income derived from interest on capital invested by the claimant;

    o   any payment made by the Secretary of State for the purpose of pensioner's Christmas bonus or winter fuel awards;

    o   any payment made under an insurance policy taken out to insure against non-payment under a consumer credit agreement or hire purchase agreement but only to the extent of discharging liabilities under such agreements.

- Disregarded in part:

    o   the first £20 per week of any regular payment made by a charitable or voluntary organisation;

    o   the first £10 per week of a War Disablement Pension or a War Widow's Pension or a pension payable under a similar scheme;

    o   the first £20 of any income from boarders or lodgers who reside with the claimant and who are provided with meals by the claimant. A further disregard of 50% of payments from boarders exceeding the £20 disregard will also be applied (i e a boarder pays the claimant £50 per week, the first £20 is disregarded, plus a further £15 will be disregarded (50% of the excess income from a boarder) leaving an assessed income from the boarder of £15);

    o   the first £4 of any income from a lodger who resides with the claimant (and is not provided with meals) plus a further £11.95 where the lodger's payments to the claimant include an amount for heating;

○ the first £15 for Housing Benefit and Council Tax Benefit of any maintenance payment received in respect of a dependent child of the claimant's family (regardless of whether these are voluntary payments, payments under an order of the court or payments under the provisions of a child support liability).

• Disregarded in part for Housing Benefit and Council Tax Benefit:

○ the first £15 of Widowed Parent's Allowance.

• Disregarded for Income Support and income-based Jobseekers Allowance until the case is transferred to Child Tax Credit:

○ an additional £10.45 per week where the claimant has a child under the age of one.

The assessment of non-dependants' income　　　　　2.34

Where a claimant claims for assistance with housing costs by way of Income Support, income-based Jobseekers Allowance, Housing Benefit and Council Tax Benefit, any award of benefit to accommodate such housing costs will be reduced in the case of a claimant who has a non-dependant living with him. The assessment of the non-dependant's income will be based on the gross income of the non-dependant (i e there are no provisions for assessing the net income of a non-dependant when applying the non-dependant deduction) (see **CHAPTER 9**).

Assessment of means for tax credits　　　　　2.35

Assessment of means for tax credits is very different from the system with means-tested benefits. In most cases, in common with tax assessments, income will be assessed for the purpose of an award on the previous year's income, although for the introduction of the new tax credits in April 2003 this was based on income for 2001/02. For claims for 2006/07, assessment will be on income for 2005/06. HM Revenue & Customs (HMRC) will therefore issue a provisional decision at the beginning of the tax year and a reconciliation will be carried out at the end of the year (see below).

The assessment of income is based closely on income tax rules, and an important part of this alignment is that there is no capital limit. Instead actual income from capital will be taken into account. The basis for the assessment is *gross* income. The rules are contained in the *Tax Credits (Definition and Calculation of Income) Regulations 2002 (SI 2002 No 2006)*. The regulations separately define nine types of income, which are then added together:

• pension income;

- investment income;
- property income;
- foreign income;
- notional income;
- employment income;
- Social Security income;
- student income; and
- miscellaneous income.

As a general rule income is taken into account if it is taxable (for example, earnings, taxable Social Security benefits and private pensions).

The important disregards of income include:

- statutory maternity pay – the first £100 per week;
- first £300 per year income from pensions, investment, property and from abroad;
- all interest on ISAs and PEPs;
- child benefit, Disability Living Allowance, Severe Disablement Allowance;
- maintenance; and
- income of children.

Tax credits are based on the income of a single applicant or the joint income of a couple. If a lone parent were a member of a couple in the previous year, the assessment would be based on only his income in the previous year.

At the end of the tax year, the provisional award is to be reconciled against actual income for the year. There could be an overpayment to be repaid or further tax credit due.

If income rises or falls during the year a claimant can choose to have an award amended based on a forecast of current year's income. However, there is no obligation to notify changes of income until the end of the tax year. So, for example, if there has been a drop in earnings this can be taken into account straight away, or the claimant can wait until the end of the year and receive a lump sum payment at that stage. Conversely, if income rises this can be taken into account straight away, or an overpayment may arise at the end of the year.

From April 2006, if income has risen by up to £25,000 in the current year, then this increase will be ignored in the reconciliation. This disregard was previously only £2,500, which led to many claimants being assessed as having been overpaid tax credits if their income had risen year on year. If the increase is more than the £25,000, then it is only the amount over £25,000 that is taken into account. As the income assessment is an annual one, the £25,000 disregard is applied to annual income. Therefore, a significant rise in income towards the end of the year is unlikely to exceed that figure.

There is a requirement to notify certain changes of circumstances within three months (*Tax Credits Act 2002, s 6*), and failure to do so attracts a penalty. Such changes include a change in the number of adults heading the household (i e becoming a member of a couple, or becoming a lone parent), and eligible childcare costs ceasing or reducing significantly.

There is no requirement to notify of other changes of circumstances, although failure to do so could result in the loss of some tax credit (increases in the maximum figure only take effect from the date of change if notified within three months), or in an overpayment (changes reducing entitlement take effect from the date of change).

Overpayments can be recovered from the next year's tax credit award, or by treating it as an underpayment of tax and taking it back through the PAYE system, or issuing a demand for payment within 30 days.

3   Claiming for the Family

Introduction   3.1

Claimants can only claim benefit for members of their family who are deemed
to be members of the claimant's 'family unit'. In most cases, this will be the
claimant, his partner (this means an opposite sex or same sex partner whether
married, unmarried, civil partners or living together with the claimant as if
they were married or civil partners) and dependent children for whom the
family receives Child Benefit. However, if a child is not living with the
claimant, or a child is living with the claimant but the claimant or his partner
does not receive Child Benefit for that child; or if a member of the family is
temporarily absent from the claimant's family unit etc, the rules relating to
membership of a claimant's 'family unit' become much more complicated and
are confusing for even the most experienced of advisors. The most common of
these problems are addressed below. (For details and discussions of more
complex issues, see *Tolley's Social Security and State Benefits Looseleaf, Chapter 5*.)

Where a couple are living together – as a same or opposite sex couple – then
either partner can make the claim for a means-tested benefit. All claims for a
means-tested benefit will be based on a joint financial assessment of a couple
regardless of who actually makes the claim. However, it is always best for the
partner who may attract most benefit to make the claim. For instance, if one of
the partners is incapable of work through sickness or disability, then it should
be that partner who makes the claim, because he or she may at some point
attract an extra disability premium.

The effect of the *Civil Partnership Act 2004*, and the regulations made as a result
of it, is broadly to put civil partners and same sex couples in the same situation
as married or unmarried opposite sex couples in all aspects of the benefits and
tax credit system.

Assessment of the family unit   3.2

The rules relating to the assessment of a family unit are contained in the
general regulations relating to the specific benefit in question, but are directed
by *section 137* of the *Social Security Contributions and Benefits Act 1992* and
section 3 of the *Tax Credits Act 2002*, both of which were amended by the *Civil
Partnership Act 2004*. However, the provisions of each set of individual regulations are very similar, taking into account three elements and principles
establishing the circumstances in which any person will be treated as a member
of a claimant's family unit:

- *Couples* – Describing when a couple is treated as such for the purposes of claiming benefits.

- *Children* – Prescribing where a child will be treated as a member of the claimant's family and where a claimant might be treated as responsible or not responsible for a child of the family.

- *Young people* – Prescribing when a child, having attained the age of 16, may or may not be deemed to be a member of the claimant's family.

The regulations relevant to the assessment of a family unit are as follows:

- Chapter 6: Income Support – *Income Support (General) Regulations 1987 (SI 1987 No 1967), Regulations 2, 14–16.*

- Chapter 7: Income-based Jobseekers Allowance – *Jobseeker's Allowance Regulations 1996 (SI 1996 No 207), Regulations 1, 76–78.*

- Chapter 8: Tax Credits – *Child Tax Credit Regulations (SI 2002 No 2007), Regulations 2–5.*

- Chapter 9: Housing Benefit and Council Tax Benefit – *Housing Benefit (General) Regulations 1987 (SI 1987 No 1971), Regulations 12–15; Council Tax Benefit (General) Regulations 1992 (SI 1992 No 1814), Regulations 2, 5–7.*

Married couples and civil partners   3.3

A couple, for Social Security purposes, is defined as a man and a wife who are married to each other and who are living together as a couple in the same household, or as a same sex couple who are civil partners and living together. For tax credits purposes, the definition is of a married couple who are not separated in circumstances where this situation is likely to be permanent. It is suggested that the effect of these two definitions is very similar.

A polygamous marriage means a marriage where one party is married to more than one person in a country which permits polygamy.

Unmarried couples   3.4

A couple who are members of the opposite sex who are living together as man and wife in the same household will be treated for the purposes of the assessment of means-tested benefits and tax credits as if they were a married couple. In the same way, a couple of the same sex who are living together as if they were civil partners are treated as a couple for benefit purposes.

There are some situations where a couple who are married share the same house, but no longer live as a couple, in which case they may not be treated as members of the same family unit. The same could apply to civil partners whose relationship has ended.

There are other situations where couples are separated and not living together for temporary periods, where they may still be treated as members of the same family unit.

There are also situations where a couple are separated temporarily and want to live together as a family unit but are not treated as members of the same family unit.

A person can only ever be treated as a member of a couple in one household so, if a person shared his home in one house with one partner for part of a week and shared his home in a different house with another partner for part of the week, a decision would have to be made as to which household that person was to be treated as a member of. This situation was the subject of Commissioner's decision *R(SB)8/85* where the male claimant lived with his wife and family at weekends and a different partner during the week.

A family unit may also exist where one member of a couple is absent, provided that the absence is temporary, for example, where the claimant's partner is working away from home, or is studying at a college or university elsewhere in the country, or is in hospital or on holiday etc.

However, if a partner is absent from the claimant's home, and that absence is one that may continue indefinitely, the absent member of the couple is unlikely to be a member of the claimant's family unit for the purposes of the assessment of entitlement to a means-tested benefit.

For instance, if a couple have separated and one member of the couple considers the separation to be only temporary, but the other member of the couple does not, it would be unlikely that the couple would be treated as members of the same family unit. A further example of periods of indefinite absence from the home was considered in Commissioner's decision *R(SB)19/85* where a couple did not want to be separated, nor did they wish to declare themselves separated, but unfortunately they were. This was due to the claimant living in London and his wife living in Manchester to continue with her renal dialysis (though she intended to move to London to join her husband as soon as he found appropriate housing for her medical requirements). Although the Commissioner accepted that the separation was clearly a temporary arrangement, he found the couple not to be living together as members of the same household during the relevant period of temporary absence.

Therefore, the question of membership of the family unit relies on there being a clear intention by both parties who are separated temporarily to resume living together, and those intentions must be within the control of both parties.

Effect of cohabitation   3.5

Cohabitation is difficult to establish by any one factor. There has been a myth for many years relating to the number of nights a partner stays over with a claimant as being the test of whether a couple are cohabiting. There are several tests laid down by Social Security Commissioners and the courts over the years to help to establish cohabitation and this myth is not one of them.

The test must look at six factors which could establish whether or not a couple are 'living together as man and wife' for the purpose of an assessment of entitlement to means-tested benefits. These factors are as follows:

- Are the man and woman members of the same household?

- Is the relationship between the couple a stable one?

- Does the couple pool money to accommodate the cost of living?

- Is there a sexual relationship?

- Are there any children of the couple living in the household, and if so do the family present themselves as a family unit?

- How is the couple seen in public – are they perceived by the public to be a couple?

These six factors were established by case law long before the passing of the *Civil Partnership Act 2004*. It is clear, however, that the same tests should be applied to same sex couples. It is too early for there to have been any case law to determine how, if at all, these tests should be varied to apply to same sex couples. Cohabitation can only be established when applying a test of this nature, which may or may not show a true reflection of a relationship.

All six factors above need to be considered by the benefit authority when trying to prove a case of cohabitation, and if two or more of the above six factors are established, then cohabitation will most likely have been established.

Members of the same household   3.6

A couple who are simply 'sharing a roof' will not satisfy the test of living together as a couple. The reasons for this arrangement are of equal significance in establishing whether a couple sharing a home are doing so for reasons other than cohabitation. For example, in *Robson v Secretary of State for Social Services*

(1981) 3 FLR 232, two disabled people who were both living in the same house, for reasons of mutual care, support and companionship, were held not to be cohabiting.

In practical terms, further consideration needs to be given to the more day-to-day living activities of living in the same house. For example, pooling resources for food and domestic bills, eating together, watching television together, sharing social activities etc. These things are not conclusive evidence of cohabitation, as many friends, relatives and flatmates sharing accommodation will also engage in such activities; and by the same token a married couple may not do such things together.

Therefore, establishing details of any formal arrangements, like rotas for domestic duties, agreements, and additional considerations which might occur when two people who are not cohabiting but are living under the same roof, may be of assistance. This information is highly relevant when compared with those informal arrangements or expectations of relying on a partner to share such responsibilities which a couple living together as man and wife may have.

Stable relationship   3.7

Clearly what constitutes stability is a matter of degree. In many cases, the intention to remain together, a primary characteristic of a marriage or civil partnership, will be lacking. A lesser intention than this will clearly suffice for cohabitation; if any sort of intention is required, it need be no more than willingness to stay together for the time being.

There could, of course, be other reasons for the willingness to maintain living arrangements, for example, the need for care, companionship, the inability to afford to live elsewhere, or difficulty in securing appropriate accommodation etc.

In the situation of a marriage or civil partnership breakdown, it may be impractical for one of the couple to move out; this could be due to financial difficulties, shared liabilities, shared responsibilities etc.

A further persuasive indicator of non-cohabitation might be where one or both parties have sought legal advice concerning a relationship breakdown or have commenced legal proceedings. Equally, one or both parties may be able to show that they are actively looking for alternative accommodation and for the time being have no choice but to remain in the same accommodation as that of a former partner or spouse.

Where a couple continue to share living and domestic arrangements, in the same manner as prior to the relationship breakdown, they will be deemed to be living together as a couple. Non-cohabitation would only apply in circumstances where the couple can show that they are maintaining separate households, albeit under the same roof, and, wherever possible, that they are taking steps to live apart.

Financial arrangements   3.8

There are two considerations relating to financial arrangements which are frequently the deciding factors in the assessment of cohabitation. This is of particular relevance where the claimant spends the majority of his time as a member of the household or with the alleged partner. The points that must be established are as follows.

In determining whether there is a genuine relationship between the parties it would need to be established whether the 'landlord' would be prepared to allow the 'lodger' to stay in the event of the 'lodger' no longer having entitlement to benefit. If the 'landlord' would allow the 'lodger' to remain, despite the fact that the 'lodger' would not be able to support himself, then this may indicate cohabitation.

If, however, the 'lodger' was under pressure to make up any arrears of payments, or faced losing his home in the event of his not being able to accommodate his living cost, then this may support the relationship being other than that of cohabitation.

If the claimant is making payments towards his lodgings, either by way of rent or sharing household expenses, then the manner, frequency, method or arrangement could be significant in establishing whether the relationship is other than cohabitation. For instance, if the claimant is paying by way of pooling income and expenditure, then such pooling of resources could imply cohabitation. However, if the claimant makes a fixed, weekly/fortnightly contribution or other fixed agreement, i e 50/50 sharing of bills etc, then this may indicate that the relationship is something other than cohabitation.

The sexual relationship   3.9

Benefit officers should not question the claimant about the existence of a sexual relationship, but if the information is volunteered it can be used in the assessment and may well be persuasive. However, in an appeal the tribunal does have a duty to ask such questions in order to satisfy the test of the relevant factors of the relationship. Sexual relations are a poor guide as there may be a total absence of sexual relations in many marriages or civil partnerships, and the fact that the claimant is having a sexual relationship with a partner will not be sufficient evidence of cohabitation in the absence of other factors.

Other information of relevance would be whether the 'lodger' or 'landlord' has had other partners during the period of the alleged period of cohabitation.

Furthermore, a claimant volunteering such information would imply that cohabitation was most likely not present.

There are no regulations or legislation permitting or disallowing a person in receipt of any benefit to have a sexual relationship; there is no specified number of nights in a week that a partner is allowed to stay over.

The presence of a sexual relationship must be considered along with all other factors and elements of the relationship. If, however, the parties have an established relationship and have been living in the same house for a significant period of time and the woman takes the man's name, as was the case in Commissioner's decision *R(G)1/79*, then the presence of a sexual relationship could be inferred.

Children   3.10

If there are children, especially children of the couple, being cared for by the couple, this would be a strong indication of cohabitation (subject to the considerations above). How a child relates to a partner of the claimant may be a further indication of cohabitation, as it is unlikely that a child would be as comfortable with a visiting partner as he would be with a partner who resided with the family, either all or most of the time.

A visiting partner would be unlikely to avail himself for collecting a child or taking a child to school or playgroup, whereas a cohabiting partner may well do this, in particular where the other 'parent' is caring for another child or working. The adoption of a partner's name is a very strong indication of cohabitation.

Public repute   3.11

If the couple present themselves in public as a couple, sharing activities such as socialising together, going to the pub together, sharing the same friends, visiting each other's families, going on holiday together etc, this would be a strong indication of cohabitation, unless either one of them is engaged in a relationship with another person.

However, because a couple do not present themselves socially as a couple, it does not mean that they are not living together.

Dependent children   3.12

Where a claimant is responsible for a child who is a member of his household, that child's status in the family unit will need to be established. It is not necessary for the child to be a son or daughter of the claimant, whether natural or by adoption. What is required is that the claimant should be 'responsible for' the child. This test is similar to that for Child Benefit.

In most cases, the claimant will be in receipt of Child Benefit for a child who is a member of his household. However, this might not always be the case, for example, where the child's parents are separated and the child spends an equal amount of time with each parent. In these circumstances a further test of whether a claimant might be treated as 'responsible for' the child must be applied.

In cases where a couple have separated and there is shared care of a child, only one person can claim Child Benefit – the decision relating to this is an HMRC decision and not open to appeal.

What must be established is the question of whether the child 'normally lives' with the claimant (for tax credits, Housing Benefit or Council Tax Benefit) or whether the child 'usually lives' with the claimant (for Income Support and income-based Jobseekers Allowance).

Is the child 'normally living' with the claimant?   3.13

The term 'normally living' means that the child spends more time with the claimant than anyone else. In a case where the child spends equal time (3.5 days) with each parent, the claimant will be treated as 'responsible' where:

• the claimant is in receipt of Child Benefit;

• Child Benefit is not being paid at all and the claimant has applied for Child Benefit; or

• no one has applied for Child Benefit, or both parents have applied for Child Benefit and it appears to the benefit office that the claimant has the greater amount of responsibility for the child (i e the claimant is the person who seems to take the greatest parental responsibility for the child, for example, takes the child to the dentist and/or doctor, or deals with problems at school, or cares for the child when he is ill etc).

Does the child 'usually' live with the claimant?   3.14

The child will be deemed usually to live with the claimant where:

• the claimant is in receipt of Child Benefit;

• Child Benefit is not being paid at all and the claimant has applied for Child Benefit; or

- no one has applied for Child Benefit, or both parents have applied for Child Benefit and it appears to the benefit office that the child's normal place of residence is with the claimant (e g the claimant's address is the one that the child has provided for the purpose of registration and place of contact with the school, doctor, hospital etc).

Where the claimant is treated as 'responsible for' a child, that child will be deemed to be a member of the claimant's household even during periods of temporary absence.

Membership of the household   3.15

A person will *not* be deemed to be a member of the claimant's household in the assessment of benefit entitlement if the following circumstances apply.

The circumstances listed below apply to the assessment of all means-tested benefits.

- The dependant:

  o   is a child who is being fostered by the claimant or his partner under statutory provisions applied by the courts or Social Services;

  o   is a child who has been placed with the claimant or his partner prior to adoption – this rule applies in all circumstances, regardless of whether the child has been placed with the claimant or his partner by an order, agency, local authority etc, or not;

  o   is a child or other dependant (for example, a partner) who is absent from the claimant's home and does temporarily intend to return.

The circumstances listed below apply only to the assessment of Income Support and income-based Jobseekers Allowance.

- The member of the household:

  o   is the claimant and/or his partner who is detained in custody pending trial or sentence or under a sentence imposed by the court (including periods of temporary release from prison);

  o   is the claimant who is abroad for a period of more than four weeks (other than in prescribed circumstances, i e receiving medical treatment etc);

  o   is the claimant or his partner who is permanently in residential accommodation, a care home or nursing home. In these circumstances each member of the couple will be treated as a single person in the assessment of entitlement to benefit;

○ is a child who is detained in custody pending trial or sentence or under a sentence imposed by the court. However, if the child is allowed home for any periods, then the child will be treated as a member of the claimant's household, but only on the days that the child lives at home and benefit will be assessed for the child at a daily rate;

○ is a child who is living with the claimant for the purpose of attending school or college, and his parental or usual home is elsewhere. In this instance the child will remain a member of the household of his parental/usual home;

○ is a child or other dependant who has been absent from Great Britain for a continuous period of more. than eight weeks, but only to the extent that such dependants were treated as temporarily absent during the preceding eight weeks (i e the person absent from Great Britain was a child needing medical treatment abroad or the person taking that child abroad for the medical treatment).

The circumstances listed below apply only to the assessment of Income Support, income-based Jobseekers Allowance, Housing Benefit and Council Tax Benefit.

- The member of the household:

○ is the claimant, his partner or a child who is living away from other members of his family and his absence is likely to exceed 52 weeks;

○ is a child who has been boarded out with someone other than the claimant prior to adoption;

○ is a child who is not living with the claimant and is being looked after by, or in the care, of the local authority. However, if the child lives with the claimant (for example, at weekends, or during the holidays) then the child will be treated as a member of the claimant's family, but only on the days that the child lives at home.

The circumstances listed below apply only to the assessment of Income Support and income-based Jobseekers Allowance.

- The member of the household:

○ is a child who has been in hospital or in a local authority home for a continuous period of more than twelve weeks because of physical or mental handicap or physical or mental illness, and the claimant and/or other members of the claimant's household have not been in regular contact with the child. If, however, there has been regular contact with the child by the claimant and/or other members of the family, the child will continue to be a member of the claimant's household during a period of up to 52 weeks of absence;

○   is a child or partner who has been in hospital or in a local authority home for a continuous period of more than 52 weeks because of illness or disability. (However, for Income Support only, if the claimant is still in regular contact with the child, the 52-week period may be extended.)

In the above circumstances the twelve or 52-week period for the purpose of Income Support and income-based Jobseekers Allowance commences from the day the child went into hospital or the home; or where the claimant was not in receipt of the benefit he has claimed at that time, the twelve or 52-week period commences on the date of claim for Income Support or income-based Jobseekers Allowance.

Eligible childcare costs 3.16

This applies to the assessment of maximum credit for Working Tax Credit (see **CHAPTER 8 TAX CREDITS**) and the assessment of disregarded income for Housing and Council Tax Benefit (see **CHAPTER 9 HOUSING BENEFIT, COUNCIL TAX BENEFIT AND DISCRETIONARY HOUSING PAYMENTS**).

Some parents who are working may be entitled to additional childcare costs to be included in their assessment of entitlement to a tax credit, and/or childcare costs incurred to be disregarded from their assessment of income for the purpose of calculating entitlement to Housing and Council Tax Benefit.

However, this only applies in certain circumstances, which are set out below.

The childcare costs must be paid by the claimant to an authorised provider of childcare (i e a registered childminder, nursery, organised after-school club or any other provider of childcare that holds a certificate of authorisation, including a childcarer approved to provide childcare in your own home) in respect of a dependent child who is under the age of 15 (or 16 if the child is disabled and either registered blind or receiving Disability Living Allowance care component). The payments of childcare costs must be paid by commercial arrangement and the claimant must be:

- a single parent working more than 16 hours; or

- a member of a couple who are both working for 16 hours or more, or where one parent is working for at least 16 hours and the other parent is incapacitated (i e has been sick and incapable of work for more than 28 weeks, or in receipt of Severe Disablement Allowance, Disability Living Allowance or Attendance Allowance).

How childcare costs are assessed   3.17

The assessment of childcare costs will be determined by the use of a formula that will depend on whether the childcare fees are paid monthly or otherwise.

Where childcare fees are paid monthly, the formula used will simply multiply the regular monthly fees by twelve and divide by 52 weeks. So, for example, if the charges are £250 per month, this will be multiplied by twelve and divided by 52, providing a weekly eligible childcare charge of £57.69 per week.

If the charge is variable (this often being the case as childcare charges are higher in the school holidays than in term time) the formula will take the last twelve months' fees and divide that by 52. So, if the claimant has paid £3,200 in the previous year for childcare fees this will be divided by 52, giving an eligible childcare cost of £61.54 per week.

If the childcare is charged weekly, then the average weekly figure is taken based on the last complete four weeks.

If the claimant has only just started work and begun paying childcare charges, or has not paid such charges for a long enough period for the formula to be implemented, then childcare charges can be estimated based on what the childcare provider confirms in writing to be the expected future childcare charges.

4 Claims, Decisions and Appeals

Introduction

4.1

The Social Security and tax credit system is very much claimant-led and relies on the claimant making the correct claim, in the correct manner to the correct office at the correct time. Once a claim has been made for a benefit or tax credit, the claimant will be notified of his rights of appeal by being advised in every letter issued to him of what he can do if he is not happy with a decision.

The relevant regulations dealing with claims are the *Social Security (Claims and Payments) Regulations 1987 (SI 1987 No 1968) (SSC&P Regs 1987)* which set out the general procedures to be followed. Each particular benefit has its own claim form. For tax credits the relevant provisions are found in the *Tax Credits Act 2002 (TCA 2002)* and the *Tax Credits (Claims and Notifications) Regulations 2002 (SI 2002 No 2014)*.

Most can be claimed from a local Department for Work and Pensions (DWP) office; quite a number are administered from centralised units in different parts of the country, and the local DWP offices have no say in how they are handled. Tax credits can be claimed on forms from the HM Revenue & Customs (HMRC) Tax Credits Office. There is a telephone helpline available (0845 300 3900). Claims can also be made online at www.hmrc.gov.uk/taxcredits. The website includes a calculation package.

It is, however, important to note that a local DWP office is authorised to act as a receiving office for any claim for a Social Security benefit (with the exception of Housing and Council Tax Benefit). Therefore a claimant may register all claims locally and the DWP will undertake to pass that claim on to the relevant office for its assessment and administration. There is also provision for the claimant to register any claim for benefit at any local authority office displaying a 'ONE' sign.

- Benefits administered by the local Social Security office (Jobcentre Plus):

    o   Income Support;

    o   Industrial Injuries and Incapacity Benefits;

    o   maternity benefits;

    o   income-based Jobseekers Allowance; and

    ○   contributory Jobseekers Allowance.

- Benefits administered by the HMRC Tax Credits Office:

    ○   Working Tax Credit;

    ○   Child Tax Credit; and

    ○   Child Benefit.

- Benefits administered by the local authority (the council):

    ○   Housing Benefit;

    ○   Council Tax Benefit; and

    ○   Home Renovation Grants.

- Benefits administered by a central DWP office:

    ○   Carer's Allowance;

    ○   State Retirement Pensions; and

    ○   Bereavement Benefits.

- Benefits administered by a regional DWP office:

    ○   Disability Living Allowance; and

    ○   Attendance Allowance.

Claims   4.2

Social Security benefits   4.3

Section 1 of the *Social Security Administration Act 1992* (*SSAA 1992*) provides that no person will be entitled to a benefit unless he makes a claim for it in the manner, and within the time, prescribed by the regulations. The *SSC&P Regs 1987* contain the detailed rules for making a claim. *Regulation 4* requires all claims to be in writing, and:

- in the case of claims for Income Support or Jobseekers Allowance, on the approved claim form;

- in the case of other benefits, either on the approved claim form or in such other manner as the Secretary of State may accept as sufficient.

Additionally, in respect of a claim for a means-tested benefit, all information and evidence required by the form must be supplied, as the claim will otherwise be defective.

The claimant must also provide his National Insurance (NI) number (and his partner's NI number too if he is claiming for her). If the claimant does not know his NI number, evidence must be provided which will enable it to be traced; if he has not got one he must apply for one and provide sufficient information and evidence for one to be allocated (i e full name, any previous name, current address and date of birth).

Note: it is important to be aware that if the claimant is claiming a non means-tested benefit such as Carer's Allowance or Incapacity Benefit, he must, if he has dependants, make a separate claim for the dependant's addition to that benefit.

Every claim is to be delivered or sent to the appropriate office and the date of claim is normally the date when the claim is received in that office. If the claim is defective in some way, and is then referred back to the claimant for amendment or for further information, or for an approved form to be completed, the original date of receipt will still be treated as the date of claim, provided the claimant supplies the required information/form within one month or such longer time as the Secretary of State considers reasonable.

With regard to claims for Jobseekers Allowance, the claimant should take completed forms and full supporting evidence and documents to his initial interview with the jobseekers' adviser. If he does not do so, he will be asked to supply them within seven days. A discretionary extension may be possible up to a maximum of a month or longer if, for example, the claimant is unable to meet the requirements because:

- he has physical, learning, mental or communication difficulties;

- the evidence required does not exist;

- the claimant would risk physical or mental harm to obtain the evidence; or

- the evidence can only be obtained from a third party and this is impracticable.

With regard to other claims, once a valid claim has been made, every claimant must provide such supporting evidence as may be required by the Secretary of State, e g certificates, documents, information etc, within one month, or such longer period as is reasonable. If he fails to do so, a decision will be made on the basis of the evidence actually provided. That decision is obviously likely to be unfavourable, but the claimant will have a right of appeal to a tribunal.

In certain circumstances, if it appears that the claimant has mistakenly claimed the wrong benefit, the Secretary of State can treat a claim for one benefit as if it were made for another, i e substitute or add the correct benefit. (*SSC&P Regs 1987, Reg 9, Sch 1*). These benefits include:

Benefit claimed	*Alternative benefit*
Incapacity Benefit	Severe Disablement Allowance
Severe Disablement Allowance	Incapacity Benefit
Maternity Allowance	Incapacity or Severe Disablement Benefit
Retirement Pension	Bereavement Allowance
Bereavement Allowance	Retirement Pension
Disability Living Allowance	Attendance Allowance
Attendance Allowance	Disability Living Allowance

Claims for tax credits   4.4

In a similar way to claims for Social Security benefits, entitlement to tax credits depends on a claim being made (*TCA 2002, s 3(1)*). Couples are required to make joint claims. Claims must be in writing, or can be made online, on an approved form. The claim must include the information requested on the form, including the claimant's NI number, or information to enable the NI number to be ascertained, or can include an application for an NI number.

A claim can be backdated by up to three months, or to the start of the tax year if less than three months before. Claims can also be made in advance for the tax year that they relate to, and, in respect of WTC, can be made up to seven days before the claimant starts a job.

Claimant unable to act   4.5

If a claimant is unable, through either physical or mental disability, to look after his own affairs he can appoint someone (who will be called an appointee) to act on his behalf for the purpose of making a claim, appealing against a decision, or simply collecting his benefit.

The appointee will need to make an application in writing to the Secretary of State for benefits claimed and administered by the DWP to the Inland Revenue in respect of a tax credit claim, and to the benefits department of the local authority for Housing and Council Tax Benefit. The appointee will be issued with a certificate of appointee status by the Secretary of State or HMRC; the local authority will simply write to the appointee to confirm that appointee status has been granted.

It must, however, be noted that even where the appointee has a certificate of appointee status, a separate application must be made to a local authority for the purpose of Housing and Council Tax Benefit claims.

Appointee status can be awarded for a fixed period or for an indefinite period and may be reviewed at any time.

Once an appointment has been made the appointee takes the place of the claimant from a legal point of view. As such the appointee will hold the same responsibilities and obligations as a claimant.

Decisions   4.6

Once a claim for a benefit has been properly made, and all necessary supporting evidence supplied, the Secretary of State has an obligation to make a decision within 14 days or as soon as is practicable thereafter. Obviously, it is often not practicable for a decision to be made within 14 days, and some reasonable latitude should be granted. Nevertheless, there is a statutory duty to come to a decision, and if there is substantial delay in dealing with a claim for no apparent reason an application for judicial review may have to be considered.

The decision of the Secretary of State should be in writing and should set out the reasons for it, or should inform the claimant of his right to request a statement of the reasons for it. In all cases the claimant should also be notified of his right to appeal (see **4.23** et seq below).

In the case of tax credit awards, HMRC will make a provisional award as soon as possible after the claim is made. This provisional award will be subject to change during the tax year if circumstances change. At the end of the year a final decision will be issued, based on the actual income the claimant has received during the year in question. The claimant has a right of appeal to an appeal tribunal.

Interplay of different benefits   4.7

If the claimant has claimed Income Support, Pension Credit or income-based Jobseekers Allowance, he will be invited to register a claim for Housing Benefit and/or Council Tax Benefit. This should be done by completing Form NHB1. However, by completing this form the claimant has not provided enough information for the local authority to process the claim – he must actually complete a local authority form to do this.

In theory, the completed NHB1 should be passed to the local authority, who, on receipt should issue the claimant with a benefit claim form, which, if completed and returned to them within one month of being issued, will ensure the claimant's entitlement to Housing and Council Tax Benefit from the date on which his entitlement to Income Support, Pension Credit or income-based Jobseekers Allowance commenced.

If the claimant has also claimed a non means-tested benefit which is administered by the DWP, such as Incapacity Benefit, Carer's Allowance or retirement pension, the Income Support, Pension Credit or Jobseekers Allowance section will work in conjunction with the relevant department to assess entitlement.

The claimant will have to complete his application form for the non means-tested benefit at the same time as completing an Income Support, Pension Credit or Jobseekers Allowance claim form. Only when his claim for the non means-tested benefit has been calculated will his Income Support, Pension Credit or Jobseekers Allowance entitlement be assessed. If he is found to be entitled to Income Support, Pension Credit or Jobseekers Allowance he will receive one payment from the non means-tested department, comprising both the non means-tested benefit and his Income Support, Pension Credit or Jobseekers Allowance top-up.

A similar administrative procedure is followed for all claims received by the DWP. When claims are received they will be date-stamped on the day of receipt and any benefit entitlement will commence from that date, unless the claim form has been sent to the claimant by post, or collected by the claimant from the DWP, in which case the claim form will be date-stamped with the date of posting or collection. Provided the claimant returns the form with the necessary supporting evidence to enable the DWP to make a decision within 14 days, entitlement will start from the date stamped on the form.

Once a claim form has been received by the DWP it will be passed to an assessment officer, who will enter all the relevant information into a computer system. If there are any problems with a claim each assessment officer is responsible to a senior assessment officer to whom he can refer. Should a claimant have any complaints or questions about his claim, he should initially contact the assessment officer who is dealing with his claim.

Change of circumstances 4.8

Where a claimant's entitlement to benefit has been assessed and his circumstances then change, he will be under an obligation to disclose that change to each benefit authority which has made an award of benefit to him. Notification should be in writing or by telephone. Therefore, if the claimant is in receipt of Income Support, Pension Credit, Housing Benefit, Council Tax Benefit and Incapacity Benefit and he has a change of circumstances, he must write to each of the individual benefit offices to notify them of that change. A claimant must notify each benefit authority immediately, because his failure to do so is an offence for which he could face prosecution and may lead to a recoverable overpayment (see **CHAPTER 5 OVERPAYMENTS AND RECOVERY**).

For tax credits, some changes must be notified to HMRC within three months, otherwise a penalty may be imposed. These are:

- where a claim is made as a couple, and they separate;

- where a claim is made as a single person, and that person becomes part of a couple; and

- where the childcare element of WTC is being paid, and either the childcare costs cease for at least four weeks, or there is a reduction in the weekly childcare costs of more than £10 per week for a four-week period.

Other changes that affect how much tax credit is due should also be notified. Any increases in entitlement will only be backdated by three months, whereas reductions will take effect from the date of the change.

Challenging decisions   4.9

Decision making and appeal rights – tax credits   4.10

The decision-making and appeal process for tax credits is in many ways less complex than the system that applies to Social Security. This is partly due to the system of annual awards, based on the income for a whole year. Decisions are made by HMRC. The process starts with an 'initial decision' (*TCA 2002, s 14*) on entitlement to an award. Before making this, HMRC can require the claimant to provide further information or evidence necessary.

Once an award has been made, it can then be 'revised' following a change of circumstances, or if HMRC has reason to believe that the award is incorrect for some reason (*sections 15–16*). Usually at the end of the year HMRC will issue a 'final notice', which sets out the details of income and other circumstances on which the award of tax credits was based for that year. The claimant is required to either confirm the details as accurate (based on the actual income received during the year), or to provide details of any differences. This will commonly be, for example, because someone's income was different from the figure used to estimate the tax credit entitlement (*section 17*). As a result of the declaration received from the claimant, HMRC may choose to enquire into his circumstances further, before making a final decision (*section 19*). Once satisfied, a final decision on someone's entitlement is issued (*section 18*).

If a decision on someone's income tax liability gives rise to a doubt about the accuracy of his tax credit award, then HMRC may revise the tax credit award (*section 20*).

All notices from HMRC about tax credit decisions must inform the claimant of his right to appeal, within 30 days, to an appeal tribunal. An appeal must include details of the grounds for appeal.

Decision making and appeal rights – Social Security 4.11

The *Social Security Act 1998 (SSA 1998)* brought about new provisions for the making of decisions and the determination of appeals in relation to Social Security Benefits, Child Support, Vaccine Damage Payments and War Pensions; and the *Child Support Pensions and Social Security Act 2000 (CSPSSA 2000)* incorporated these changes into the Housing Benefit and Council Tax Benefit procedure from July 2001.

These changes modernised the Social Security system, streamlining systems of claims, decisions, reviews and appeals. The Acts revoked all functions of the adjudication officer, replacing them with decisions of the Secretary of State.

The *Social Security and Child Support (Decisions and Appeals) Regulations 1999 (SI 1999 No 991)* and the *Housing Benefit and Council Tax Benefit (Decisions and Appeals) Regulations 2001 (SI 2001 No 1002)* provide the relevant legislation for these changes.

The Secretary of State (i e an officer authorised to make decisions on his behalf, known as a decision maker) will make decisions relating to:

- the initial decision (following the receipt of any claim);
- applications for review;
- applications for decisions to be superseded;
- whether to suspend or terminate an award of benefit; and
- whether the appeal tribunal should consider an application for appeal.

The principal legislation and guiding regulations referred to are as follows:

- *SSA 1998;*
- *CSPSSA 2000;*
- *Social Security (Transfer of Functions, etc) Act 1999;*
- *Social Security (Recovery of Benefits) Act 1997;*
- *Social Security Contributions and Benefits Act 1992 (SSCBA 1992);*
- *SSAA 1992;*
- *Social Security and Child Support (Decisions and Appeals) Regulations 1999 (SI 1999 Nos 991, 1466, 1632, 1670);*

- *Social Security Commissioners (Procedure) Regulations 1999 (SI 1999 No 1495);*

- *Housing Benefit and Council Tax Benefit (Decisions and Appeals) Regulations 2001 (Si 2001 No 1002);* and

- *Social Security Commissioners (Procedure) (Amendment) Regulations 2001 (SI 2001 No 1095).*

Secretary of State decisions   4.12

Legislation provides for the Secretary of State to make decisions in respect of any claim for benefit, any request for a review of a decision relating to benefit (i e to replace an original decision), any request to supersede a decision (i e replace an earlier decision with a new decision part way through a claim) and a decision as to whether any application for appeal should be referred to the appeal tribunal.

In most cases the Secretary of State will decide an issue without the need to refer a matter for further 'expert' consideration. However, where a decision relates to a claim for Industrial Injuries Benefit under *Part V* of the *SSCBA 1992*, the Secretary of State may refer an issue relating to the extent of an injury or any disablement arising from it, (including an industrial disease) to a medical practitioner experienced in dealing with such issues.

In making his decision the Secretary of State must have regard to any medical reports provided and the experience of any medical practitioner who has provided a report. *(SI 1999 No 991, Reg 12)*.

The Secretary of State will not only make decisions in relation to the entitlement to benefit – once a decision is made that a claimant is entitled to benefit, there will be a further step to resolve relating to whether that benefit should be paid to the claimant, and if so, from what date.

Decisions relating to the suspension
of benefit   4.13

Where the Secretary of State has decided that a benefit is payable, he may further suspend any payment of that benefit, in whole or in part in circumstances which are as follows:

- there is a question relating to whether a person claiming Jobseekers Allowance is or was available for employment and actively seeking work;

- there is a question relating to the claimant's entitlement to benefit;

- where it appears that the decision may have to be revised or superseded;

- where it appears that there may be an overpayment of another benefit due to be recovered from the amount paid or payable;

- the address from which the claimant made his claim for benefit is different from the last address that the claimant provided to the benefit department;

- an appeal is pending against an appeal tribunal, Commissioner or court (be it the claimant's appeal or an appeal in a different case), and it appears that the effect of the decision subject to appeal would have an impact on the decision made in any particular case.

(*SI 1999 No 991, Reg 16; SI 2001 No 1002, Reg 11*).

Information and evidence   4.14

In making any decision relating to benefit entitlement, the Secretary of State will require a basic amount of information and evidence. This will generally be provided by way of a full completed application form along with specified information and evidence requested on the application form (e g proof of NI number, proof of any income, proof of any savings and capital or proof of mortgage liability or rent etc).

Where required evidence is not provided, the claimant's payment of benefit may be suspended.

Where a question arises in relation to the claimant's entitlement to benefit, which results in a suspension of benefit entitlement, including the claimant's failure to supply supporting evidence and information that might be required, the Secretary of State will issue a notification to the claimant to the effect that he must supply the information or evidence within one month of the issue of that notification (although an extension of this period may be awarded where the claimant is able to satisfy the Secretary of State that an extension of time is reasonably required).

Where evidence is requested that either does not exist or it is impossible for the claimant to obtain it (even with an extension of time) the claimant must advise the Secretary of State, giving as much detail as possible as to why this is the case, within one month of the issue of that notification requesting information or evidence.

If the claimant's reasons for not supplying the required evidence are compelling then benefit may be paid in the absence of this evidence. (*SI 1999 No 991, Reg 17*).

Where a claimant fails to comply with the requirements of evidence (or has no good reason for not providing the evidence) within one month of his being told what evidence is required, and his payment of benefit has been suspended in whole (not in part), the claimant's entitlement to the benefit will be terminated from the date on which the payment was suspended. (*SI 1999 No 991, Reg 18; SI 2001 No 1002, Reg 14*).

If a claimant does not provide sufficient information and evidence with his claim for Income Support to provide for an assessment of entitlement to housing costs, the Secretary of State's decision will exclude any entitlement to housing costs from an award of Income Support. For example, if the claimant's entitlement to Income Support with housing costs would have been £100 per week, but without the housing costs his entitlement is £70 per week, the Secretary of State will make a decision to the effect that the claimant is entitled to Income Support of £70 per week). (*SI 1999 No 991, Reg 13(1)*).

If a claimant does not provide sufficient information and evidence with his claim for Income Support or Jobseekers Allowance or Housing or Council Tax Benefit to provide for an assessment of entitlement to benefit for a dependent child, or for assessment in consequence of reduced income due to a trade dispute, the Secretary of State's decision will exclude any entitlement to benefit in respect of these circumstances, thus producing a lower award of benefit. (*SI 1999 No 991, Reg 13(2)(i)–(ii), Reg 15; SI 2001 No 1002, Reg 11(1)*).

If a claimant does not provide sufficient information and evidence with his claim for Income Support or Housing or Council Tax Benefit to provide for an assessment of entitlement to a severe disability premium, the Secretary of State's decision will exclude any entitlement to this premium in an award of Income Support. For example, if a claimant who is living alone and has no one claiming Carer's Allowance for him, has been awarded a Disability Living Allowance Care Component, but does not provide a notification of award, then even though technically he would be entitled to a severe disability premium in his assessment of Income Support, this premium will be excluded from any assessment of entitlement. (*SI 1999 No 991, Reg 13(2)(iii); SI 2001 No 1002, Reg 11(1)*).

All notifications of entitlement will be issued to the claimant in writing within 14 days of the date on which the benefit department received the claim. The claimant, in all cases will have one month, from the date of issue of any notification/determination to either respond to any requests for further information, or to request a revision of any determination.

Secretary of State revisions   4.15

The Secretary of State may revise a decision either of his own initiation or following an application from the claimant. Where a revision is either initiated or requested within one month of the issue of any notification or decision, the decision revised will be deemed to be the original decision, and as such any revised decision will be effective from the date of the original decision.

Decisions subject to time limitations 4.16

Under the legislation, decisions may be revised by the Secretary of State where:

- the Secretary of State commences action leading to the revision within one month of the date of the original decision; or

- the claimant makes an application in writing to the benefit authority for a revised decision within one month of the date of the original decision. However, if the claimant has not been provided with reasons for the decision, he may, within one month of the original decision, make an application for written reasons. The claimant's application for a revised decision must then be made within six weeks of the date of issue of the original decision.

Where the Secretary of State requires any further information to consider the application for review such evidence and/or information must be provided within one month of it being requested.

Late applications for revision 4.17

Time limited applications may be extended where an application is made within 13 months of the date of issue of the original decision and the late application provides details of:

- the decision which the late application is in respect of; and

- grounds on which the late application is sought, including reasons for the late application.

An extension of time will only be granted where the claimant satisfies the Secretary of State that it is reasonable to grant the application, that the application has merit and that there are special circumstances which directly relate to the reason for the late application (special circumstances do not include ignorance or misunderstanding of the law or time limits, nor do they include a Commissioner or a court having taken a different view of the law than originally applied to the claimant's case at the time of the original decision).

An application for an extension of time which is refused cannot be revised.

Decisions that can be revised at any time   **4.18**

The Secretary of State may revise a decision either of his own initiation or following the application from a claimant outside of the limited period of one month where:

- a decision of the Secretary of State arose from an official error;

- a decision was based on a mistake as to or in ignorance of a material fact and, as a result, the decision was more advantageous to the claimant than it should have been;

- the decision was not to award Jobseekers Allowance (due to the implementation of sanctions and penalties);

- the decision was to award benefit to a claimant or member of his family, where it is established that the claimant or family member is entitled to, or receives an increase in entitlement to another relevant benefit;

- the decision is one for which the claimant has no right of appeal; and

- the claimant has had a relevant change of circumstances since the date of his original application.

The *SSA 1998* provides that the Secretary of State is only required to consider matters in a revision which have been raised either by the claimant or by himself. This means that an entire claim may not be looked at, only issues mentioned in the application for revision.

A revised decision in respect of an application will usually take effect from the effective date of the original decision. Where this means that the claimant is entitled to more benefit, arrears should be paid. This is a crucial advantage of fitting an application into the grounds for a revision, rather than a supersession. Superseded decisions usually only take effect from when the request for supersession was made.

Supersessions   **4.19**

Where the Secretary of State has made a decision relating to a claim or a revision, he may, in certain circumstances, decide to supersede the decision (i e make a further decision to replace the original decision).

The Secretary of State may supersede decisions, either on his own initiative or on application, in the following circumstances:

- there has been a relevant change of circumstances, or it is anticipated that a relevant change of circumstances will occur (provided that the change of circumstances does not relate to the repayment of a Social Fund loan or a period of absence from a residential/nursing home that will be for less than one week);

- the decision being superseded was erroneous in law and a period of more than one month has passed since the date of the original decision;

- the decision was made by an appeal tribunal or Commissioner and was based on ignorance or mistake as to material fact;

- a relevant benefit was awarded following which the claimant or a member of his family has become entitled to another benefit or relevant increase of award of another benefit;

- the original decision was to award Jobseekers Allowance, which is subsequently determined not to be payable (due to the implementation of sanctions and penalties);

- the Secretary of State receives further information or evidence or does not receive requested further information or evidence, resulting in the earlier decision being superseded.

Once an application is made for a decision to be superseded, the decision maker (or tribunal) should initially consider whether one of the grounds for supersession (e g a material change of circumstances) has occurred. It is not enough that the present decision maker takes a different view of the evidence. If the decision maker does not consider that the decision should be changed, then the original decision will still apply. However, this new decision (i e the decision not to supersede) carries a fresh right of appeal.

Decisions against which no right of appeal lies cannot be superseded.

The effective date of supersession in cases where decisions are superseded in consequence of a change of circumstances will be either:

- The effective date of the change of circumstances, where the claimant has notified the benefit authority of the change within one month of the change of circumstances occurring.

  For example, if the claimant is notified of his entitlement to Disability Living Allowance on 21 November, and he advises (in writing) the Income Support department of this award on or before 20 December, his Income Support determination may be superseded with a decision to award a disability premium from 21 November.

- The date on which the benefit authority was notified of the change of circumstances in all other cases.

For example, if the claimant is notified of his entitlement to Disability Living Allowance on 21 November, and the claimant advises (in writing) the Income Support department of this award on 22 December, his Income Support determination may be superseded with a decision to award a disability premium from the week following 22 December.

Suspension and termination   4.20

Once a decision has been made that the claimant is entitled to an award of benefit, the Secretary of State may suspend that award, in full or in part, in certain circumstances.

A decision to suspend benefit will result in the claimant not being paid any benefit at all, or only being paid benefit at a reduced rate. However, the claimant will be notified in writing of any decision to suspend benefit, and the notification will include full reasons why the decision has been made (the claimant will have the right to request that the decision to suspend benefit be reviewed).

The Secretary of State may decide to suspend an award of benefit, in full or in part, where:

- there is a question relating to whether a person claiming Jobseekers Allowance is or was available for employment and actively seeking work. This may apply where the claimant was late in signing on as available for work, or where the claimant places restrictions on the type of work or training which he is prepared to do, or where the claimant places restrictions on the hours that he is willing to work, or where he is unable to show that he has complied with the requirements of any part of his Jobseekers agreement;

- there is a question relating to the claimant's entitlement to benefit, i e where he has failed to supply sufficient information and evidence with his original claim, or where the claimant has failed to provide a medical certificate or attend a medical examination, or where the Secretary of State has any other reason to believe there may be a question relating to entitlement to benefit;

- it appears that the decision may have to be revised or superseded. This will most frequently be applied where the Secretary of State is aware of a change of circumstances or aware of a pending change of the claimant's circumstances, e g the claimant has been found fit for work, the claimant is going abroad, the claimant is in hospital, the claimant is starting work etc. This may also be applied where the Secretary of State is aware of a tribunal decision, which he intends to appeal against;

- it appears that there may be an overpayment of another benefit due to be recovered from the amount paid or payable. For example, the claimant has been in receipt of Income Support and also qualifies for another benefit such as Carer's Allowance. There could well be an overlap in entitlement giving rise to an overpayment of Income Support. In this scenario the Secretary of State may suspend payments of Carer's Allowance while establishing the amount of benefit to be recovered from Income Support;

- the address from which the claimant made his claim for benefit is different from the last address that the claimant provided to the benefit department. So for example, if the claimant's NI number shows on the computer as being registered to a previous address, his entitlement to benefit will be suspended until such time that he notifies the Secretary of State in writing, providing the date that he moved etc;

- an appeal is pending against an appeal tribunal, Commissioner or court (be it the claimant's appeal or an appeal in a different case), and it appears that the effect of the decision subject to appeal would have an impact on the decision made in any particular case. For example, the interpretation or definition of the qualifying conditions for a particular premium is the subject of an appeal, or the descriptors of incapacity become a subject of an appeal etc.

Failure to attend a medical examination 4.21

Where a claimant fails to attend a medical examination at the direction of the Secretary of State, and his claim for benefit is in consequence of his being incapable of work, benefit will be suspended in full or in part, but only where the claimant fails to attend the medical examination without good cause on two consecutive occasions, in which case benefit will be terminated from the date on which payment was suspended. (*SI 1999 No 991, Reg 19*).

Making payments of suspended benefit 4.22

Payments of suspended benefit will be made where the Secretary of State is satisfied that any questions regarding the claimant's entitlement to benefit have been resolved and that the suspended benefit is properly payable. Therefore, where the Secretary of State notifies the claimant that he requires further information/evidence and the claimant complies with the request within one month of issue, benefit entitlement will be assessed from the date on which the suspension commenced.

In the case of benefit suspensions due to the claimant's failure to inform the benefit authority of a change of address, suspended benefit will be paid from the date that the claimant notifies the Secretary of State, in writing, of his change of address.

In the case of benefit suspension arising from a pending appeal, payment of suspended benefit will be made if, within one month of receipt of a decision relating to that appeal, the Secretary of State does not notify the claimant, in writing, that he has either asked for a statement of reasons for the decision, or within one month of receipt of a statement of reasons, made an application for leave to appeal against the decision. (*SI 1999 No 991, Reg 20*).

The claimant will receive written notification of the Secretary of State's decision within 14 days (or as soon as possible thereafter) of his claim and accompanying evidence having been received. The decision relating to the claim will be sent, in writing, to the claimant. If the claimant is not happy with the decision of the Secretary of State, then he may make an application for the decision to be revised or superseded.

Rights of appeal 4.23

Secretary of State decisions fall into two groups, namely:

- decisions against which an appeal lies (*SI 1999 No 991, Reg 26*); and
- decisions against which no appeal lies (*SI 1999 No 991, Reg 27, Sch 2*).

Most decisions of the Secretary of State, or a local authority for Housing Benefit and Council Tax Benefit, will be decisions which can be appealed to an appeal tribunal, with the exception of those which fall within the exclusions listed below. If an appeal against a decision to which no appeal lies is registered, the appeal will be 'struck out' by the clerk of the tribunal.

There will be no right of appeal against decisions relating to the following:

- *Child Benefit* – A child's temporary absence abroad and the disregarding of certain days absence abroad; a child's attendance at a recognised educational establishment; any discretionary decision relating to contributions and expenses in respect of a child.

- *Claims and payments* – Any decision made under the *Social Security (Claims and Payments) Regulations 1979 (SI 1979 No 628)*, except the time for claiming benefit; the validity of a claim; the payment of withheld benefit; the right to payment of benefit where payment is not obtained within twelve months; the amount deductible by way of housing costs; the amount of miscellaneous housing costs payable direct to a third party; the direct payment to a third party of benefit payable to or in respect of residents in hostels; payments of benefit direct to the claimant's landlord; the direct payment out of benefit for fuel costs, water charges, child support maintenance (actual liability and arrears); and the priority of deductions for gas and electricity.

- *Contracted-out pension schemes* – Relating to annual increase of guaranteed minimum pensions.

- *Decisions depending on other cases*.

- *Deductions* – Deductions from Income Support, except where the deduction relates to community charges or council tax deductions from Income Support, or the appeal at issue is in relation to whether there is sufficient benefit for deductions to be made or the priority awarded to any deduction.

- *Expenses* – Whether to pay expenses to any person who is directed to attend an interview concerning his entitlement to benefit.

- *Guardian's Allowance* – Giving notice to surviving parents who are in prison or legal custody.

- *Income Support, Social Fund payments and Jobseekers Allowance* – Applications for benefit from claimants under the age of 18 where there is incomplete evidence.

- *Income Support, Housing and Council Tax Benefit* – Increases in Income Support due to the attainment of a particular age.

- *Industrial Injuries Benefit* – Disablement pension increases; or period of payment of an increase for Constant Attendance; or further increases for exceptionally severe disablement; and whether a person might be treated as incapable of work, even though he has worked after an industrial injury.

- *Invalid Vehicle Scheme* – The issue of certificates for the invalid vehicle scheme.

- *Jobseekers Allowance* – The time or day of the week that a claimant is to attend at a job centre or sign on.

- *Payments on account, overpayments and recovery* – Any matter except: the offsetting of any interim payment made in anticipation of an award of benefit; the overpayment of an interim payment; the offsetting of a prior payment against a subsequent award; whether a payment in excess of entitlement has been credited to a bank or other account; the sums to be deducted in calculating recoverable amounts; treatment of capital to be reduced; determining, revising or superseding decisions relating to a claimant's protected earnings; from whom an overpayment of Housing Benefit should be recovered; or whether payments should be paid to a landlord.

- *Persons abroad* – Whether to allow a person to avoid disqualification for receiving benefit during a period of temporary absence from Great Britain longer than that specified in the regulations.

- *Reciprocal agreements* – Any reciprocal agreement with countries outside the United Kingdom.

- *Social Fund awards* – In relation to the recovery of Social Fund awards.

- *Suspension* – Benefit which has been suspended or terminated.

- *Up-rating* – The alterations of benefit rates in consequence of an up-rating order.

An appeal may be brought by the claimant, an appointee who has been appointed by the Secretary of State, or a person who has made the claim for Attendance Allowance or Disability Living Allowance on behalf of a person who is terminally ill, or in the case of an appeal relating to a pension scheme, the employer or his member, trustee or manager. (*SI 1999 No 991, Reg 25*).

Time limits for bringing an appeal   4.24

A late appeal may be made in certain circumstances, but must be made within 13 months of the date of the decision in respect of which the appeal lies. This provision extends the prescribed time for bringing an appeal by twelve months. A decision on whether to accept the late appeal is initially made by the decision maker or local authority. A decision maker can accept a late appeal if it is 'in the interests of justice'. If not accepted, it must be passed to a legally qualified panel of the appeal tribunal. An extension of time will not be allowed unless the tribunal is satisfied that:

- if the application was granted there would be reasonable prospects of success; or

- it is in the interests of justice that the application be granted because:

  o   there are exceptional special circumstances which are relevant to the application; or

  o   there are special circumstances which arose in consequence of the claimant, his spouse or dependant having died or suffered serious illness, or the applicant was not resident in the United Kingdom, or the normal postal services where disrupted.

The reasons for the late application must be as a result of those special circumstances, which resulted in it not being practical for the application to be made within one month of the decision. However, consideration will be given to the time which has elapsed between the expiry of an 'in time' application and the special circumstances being of compelling weight.

Where consideration is given to the interest of justice, no consideration will be given to the claimant's misunderstanding or ignorance of the law, regulations or time limits, or that a Commissioner or court has taken a different view of the law than that applied at the time of the decision. An application for an extension of time, which has been refused, may not be reviewed. (*SI 1999 No 991, Reg 32; SI 2001 No 1002, Regs 5, 15*).

Applications for appeal   4.25

Applications for appeal must be made by:

- the claimant;

- an appointee who has been appointed by the Secretary of State; or

- a person who has made the claim for Attendance Allowance or Disability Living Allowance on behalf of a person who is terminally ill;

or, in the case of an appeal relating to a pension scheme, by:

- the employer;

- his member, trustee or manager; or

- a representative to whom the appellant has provided his written authority.

The appeal must be in writing, in a signed and completed prescribed appeal form (or by signed letter which identifies the claimant's name, NI number, date of decision, the benefit that the appeal is in respect of, grounds for appeal and reasons for appeal) and delivered to the benefit office which issued the decision which is the subject of the appeal.

Where the application for appeal contains the minimum required information (as above) but the Secretary of State feels that further information will be required in order for the appeal to proceed, he will issue a notification requesting further particulars to which the appellant must respond within 14 days of its issue.

Any issue as to the validity of an appeal will be passed to the appeal tribunal for determination by a legally qualified appeal panel member.

If the appellant, prior to the determination of the legally qualified panel member, provides further particulars, then that further information must be taken into consideration by the panel member in reaching a decision. (*SI 1999 No 991, Reg 33*).

The *SSA 1998* and the *CSPSSA 2000* provide that the tribunal is not required to consider matters in an appeal which have not been raised either by the claimant or the Secretary of State/local authority. This means that the entire claim may not necessarily be looked at – only issues mentioned in the appeal. The appeal tribunal shall not take into account any circumstances which were not existing at the time when the decision appealed against was made.

Composition of appeal tribunal 4.26

The administration of appeals is the responsibility of the Appeals Service, an executive agency of the DWP. The appeal tribunal itself, which is appointed by the Lord Chancellor and is part of the judiciary, will consist of:

• a legally qualified person, who will be required to form part of the panel at all appeal tribunals;

• a medically qualified person who is a fully registered medical practitioner and will be required to form part of the panel where an appeal relates to Incapacity Benefit, Industrial Injuries Benefit, Severe Disablement Allowance, certificates of recoverable benefits, and vaccine damage payments (a medically qualified member will always sit with a legally qualified member);

• a financially qualified person who is an accountant and will be required to form part of a panel where an appeal relates to a difficult issue raised in respect of Child Support or relevant benefit concerning consideration of profit and loss accounts, revenue accounts, balance sheets, income and expenditure (in the case of non-profit making enterprises) and the accounts of any trust fund (a financially qualified member will always sit with a legally qualified member);

• a person deemed to meet the requirements of a disability qualification (which relate to persons experienced in dealing with the needs of disabled persons in a professional or voluntary capacity, or who are disabled themselves), who will be required to form part of a panel where an appeal relates to Attendance Allowance, Disability Living Allowance, or disability issues within tax credit claims (a disability-qualified member will always sit with a legally qualified member and a medically qualified member);

• a combination of all four prescribed qualified members where the need arises. (*SI 1999 No 991, Reg 36*).

The legally qualified member may give directions to any party to the appeal proceedings to provide further evidence, information or documents as may reasonably be required. He may also summon a witness to attend a hearing of an appeal tribunal in order to answer any questions or to produce any document relating to a matter in question at the appeal.

Every summons will provide the witness with at least 14 days' notice of his being required at the hearing. If the witness is not provided with 14 days' notice, or the witness' necessary expenses of attendance are not paid or tendered to him, he will not be required to attend in obedience to the summons.

Every witness summons will advise the witness of his right to make an application to the chairman of the tribunal to vary or set aside the summons. A chairman at the tribunal may require any witness to give evidence on oath or affirmation, which will be administered in due form. (*SI 1999 No 991, Reg 43*).

Medical examination 4.27

Where a medical question is one of the issues raised at the tribunal, the tribunal may direct that a medical examination is carried out to establish a question relating to physical or mental disablement, including the extent of that disablement and the period throughout which the claimant is likely to satisfy the disability requirement, and to assess the extent of any loss of faculty.

Such examinations may be required in an appeal relating to Disability Living Allowance, Attendance Allowance, Disabled Person's Tax Credit, Severe Disablement Benefit, Incapacity Benefit, and Industrial Injuries Benefit (including industrial diseases). (*SI 1999 No 991, Reg 41*).

Physical examinations at oral hearings 4.28

Appeal tribunals can only require a claimant to have a physical examination at an oral hearing where there is a question relating to whether a person's disablement is more than 80% for the purpose of entitlement to Severe Disablement Allowance, Disablement Benefit or Constant Attendance Allowance, or the extent of a person's disablement arising from an industrial injury or disease. (*SI 1999 No 991, Reg 52*).

Oral hearings 4.29

Procedures 4.30

Where an appeal is registered with the appeal tribunal, the benefit authority will issue a questionnaire to the appellant asking whether he would like an oral hearing or whether he is content for the hearing to proceed without an oral hearing. This questionnaire must be returned to the Appeals Service within 14 days of issue. If the appellant does not respond to this questionnaire within 14 days, his appeal may be struck out. (*SI 1999 No 991, Reg 39*).

The claimant will be given at least 14 days' notice of his appeal hearing. If any party fails to appear at the hearing, the chairman will have regard to any explanation offered for the absence, but may proceed with the hearing in that person's absence. (*SI 1999 No 991, Reg 49*).

The chairman of the tribunal will decide on the 'order of play' at the hearing, and provide a plain English explanation of the procedure to all parties to the hearing. However, all parties to the hearing will have a right to be heard, to call witnesses and to question any other person called as a witness and to address the tribunal. Any person who has a right to be heard will also have the right to be accompanied or represented by another person, regardless of whether or not that representative has professional qualifications.

In practice, at an appeal tribunal, the chairman will introduce himself and his panel. The independence of the tribunal will be explained, and the procedure to be followed. In practice it is very unusual for there to be a presenting officer for the DWP at appeal hearings. Where the appeal concerns Housing Benefit, Council Tax Benefit or tax credits a presenting officer usually attends. Most appeal hearings consist of the claimant or representative opening their case, if they choose, followed by questions from the tribunal to the claimant. If there are witnesses then they too will be questioned. Once all issues have been covered, the claimant or representative should be given the opportunity to make final submissions. The claimant and others will then be asked to return to the waiting room, while the tribunal consider their decision. It is usual practice to notify the claimant of the decision on the day, although this is not a requirement, and may be inappropriate in difficult cases.

Postponements and adjournments 4.31

All applications for postponements must be in writing to the clerk of the tribunal stating reasons for the request to postpone a hearing. The clerk of the tribunal may decide to grant or refuse the request, or he may pass the request on to the legally qualified panel member for a decision.

If the request is refused, the clerk must notify the applicant in writing. He must also place the request for a postponement and his letter of refusal before the appeal tribunal, who may decide to grant a postponement at any time before the commencement of the hearing of their own motion, or grant an adjournment of their own motion following the commencement of the hearing.

Where a hearing is adjourned and it is not practicable, or would cause undue delay, to reconvene before a panel of the same members, the appeal may be placed before a new panel by way of a complete rehearing. (*SI 1999 No 991, Reg 51*).

Decisions of appeal tribunals 4.32

Decisions will be recorded in summary and signed by the chairman. The decision will always advise all parties to the proceedings of:

- their right to request a copy statement of the reasons for the decision, which they must apply for within one month of the date of issue of the decision; and

- conditions governing appeals to the Commissioner.

A late application for a statement of reasons may be made in certain circumstances, but must be made in writing to the legally qualified panel member within 13 months of the date of the decision in respect of the appeal in question. This provision extends the prescribed time of one month for bringing an appeal by twelve months. However, an extension of time will not be allowed unless the tribunal are satisfied that it is in the interest of justice that the application be granted because:

- there are exceptional special circumstances which are relevant to the application; or

- there are special circumstances which arose in consequence of the claimant, his spouse or dependant having died or suffered serious illness, or the applicant was not resident in the United Kingdom, or the normal postal services where disrupted.

The late application must be due to those special circumstances, which resulted in it not being practical for the application to be made within one month of the decision. However, consideration will be given to the time which has elapsed between the expiry of an 'in time' application and the special circumstances being of compelling weight.

Where consideration is awarded to the interest of justice, no consideration will be awarded to the claimant's misunderstanding or ignorance of the law, regulations or time limits, or that a Commissioner or court has taken a different view of the law than that applied at the time of the decision. An application for an extension of time which has been refused may not be reviewed. (*SI 1999 No 991, Reg 54*).

Record of the hearing   4.33

The clerk to the tribunal will keep a copy of the chairman's record of the appeal hearing for a period of six months from the date of the decision of the appeal. During this time any party to the proceedings may make a written request for a copy of the record of the hearing – such applications should be made directly to the clerk of the tribunal.

Setting aside decisions   4.34

An application for setting aside a decision of the tribunal may be made in writing to the legally qualified panel member of the appeal tribunal, who may set aside a decision in the following circumstances:

- a document was not sent to or received at the appropriate time (i e 14 days before the hearing) by a party to the proceedings; or

- a party to the proceedings or his authorised representative was not present at the hearing. However, this will only apply where the party and/or his representative actually indicated beforehand that they wished to be present at the hearing.

Applications to set aside any decision of the tribunal must be made within one month of the issue of the decision. However, where the party requests written reasons for the decision, the prescribed time of one month in which the claimant must register a request to set aside a decision will be extended by 14 days. (*SI 1999 No 991, Reg 57*).

Leave to appeal to the Commissioner   4.35

An application for leave to appeal to a Commissioner must be made directly to the legally qualified panel member of the appeal tribunal on the grounds that the decision of the tribunal was erroneous in law. Such applications must be made within one month of the date of the issue of the decision of the tribunal (but may be extended by 14 days where reasons for the decision have been requested).

If the application for leave to appeal is granted, the legally qualified panel member may direct that the appeal be reheard by another appeal tribunal rather than grant leave to appeal to the Commissioner. This situation will arise where the panel member agrees that the decision of the tribunal was indeed erroneous in law.

If the application for leave to appeal to the Commissioner is refused or rejected, then the appellant may make an application to the Commissioner directly requesting leave to appeal. Applications for leave to appeal to the Commissioner must be made within one month of the date of issue of the decision refusing leave to appeal. (*SI 1999 No 1495, Reg 9; SI 2001 No 1095*).

An application to the Commissioner for leave to appeal must contain the following:

- the name and address of the applicant;

- the grounds on which the applicant intends to rely;

- the address for sending notices and documents;

- copies of the decision of the tribunal and reasons for the decision; and

- the chairman's notice of refusal or rejection of leave to appeal.

Appeals to the Commissioner   4.36

An appeal lies to a Commissioner from any decision under *sections 12* and *13* of the *SSA 1998*, including on tax credit appeals on the grounds that the decision of the tribunal was erroneous in law (subject to the claimant having made an application for leave to appeal).

If each of the principal parties to the case (the claimant and the benefit authority) consider the decision to be erroneous in law, then the Commissioner may set aside the decision and refer the case to a differently constituted tribunal with recommendations for its determination.

Where the Commissioner holds that the decision was erroneous in law, he will set the decision aside and give the decision which he considers to be correct, without making fresh findings of fact; or make new findings of fact; or refer the case to a tribunal with directions for its determination. (*SI 1999 No 1495, Reg 5*).

Appeals to the Court of Appeal   4.37

An application must be made to the Commissioner for leave to appeal on a point of law, in writing, stating the grounds of the appeal, within three months of the date of issue of the Commissioner's decision. (*SI 1999 No 1495, Reg 33*).

If leave is granted then an appeal to the Court of Appeal may proceed within three months of the Commissioner having granted leave.

If leave is refused by the Commissioner, then an application to the court for leave must be made within six weeks of the date of issue of the Commissioner's decision refusing leave to appeal. (*SSA 1998, s 15*).

An application to the court for leave to appeal must contain the following:

*   the name and address of the applicant;

*   the grounds on which the applicant intends to rely;

*   the address for sending notices and documents;

*   copies of the decision of the tribunal and reasons for the decision;

*   the chairman's notice of refusal or rejection of leave to appeal;

*   copies of the Commissioner's decision; and

*   the Commissioner's notice of refusal to grant leave to appeal.

Backdating Social Security benefits   4.38

The period for backdating all Social Security benefits is limited to either one or three months (with the exception of Housing Benefit and Council Tax Benefit where backdating may be allowed for a period of up to 52 weeks). For Pension Credit there is a concession allowing claims to be backdated by up to 12 months.

Automatic backdating for three months applies to the following benefits:

- Child Benefit;

- Guardian's Allowance;

- Incapacity Benefit;

- Industrial Disablement Benefit;

- Carer's Allowance;

- Maternity Allowance;

- Reduced Earnings Allowance;

- Retirement Pension;

- Pension Credit;

- Widow's Benefit; and

- dependants' increases for those benefits.

Applications for benefit to be backdated for three months in respect of means-tested benefits (other than Pension Credit) will only be accepted on the grounds that the claimant:

- had difficulty in communicating and it was impractical to obtain assistance;

- was caring for an ill or disabled person and it was impractical to obtain assistance;

- had a domestic emergency and it was impractical to obtain assistance;

- received misleading information or advice from a government office;

- received misleading written advice from an adviser;

- received financial information from a bank or an employer leading him to believe that he would not qualify;

- was prevented from attending the benefit office by adverse weather conditions; or

- was ill or disabled and it was impractical to obtain assistance.

Where the claimant can show that he satisfies one of the above grounds, he will also have to show that continuously, throughout the period of backdating, he could not reasonably have been expected to claim earlier.

Administrative backdating for up to one month 4.39

Means-tested benefits may be backdated for one month, provided the claimant can show that the reason for his not claiming earlier fell in to one of the following situations:

- the office from which the claimant should have claimed was closed and there was no alternative;

- the claimant was unable to attend the office because of difficulties with his usual mode of transport and there was no reasonable alternative available;

- there were adverse postal conditions;

- the claimant had been receiving another benefit and was not advised in advance that his benefit had expired;

- a claim for a tax credit was made within one month of previous entitlement to Income Support or Jobseekers Allowance;

- the claimant had ceased to be a member of a couple within one month of the claim;

- within one month before the claim, the claimant's partner, parent, child, brother or sister had died.

Special backdating rules for particular benefits 4.40

Where a benefit award depends on the award of another qualifying benefit, special rules apply. Backdating is dependent on the claimant having registered a claim when he originally thought that he would qualify and because of the linking benefit rule his application was refused. In such cases provided the claimant makes a further claim within three months of entitlement to the qualifying benefit the linking benefit can be backdated.

This rule relates to the following benefits:

- Disabled Person's Tax Credit (prior to April 2003);

- Carer's Allowance;

- Social Fund, Maternity and Funeral Payments;

- Severe Disablement Allowance; and

- Incapacity Benefit.

Discretionary backdating by the Secretary of State   **4.41**

Discretionary backdating by the Secretary of State for more than three months can be applied in two cases:

- *regulation 4(1)* of *SSC&P Regs 1987* provides that a claim shall be made on an approved form or 'in such other manner, being in writing as the Secretary of State accepts as being sufficient in the circumstances'. (This does not apply to Income Support or Jobseekers Allowance which must be made on a specified form.) Subject to these exceptions, a letter enquiring about a particular benefit could be treated as a claim. In such cases benefit could be backdated to the date of the letter;

- under *regulation 9(1)* of *SSC&P Regs 1987* the Secretary of State can treat a claim for one benefit as a claim for another specified benefit and there could be unlimited backdating.

Such applications are at the discretion of the Secretary of State and consequently there is no right of an appeal to an appeal tribunal. The only remedy would be an application for Judicial Review.

5 Overpayments and Recovery

(*Social Security Administration Act 1992 (SSAA 1992), ss 71–78; Social Security (Payments on Account, Overpayments and Recovery) Regulations 1988 (SI 1988 No 664); Social Security (Payments on Account, Overpayments and Recovery) Amendment Regulations 2000 (SI 2000 No 2336)*).

Introduction   5.1

On occasions it will be discovered that a claimant has received more benefit than he should have done. This usually happens either because he has received Income Support and another benefit at the same time, without that other benefit being off-set against his Income Support as it should have been; or because he has continued to receive a benefit for a longer period than he should; or simply because his benefit entitlement was incorrectly calculated in the first place so that, for instance, instead of getting £85 per week he has been getting £95.

The legal consequence of such errors, in particular whether the claimant has to repay the amount overpaid, depends on how the error arose in the first place and what sort of error it is. In certain circumstances, the benefits authority can recover an overpayment of benefit even where there has been no fault or neglect on the part of the claimant.

The three most common situations where overpayments can occur are where the claimant:

• has received a means-tested benefit together with one or more other non means-tested benefits covering the same period of time and, because of the rules on overlapping benefits, one should have extinguished or reduced the other (for example, a claimant's incapacity award, which he is claiming in addition to Income Support, increases after 28 weeks, and the Income Support department fail to take this increase into account and carry out an adjustment to the claimant's benefit award);

• continues to be paid benefit for longer than he should (for example, he starts work and is no longer entitled to Income Support); and

• has his entitlement incorrectly calculated so that he receives more each week than he should (for example, a dependent child was included in the claimant's assessment of entitlement to benefit, but that dependent child has left school and started work).

Overlapping benefits rule   5.2

An example of the overlapping benefits situation is where a claimant has claimed Income Support and Child Benefit at the same time and payments of Income Support are made by the local DWP to the claimant, while the Child Benefit claim is being processed by the Child Benefit Centre. Then, after several weeks, the claimant receives a payment for arrears of Child Benefit. The claimant may well assume, and usually does, that as the giro has been sent to him, he is entitled to have it in addition to the Income Support, and so spends it.

The Child Benefit payment has to be taken into account in full as income when calculating entitlement to Income Support, and so there has been an overpayment of Income Support for the weeks covered by the Child Benefit arrears. In other words, if the claimant has been on Income Support of £45 per week, after six weeks he will have received £270. If he then receives a payment of £90 for Child Benefit arrears covering those same six weeks, his Income Support entitlement reduces to £30 per week, because he cannot have both the Income Support and the Child Benefit – one must be set off against the other.

There are other situations where Income Support will overlap with another benefit which should have been taken into account but for some reason was not. The rule is absolutely clear: if it is established that the two benefits have incorrectly been paid to the claimant for the same period then the claimant must repay, even though there has probably been no fault or neglect at all on his part. This is stipulated by *section 74(1)* of the *SSAA 1992*, which says:

> 'Where—
>
> (a)   a payment by way of prescribed income is made after the date which is the prescribed date in relation to the payment; and
>
> (b)   it is determined that an amount which has been paid by way of Income Support would not have been paid if the payment had been made on the prescribed date,
>
> the Secretary of State shall be entitled to recover that amount from the person to whom it was paid.'

'Prescribed' means prescribed by regulations, the relevant regulations being the *Social Security (Payments on Account, Overpayments and Recovery) Regulations 1988*. The words 'would not have been paid' in *section 74(1)(b)* above are to be taken as meaning 'should not have been paid', i e it is to be assumed that the appropriate amount of Income Support would automatically have been withheld as soon as the other benefit was awarded.

An overpayment could also occur if, for example, the claimant has been on Income Support and then receives arrears of maintenance. His Income Support will have been calculated without reference to any maintenance, and so when a lump sum is received it will be necessary for the Income Support to be adjusted. (There are special rules to deal with this situation, which are discussed in **CHAPTER 2 ASSESSMENT OF MEANS**.)

Payment continuing for too long   5.3

The second situation where an overpayment can arise is where the claimant continues to receive payment of a benefit, or an increase in a benefit for a dependant, for longer than he should, for instance, because he no longer satisfies the conditions for payment. Examples of this are numerous, but would cover the case of a claimant starting full-time work while on Incapacity Benefit or Income Support; continuing to receive Child Benefit even though the child had left school and started work or obtained a placement on a youth training course; or continuing to receive an increase for a dependent wife after a separation.

Whether any overpayment is recoverable in this type of case does depend on whether there has been fault on the part of the claimant; whether he maintains that he did tell the benefit authority of the change in circumstances; and, where he did, whether he did so effectively in writing as the regulations prescribe.

Section 71(1) of the *SSAA 1992* prescribes that:

'Where it is determined that, whether fraudulently or otherwise, any person has misrepresented, or failed to disclose, any material fact and in consequence of the misrepresentation or failure—

(*a*)   a payment has been made in respect of a benefit to which this section applies; or

(*b*)   any sum recoverable by or on behalf of the Secretary of State in connection with any such payment has not been recovered,

the Secretary of State shall be entitled to recover the amount of any payment which he would not have made or any sum which he would have received but for the misrepresentation or failure to disclose.'

Assuming the overpayment can be proved, it is then necessary to establish that it is recoverable, and to do this it must be shown that someone – not necessarily the claimant because an overpayment can be recovered from whoever is legally liable to repay (which may be the claimant, a partner who was living with the claimant at the time of the overpayment occurring, an appointee, the person to whom the payment was made etc) – must have, whether fraudulently or otherwise, (i) misrepresented; or (ii) failed to disclose a material fact, and as a result an overpayment of benefit must have occurred.

Fraudulently or otherwise 5.4

The words 'fraudulently or otherwise' make it clear that dishonesty is not an essential ingredient. An innocent misrepresentation will result in an overpayment being recoverable just as surely as a fraudulent misrepresentation. This was confirmed in *Page v Chief Adjudication Officer (1991) Times, 4 July* (a decision on identical wording in the *Social Security Act 1986*), where the Court of Appeal held that the words 'fraudulently or otherwise' were plain and unambiguous and included an innocent misrepresentation.

An innocent failure to disclose will also lead to a recoverable overpayment, in the sense that carelessness, as opposed to deliberately withholding information, will lead to the same result. However, there must be some degree of responsibility on the part of the claimant in that he must know the fact which should be disclosed.

Misrepresentation 5.5

A misrepresentation is something that the claimant does knowingly and is, therefore, positive; whereas a failure to disclose may be an innocent action, which is negative, although the two may be said to overlap to some extent. For instance, the untrue statement 'I am not working' is both a misrepresentation and a failure to disclose the true facts. Any positive statement, whether in writing or oral, which is untrue will constitute a misrepresentation. There would be no defence that the maker did not know the true facts when he made the statement; it is sufficient that there is a misrepresentation, whether known to him or not. (Compare the position on failure to disclose – see **5.6** below.)

So if a claimant says 'my wife is not working' he may believe that to be true, but if in fact it is not true he will be guilty of misrepresentation. To avoid liability he should have said 'I believe my wife is not working'. This, of course, will also apply to claimants who have a partner and are not aware that the partner has savings and capital and/or the amount of those savings and capital. This is because in signing a claim for benefit the claimant is declaring in all cases that the information that he is providing is true, correct and complete, and in signing such a declaration the claimant's lack of knowledge is no bar to recovery if any of the answers are in fact wrong.

An innocent misrepresentation can be made even if the claimant lacks the necessary knowledge or mental capacity. For example, an elderly claimant, who is confused and in a nursing home, may have signed a Pension Credit claim form which has been completed on his behalf by nursing staff. If it later transpires that he has substantial assets which had not been disclosed, there will be a recoverable overpayment if the claimant has no appointee acting on his behalf, because he will be the only person entitled to claim. If he signs the claim form he will be deemed to be responsible for its contents and must be assumed to have been capable of making the claim.

Failure to disclose 5.6

A failure to disclose requires that the claimant knows, or is in a position where he ought to have known, the fact which should have been disclosed. A person cannot be held liable for failing to disclose what he did not know. There is, however, a fine line between what the claimant ought reasonably to have known and what he knows.

For instance, a claimant who completes a claim form for a means-tested benefit is required to answer questions in relation to his partner's circumstances, income and capital. Therefore, if he is unsure of any questions raised on the claim about his partner's circumstances, then he is under an obligation to clarify that information prior to signing a declaration.

Failing to do something connotes a breach of an obligation to do it, and it had been held by Social Security Commissioners and the courts that, in order to establish a failure to disclose, the benefit authority must establish that non-disclosure must have occurred in circumstances 'in which ... disclosure by the person in question was reasonably to be expected' (see *R(SB)21/82* and *R(SB)28/83*). However, a recent tribunal of Commissioners, in *CIS/4348/2003*, has overruled this long-established approach, and held that the obligation to disclose material facts is absolute, even if the claimant did not realise the matter was relevant.

The fact to be disclosed must be 'material', i e a fact which is relevant to the matters in issue, and the overpayment must be made 'in consequence of the misrepresentation or the failure to disclose', so that if there is a break in the chain of causation this will be relevant as to whether there has been a recoverable overpayment at all, or possibly as to the amount thereof. If, for instance, a claimant could show that, even though he had failed to disclose, some other factor had intervened to cause the overpayment, then he would avoid liability.

In Commissioner's decision *CIS/159/90*, the claimant was receiving Supplementary Benefit and claimed Child Benefit for her son who was born in July 1987. In October 1987, she was sent an order book by the Child Benefit Centre but did not tell the local office. However, the local office was notified by the Child Benefit Centre of the award, but they failed to act on this and continued to pay the claimant the same amount of Supplementary Benefit. The Commissioner held that even though the claimant had failed to disclose, the subsequent overpayment was not recoverable, as it was not in consequence of the failure to disclose.

To whom must disclosure be made? 5.7

Disclosure should be made directly to the benefit authority that is paying the benefit. If the claimant is paid benefit from a number of different benefit offices, disclosure must be made to each office.

If a claimant informs an office that is not dealing with the benefit issue in question – for example, informing the local Social Security office about an issue relating to Disability Living Allowance – the claimant is entitled to assume initially that his disclosure has been effective, but then if he continues to receive benefit as before, so that it is clear that his disclosure has not got through to the people who are actually paying him, he must try again and do his best to ensure that his disclosure is effective. How long he is entitled to wait before trying again is not certain, as each case will depend on its own facts, but, in most cases, probably no more than a few weeks.

Any overpayment arising where the claimant has disclosed the required information to the benefit office dealing with the claim will clearly be in consequence of an official error (i e the benefit department failing to act on the information provided to them).

Disclosure only to the Post Office where the claimant cashes his benefit payment will never suffice for the purpose of disclosure to the benefit authority.

By whom must disclosure be made? 5.8

Normally it will be the claimant who makes disclosure and it always remains his duty to do so. It is, however, permissible for disclosure to be made by a third party on his behalf, e g by a relative or appointee, provided:

- the information is given to the relevant office;

- the claimant knows the information has been given; and

- it is reasonable for the claimant to believe that it is not necessary for him to take any action himself.

Casual or incidental disclosure, for example, in the course of a third party making a separate claim for himself, will not, however, be sufficient, as this would not be made on behalf of the claimant.

From whom can recovery be claimed? 5.9

Section 71(3) of the *SSAA 1992*, provides:

'An amount recoverable under subsection (1) above [see **5.3** above] is in all cases recoverable from the person who misrepresented the fact or failed to disclose it.'

So if the misrepresentation or failure to disclose is the responsibility of the claimant, then he must repay. If the responsibility lies with a third party such as a relative, then the overpayment can be recovered from that person.

Calculating the overpayment 5.10

If it is determined that there has been a recoverable overpayment, the amount of the overpayment must be calculated. Effectively, the amount overpaid will be the difference between the amount actually paid and what would have been paid if the misrepresentation or failure to disclose had not occurred. Usually this will be straightforward. If, for example, the claimant's right to a particular benefit ceased on a known date, then obviously any payments made to him after that date will have to be repaid. On other occasions, however, where perhaps it is alleged that the claimant has been working, it can be difficult to be certain about the amount overpaid as there may be a factual dispute as to how often or for how long the claimant has worked, and what he has earned. In addition, it must be borne in mind that, even after the amount of the overpayment has been assessed, the claimant may be entitled to an off-set.

Under the *Social Security (Payments on Account, Overpayments and Recovery) Regulations 1988 (SI 1988 No 664)*, there can be deducted from an overpayment any off-set. Such off-sets apply where, for example, it is determined that the claimant is entitled to a particular benefit for a period but he has already received a different amount of benefit, for the same period; or where he has received an increase for a partner and it is then decided that his partner was entitled to benefit in her own right. Such payment can then be set off against any arrears of entitlement under the second decision and treated as properly made on account of it. However, there can be no off-set if the original payment was obtained as a result of a failure to disclose or misrepresentation, i e it was a recoverable overpayment.

Regulation 13(1)(b) states that there can be deducted from any recoverable overpayment of Income Support:

'... any additional amount of Income Support ... which should have been determined to be payable—

(i) on the basis of the claim as presented to the adjudicating authority, or

(ii) on the basis of the claim as it would have appeared had the misrepresentation or non-disclosure been remedied before the determination ...'

129

Therefore, if all the required facts were before the decision maker at the date of claim, or they would have been but for the misrepresentation or failure to disclose, any further Income Support which the claimant should have been awarded can be set off against any overpayment. For example, if the information provided by the claimant revealed entitlement to a premium but no premium was awarded; or if the claimant failed to disclose that he was working ten hours a week and the award was calculated as if he was not working, the overpayment should be reduced by the earnings disregard.

Misrepresentation/failure to disclose capital 5.11

There is a special rule relating to misrepresentation as to, or failure to disclose, capital when claims have been made for Income Support, Working Families Tax Credit, Disabled Person's Tax Credit, Housing Benefit or Council Tax Benefit. This provides that the capital is to be treated as having been reduced at the end of each 13-week period by the amount of benefit overpaid during that period. So eventually there will come a time when the capital reduces below the appropriate limit.

There is a formula for reducing notional capital over a period of time; it is considered unreasonable to treat the claimant as continuing to keep the capital while depriving him of benefit and therefore the theory is that he will spend part of his capital each week in order to live, and so his capital will steadily diminish.

For instance, where a claimant is paying more rent in consequence of his capital, then he should be treated as spending some of that capital on his rent, and thus diminishing his capital amount. Where the claimant does not qualify for any other means-tested benefit because he has too much capital, then the amount of that means-tested benefit, which he would have been awarded but for the capital, will also diminish his capital, as in theory he would have to subsidise his living expenses from his capital.

An initial assessment of diminishing capital would not have to be carried out until the claimant makes a further claim for benefit at least 26 weeks after the initial assessment. However, after this point the diminishing capital rule comes into force.

Overpayments – who decides? 5.12

The questions of:

- whether there has been an overpayment;
- if so, how much has been overpaid; and

130

- whether it is recoverable,

are for determination by the Secretary of State, with a right of appeal to a tribunal.

On the other hand, the question (or enforcement) of actual repayment is not open to appeal. The Secretary of State will either recover the overpayment from the claimant's future weekly benefit payments at no more than the maximum rates set out in the *Social Security (Payments on Account, Overpayments and Recovery) Regulations 1988 (SI 1988 No 664)*, or if the claimant is not on benefit, will take civil proceedings if it is considered these will be effective. The tribunal has no jurisdiction over these issues.

The power of the Secretary of State to order repayment of a recoverable overpayment is discretionary, to be exercised on the merits of the case.

It may be argued, where someone has been overpaid benefit for a period, that he should have claimed another benefit for this same period, and that the overpayment should be reduced on account of this underclaim. For example, if someone has been overpaid Income Support for a period when he was working, it may be that he would have been entitled to a tax credit award for the same period if he had made a claim. This sort of off-setting argument can be worth pursuing, but it is important to understand the legal basis.

In the above example there was no actual entitlement to an award of tax credit, since no claim was in fact made. A tribunal has no jurisdiction to reduce the overpayment of Income Support on that basis. However, the Secretary of State has the power to use his discretion, in this sort of case, not to recover the full amount of the overpaid benefit. He may be persuaded to limit recovery to the net amount by which the public purse is short. In other words, if there was an overpayment of Income Support of £5,000, and for the same period the claimant could have been entitled to a tax credit of £3,000 if a claim had been made, the Secretary of State has the power to recover only the net balance of £2,000. This is not a matter that carries a right of appeal to an appeal tribunal – it is a matter within the discretion of the Secretary of State. In practice, it appears that since the separation of administration of the Social Security and tax credit systems, the above argument for the creative use of discretion has become less successful.

It should be emphasised that a conviction for fraud does not extinguish any overpayment, except to the extent that the court orders repayment. Any balance not ordered to be repaid still remains recoverable from the claimant.

Incorrect award of benefit 5.13

The third possible situation where an overpayment will arise is when the claimant has made a claim for benefit, has not misrepresented or failed to disclose any material fact, but has simply been awarded the wrong amount by mistake, for example £95 per week instead of his correct entitlement of £85 per week. If the resulting overpayment is due to an official error by the benefit authority, then the claimant will not be required to repay. He is entitled to assume that his claim will be properly processed and the correct amount paid to him, and is under no duty to verify the amount.

Overpayments of Housing Benefit   5.14

Overpayments of Housing Benefit frequently arise. The authority will often try to recover these overpayments from the claimant. In many cases this will lead to rent arrears for the claimant, especially where the award of benefit has been paid directly to the claimant's landlord.

The law on whether overpayments of Housing or Council Tax Benefit may be recovered by the local authority is very different from the rest of Social Security. For Social Security benefits the test is, effectively, whether the overpayment was caused by the claimant – only then can the payment be recovered. For local authority benefits the test is reversed. Virtually all overpayments can be recovered *unless* they are caused entirely by the benefit authority, and even then may still be recoverable.

Summary   5.15

There are basically three types of overpayment:

- *Claimant error* – Where the claimant has made a genuine mistake in his application or has neglected to notify a change in circumstances. For example, he genuinely does not know how much income his non-dependant is in receipt of. This type of overpayment will be recoverable from the claimant.

- *Claimant fraud* – Where the claimant fails to disclose a material fact, a change in circumstances or income etc. This type of overpayment will always be recoverable from the claimant, and may lead to the claimant being prosecuted.

- *Official error* – Where the authority or DWP have made a mistake or has failed to act on information received in respect of a claim at an appropriate time.

All overpayments are recoverable from the claimant unless the overpayment is an official authority error and it was not reasonable for the claimant to know at the time that he was being overpaid.

An overpayment may arise due to a combination of factors. For example, on 1 July a claimant starts to receive an increase in his income. On 21 July he notifies the local authority of this increase, but the authority, due to a backlog of work, fail to take any action to adjust his benefit until 21 August. The overpaid benefit from 1–21 July will be classified as claimant error, since the claimant failed to notify the authority promptly. However, the further delay of one month before the benefit is changed is not caused by the claimant, and would be seen as official error. Even the official error part, however, may be recoverable, since the authority are likely to consider that the claimant should have realised that this further month of unaltered benefit was an overpayment.

It is important to consider carefully what conclusion a reasonable claimant should have reached in the above type of situation, when benefit does not immediately alter. Depending on such issues as the significance of the change notified, the claimant's prior working knowledge of the workings of the benefit system, and his experience of the local authority's administration, it may be that he could not have been expected to realise that there was an overpayment.

In such cases it is always advisable to obtain full reasons for how the overpayment occurred directly from the local authority, so that any notification of overpayment can be challenged if necessary.

Offsetting Housing Benefit overpayments   5.16

As with all other Social Security benefits, the local authority must offset any notional entitlement to Housing Benefit of the claimant had the correct information been disclosed to the benefit authority.

Changes of circumstances and fraud   5.17

If the claimant or any member of his family or household has a change of circumstances, he is under a duty to notify the authority of that change of circumstances: for example, the claimant was on Income Support and now receives Jobseekers Allowance: or that he was on Incapacity Benefit topped up with Income Support, but now is on Incapacity Benefit and Industrial Injuries Disablement Benefit; or that the claimant was receiving Widow's Pension and is now receiving retirement pension; or that he has had an increased award of occupational pension, etc.

Failure to advise the council of this change as soon as it occurs may result in the claimant's benefit being withdrawn or cancelled. Furthermore, it is now an offence under the *Social Security Administration (Fraud) Act 1997 (SS(F)A 1997)* and *section 16* of the *Social Security Fraud Act 2001 (SSFA 2001)* to fail to disclose such information, and the claimant, or any other person with a duty to disclose, could be prosecuted.

If a landlord is receiving direct benefit payments from the local authority, he too is under a duty to notify the authority of any change in the claimant's circumstances known to him, or that he could reasonably be expected to know. Failure to do so could lead to prosecution under the *SS(F)A 1997* and *section 16* of the *SSFA 2001*.

The *SS(F)A 1997* also provides the power for the local authority to enter any commercial premises in order to inspect documents relating to a benefit claimant. This means that the local authority will have the power to enter the premises of persons whom they believe may hold information and evidence relating to the claimant's claim for Housing and/or Council Tax Benefit.

However, the local authority may only do this where it holds a warrant for the inspection of a file and may only inspect the file relating to a named individual's claim for Housing or Council Tax Benefit.

On entering any premises the local authority may question any person found on the premises whom they reasonably believe may hold information relating to a claimant's entitlement to benefit.

Where a tenant agrees that there has been an overpayment, in consequence of fraud, he will be given the option to repay that overpayment, plus 30% as a penalty as an alternative to prosecution. This 30% may also be recovered from the landlord.

For instance, if there has been an overpayment of £280, there will be a standard £84 administrative penalty, making the overpayment £364. If benefit were paid directly to the landlord in respect of that tenant or any other benefit claimant, then the amount recovered from the landlord's cheque in respect of Housing Benefit payments would be £364.

The penalty may also be deducted from ongoing entitlement to benefit payable to the landlord.

If the claimant does not agree to a penalty, he may be prosecuted, and on conviction could be sentenced to between six months' and seven years' imprisonment or fined or both.

If a third party, i e a landlord or appointee, is also guilty of failing to disclose information which he was aware of, which is instrumental to the fraud, that third party can also be prosecuted and may face the same sentence.

Methods of recovering payments 5.18

The regulations give the local authority a range of methods of recovering overpayments.

From ongoing benefit payments   5.19

Overpayments can be recovered by the authority making deductions from a claimant's ongoing benefit entitlement. The maximum rate of deduction is £11.60 per week in cases of fraud, or £8.70 per week in other cases. It is open to an authority to deduct lesser amounts if the claimant would otherwise suffer hardship.

From the claimant's partner   5.20

Recovery can be made from benefit paid to a partner, providing people were a couple when the overpayment was made, and remain so when recovery takes place.

From a landlord   5.21

Recovery can be made from a landlord where benefit was paid directly to the landlord originally. This can be from benefit paid to the landlord personally, from benefit paid on behalf of the claimant, or from benefit paid on behalf of other claimants.

Amended rules implemented on 3 November 1997 allow the Housing Benefit department to recover overpayments from ongoing payments made to a landlord in respect of other tenants who have not been overpaid.

The rules on recovering overpayments from benefits paid to a landlord in respect of any other tenant were implemented under *section 16* of the *SS(F)A 1997*, which took effect from 3 November 1997.

Where recovery of benefit in this way is implemented, the authority will notify the landlord of the benefit payments made in respect of each tenant, but withhold any amount in respect of overpaid benefit incurred by previous benefit claimants.

The authority must apply their discretion in deciding from whom to recover the overpayment. Therefore, the authority cannot have a general 'policy' of recovering all overpayments of benefit that are paid to a landlord, from the landlord.

In applying its discretion to any matter, the authority must demonstrate that it has considered the merits of each individual case. Where the authority does not take this action its decision may be open to judicial review as it would not have complied with the principles of administrative law.

Where an overpayment is recovered from a local authority tenant, some authorities do this by way of adjusting the rent account to show the tenant in arrears. DWP guidance makes clear to local authorities that a recovered overpayment is not legally the same as rent arrears, and could not be used as the basis for possession proceedings on the grounds of rent arrears. Therefore, an authority must ensure that it can separately identify any recovered overpayments within the rent account.

In the case of overpayments recovered from a non-local authority landlord by deductions from ongoing benefit, regulations provide that where the landlord has been guilty of fraud, then the tenant should still be treated as having paid his rent. In other cases where a lump sum is recovered from a landlord, regulations provide that these can be deducted from a tenant's rent account, and properly be treated as rent arrears. There is some doubt as to the validity of this regulation.

From other benefits 5.22

The authority can request that the DWP recover an overpayment of Housing or Council Tax Benefit by deductions from other Social Security benefits.

By court action 5.23

The authority may either sue the claimant in the county court for a debt, or simply register the overpayment as a judgment, which can then be recovered.

Overpayments of tax credits 5.24

The system of awarding tax credits on a provisional basis, at the beginning of the year and based on the previous year's income, makes frequent overpayments inevitable. When the assessment is finalised at the end of the year it is highly likely that in many cases income will have gone up compared to the previous year, so as to create an overpayment. In order to reduce this problem, the rules were changed from April 2006 so that only an increase in income of over £25,000 from one year to the next will trigger an overpayment. In addition, of course, overpayments will take place due to failures to notify changes of circumstances, other claimant errors, as well as errors by HMRC.

Section 28 of the *Tax Credits Act 2002* (*TCA 2002*) provides that HMRC has discretion to recover all or part of any overpayment. In the case of overpayments made to couples, both partners are jointly and severally liable to repay the amount, unless HMRC decides to apportion the overpayment between the parties. Claimants are issued with a notice specifying the amount of the overpayment, and how it is to be recovered. This can be:

- as an outstanding tax liability;
- by deductions from an ongoing tax credit award; or

• by adjustment of the claimant's tax code under PAYE.

An overpayment of Child Tax Credit and/or Working Tax Credit will arise when HMRC determines that more tax credit has been paid in a year than the claimant was entitled to receive. HMRC then has the right to recover some or all of the overpayment. There is no right of appeal against having the overpayment recovered, but the underlying decision on the amount of tax credit due can be challenged.

Likely situations creating overpayments are:

• income rises by more than £2,500 year on year for years prior to 2006/2007, and of more than £25,000 from April 2006;

• failure to inform the Inland Revenue of a change of circumstances reducing entitlement;

• giving incorrect information; and

• official errors.

In most cases, overpayment decisions will not be made until after the end of the year. An exception will be where someone no longer meets the conditions of entitlement.

Mid-year reductions   5.25

A particular problem that has arisen recently is where HMRC considers that someone's circumstances currently are significantly different from the year of assessment and that, therefore, the current level of payment is leading towards a large overpayment. *Section 28(5)* of the *TCA 2002* empowers them to 'amend' the current award in order to 'reduce' or 'eliminate' a likely overpayment. This does not generate a decision, and therefore does not produce any appeal rights.

HMRC policy has been to reduce an award so as to prevent the overpayment by the end of the year, or to stop payment altogether, where it considers someone to have been already overpaid. This can have drastic results for claimants, who may have budgeted according to the previous level of tax credits. The HMRC Code of Practice (COP26) should be referred to for guidance.

Where the 'overpayment' is due to official error, or where there will be hardship, policy is to restart some 'additional' payments up to the end of the year. These payments will, themselves, contribute to the overpayment.

Methods of recovery   5.26

Overpayments may be reclaimed in a variety of ways:

- from claimant and/or partner where joint claim;
- subject to discretion in cases of official error or hardship;
- from ongoing tax credit award;
- through PAYE;
- by demand for payment; and/or
- by court action.

The Code of Practice sets out the policy, and states:

- the rate of recovery from maximum awards will be 10%;
- recovery from other claimants will be 25%;
- claimants receiving only the family element of Child Tax Credit will suffer 100% reduction.

Consideration will be given to recovering only some, or none, of an overpayment in cases of hardship, or official error.

Although there is no right of appeal, there is recourse to the HMRC adjudicator, or the Parliamentary Ombudsman: see details at www.adjudicatorsoffice.gov.uk and www.ombudsman.gov.uk.

Interest   5.27

It is possible to charge interest at 6.5% (or bank base rate + 2.5%) where overpayment has been caused by 'fraud or neglect'. Interest can be charged from 30 days after decision terminating award, or final date for confirming actual income for year. Decisions to charge interest are open to appeal.

6   Income Support

Introduction   6.1

(Income Support (General) Regulations 1987 (SI 1987 No 1967)).

Income Support (IS) is a means-tested benefit and provides a weekly cash sum to top up a claimant's income to a minimum level as prescribed each year by the Secretary of State. It also operates as a passport to some other benefits, such as free dental treatment, free prescriptions, vouchers for spectacles, maximum Housing Benefit for rent and Council Tax Benefit.

IS is available to those under 60 who are not in full-time work and are not required to sign on as available for work. For example, people who are incapable of work through sickness or disability, people bringing up children on their own and people who are unable to work because they are caring for a disabled person. For people aged 60 or over IS was replaced from October 2003 by Pension Credit.

Basic rules   6.2

Who can claim?   6.3

Note the following points:

- a claimant must be habitually resident in the UK and must not be subject to immigration control;

- a claimant must be aged under 60 and have less than £16,000 in savings, investments and capital. Prior to April 2006, this figure was £8,000;

- a person in full-time higher education is not normally able to claim IS, although this rule will not apply if the claimant is a lone parent or a disabled student;

- in order to claim IS, a person will normally have to fall within one of the following groups:

  ○ people who are sick, disabled or pregnant;

  ○ single parents with dependant children under the age of 16; or

  ○ people receiving Carer's Allowance to look after a disabled person, or carers looking after a person who is receiving Attendance

Allowance or Disability Living Allowance paid at the middle or higher rate for attendance needs;

- a person must not be working or must be working for less than 16 hours per week to satisfy the qualifying conditions for IS, although a claimant's partner can be working for up to 24 hours a week;

- people on strike can claim IS, but will only be awarded an amount for their dependants and this will be at a reduced rate.

How Income Support is calculated   6.4

A claimant's IS or income-based Jobseekers Allowance is calculated by first of all working out an *applicable amount*. This is made up of three parts as set out in **6.5–6.18** below.

Personal allowances   6.5

These are amounts intended to cover a person's day-to-day living expenses (e g food, water rates, fuel, clothing, etc). These amounts are worked out on a fixed scale depending on a claimant's age and circumstances (*SI 1987 No 1967, Reg 17, Sch 2*).

Where a couple are living together as if they were married or in a civil partnership, either partner can make the claim for IS. It is always best for the partner who may attract most benefit to make the claim. For instance, if one of the partners is incapable of work through sickness or disability, that partner should make the claim because he may, at some point, attract an extra disability premium.

Traditionally there have been additional allowances paid in respect of dependent children. The introduction of the Child Tax Credit will eventually transform IS and Jobseekers Allowance into 'adult only' benefits. Although the tax credits were introduced from April 2003, the change to IS and Jobseekers Allowance has been phased in. For claims prior to April 2004, these benefits continued virtually unchanged, including allowances for dependent children. For new claims from April 2004, no allowances are paid in respect of dependent children and claimants will have to make appropriate claims for Child Tax Credit. Claimants already receiving IS in respect of children in April 2004 will be changed over onto the new system in a phased process at some point during 2006.

Premiums   6.6

These are extra amounts of benefit which some people will be able to claim and which are paid in addition to any personal allowances. There are different premiums for different groups (*SI 1987 No 1967, Reg 17, Sch 2*). They are also applicable to the calculation of income-based Jobseekers Allowance (**CHAPTER 7 INCOME-BASED JOBSEEKERS ALLOWANCE**), Housing Benefit and Council Tax Benefit (**CHAPTER 9 HOUSING BENEFIT, COUNCIL TAX BENEFIT AND DISCRETIONARY HOUSING PAYMENTS**).

Family   6.7

This is paid to any families that have dependent children for whom they claim Child Benefit, including lone parents. There is only one premium payable regardless of the number of children. This is always paid in addition to any other premium. From April 2004, this will no longer be paid for new claims and will be phased out for existing claims as claimants are shifted onto Child Tax Credit.

Disabled child   6.8

This is payable for each dependent child who is blind or in receipt of Disability Living Allowance, and is only paid if the child has less than £3,000 capital. This is always paid in addition to any other premium. From April 2004, this will no longer be paid for new claims and will be phased out for existing claims as claimants are shifted onto Child Tax Credit.

Pensioner   6.9

IS for pensioners (also known as Minimum Income Guarantee (MIG)) was replaced from October 2003 by the new Pension Credit (see **CHAPTER 25 PENSION CREDIT**).

Enhanced pensioner   6.10

IS for pensioners (also known as MIG) was replaced from October 2003 by the new Pension Credit (see **CHAPTER 25**).

Higher pensioner   6.11

IS for pensioners (also known as MIG) was replaced from October 2003 by the new Pension Credit (see **CHAPTER 25**).

Disability premium   6.12

This is payable if the claimant or his partner is aged under 60 and:

- is registered blind;
- the claimant (but not his partner) has been incapable of work for at least 52 weeks;

- has an invalid carriage, car or private car allowance from the DWP;
- is getting either Disability Living Allowance or Severe Disablement Allowance.

There is one rate payable for single people and a higher rate payable for couples. Only one premium is payable even if both partners qualify. This can be paid in addition to a family premium, disabled child premium, carer's premium or severe disability premium or enhanced disability premium.

Enhanced disability premium   6.13

This premium is payable if the claimant, partner or dependent child receives the highest rate care component of Disability Living Allowance and are aged less than 60. The premium ceases once the disabled person reaches 60. The premium is not paid for a child with capital over £3,000, nor if the claimant or partner (whichever is disabled) has been in hospital over six weeks.

Severe disability premium   6.14

This is payable to a claimant who is severely disabled, provided that he is receiving Attendance Allowance or the middle or higher rate Disability Living Allowance care component (for himself and not a child), no one is receiving Carer's Allowance for him and he is defined as living alone. (This means that there are no non-dependants over the age of 18 living in the house. Any boarders with a liability to make payments to the claimant on a commercial basis, who are not close relatives, will be ignored.) If both partners qualify then they can both get a single person's rate. It is paid in addition to other premiums. The claimant must qualify for a disability premium or a higher pensioner premium to attract this additional premium.

Carer's premium   6.15

This is payable if the claimant or partner gets Carer's Allowance, or would be entitled to Carer's Allowance but is getting another benefit instead. This is always payable in addition to any other premium to which the claimant may be entitled.

Bereavement premium   6.16

This is payable to single claimants aged 55–60 who previously qualified for, or were awarded, Bereavement Allowance, where that award has expired (see **22.5**) and:

- the claimant's spouse died on or after 9 April 2001; and
- the claimant is a single person (not a member of a couple); and

- the claimant claims IS within eight weeks of the date of expiry of the Bereavement Allowance award.

Premiums for homeless people   6.17

A homeless person will not be paid any premiums to which he would be entitled in normal circumstances. However, any premiums will come into payment from the day on which the claimant notifies the DWP that he is no longer homeless.

Housing costs   6.18

These are extra amounts of benefit which may be payable to claimants who have housing costs for the place where they live by way of mortgage interest payments or home improvement loan interest payments (*SI 1987 No 1967, Reg 17, Sch 3*).

Eligible interest payments will only be met on loans up to a total of £100,000.

Eligible interest payments include:

- interest payments on mortgages and loans to acquire an interest in the property where the claimant lives;

- interest payments on remortgages, but only to the value needed to pay off an original mortgage. For example, a claimant had a mortgage of £50,000 and took a new mortgage of £70,000, (the additional £20,000 being needed to pay off debts and buy a car) – interest payments will only be eligible on the first £50,000 of the mortgage;

- interest payments on loans secured on the property where the claimant lives which were essential and taken out for the purpose of:

  o provision of bathroom facilities, including any necessary plumbing and hot water supply;

  o repairs to heating systems and unsafe structural defects (note that if the loan is taken out for the installation of a heating system, such loans will not be eligible for assistance, but if the loan is to repair or replace (where essential) the heating system such loans will be eligible for assistance);

  o provision of damp proofing, home insulation, ventilation, natural lighting and drainage facilities;

  o facilities for preparing and cooking food;

  o provision of electric lighting and sockets;

143

○   storage facilities for fuel and refuse;

○   adaptations for disabled persons; and

○   providing separate bedrooms for children over the age of ten of different sexes who are part of the claimant's family.

Claimants who are over the age of 60 have been entitled to housing costs from the commencement of their claim for IS. This principle continues now that IS for people over 60 has been replaced by Pension Credit. The claimant will qualify for 100% of any eligible interest at an interest rate as set by the Secretary of State.

Claimants under the age of 60 who took out the mortgage or loan prior to 2 October 1995 will not qualify for any assistance with interest payments for those loans for the first eight weeks of claiming IS. For the next 18 weeks of claiming IS the claimant will only qualify for 50% of any eligible interest payments, thereafter in the 27th week the claimant will qualify for 100% of any eligible interest at an interest rate as set by the Secretary of State.

Claimants under the age of 60 who took out the mortgage or loan after 2 October 1995 will not (in most cases) qualify for any assistance with eligible interest payments for those loans for the first 39 weeks of claiming IS. However, in the 40th week of claiming benefit the claimant will qualify for 100% of any eligible interest at an interest rate as set by the Secretary of State.

Claimants are exempt from the 39-week waiting period and are subject to the rules for pre-October 1995 mortgages in the following situations:

• a lone parent claiming IS because of abandonment by a partner, or because the partner has died;

• carers;

• prisoners on remand;

• where payments under a mortgage protection policy have been refused due to a pre-existing medical condition or HIV.

These rules on waiting periods only apply at the start of a claim. Some periods prior to the claim, such as when the claimant was receiving IS or Jobseekers Allowance as part of a couple prior to splitting up, may be taken into account in the waiting period.

Where housing costs are included in an IS assessment, a claimant will have non-dependant deductions made for any persons living in the house who are over the age of 18. These non-dependant deductions are set at six rates depending on the source and level of gross income that the non-dependant has. (See **CHAPTER 9** for further details of non-dependant deductions.)

Income   6.19

All the income that a claimant has will be assessed in the same way as all means-tested benefits (see **CHAPTER 2 ASSESSMENT OF MEANS**) but generally the following will be taken into account:

- earnings;

- other income from sources such as other State benefits, periodical payments from trust funds (other than trusts of personal injury compensation), payments from occupational pensions etc;

- maintenance payments;

- tariff income from capital.

There is some scope for elements of income to be disregarded. Where the claimant is a lone parent or attracts a disability premium, the first £20 of his earned income will be disregarded. If the claimant is a member of a couple the first £10 of the joint earned income will be disregarded, regardless of whether one or both members of the couple are working. In all other cases only the first £5 of the claimant's earned income will be disregarded. There is also scope for other items of income to be disregarded, such as the first £10 of child maintenance payments under the 2003 CSA rules, and 100% of payments of Attendance Allowance, Disability Living Allowance etc. (*SI 1987 No 1967, Reg 40(2)*; for a full list of sums disregarded, see *Schedule 9*.)

From April 2004, the IS applicable amount no longer includes amounts for dependent children, although in some cases this will be phased out. Once an IS claim no longer includes any allowances for children, then any Child Benefit and Child Tax Credit will also be disregarded from the income assessment.

Capital   6.20

If the claimant and partner jointly have savings, investments or capital of £16,000 or more, there will be no entitlement to IS.

In all cases, there will be a disregard of capital of the claimant and partner to the value of £6,000 (*SI 1987 No 1967, Reg 46, Sch 10*).

All the capital of the claimant and partner will be assessed in line with all other means-tested benefits. Where the claimant is under the age of 60 and savings are assessed to be in excess of £6,000, then a tariff income will be applied in respect of these savings. This tariff income will be assessed at £1 per week for every £250 (or part) by which the claimant's capital exceeds £6,000. (See **CHAPTER 2**.)

EXAMPLE

A claimant and partner under the age of 60 have savings, capital and investments to the value of £8,300. The first £6,000 will be ignored and the remaining £2,300 will attract a tariff income of £10 per week. This amount will be added to the claimant's weekly income for the assessment of entitlement to IS.

Disregarded capital   6.21

Certain types of capital can be totally disregarded so that they do not come into the calculation at all – the fact that the claimant owns all or any of them will not affect his entitlement to IS. These are listed in full in *Schedule 10* of the *Income Support (General) Regulations 1987 (SI 1987 No 1967)* (see **CHAPTER 2**).

Capital taken into account   6.22

If the capital does not fall within any of the disregards set out in the schedules to the regulations, the next question is whether it is of such a nature that it has to be taken into account.

Capital includes all assets of any kind owned by the claimant and will thus include money saved in the home, bank or building society accounts, premium bonds, stocks and shares, unit trusts, items of value such as paintings, stamp collections etc. Also included will be items such as debts or other courses in action which have a market value and can be sold, even though they may not be payable until some future date (see **CHAPTER 2**).

The final calculation   6.23

The final part of the calculation involves comparing income with the applicable amount:

- if the income is *greater* than the applicable amount, then the claimant will *not* be entitled to IS;

- if the income is *less* than the applicable amount, then the claimant will be awarded the difference by the way of an IS or income-based Jobseekers Allowance award.

EXAMPLE

Christopher and Andrea are a couple who are both under 60. They have twin daughters aged 8 and Andrea's brother, aged 30, who is severely disabled and in receipt of IS and Disability Living Allowance high rate care component, lives with them.

They live in their own home which they bought in 1981 and have an endowment mortgage of £60,000.

Christopher was recently made redundant and receives a small occupational pension of around £120 per month. Andrea receives Carer's Allowance (see **CHAPTER 19 CARER'S ALLOWANCE**) for looking after her brother and Child Benefit for the children. They also receive Child Tax Credit of £119.42 per week. She also gets the middle rate Disability Living Allowance care component for one of her daughters. The couple have savings of £7,850.

Because Andrea is the only member of the couple who might qualify for IS (as a carer) she must make the claim for this benefit for the family. (For the purposes of this example a standard interest rate of 5% has been used.)

IS will be calculated as follows.

Applicable amount		*Income*	
Personal allowances			
Couple	£90.10	Carer's Allowance	£46.95
		Child Benefit (disregarded)	£29.15
		Tariff income	£8.00
Premiums		Occupational pension	£27.62
Carer's premium	£26.35	DLA for daughter (disregarded)	£0.00
		Child Tax Credit (disregarded)	£0.00
Sub total A	**£116.45**	**Total**	**£82.57**

Housing costs	
Mortgage interest payments	
@ 50% eligible (5.00%)	£28.84
less non-dependant deduction	£7.40
	£21.44
Sub total B	**£137.89**
@ 100% eligible (5.00%)	£57.68
less non-dependant deduction	£7.40
	£50.28
Sub total C	**£166.73**

- For the first eight weeks of claiming IS there will be no entitlement to any housing costs, so IS entitlement will be £33.88 per week, i e applicable amount @ sub total A: £116.45 less assessable income £82.57 = £33.88 per IS award.

- For the next 18 weeks of claiming IS the couple will qualify for eligible interest payments of 50% (less a non-dependant deduction for Andrea's brother). IS entitlement will be £55.32 per week, i e applicable amount @ sub total B: £137.89 less assessable income £82.57 = £55.32 per week IS award. (Eligible interest payments will be paid directly to the mortgage lender.)

- In the 27th week of claiming IS the couple will qualify for eligible interest payments of 100% (less a non-dependant deduction for Andrea's brother). IS entitlement will be £84.16 per week, i e applicable amount @ sub total C: £166.73 less assessable income £82.57 = £84.16 per week IS award. (Eligible interest payments will be paid directly to the mortgage lender.)

Those who cannot normally claim Income Support

6.24

Full-time education

6.25

A claimant in full-time education will not be able to claim IS, unless he satisfies one of the special criteria outlined below:

- he is under 19 and in full-time education (i e a course of study which lasts for more than twelve hours per week or a course which is defined by the educational establishment as being a full-time course) and:

  ○ he has a dependent child;

  ○ he is so handicapped that he would be unlikely to get a job in the next twelve months;

  ○ he is an orphan with no one acting as a parent;

  ○ he is estranged from his parents (i e he has severed all ties with his parents or the person acting as his parent, either through his choice, his parents' choice or because the relationship with his parents has irretrievably broken down);

  ○ he lives apart from his parents who are not able to support him because they are in prison, or mentally or physically disabled, chronically sick or unable to come to the UK because of immigration laws; or

  ○ he is a refugee and has started a course to learn English in order to obtain employment during his first year in the UK;

- he is over 19 in full-time education (i e a course of study which is over 21 hours per week or which is defined by the college as being a full-time course) and:

  ○ he is a single parent or foster parent and is responsible for looking after a child;

  ○ he is getting a training allowance;

  ○ he is caring for dependent children under 16; or

  ○ he is a disabled student and would qualify for a disability premium or a severe disability premium.

(*SI 1987 No 1967, Reg 13.*)

16–17 year olds   6.26

A claimant must normally be over the age of 18 to claim IS although in certain circumstances a 16 or 17 year old will be eligible to claim. A 16–17 year old will be entitled to IS if he falls into one of the following categories, namely:

- a single parent with a dependent child under the age of 16;

- looking after a child under the age of 16 while the child's parent is ill or temporarily away from home;

- one of a couple who have a child under the age of 16 for whom he can claim (although in these circumstances he would still have to register with the careers office or youth training scheme);

- a disabled student;

- pregnant and unable to work for a period starting eleven weeks before the baby is due and up to seven weeks after the baby is born;

- caring for a person who is receiving Attendance Allowance or Disability Living Allowance care component; or

- blind.

If a 16–17 year old has been looked after by a local authority in England and Wales since October 2001, he cannot usually claim IS. Instead the local authority should support and accommodate him.

Note: If a young person is suffering exceptional hardship and does not qualify for a bridging allowance, for example because he has exhausted his bridging allowance period of 40 days in a 52-week period, he may be considered for payment under *section 17* of the *Children Act 1989* (a section 17 payment – section 12 in Scotland) from Social Services as a temporary measure to alleviate an immediate financial problem. Such payments are made to 'children in need' as defined in *section 17(10)* of the *Children Act 1989*:

'... a child shall be taken to be in need if:

(*a*) he is unlikely to achieve or maintain, or to have the opportunity of achieving or maintaining, a reasonable standard of health or development without the provision for him of services by a local authority under this Part;

(*b*) his health or development is likely to be significantly impaired, or further impaired, without the provision for him of such services; or

(*c*) he is disabled ...'

Such payments can meet a wide variety of needs, for example food, clothing, fuel bills, help in the home, contributions towards holidays and help for young people who are leaving or have left local authority care to establish themselves in the community. There is no set rate as to how much can be claimed as the awards are made at the discretion of the Social Services. Applications should be made to the Social Services duty officer. Furthermore, if a young person has been in Social Services care for 13 weeks or more since attaining the age of 14, financial assistance must be awarded by Social Services (*Children (Leaving Care) (England) Regulations 2001 (SI 2001 No 2874)*).

Young people living at home in further education   6.27

Young people in non-advanced education (i e to A-Level) up to the age of 19 who are still in receipt of Child Benefit and who are not estranged from their parents will be treated as dependent children, and as such will not be able to claim IS in their own right. However, a claim for IS can sometimes be made during what is called 'the Child Benefit extension period'.

If a young person does not qualify for IS, he may nevertheless meet the conditions for getting Jobseekers Allowance while he is 16–17 years old.

People on strike or involved in an industrial dispute   6.28

A claimant who is on strike for more than seven days can claim IS but will not be awarded anything for himself and will only receive a reduced amount for his dependants, namely personal allowances for any dependent children, plus any family premium and disabled child premium etc.

IS cannot be claimed until a claimant has been involved in a trade dispute for at least seven days.

Where the claimant has a partner who is not involved in the trade dispute, he will have his personal allowance reduced by 50% and 50% of the value of the value of any premiums payable in respect of the couple.

A claimant receiving IS while involved in a trade dispute will be assumed to be receiving a strike pay of £31.00, which is treated as income, whether it is received or not. On returning to work, a claimant is eligible for IS for the first 15 days back at work, as a loan.

Note: A claimant on strike, even if he is receiving IS for his dependants, will not be eligible for any payment from the Social Fund.

(*Social Security Contributions and Benefits Act 1992, s 126(3); SI 1987 No 1967, Reg 5(4).*)

Benefits for those in hospital   6.29

From April 2006, there is no longer any reduction in benefit for a claimant who is in hospital. After a partner has been in hospital 52 weeks, the claimant will be treated as a single person.

Where a claimant is in hospital for 28 days or more, he will have any award of severe disability premium withdrawn along with any award of Disability Living Allowance (see **CHAPTER 23 DISABILITY LIVING ALLOWANCE**) or Attendance Allowance (see **CHAPTER 24 ATTENDANCE LIVING ALLOWANCE**).

Any person receiving a carer premium as a carer of a disabled person in hospital will lose entitlement to Carer's Allowance (see **CHAPTER 19**) once the disabled person has been in hospital for 28 days. However, he will not lose the carer premium for a further eight weeks following the withdrawal of the Carer's Allowance.

People in residential care and nursing homes 6.30

Where the claimant has a partner and the claimant or his partner go into a residential care/nursing home on a permanent basis, each member of the couple will be assessed for benefit individually, that is to say, each member of the couple will be assessed as though he or she were a single person. However, if they are a married couple then the DWP may seek a contribution from either partner to maintain the other who will be treated as a liable relative.

If the claimant or his partner goes into a residential care/nursing home for a temporary period, the couple's income will be assessed jointly, and their applicable amount will either be:

- a couple's applicable amount under the normal rules; or

- separate applicable amounts for a single person,

whichever is the greater.

So, for example, if a husband suffers serious injury in an industrial accident and as a result has to go into a residential care home, he would qualify for Incapacity Benefit and in addition, because he will be entitled to a disability premium, he will also receive IS.

If, however, he were to claim as a single person, he would only receive the single rate of disability premium, and if his wife were to claim IS as a single person, she would only qualify for a personal allowance of £57.45, but if they claim as a couple, they will qualify for the rate of disability premium payable for a couple and so the total award will be higher than if they both claimed as single individuals.

When assessing capital for a claimant in a residential care/nursing home the value of his own home will be disregarded and not taken into account as capital if:

- the claimant is in the home temporarily;

- the claimant's partner or spouse or relative, who is either aged over 60 or who is disabled, lives in the property;

- the claimant is trying to dispose of the property (see **CHAPTER 2**); or

- the claimant has been in the home less than twelve weeks.

A claimant should always be left with £19.60 per week for his personal expenses when in any kind of residential care/nursing home. This is in order that the claimant can afford personal items such as toiletries and clothing etc.

(See **CHAPTER 11 ASSESSMENT OF MEANS IN COMMUNITY CARE**.)

How to claim   6.31

Claims should be made by completion of a claim Form A1, which can be obtained from the claimant's local DWP office. With the claim Form A1 the claimant will be provided with a number of additional forms, namely NHB 1 (for the purpose of indicating intention to claim Housing and/or Council Tax Benefit) and a Form MI12 for the purpose of claiming entitlement to mortgage or home improvement loan interest payments.

Claim forms will be dated at the time of issue and a date for the return of the form will also be identified on the claim form. Benefit will be paid from the date of issue of the form, provided the form is completed and returned to the DWP with all required evidence and information by the date so prescribed.

Claimants will be required to provide evidence of their own and their partner's National Insurance numbers (e g a letter from HMRC or the DWP), identity (e g birth certificate, passport etc) and proof of residence (e g a recent utility bill etc), along with evidence of any income and capital that the claimant or partner has. This evidence must be by way of original documents (not photocopies). Until this evidence is provided a valid claim will not be treated as made. There are some limited exceptions where there is a good reason for the information not being supplied.

Most claimants claiming IS for the first time will receive a home visit from an officer of the DWP within two weeks of their claim being registered. The purpose of this visit is to check through the claim with the claimant and to obtain any evidence that the claimant has not been able to provide at the time of registering the claim.

Payments of IS will generally be made directly into the claimant's bank account. However, a claimant may request that benefit be paid by way of a benefit payment book, and in such circumstances payments of this benefit will be paid weekly or fortnightly.

Challenging decisions   6.32

Once benefit has been assessed, the claimant will be sent a full written decision in respect of the claim. If a claimant is not happy with the decision for whatever reason, he will need to ask that the decision be revised. Such applications for revision must be made in writing and delivered to the decision maker within one month of the date of the original decision having been issued.

The decision maker will look at the claim again and take into account any new information that the claimant has raised in his application for revision. The decision maker will then issue a further decision, and if the claimant is not happy with that decision, he may appeal to the Appeals Service, but must do so within one month of the date of issue of the most recent decision (see **CHAPTER 4 CLAIMS, DECISIONS AND APPEALS**).

Common problems   6.33

1. The claimant has claimed IS for the first time, and has claimed other Social Security benefits at the same time, none of which are in payment at the time of registering the claim for IS.

At the time of registering the claim for IS the claimant should identify all other benefits that he has claimed (even where these benefits are not yet being paid). Once entitlement to any other benefit has been determined, the claimant must advise the DWP office paying IS, in writing, of that additional award of benefit. This must be done within one month of the decision relating to the other benefit award having been sent to the claimant.

In such circumstances the amount of IS to which the claimant is entitled will be reviewed and adjusted to take into account the additional income from the date that it was awarded. This procedure is also the same if the additional benefit is Disability Living Allowance or Attendance Allowance because, although these benefits are disregarded as income, their award could mean that the claimant is entitled to more premiums, thus resulting in an increased award of IS.

2. The claimant has been receiving IS as a person incapable of work, but following a recent medical assessment, has been found fit for work.

If a claimant in receipt of IS is found fit for work following a medical assessment, he will no longer be entitled to IS unless he has an alternative route for claiming this benefit (i e he is a lone parent, he is caring for a disabled person etc). If the claimant does have an alternative route to claim IS he will have to register a new claim for an assessment under the new qualifying criteria.

If the claimant does not have an alternative route to claim IS, he will have to sign on to claim Jobseekers Allowance (see **CHAPTER 7**). Alternatively, the claimant may wish to appeal against the decision relating to his fitness for work

– by doing so his entitlement to IS will continue, but his personal allowance will be reduced by 20% until such time as the outcome of the appeal is established. If the claimant's appeal is successful he will have any reduced benefit reinstated and paid back to him. However, if the appeal is not successful the claimant will then be required to sign on as available for work in order to secure continued entitlement to benefit. Furthermore, for the period that a claimant has been waiting for the outcome of his appeal he will not have been credited with any National Insurance contributions.

It is, however, possible for a claimant to claim Jobseekers Allowance and appeal against the decision to find him fit for work, but in applying for Jobseekers Allowance the claimant will have to show that he is available and actively seeking work. If the claimant has to place restrictions on the type of work that he is able to do in consequence of his disability, he should not be penalised if these restrictions are reasonable and are supported by way of medical evidence from his GP.

If, following a successful appeal, the claimant wishes to reclaim IS, he will be treated as a continuous claimant and will not have any lost entitlement to benefit (i e disability premiums etc) as IS will be reinstated from the date that it ceased to be paid (see **CHAPTER 7** for Jobseeker Allowance view of this problem).

Checklist 6.34

Claim specification	Details
Basic entitlement conditions	Claimant must not be working, or working for less than 16 hours per week. Any partner, if working, must be working for less than 24 hours per week. Claimant and partner must have less than £16,000 in savings and capital, and be habitually resident in the UK. Claimant must be either incapable of work, or caring for a severely disabled person or caring for a dependent child under the age of 16. Entitlement is wholly subject to a means test of the family unit.
Dependant additions	Additions for a dependent partner and homeowner housing costs are included in any assessment of entitlement to this benefit.
Where to claim	Claims must be made using a prescribed IS application form obtainable from local DWP.

Claim specification	Details
Work-focused interviews	The Secretary of State may require any claimant to attend a work-focused interview to establish the employability of the claimant at any time. If the claimant does not attend his entitlement to benefit will be suspended until he does attend the interview.
How difficult is the claim form to complete?	Quite simple, requiring factual information about the claimant and family and comprehensive details regarding income and capital. The claimant will also have to provide proof of all income and capital with this claim. This is a long form requiring approximately 45–60 minutes for completion.
Changes of circumstances that need to be notified	Any changes in the claimant's circumstances at all, including people moving into or out of his home, changes in hours of work, changes in income and capital, going into or out of hospital, changes in disability etc. Any changes of address and if the claimant or partner claims or receives any other benefits or sources of income or capital.
Frequency of periodic reviews	Reviews can be carried out at any time – there is no specific requirement for a fixed-term review.
Time limits for reviews and appeals	Applications must be made within one month of the date that the decision under review/appeal was issued.
Benefit reductions	Benefit entitlement is reduced if the claimant or dependent goes into hospital and is an in-patient for more than 52 weeks. Benefit will be withdrawn in most cases if the claimant or partner goes abroad for more than 28 days.
Other linked benefits	Can be claimed in addition to Housing Benefit and Council Tax Benefit. Otherwise this benefit is paid as a top-up to any other Social Security benefit. Also gives rise to possible entitlement to Social Fund payments and NHS benefits, such as free prescriptions, dental treatment, sight tests etc, and free school meals for children of school age.

Claim specification	Details
Attracting a NICs credit	Yes.
Taxable	No.

7 Income-based Jobseekers Allowance

(Jobseekers Allowance Regulations 1996 (SI 1996 No 207)).

Introduction
7.1

There are two elements of Jobseekers Allowance (JSA), namely:

- *Contributory Jobseekers Allowance* – Entitlement is conditional upon a claimant having paid sufficient National Insurance contributions (NICs) prior to becoming unemployed. This benefit is not the subject of a detailed means test and is payable for up to six months (see **CHAPTER 16 CONTRIBUTORY JOBSEEKERS ALLOWANCE**).

- *Income-based Jobseekers Allowance* – For those people who are unemployed but available for and seeking work, and either do not or no longer qualify for contributory JSA or need to claim additional benefit because they have dependants and/or housing costs. This benefit is subject to a full and comprehensive means test, but can be paid for as long as a claimant satisfies all the qualifying conditions of entitlement.

Basic rules
7.2

Income-based JSA is a means-tested benefit and provides a weekly cash sum to top up a claimant's income to a minimum level as prescribed each year by the Secretary of State. It also operates as a passport to some other benefits, such as free dental treatment, free prescriptions, and vouchers for spectacles, and maximum Housing Benefit for rent and Council Tax Benefit. This benefit is similar in structure to Income Support, though governed by a separate set of regulations. There are the same three elements to the formula needed to assess entitlement to the amount of payment that a claimant may receive, i e personal allowances, premiums and housing costs assessed in the same way as for Income Support (see **CHAPTER 6 INCOME SUPPORT**). However, there are additional rules relating to securing entitlement.

Who can claim?
7.3

A claimant must:

- be habitually resident and living in the UK;

- have less than £16,000 in savings, investments and capital;

- either not be working or working for less than 16 hours per week, and where the claimant has a partner, the partner must not be working or working less than 24 hours per week;

- be available for employment;

- be actively seeking employment;

- have entered into a jobseekers agreement.

Note: Where a claimant is a member of a couple generally, both members of a couple must sign all documentation and meet the qualifying conditions in relation to claims for income-based JSA.

Available for employment 7.4

If claiming JSA for the first time following a period of full-time employment, for the periods of between one and 13 weeks of claiming JSA the claimant may only need make himself available to undertake work of a similar nature to his previous job, or his 'usual occupation' and/or work that he is suitably qualified to do. The length of this 'permitted' period is for the Jobcentre Plus officer to decide (see **CHAPTER 16**).

However, in all other cases (i e new claimants who have not previously worked or claimants who have been claiming JSA for 13 weeks or more) claimants must satisfy the very strict rules of making themselves available for all work.

This requirement involves a claimant being able to take up a job immediately, should one become available. There are, however, some exceptions to this rule, in particular where a claimant is unable to start work immediately because of caring responsibilities, i e a single parent who needs to make provision for the care of dependent children, a person caring for a disabled person who needs to make provisions for someone else to care for the disabled person, or if the claimant is working voluntarily for a charitable organisation. In these circumstances the claimant would have to be available to start work at 48-hours' notice, or one week, in the case of voluntary work.

If the claimant is already working part time (i e less than 16 hours per week) and is required to give notice to an employer, then restricting his immediate availability for employment to the required period of notice will also be allowed.

Additionally, the claimant must be available and prepared to work for at least 40 hours per week, but must be prepared to accept employment of less than 40 hours per week. The requirement for availability relates to paid work for an employer, therefore if a claimant is only looking for self-employed work he will not satisfy this test.

The requirement of availability must be satisfied for each individual week of claiming benefit, however, again there are some exceptions to this rule where a claimant will be treated for a short period as available for work in a week that he is not. These are quite prescribed circumstances; the main exceptions are as follows:

- for up to two weeks during a twelve-month period where the claimant has a short period of sickness;

- for one week from the date of discharge from a remand centre or prison;

- for a maximum of up to eight weeks where the claimant is a part-time firefighter, crewing or launching a lifeboat, assisting others as a volunteer in emergency situations for the benefit of others, caring for someone else's child because the child's parents/guardians are ill or temporarily away from home, or caring for a member of the family who is ill and needs to be cared for; or

- for up to one week where the claimant needs to deal with a domestic emergency or following the death or serious illness of a close friend or relative.

(SI 1996 No 207, Regs 53–55.)

Note: There is no provision for a claimant to be treated as available for work in any week that he has taken to go away on holiday. However, if the claimant agrees that he will continue to be available for work and to seek work while away on holiday (in the UK) he may still qualify for benefit. In these circumstances the claimant will have to notify Jobcentre Plus of his intention to go on holiday before he goes, and he will be required to complete a holiday form giving details of how he can be contacted should a job become available.

Actively seeking work 7.5

A claimant will be required to demonstrate that he has taken steps to find employment and/or improve his prospects of finding employment during each week that he is claiming benefit. This may include:

- making applications for employment (oral or written);

- attending the jobcentre or other recruitment agency to see if any suitable jobs are being advertised;

- registering with an employment agency, either in person or by registration on the internet;

- looking for job vacancies in newspapers, magazines or employers' vacancy bulletins;

- securing assistance with the preparation of a CV; and

- attending a job club.

A claimant will be required to show that he has complied with the requirements to take 'steps' (which means that a claimant must show that he has taken at least two steps) to find or increase his prospects of securing employment each week.

Claimants may also be required to change the steps, or increase the steps, that they are taking to find employment, where after a period of time the steps that they have been taking have proved to be unsuccessful.

Furthermore, the claimant must show that the steps that he is taking to secure employment are such that his chances of securing employment are reasonable and realistic, for example an unskilled claimant applying only for skilled work would not have reasonable prospects of securing employment.

Written jobseekers agreement   7.6

The agreement will set out the steps that a claimant agrees to take to find work or to increase his prospects of finding work.

Payment of benefit will require a jobseekers agreement to be signed by both the claimant and an officer of Jobcentre Plus. However, the Jobcentre Plus officer will not sign the agreement unless he is satisfied that the contents will satisfy the requirements of availability and actively seeking work. If there is a dispute over the proposed agreement, either party can refer it to the Secretary of State for a decision.

The Secretary of State should make a decision within 14 days, giving such directions, as he feels appropriate – any such directions will be binding. If the claimant disagrees with the decision or directions then he will be able to appeal to the Appeal Service (see **CHAPTER 4 CLAIMS, DECISIONS AND APPEALS**).

After the agreement has been signed, it may subsequently be changed to take into account any changes in the claimant's circumstances or changes in the job market.

An employment officer can, at any time, issue a formal direction requiring the claimant to take specific steps to improve his chances of finding employment. Such a direction can not only be used to enforce an existing obligation, but could also require the claimant to take additional steps, e g attend a course to improve his skills or qualifications. If the claimant fails to comply with any such direction he will have his benefit suspended for two weeks, but he will be able to apply to appeal against such a decision (see **CHAPTER 4**).

Suspensions of benefit 7.7

If JSA is not awarded because the Jobcentre Plus officer is making further enquiries into the claimant's entitlement to the benefit, under the direction of the Secretary of State, he may suspend any entitlement to JSA pending the outcome of that enquiry.

Once a decision is made about entitlement, benefit will be paid, but only from the date of the decision. In these cases there will generally be a gap between the date of claim and the date of the award. Any benefit that has been suspended during the decision-making process will not be released to the claimant unless he makes a written request (see **CHAPTER 4**).

If the claimant loses his job through misconduct, leaves his employment without good cause or fails to make himself available for work, he could have his benefit suspended for a minimum period of seven days or up to a maximum period of 26 weeks. However, when deciding the period of disqualification, the Employment Service must specifically exclude pay levels from being taken into account in deciding 'just cause' to suspend benefit.

A claimant who fails to attend or complete a training scheme or employment programme will have a fixed disqualification from benefit entitlement for two weeks (or four for persistent offenders).

During periods for which JSA is suspended in consequence of disqualification, the claimant may apply for a hardship payment. However, the claimant will only qualify for a hardship payment if he can show that he or a member of his family would suffer hardship as a result of disqualification.

Hardship is not defined in the regulations but guidance provides that hardship may occur where a claimant does not have, or does not have access to, (e g by way of a bank overdraft facility or credit card facility) sufficient means to accommodate his essential requirements of life, for example food, fuel, heating and accommodation.

If hardship can be established, no payment will be made for the first two weeks (unless the claimant or partner is pregnant, or the claimant has dependent children, or care responsibilities or the claimant is sick or disabled).

The hardship payment will be the amount of benefit that the claimant would otherwise receive, but the personal allowance attributable to the claimant will be reduced by 20% if the claimant or his partner is pregnant or if a member of the claimant's family is seriously ill, or 40% in any other case.

New Deal 7.8

The New Deal is a government project which looks to secure training and employment for young people who are unemployed and for people who may have difficulty in finding employment, i e those who have been out of work for more than two years, disabled claimants, claimants over the age of 50 and lone parents.

Gateway 7.9

If the claimant joins the New Deal voluntarily or because he has to, he will be placed on the Gateway. This will offer assistance in job search, training and choosing the right New Deal option. Activities in the Gateway scheme will form part of the claimant's jobseekers agreement.

If, in the Gateway scheme, the claimant does not comply with his jobseekers agreement, or he refuses a job without good cause, or he is sacked for misconduct etc, he could have a benefit sanction of as little as seven days or up to 26 weeks (in most cases the full 26 weeks will apply). If the claimant in the Gateway scheme does not sign his jobseekers agreement he will not receive any benefit at all.

There are four options available under the New Deal and a claimant who is aged under 26 will have to choose one of them if he has been unemployed for more than six months and is directed to join the New Deal scheme. These options are set out below.

Employment option 7.10

Upon taking this option the claimant will be classed as an employee and will have to sign off JSA. The claimant should get a wage of at least £60 per week if he is working for more than 30 hours, or at least £40 per week if he is working between 24 and 29 hours each week.

Environment task force or voluntary sector option 7.11

On these two options the claimant can either be paid a wage or an allowance. If the claimant receives a wage his benefits will be the same as on the employment option (above).

If the claimant receives an allowance, he will receive his JSA plus £400 (£15.38 per week) paid in instalments over six months (usually paid fortnightly).

Full-time education and training option 7.12

The claimant will be paid an allowance at the same rate as his previous JSA.

He should still be entitled to all the other benefits which he was previously receiving at the same rate as before.

The course provider should meet the following costs:

- books and equipment; and
- reasonable travel costs.

There is also a discretionary fund that the claimant can apply to for:

- special equipment and clothing needs;
- exceptional costs of travel (if his travel costs are particularly high);
- accommodation costs if the claimant is training away from home; and
- childcare (if the course provider does not have its own facilities).

Sanctions and penalties   7.13

If the claimant does not co-operate with the New Deal he is likely to lose benefit. Once the claimant has started an option any sanction will initially be for two weeks and four weeks if this happens again.

The sanctions apply if the claimant:

- refuses or fails to take up his place on an option without a good reason;
- leaves his option early without a good reason; or
- loses his place on an option through misconduct.

How income-based Jobseekers Allowance is calculated   7.14

A claimant's income-based JSA is calculated by first of all working out his *applicable amount*. This is made up of three parts in the same way as for Income Support (see **6.5** et seq).

These parts are as follows.

Personal allowances   7.15

These are amounts intended to cover a person's day-to-day living expenses (e g food, fuel, clothing, etc). They are worked out on a fixed scale depending on a claimant's age and circumstances.

Traditionally there have been additional allowances paid in respect of dependent children. The introduction of the Child Tax Credit will eventually transform Income Support and JSA into 'adult only' benefits. Although the tax credits were introduced from April 2003, the change to Income Support and JSA has been phased in. For claims prior to April 2004, these benefits continued virtually unchanged, including allowances for dependent children.

For new claims from April 2004, no allowances will be paid in respect of dependent children and claimants will have to make appropriate claims for Child Tax Credit. Claimants already receiving JSA in respect of children in April 2004 will be changed over onto the new system in a phased process during 2006.

Premiums   7.16

These are extra amounts of benefit which some people will be able to claim and which are paid in addition to any personal allowances. There are different premiums for different groups (see **6.6–6.17** for full qualifying conditions):

- *Family* – Paid to any families that have dependent children for whom they claim Child Benefit (replaced by Child Tax Credit from April 2004).

- *Disabled child* – Paid in respect of blind or disabled children of the claimant's family.

- *Pensioner* – Paid where the claimant or partner is aged between 60–74.

- *Enhanced pensioner premium* – Paid where the claimant or partner is aged between 75 and 79.

- *Higher pensioner* – Paid where the claimant or partner is aged 80 or over, or aged 60 or over and disabled.

- *Disability premium* – Paid where the claimant or partner is aged under 60 and disabled.

- *Enhanced disability premium* – Paid where the claimant, partner or child are receiving the higher rate care component of Disability Living Allowance.

- *Severe disability premium* – Paid to a severely disabled person living alone and who does not have any one particular person caring for him.

- *Carer's premium* – Paid where a claimant or partner is caring for a severely disabled person.

- *Bereavement premium* – Paid to claimants aged 55–60 on expiry of Bereavement Allowance awards.

Premiums for homeless people   7.17

A homeless person will not be paid any premiums to which he would be entitled in normal circumstances. However, any premiums will come into payment from the day on which the claimant notifies the DWP that he is no longer homeless.

Housing costs 7.18

These may be paid to homeowners who are liable to pay interest on a mortgage or home improvement loan for the place where they live (see **6.18** for specific qualifying rules).

Where housing costs are included in an income-based JSA calculation a claimant will have non-dependant deductions made for any persons living in the house who are over the age of 18. These non-dependant deductions are set at six rates depending on the source and level of gross income of the non-dependant. (See **CHAPTER 9 HOUSING BENEFIT, COUNCIL TAX BENEFIT AND DISCRETIONARY HOUSING PAYMENTS** for more specific rules and rates.)

Income 7.19

All the income that a claimant has will be assessed as with all means-tested benefits (see **CHAPTER 2 ASSESSMENT OF MEANS**) but in general the following will be taken into account:

- earnings;
- other income;
- maintenance; and
- tariff income from capital.

There is some scope for elements of earned income to be disregarded, i e if the claimant is a lone parent or attracts a disability premium, the first £20 of his earned income will be disregarded. If the claimant is a member of a couple the first £10 of the joint earned income will be disregarded, regardless of whether one or both members of the couple are working. In all other cases only the first £5 of the claimant's income will be disregarded. There is also scope in *regulation 103(2)* of the *Jobseeker's Allowance Regulations 1996 (SI 1996 No 207)* for other items of income to be disregarded such as 100% of any Attendance Allowance, Disability Living Allowance etc. For a full list of sums disregarded see *Schedule* 7 of the 1996 Regulations.

From April 2004, the Income Support applicable amount no longer includes amounts for dependent children, although in some cases this will be phased out. Once an Income Support claim no longer includes any allowances for children, then any Child Benefit and Child Tax Credit will also be disregarded from the income assessment.

Capital 7.20

All the claimant's and his partner's savings and capital will be assessed in line with all other means-tested benefits (see **CHAPTER 2**). If the savings and capital are assessed to be in excess of £6,000, then a tariff income will be applied in respect of any savings or capital between £6,000 and the £16,000 capital limit. This tariff income will be assessed at £1 per week for every £250 (or part) by which the claimant's capital exceeds £6,000.

The final calculation   7.21

The final part of the calculation involves comparing income with the applicable amount:

- if the income is *greater* than the applicable amount, then the claimant will *not* be entitled to income-based JSA;

- if the income is *less* than the applicable amount, then the claimant will be awarded the difference by the way of an income-based JSA award.

EXAMPLE

Peter and Karen are a couple who are both under 60. They have two sons aged 12 and 17. The latter is in further education and is still a dependent child. They receive Child Benefit and Child Tax Credit for both children.

They live in rented accommodation paying a rent of £60 per week to a housing association.

Peter has recently been made redundant and Karen is working twelve hours per week and has a net income from this employment of £55 per week. Peter is now claiming income-based JSA but does not have sufficient NICs to qualify for contributory JSA. The couple have savings of £6,790.

Income-based JSA will be calculated as follows:

➡

Applicable amount		Income	
Personal allowances			
Couple	£90.10	Karen's earnings	£55.00
		less income disregard	£10.00
		Assessable earned income	£45.00
Premiums		Child Benefit (disregarded)	£29.15
none		Child Tax Credit (disregarded)	£78.36
		Tariff income	£4.00
Total	**£90.10**	**Total**	**£49.00**

The award of income-based JSA to which Peter and Karen will be entitled will be £41.10 per week, i e applicable amount of £90.10 less assessable income £49.00 = £41.10 per week.

(For an example demonstrating mortgage interest payments, see **6.23** above.)

Job Grant 7.22

From October 2004 the previously available 'back to work bonus' was abolished, and replaced by a new Job Grant.

Job Grant is aimed at helping people who have been in receipt of Income Support, Jobseekers Allowance, Severe Disablement Allowance or Incapacity Benefit for six months or more when they leave benefit to start full-time work. Claimants receiving benefit for six months or more may be eligible for a payment of £100 (£250 for lone parents and couples with children), and four weeks' additional assistance with rent or mortgage interest. Claims should be made to Jobcentre Plus, on leaflets JSP1 or WK1. These grants are payable under the *Employment and Training Act 1973, section 2*.

How to claim 7.23

Before claiming JSA a claimant and any partner must either attend their local jobcentre to make an appointment to 'sign on' for JSA, or telephone Jobcentre Plus to make an appointment to sign on. At this point the claimant will be provided with a jobseekers claim pack containing a contributory JSA claim form, an income-based JSA claim form along with a number of additional forms: a JSANHB 1 (for the purpose of indicating intention to claim Housing and/or Council Tax Benefit) and a Form JSAMI12 for the purpose of claiming entitlement to mortgage or home improvement loan interest payments.

The first appointment for a jobseekers interview should be within five days of a claimant first contacting Jobcentre Plus. Any assessment of entitlement to benefit will be considered from the date that the claimant made the appointment to 'sign on'. Claimants signing on for the first time will be required to provide proof of their last wage and provide their Form P45. They will also be required to provide evidence of their own and their partner's National Insurance numbers (e g a letter from HMRC or the DWP), identity (e g birth certificate, passport etc) and proof of residence (e g a recent utility bill etc), along with evidence of any income and capital that the claimant or partner has. This evidence must be by way of original documents (not photocopies).

At the initial jobseekers interview the claimant will meet an adviser who will go through the requirements of availability for work, and what is required of the claimant by way of taking appropriate steps to find work. At this point the claimant and the advisor will jointly draw up a jobseekers agreement. (The initial jobseekers interview can take several hours.)

Once the jobseekers agreement is in place and agreed and signed by both parties, the claimant will be given a future signing-on day (usually at intervals of two weeks, but this can be as frequent as daily in special circumstances) which the claimant must keep in order to be paid any continuing entitlement to benefit.

If the claimant is not able to attend the jobcentre every two weeks because:

- the claimant has mobility problems in consequence of a physical disability;

- the journey one way to the jobcentre by public transport will take more than one hour;

- attending the jobcentre will result in the claimant being away from home for more than four hours;

- the claimant does not have access to public transport and the journey on foot exceeds three miles in reasonable terrain (or less where the claimant's health and wellbeing may be affected by such a long journey on foot),

the claimant will be able to make an application to sign on by post. Signing on by post is allowed for the fortnightly signings only.

The claimant will still have to attend the jobcentre for his initial interview and subsequent 13-weekly restart interviews (see below) unless this would result in his being away from home for eight hours or more. In such circumstances the claimant must request that Jobcentre Plus provides a home visit for the purpose of conducting an interview.

Most signing-on days will involve attendance at the jobcentre office of about 30 minutes. However, the claimant will be required to attend a more detailed appointment every 13 weeks.

The 13-week interview is known as a restart interview, where the claimant will revisit his jobseekers agreement to see if there is anything that he can do to improve his prospects of finding work. He will also have to produce evidence to show what he has been doing in the previous 13-week period to find work. He may, of his own motion, decide to alter his jobseekers agreement, but this must be agreed by the benefit officer. Where the benefit officer feels that improvements or changes need to be made he may direct that the jobseekers agreement be amended or changed (this often occurs at a second or third restart interview, where after at least 26 weeks all the claimant's attempts to secure work have failed).

Payments of income-based JSA will generally be made fortnightly in arrears directly into the claimant's bank account. However, a claimant may request that benefit be paid by way of Giros, and in such circumstances payments of this benefit will be paid fortnightly. No benefit will be paid in respect of the first three days of unemployment, unless the claimant was receiving an alternative earnings replacement benefit or Income Support immediately before claiming JSA.

Challenging decisions   7.24

Once benefit has been assessed, the claimant will be sent a full written decision in respect of the claim. If a claimant is not happy with the decision for whatever reason, he will need to ask that the decision be revised. Applications for revision must be made in writing and delivered to the decision maker within one month of the date of the original decision.

The decision maker will look at the claim again and take into account any new information that the claimant has raised in his application for revision. The decision maker will then issue a further decision, and if the claimant is not happy with that decision, he may, in certain circumstances, appeal to the appeal tribunal, but must do so within one month of the date of issue of the most recent decision (see **CHAPTER 4**).

Common problems   7.25

1. The claimant has been dismissed from employment but his employer alleges that he was dismissed because of gross miscon-

duct. The claimant, having made a claim for JSA, has been advised that his entitlement to benefit has been suspended for 26 weeks.

The claimant must request a revision of the decision to suspend benefit and provide a detailed explanation of the circumstances surrounding his dismissal. If the claimant was employed for more than a year, or if the dismissal was for reasons of discrimination, the claimant has a right to appeal to an employment tribunal. Registering the appeal with the employment tribunal will be persuasive evidence of relevance that can be taken into account by the DWP when revising the claimant's benefit suspension. Alternatively, if the claimant has not been employed for long enough to appeal to an employment tribunal, the claimant should provide any evidence to support his claim for unfair dismissal, which may include statements from any witnesses, authorising the DWP to contact any potential witnesses and obtaining references from previous employers etc (see **CHAPTER 4**).

2. The claimant has been receiving Income Support as a person incapable of work, but following a recent medical assessment has been found fit for work. He intends to appeal against this decision but in the mean time he needs to sign on as available for work in order to receive his full entitlement to benefit.

It is for a claimant to claim JSA and appeal against the decision to find him fit for work, but in applying for JSA the claimant will have to show that he is available and actively seeking work. If the claimant has to place restrictions on the type of work that he is able to do in consequence of his disability, he should not be penalised if these restrictions are 'reasonable' and do not considerably reduce his prospects of finding work.

For instance, if the claimant's physical disability prevents him from being able to undertake manual work and this is supported by a letter from his GP, then this restriction will be deemed reasonable. If the claimant's disability is a mental incapacity which results in the claimant only being able to undertake work where he is supervised and/or prompted continuously, and again the claimant's GP supports this requirement in the working environment, then this restriction will be deemed reasonable.

In such circumstances the claimant will normally be referred to a Disability Employment Adviser (DEA) who will give practical advice and assistance on the type of work that might be available to a claimant with disabilities, or alternatively the claimant can ask to be referred to a DEA of his own motion.

If, following a successful appeal, the claimant wishes to reclaim Income Support, he will be treated as a continuous claimant for Income Support and will not have any lost entitlement to benefit (i e disability premiums etc) as Income Support will be reinstated from the date that it ceased to be paid.

However, any payments of JSA that have been made to the claimant during the period while waiting for an appeal will be offset against any arrears of Income Support due to be paid to the claimant (see **CHAPTER 6** for an alternative Income Support remedy to this problem).

Checklist 7.26

Claim specification	Details
Basic entitlement conditions	Claimant must not be working, or working for less than 16 hours per week. Any partner, if working, must be working for less than 24 hours per week. Claimant and partner must have less than £16,000 in savings and capital and be habitually resident in the UK. Claimant must be available for and actively seeking full-time work and be required to enter into a jobseekers contract. Entitlement is wholly subject to a means test of the family unit.
Dependant additions	Additions for a dependent partner and homeowner housing costs are included in any assessment of entitlement to this benefit.
Where to claim	Claims must be made in a prescribed JSA application form obtainable from the local DWP or jobcentre. A claimant must also attend an initial jobseekers interview and enter into a written jobseekers agreement which is contractually binding.

Claim specification	Details
How difficult is the claim form to complete?	The means test form is quite simple, requiring factual information about the claimant and family, and comprehensive details regarding income and capital. The claimant will also have to provide proof of all income and capital with this claim and evidence of his last payment details. This is a long form requiring approximately 45–60 minutes for completion. The claimant will also be required to state what he intends to do to find work and how he will do this. This is often quite difficult as whatever the claimant says he will do, he must do, otherwise his benefit entitlement could be suspended. Both members of any couple must sign all forms and agreements.
Changes of circumstances that need to be notified	Any changes in the claimant's circumstances at all, including people moving into or out of his home, changes in hours of work, changes in income and capital, going into or out of hospital, going on holiday, changes in disability etc. Any change of address and if the claimant or partner claims or receives any other benefits or sources of income or capital. The claimant must also notify of any changes that he wishes to make to his jobseekers agreement and these must be agreed with the jobcentre before they are implemented.
Frequency of periodic reviews	Reviews can be carried out at any time. However, most claimants will be required to sign on every two weeks, and in effect this requirement produces a fortnightly review. The claimant will have a more detailed review carried out every 13 weeks by attending a restart interview.
Time limits for reviews and appeals	Applications must be made within one month of the date that the decision under review/appeal was issued.

Claim specification	Details
Benefit reductions	Benefit entitlement is reduced if the claimant's partner goes into hospital and is an in-patient for more than 52 weeks. If the claimant goes into hospital and his period of sickness is likely to exceed two weeks, he will no longer qualify for this benefit and will have to claim IS as an alternative. Benefit will be withdrawn in most cases if the claimant is not available for work in any benefit payment week. If the jobseekers agreement is not complied with, the claimant will have benefit entitlement suspended for a fixed period.
Other linked benefits	Can be claimed in addition to Housing Benefit and Council Tax Benefit. Otherwise this benefit is paid as a top-up to any other Social Security benefit. Also gives rise to possible entitlement to Social Fund payments and NHS benefits, such as free prescriptions, dental treatment, sight tests etc and free school meals for children of school age.
Attracting a NICs credit	Yes.
Taxable	No.

8 Tax Credits

Introduction 8.1

Two new tax credits were introduced in April 2003. While many people are better off under this new system, there has been a great deal of administrative confusion over the implementation of the scheme. In the first two years, many people were overpaid tax credits, often through no fault of their own. The process of HMRC recovering overpayments, and reducing people's ongoing awards in order to do so, has caused considerable hardship. Recently, reforms have been announced that will come into effect during 2006 and 2007 to reduce the number of overpayments and to ease the problems caused by their recovery.

- **Working Tax Credit (WTC)**

  ○ a means-tested credit for working adults;

  ○ WTC brought together adult elements in the former Working Families Tax Credit and Disabled Person's Tax Credit;

  ○ WTC extends entitlement to non-disabled people without children.

- **Child Tax Credit (CTC)**

  ○ a means-tested credit for low-income families with children, whether in or out of work;

  ○ CTC brought together in one payment existing means-tested support for children.

In separating out support for adults from support for children, the stated aims were:

- to make work pay for those in low-income households, including those without children, through the WTC;

- to tackle child poverty through the CTC and Child Benefit; and

- to provide a common framework for assessing entitlement to tax credits based more closely on income tax rules, integrating the tax and benefit systems to bridge the divide between work and welfare.

Legislation 8.2

The primary legislation is the *Tax Credits Act 2002 (TCA 2002)* which received Royal Assent on 8 July 2002. The Act provides a framework for the WTC and the CTC. Much of the detail is contained within the regulations, the most important of which are:

- *Working Tax Credit (Entitlement and Maximum Rate) Regulations 2002 (SI 2002 No 2005);*

- *Tax Credits (Definition and Calculation of Income) Regulations 2002 (SI 2002 No 2006);*

- *Child Tax Credit Regulations 2002 (SI 2002 No 2007);*

- *Tax Credits (Income Thresholds and Determination of Rates) Regulations 2002 (SI 2002 No 2008);*

- *Tax Credits (Claims and Notifications) Regulations 2002 (SI 2002 No 2014);*

- *Working Tax Credit (Payment by Employers) Regulations 2002 (SI 2002 No 2172);* and

- *Tax Credits (Payments by the Board) Regulations 2002 (SI 2002 No 2173).*

Working Tax Credit 8.3

WTC is for low-paid families with children and for disabled people with or without children who work at least 16 hours per week, and for low-paid people without children who work at least 30 hours per week. There are increased amounts for those working 30 hours or more and for disabled workers. It can include an amount for childcare costs.

Unlike for Working Families Tax Credit and Disabled Person's Tax Credit, the requirement to be in work is an ongoing one with the exception of some periods of illness and maternity leave. The number of hours worked is defined as 'the number of hours of such work he normally performs' (*SI 2002 No 2005, Reg 4*). In borderline cases the claimants should be advised to keep a careful record of hours worked in case of dispute.

Who can claim? 8.4

There are four routes to qualifying for WTC.

Route 1 – Lone parent or couple with at least one dependent child 8.5

To qualify the claimant must:

- be aged 16 or over (*TCA 2002, s 3*);

- work at least 16 hours per week (or claimant's partner must do so) (*SI 2002 No 2005, Reg 4*). This must be work done in the expectation of payment and must be expected to last at least four weeks. The claimant must be working in the week he claims, or be expecting to start a job within seven days; and

- be responsible for at least one child (*SI 2002 No 2005, Reg 4*). Definitions of 'responsible for' and a 'child' are found in the *Child Tax Credit Regulations 2002 (SI 2002 No 2007)*.

Route 2 – Claimant has a disability 8.6

To qualify the claimant must:

- be aged 16 or over (*TCA 2002, s 3*);

- work at least 16 hours per week (or claimant's partner must do so) (*SI 2002 No 2005, Reg 4*); and

- have a disability that puts him at a disadvantage in getting a job (*SI 2002 No 2005, Reg 9, Sch 1*).

Route 3 – Claimant without children over 25 8.7

To qualify the claimant must:

- be aged 25 or over; and

- work at least 30 hours per week (or claimant's partner must do so) (*SI 2002 No 2005, Reg 4(1)*).

Route 4 – Claimant over 50 8.8

To qualify the claimant must:

- qualify for the 50+ element and work at least 16 hours per week.

Disability conditions 8.9

The claimant or his partner must satisfy one of the following conditions:

1   Be in receipt of, for at least one day in the last 182, higher short-term rate of Incapacity Benefit or long-term rate, Severe Disablement Allowance or Income Support, income-based Jobseekers Allowance, Housing Benefit or Council Tax Benefit, including a disability or higher pensioner premium.

2   Be in receipt of, at the date of claim, Disability Living Allowance, Attendance Allowance or Constant Attendance Allowance, or have an invalid car from the NHS.

3   Comply with the following conditions:

   ○   be in receipt of Statutory Sick Pay, occupational sick pay, lower short-term rate of Incapacity Benefit, or Income Support for 140 days, or being credited with National Insurance contributions for incapacity for work for 20 weeks, and claim WTC within 56 days of the end of that period;

   ○   have a disability which is likely to last for at least six months; and

   ○   have gross earnings reduced by at least 20% or £15 per week compared to before the disability began.

4   Have undertaken 'training for work' in the 56 days before the claim and have been in receipt of a long-term incapacity benefit prior to the start of the training.

On a renewal claim made within eight weeks of the expiry of the previous award, following a claim based on previous incapacity under points 1 and 3 above, the condition will still be treated as satisfied.

In addition, the claimant or partner must either:

•   be undergoing a period of rehabilitation following an accident or illness; or

•   have one of the following disabilities:

   ○   when standing he is unable to keep his balance without holding on to something;

   ○   he suffers from fits, which cause him to lose consciousness at least once a year;

   ○   he is unable to walk more than 100 metres along level ground using any walking aid he normally uses;

   ○   he cannot place both hands behind his back as he would when putting on a coat or tucking a shirt into trousers;

○　　he cannot extend his arms in front of him without difficulty;

○　　he cannot extend his hands to reach his head without difficulty;

○　　he is unable to pick up a full jug and pour a glass of water without difficulty;

○　　he is registered blind or partially sighted;

○　　he cannot hear a telephone ring in the same room, or hear a person talking in a loud voice from a distance of two metres;

○　　people who know him well have difficulty understanding what he says, or vice versa;

○　　he has a mental illness for which he receives regular treatment;

○　　because of mental illness he is confused or forgetful;

○　　he cannot do the simplest addition and/or subtraction;

○　　due to mental disability he strikes people or damages property or is unable to form social relationships; or

○　　if he cannot sustain a normal eight-hour day or five-day week due to a medical condition or severe pain.

In addition, in all cases, the claimant's income must be below the relevant income threshold, or no more than a fixed amount above, and the claimant must not be subject to immigration control.

Maximum amount of Working Tax Credit   8.10

WTC is made up of:

- a **basic element**, which is always included (*SI 2002 No 2005, Reg 4*);

- a **lone parent element** in the case of a claim by a lone parent (*SI 2002 No 2005, Reg 12*);

- a **second adult element**, in the case of a joint claim, unless the only route to claiming is the 50+ route, and the claimant works less than 30 hours per week (*SI 2002 No 2005, Reg 11*);

- a **disability element** if the claimant or partner qualifies as a disabled worker – one per qualifying member of the couple (*SI 2002 No 2005, Reg 9*);

- a **severe disability element** if the claimant or partner receives the highest rate care component of Disability Living Allowance (*SI 2002 No 2005, Reg 17*);

179

- a **30-hour element** if claimant or partner works 30 hours per week (or aggregate number of hours worked by both members of a couple if 30+ (*SI 2002 No 2005, Reg 10*);

- a **50+ element** paid for the first year after return to work following a period of at least six months on Income Support, Jobseekers Allowance, Incapacity Benefit, Severe Disability Premium or retirement pension with Minimum Income Guarantee, Carer's Allowance or Bereavement Benefit (*SI 2002 No 2005, Reg 18*); and

- a **childcare element** of 80% of eligible childcare charges, subject to maximum amounts (see below), provided claimant is a lone parent, or in the case of a joint claim, both members of the couple are working 16+ hours per week, or one is and the other is incapable of work. This figure was increased from 70% from April 2006 (*SI 2002 No 2005, Regs 13–17*).

WTC Amounts		
	2006/07 **£ per year**	**Weekly equivalent** **£ per week**
Basic element	1,665	32.01
Second adult element/lone parent element	1,640	31.53
30-hour element	680	13.07
Disability element	2,225	42.78
Severe disability element	945	18.17
50+ element 16–29 hours	1,140	21.92
50+ element 30+ hours	1,705	32.78
Childcare element (80% of maximum)		
– maximum eligible cost 2+ children	15,600 (12,480)	300.00 (240.00)
– maximum eligible cost for 1 child	9,100 (7,280)	175.00 (140.00)
Threshold:		
Income threshold	5,220	100.38

	WTC Amounts	
	2006/07 **£ per year**	**Weekly equivalent** **£ per week**
Withdrawal rate – 37%		

Child Tax Credit   8.11

CTC is for families with at least one child under 16 or under 19 and still in non-advanced education. The amount depends on the age of the children and on whether any children are disabled. The maximum amount reduces as income increases above a threshold.

Who can claim?   8.12

To qualify the claimant must:

- be aged 16 or over (*TCA 2002, s 3*);

- be responsible for at least one child (the test is where the child is 'normally living' and there is no provision to split awards in shared care cases (*SI 2002 No 2007, Reg 3*)) who is:

  ○ under age 16 (*SI 2002 No 2007, Reg 2*);

  ○ aged 16 – for school leavers CTC is paid up to the end of August following their 16th birthday (*SI 2002 No 2007, Reg 4*);

  ○ under 18, not in education or work, but registered for work/training (*SI 2002 No 2007, Reg 5*); or

  ○ under 19 and in full-time non-advanced education (*SI 2002 No 2007, Reg 5*);

- have income below the appropriate threshold, or no more than a set amount above, or be in receipt of Income Support/income-based Jobseekers Allowance; and

- not be subject to immigration control.

Maximum amount of Child Tax Credit   8.13

CTC is made up of:

- a **family element** – always included (*SI 2002 No 2007, Reg 7(3)*);

- an **additional family element** where there is a child under one year (*SI 2002 No 2007, Reg 7(3)*);

- a **child element** for each child (*SI 2002 No 2007, Reg 7(4)*);

- a **disabled child element** for a child who is blind or in receipt of Disability Living Allowance (*SI 2002 No 2007, Regs 7(4), 8*); and

- a **severely disabled child element** if the child is in receipt of the highest rate care component of Disability Living Allowance (*SI 2002 No 2007, Regs 7(4), 8*).

CTC Amounts		
	2006/07 **£ per year**	**Weekly equivalent** **£ per week**
Family element	545	10.45
Additional family element	545	10.45
Child element	1,765	33.94
Disabled child element	2,350	45.19
Severely disabled child element	945	18.17
Thresholds		
First income threshold	5,220	100.38
First withdrawal rate – 37%		
Second income threshold for family elements	50,000	958.90
Second withdrawal rate – 1 in 15		

CTC Amounts		
	2006/07 **£ per year**	**Weekly equivalent** **£ per week**
First threshold for those not on income support/ income-based JSA and entitled to CTC only (i e no WTC)	14,155	272.21

Calculating the tax credits   8.14

Step 1 – Maximum WTC and/or CTC   8.15

Work out the maximum possible WTC and/or CTC for the 'relevant period' – see figures to include above. A 'relevant period' is a period during which the maximum WTC and CTC remain the same. Where there are changes, for example in the number of children, the maximum award will have to be calculated on a pro rata basis for each relevant period. This will also be the case when a claim starts after the beginning of the tax year.

Step 2 – Assess income   8.16

In most cases, income will be assessed for the purpose of an award on the previous year's income (income for 2005/06 will form the basis of the assessment for 2006/07), although for the introduction of the new tax credits in April 2003 this was based on income for 2001/02. HMRC therefore issues a provisional decision at the beginning of the tax year and a reconciliation is carried out at the end of the year (see **8.18** below). See **CHAPTER 2 ASSESSMENT OF MEANS** for rules on assessment of income.

Tax credits are based on the income of a single applicant or the joint income of a couple, including for same sex couples. If a lone parent were a member of a couple in the previous year, the assessment would be based on only his income in the previous year.

Step 3 – Work out amount payable   8.17

Compare income to the appropriate threshold(s) and apply taper (i e percentage withdrawal rate as income goes above the threshold).

- **Maximum WTC/CTC payable**

  If income is at or below the threshold of £5,220 then maximum WTC and CTC are payable. Income Support and income-based Jobseekers Allowance claimants receive the maximum rate of CTC.

- **Entitled to WTC (and CTC)**

  If income is over the threshold then the maximum amount is reduced at the rate of 37p for every pound of income above the threshold. There is a set order in which the reduction is applied, as follows:

  o   first the maximum amount of WTC excluding the childcare element is reduced;

  o   if there is still 'excess' income, the childcare element is tapered off; then

  o   the child element and disabled/severely disabled child elements of CTC are reduced leaving the family element(s); finally

  o   if income is above the second threshold of £50,000 then the family element(s) are tapered off at the rate of 1 for every £15 income exceeds £50,000. This means that everyone (over 16 and not subject to immigration control) with at least one child will receive at least some family element of CTC if total income is less than £58,175.

  (Tax Credits (Income Thresholds and Determination of Rates) Regulations 2002 (SI 2002 No 2008).)

- **Entitled to CTC only**

  Those who get CTC but not WTC or Income Support/income-based Jobseekers Allowance have a higher income threshold of £14,155 above which CTC is withdrawn at 37%. This puts them approximately on a level with others who do get WTC, and for whom CTC would only begin to be withdrawn once their WTC has been tapered off.

EXAMPLE

A lone parent with two children aged 7 and 9 who are not disabled. She works a 35-hour week with gross annual earnings of £18,500. She has no income except for maintenance and child benefit. Childcare costs average out over the year, taking into account term-time and holidays, to £75.00 per week. ➡

Step 1 – Maximum WTC and/or CTC

- WTC – £7,105

  This is the combination of the basic, lone parent, 30-hour and childcare elements.

  (£1,665 + £1,640 + £680 + £3,120 = £7,105)

- CTC – £4,075

  This is the combination of the family and two child elements.

  (£545 + £1,765 + £1,765 = £4,075)

Step 2 – Assess income – £18,500

The only income to be taken into account is her earnings as Child Benefit and maintenance are not included.

Gross income is used.

Step 3 – Work out amount payable

- Compare income with the WTC threshold and work out the difference.

  (£18,500 – £5,220 = £13,280)

- Apply the taper to the difference.

  (£13,280 x 37% = £4,913.60)

- Deduct from maximum WTC.

  (£7,105.00 – £4,913.60 = £2,191.40)

There is no deduction from CTC as the whole amount to be deducted has been taken off WTC leaving a balance. The maximum CTC will therefore be paid.

WTC payable = £2,191.40

CTC payable = £3,925.00

_____

£6,116.40 total tax credit payable

Changes of circumstances and end of year reconciliations 8.18

At the end of the tax year, the provisional award is to be reconciled against actual income for the year. There could be an overpayment to be repaid or further tax credit due.

If income rises or falls during the year a claimant can choose to have the award amended based on a forecast of current year's income. However, there is no obligation to notify changes of income until the end of the tax year. So, for example, if there has been a drop in earnings this can be taken into account straight away, or an overpayment may arise at the end of the year.

From April 2006, if income has risen by up to £25,000 in the current year, then this increase will be ignored in the reconciliation (*TCA 2002, s 7*); if the increase is more than this, then it is only the amount over £25,000 that is taken into account. This figure has been very substantially increased from the previous level of £2,500 to reduce the incidence of overpayments. As the income assessment is an annual one, the £25,000 disregard is applied to annual income. Therefore, a significant rise in income towards the end of the year is unlikely to exceed that figure.

There is a requirement to notify certain changes of circumstances within three months (*TCA 2002, s 6*) and failure to do so attracts a penalty. Such changes include a change in the number of adults heading the household (i e becoming a member of a couple, or becoming a lone parent), and eligible childcare costs ceasing or reducing significantly. From November 2006, this list of changes will be expanded to include changes in work status, or in the number of children for which the family can claim.

There is no requirement to notify other changes of circumstances, although failure to do so could result in the loss of some tax credit (increases in the maximum figure only take effect from the date of change if notified within three months), or in an overpayment (changes reducing entitlement take effect from the date of change.

Overpayments can be recovered from the next year's tax credit award, or by treating it as an underpayment of tax and taking it back through the PAYE system, or issuing a demand for payment within 30 days.

Annual reviews and renewals 8.19

All decisions made in relation to a current year's entitlement to tax credits are provisional, since it is not until the end of the tax year that a final assessment can be made. This process has been referred to as 'reconciliation', but HMRC refers to it as 'annual review'. Claimants are required to declare that the information HMRC has is correct. This will also act as a renewal claim for the following year.

The legal process   8.20

- final notice required before decision on entitlement. This requires the claimant to confirm their personal circumstances, and actual or estimated income for the preceding year. This must be done by the date specified on the notice;

- information is then used by HMRC to finalise the previous year's tax credits entitlement. This may result in an underpayment or overpayment, and will be confirmed in a final notice of entitlement;

- the information on the declaration is then used as a renewal claim for the following year. If the declaration is given by the date on the final notice, the claim is automatically backdated to the beginning of the tax year. If the declaration is late, only three months backdating is allowed;

- the new initial award may be reduced to recover an overpayment from the previous year.

The renewal process   8.21

From April to June, HMRC sends renewals packs to claimants, containing two forms:

- the *annual review form* contains details of the claimant's circumstances and income details for the previous year. Claimants have to confirm that the details are correct, or to notify any changes or inaccuracies;

- the *annual declaration form* asks for details of income – or an estimate – for the previous year. The claimant must sign a declaration that the information on the review form is correct and complete, and that the information provided on the declaration is correct, and to confirm that they are making a claim for the current year just started. This form has to be returned by 31 August. This has been brought forward by one month from previous years to reduce the period during which provisional assessments are made based on out of date information. If the form is not returned by this date, any continuing payments of tax credits will stop;

- claimants not receiving tax credits, due to a 'nil award', or those on only the family element of CTC, receive a modified annual review form, asking them to notify any changes, and to confirm that their income is still within the range stated. These claimants are not required to complete a separate declaration, and they are deemed to have declared that all information is correct.

Timetable for 2006/07 8.22

3 April 2006	From this date provisional awards of tax credits replaced the previous year's award, but at the same rate. For many claimants this meant no change. Claimants previously receiving reduced awards in order to reduce a likely overpayment may see an increase back to the correct amount. These provisional payments cease if declaration forms are not returned by 31 August 2006.
April to June 2006	HMRC issues annual review and declaration forms.
31 August 2006	This is the first deadline for returning declarations and notifying changes in circumstances. HMRC will issue reminders in July. If the declaration is returned by this date, the claimant will receive a final notice of entitlement for 2005/06, and a new award notice for 2006/07. The claim and award for 2006/07 will be backdated to April 2006. If the declaration is not returned by 31 August 2006, provisional payments will stop, and claimants will be required to repay money paid since April 2006.
31 January 2007	This is the second deadline for returning declarations and notifying actual (as opposed to estimated) income for 2005/06. This will particularly apply to self-employed people. If the declaration is returned by this date the claimant will receive a final award notice for 2005/06, and an initial award for 2006/07, backdated to April 2006. If the declaration is not returned by this date, there will be no claim from April 2006, and any new claim will only be backdated by three months.

Administration 8.23

Payment 8.24

(*Working Tax Credit (Payment by Employers) Regulations 2002 (SI 2002 No 2172)*).

WTC (apart from the childcare element) will be paid by employers. The Inland Revenue will pay the self-employed direct. CTC, together with the childcare element, will be paid direct to the main carer. Payment will be weekly or four-weekly. Payments are made into bank accounts; the Government asked banks and building societies to develop basic accounts that will be accessible through Post Offices, and which people can use without getting into debt.

Decisions   8.25

(*Tax Credits (Claims and Notifications) Regulations 2002 (SI 2002 No 2014)*).

The decision making process has been aligned with the income tax system.

On receiving a claim a decision maker decides whether to make an award and at what rate. This is a 'provisional decision'.

A provisional decision can be revised:

- if there is a change of circumstances affecting the amount of the credit, for example a new baby is born, disability or increased childcare costs;

- if income increases over £25,000, or reduces; or

- if HMRC has reasonable grounds for believing the award to be wrong (the award can cease altogether in these circumstances).

An award can be ended if any change of circumstances means that the claimant is no longer entitled, for example WTC ceases if the claimant leaves work.

A 'final decision' is made at the end of year reconciliation. A notice is sent out to the claimant specifying the circumstances and income on which the award was based. The claimant must either confirm the details or amend them. The end of year notice forms the basis for the next year's award.

Challenging decisions   8.26

TCA 2002 provides for appeals to be dealt with by the Tax Commissioners, but this provision is not to be implemented for the foreseeable future. Appeals will be dealt with and administered by the Appeals Service and heard by appeal tribunals as for Social Security benefits. (See **CHAPTER 4 CLAIMS, DECISIONS AND APPEALS**.)

Transitional arrangements   8.27

Although the normal method of assessment is based on the income for the preceding tax year, for the first year (2003/04) income for the year 2001/02 was used to enable advance claims to be made prior to the start of the new scheme.

Income Support and income-based Jobseekers Allowance claimants moved on to the new CTC from April 2004 for new claims. People already getting child additions with their Income Support or income-based Jobseekers Allowance at April 2004 will transfer onto CTC sometime in 2005.

Checklist   8.28

Claim specification	Details
Basic entitlement conditions:	
CTC	Claimant must be treated as being responsible for at least one dependent child or young person under 19. He must not be subject to immigration control. Entitlement is based on a means test of the family unit.
WTC	Claimant or partner must be working at least 16 hours per week, be over 16, and either have a disability or dependent children. Those with neither a disability nor children must be working at least 30 hours per week, and be aged at least 25.
Dependant additions	Additions for dependent children are included within the CTC, and for childcare costs within the WTC.
Where to claim	Claim forms can be obtained from the HMRC Credits Office, or from jobcentres or local tax offices. Claims can also be made online at www.hmrc.gov.uk/taxcredits.

Claim specification	*Details*
How difficult is the form to complete?	Not very complex, requiring factual information about the claimant and family, and comprehensive information about the preceding year's income.
Changes of circumstances that need to be notified	Some changes, such as becoming a lone parent or part of a couple, must be reported within three months. Penalties may be imposed for failure to do so. Other changes, such as changes in income or in family circumstances, should normally be reported to avoid any loss of credit, or avoid overpayments.
Frequency of periodic reviews	Tax credits are awarded annually.
Time limits for appeals	Appeals must be lodged within 30 days of a final assessment.
Other linked benefits	Tax credits are paid on top of most other benefits, but are taken into account as income for means-tested benefits.
Taxable	No.

9 Housing Benefit, Council Tax Benefit and Discretionary Housing Payments

(Social Security Contributions and Benefits Act 1992; Housing Benefit (General) Regulations 1987 (SI 1987 No 1971); Council Tax Benefit (General) Regulations 1992 (SI 1992 No 1814)).

Introduction 9.1

Housing Benefit (HB) and Council Tax Benefit (CTB) are means-tested benefits which are administered by the local authority for claimants who have a low income to help them to meet their rent liability or council tax liability for the place where they live.

Housing Benefit 9.2

HB is available to claimants whether or not they are working full time and can be claimed in addition to any other benefit, for example tax credits, Incapacity Benefit, pensions etc. There are, however, some circumstances where HB cannot be claimed, regardless of a claimant's income and the fact that he has to pay rent.

When Housing Benefit cannot be claimed 9.3

Certain categories of rent 9.4

(SI 1987 No 1971, Reg 7).

The claimant cannot claim HB if his partner's rent liability falls into one of the following groups:

- the tenancy is not on a commercial basis, i e could not be legally enforced;

- the liability to pay rent is to a close relative who lives in the same house. A close relative is a relative or step-relative who is a parent, child, sister or brother (or partner of any one of these). This includes an equivalent relationship arising from a civil partnership;

- the liability to pay rent is to a former partner who used to live in the same property as the claimant or his partner (i e the claimant or his partner lived with the landlord in his home, the landlord then moved out and rents his home to his former partner);

- the liability to pay rent is to a parent of a child who lives in the same property as the claimant or his partner (i e the landlord is a parent of the claimant or his partner's child);

- the liability to pay rent is to a trustee or trust of which the claimant or his partner or child is a beneficiary and the liability was created to take advantage of the HB scheme;

- the liability to pay rent is to an employer or director of a company of which the claimant or his partner is an employee and the liability was created to take advantage of the HB scheme;

- the claimant is a non-dependant of someone who lives in the same property and the liability was created to take advantage of the HB scheme (i e to prevent non-dependant deductions being made from the tenant's HB award);

- the claimant or his partner previously owned the property in the five years prior to the date of claim. (This will not apply where the claimant or his partner could not have continued to live in the property without relinquishing ownership, i e a home rescue scheme);

- the occupation of the property is a condition of the claimant or his partner's employment, e g caretakers, wardens etc;

- the claimant is a member of and wholly maintained by a religious order;

- the liability was created to take advantage of the HB scheme.

Claimants who do not have a legal liability to pay rent   9.5

(Social Security Contributions and Benefits Act 1992, s 130(1)(a); SI 1987 No 1971, Reg 6).

Claimants who do not have a legal liability to pay rent for their accommodation will not be entitled to HB for their rent, for instance claimants who live in accommodation which they will not have to leave if no rent is paid. However, this exclusion will not extend to those who do not have a liability where it is reasonable to treat them as having one, for example where a couple live in a property and only one member of the couple is the tenant, the tenant then moves out of the property and leaves his partner behind – in such circumstances, although the partner does not have a legal liability, it will be deemed to be reasonable to treat that person as liable for the rent in order that the partner can continue to live in the property.

Claimants with more than £16,000 capital 9.6

(SI 1987 No 1971, Reg 37).

Where a claimant or a couple living together as man and wife have savings or capital of more than £16,000, they will not be eligible to claim HB. The £16,000 capital limit is the same for a single claimant as it is for a couple. The only exception to this rule is where the claimant is receiving the guarantee credit of Pension Credit. In this case he is eligible for the maximum HB, whatever his capital. (See **CHAPTER 2 ASSESSMENT OF MEANS**.)

Claimants who are full-time students 9.7

(SI 1987 No 1971, Reg 47).

Claimants who are full-time students in higher education will not be eligible to claim HB in most cases. However, if a claimant has a partner who is not a full-time student, then HB can be claimed. Other cases where HB might be claimed by a full-time student are where (provided that the claimant is not in student accommodation, i e halls of residence) the student:

• has dependent children;

• is aged over 60; or

• is disabled or has been incapable of work for more than 28 weeks.

Claimants who receive housing costs from other sources 9.8

(SI 1987 No 1971, Reg 8).

Claimants who receive Income Support and housing costs will not be eligible for HB for the same housing costs. Furthermore, claimants in some local authority hostels provided by Social Services will be ineligible for benefit as their housing costs are provided under the *National Assistance Act 1948*. Claimants aged 16–17 who have been in care for 13 weeks or more since attaining the age of 14 will not be able to claim HB and Social Services will have a duty to meet their housing costs.

Basic rules 9.9

Who can claim Housing Benefit? 9.10

A claimant must:

- be habitually resident in the UK;

- with his partner, jointly have less than £16,000 in savings, investments and capital;

- have a liability to pay rent as a condition of occupying the property where he resides; and

- be occupying the property that he is claiming benefit for (but there are some exceptions – see **9.33–9.36**).

The assessment of entitlement to Housing Benefit 9.11

Once it is established that a person has a liability to pay rent (and that liability is one which is eligible for HB) the first process in the assessment of entitlement is to establish how much of that rent is eligible for HB.

This is initially determined by examining the make-up of the rent, which in many cases comprises one, two, three or four elements, i e actual rent, service charges and support charges and personal charges.

Actual rent 9.12

(SI 1987 No 1971, Reg 10).

This includes the general provision of the building or room, management and administration costs of the tenancy, provision of furniture, building repairs and other essential financial control services. The actual rent will be eligible for HB, subject to this amount being a reasonable market rent and the property being of a size that is appropriate for the needs of the claimant and his family.

A new system of local housing allowances was initially piloted in nine 'pathfinder' local authorities. These were: Blackpool, Lewisham, Coventry, Teignbridge, Brighton and Hove, Edinburgh, North East Lincolnshire, Conwy and Leeds. From April 2005, a further nine local authorities began piloting the scheme. These are: Argyll and Bute, East Riding of Yorkshire, Guildford, Norwich, Pembrokeshire, Salford, South Norfolk, St Helens and Wandsworth. In these areas, HB for the commercial private sector will be based on a standard housing allowance, set by the rent officer, based on local rent levels, in the same way that Local Reference Rents have been set up to now. The amount of this local housing allowance will be widely known and will form the basis for the HB calculation, even if the tenant's actual rent is lower. The object is to simplify the housing benefit process and to provide a clear incentive for tenants to find cheaper accommodation. These pilots will each be evaluated over a two-year period. The new local housing allowance will only apply to new claims for HB after the commencement of the pilot.

Service charges 9.13

(SI 1987 No 1971, Sch 1).

These may include essential services that are necessary in the provision of adequate accommodation, and may include heating, lighting and cleaning of communal areas, repairs and replacement of furniture, servicing of equipment etc. These service charges will be eligible for HB, subject to their being of a reasonable amount compared with other similar charges in a specific area.

Support charges 9.14

Support charges were only eligible for HB (subject to the charges being reasonable) until April 2003. Thereafter, the funds for the assistance with these costs were transferred over to a new Supporting People Budget which is administered by Social Services, Housing Services and Probation Services.

Table of potential rent elements 9.15

Rent eligible	Services eligible	Support charges eligible	Personal charges not eligible
Rent.	Communal cleaning.	No longer eligible for HB. May be funded under the Supporting People Scheme.	Provision of cleaning materials.
Administration.	Provision of laundry facilities.	Will always be deducted from any eligible rent for HB.	Personal heating, light and power.
Insurance.	Communal heat, light and power.		Water rates.

Rent eligible	Services eligible	Support charges eligible	Personal charges not eligible
Repairs, maintenance and electrical checks.	Furniture fixtures and fittings: renewal, replacement and repair.		Meals.
Property security.	Communal window cleaning.		Fuel for cooking food.
Housing management.	Communal water rates.		Personal counselling and support.
Sinking fund for long major repairs.	May be restricted if charge unreasonably high.		Provision of personal/medical/nursing care.
General administration.			Other day-to-day living expenses.
Provision of furniture.			Will always be deducted from any eligible rent for HB.
Fire equipment etc.			
Arrears collection and control.			
Property control.			
May be restricted if cost too high or property too large.			

Personal charges   9.16

(SI 1987 No 1971, Sch 1).

These may include charges for water rates, food, heating and lighting for the claimant's own rooms (not communal), nursing, medical or personal care, the cost of day-to-day living etc. These charges are not eligible for HB as they are accommodated from other sources of assistance available in the Social Security system.

Making the assessment   9.17

Once the HB department establishes all elements of a rent, the next step of the assessment will take place.

If the landlord is the local authority, or a registered social landlord, most rents will be assessed on the basis of actual eligible costs.

If, however, the landlord is a private landlord (or a housing association where the authority considers the rent to be unreasonably high or the property unreasonably large for the claimant's needs), the HB department must refer the rent for assessment to the rent officer Services, who will determine how much of the rent and services charges will be eligible for HB. The HB department is bound by the rent officer's decision regardless of the claimant's circumstances. This means that even if a claimant is on Income Support and paying a rent of £75 per week, and the rent is restricted to £50 per week by the rent officer, the HB department can only assess the claimant's entitlement to HB on the basis of a £50 rent (this is called an eligible rent), rather than that which the claimant has a liability to pay, i e £75.

In a council where the local housing allowance is being piloted, the eligible rent is based on the local housing allowance set by the rent officer.

In reaching a decision the rent officer must take into account a claimant's personal circumstances and decide whether the accommodation is too large or too expensive. In the event of a rent officer deciding that the accommodation is too large or too expensive, he will assess what he would consider to be a reasonable rent.

A claimant may request that the rent officer reconsiders his decision, in which case a different rent officer will look at the rent and the property and make a new determination. The rent officer must look at the rent afresh and his decision may result in a lower rent being set than that set by the previous rent officer. Applications for rent officer reviews must be made in writing to the HB department.

Once the eligible rent for the assessment of HB has been established, the claimant's entitlement to HB can be calculated. This will involve the application of the means test.

If, however, the claimant's rent is restricted, or the claimant has to make a contribution towards his eligible rent, he may qualify for a discretionary housing payment from a budget administered by the local authority – see **9.48** et seq below.

How Housing Benefit is calculated   9.18

A claimant's HB/CTB is calculated by first of all working out an *applicable amount*. This is made up of two parts.

Personal allowances   9.19

(*SI 1987 No 1971, Reg 16, Sch 2; SI 1992 No 1814, Reg 8, Sch 1*).

These are amounts intended to cover a person's day-to-day living expenses (e g food, water rates, fuel, clothing, etc). These amounts are worked out on a fixed scale depending on a claimant's age and circumstances.

Where a couple are living together, either partner can make the claim for HB and/or CTB. It is always best for the partner who may attract most benefit to make the claim; for instance, if one of the partners is incapable of work through sickness or disability, then it should be that partner who makes the claim, because he may at some point attract an extra disability premium.

There are additional personal allowances allocated in respect of dependent children.

Premiums   9.20

(*SI 1987 No 1971, Reg 16, Sch 2; SI 1992 No 1814, Reg 8, Sch 1*).

Premiums are additional amounts which are allocated to claimants with specific circumstances relating to family, age, disability etc. They are allocated in addition to any personal allowances. There are different premiums for different groups. They are also applicable to the calculation of income-based Jobseekers Allowance (see **CHAPTER 7 INCOME-BASED JOBSEEKERS ALLOW-ANCE**) and Income Support (see **CHAPTER 6 INCOME SUPPORT**).

The relevant premiums are:

- *Family premium* – For those with dependent children (this is increased by £10.50 per week where there is a child under one).

- *Disabled child premium* – For those who have a disabled child.

- *Disability premium* – For those aged under 60 who are disabled and in receipt of a specified disability benefit.

- *Severe disability premium* – For those who live alone, who are severely disabled and in receipt of specified disability benefits and have no one caring for them.

- *Carer's premium* – For those who have claimed Carer's Allowance because they are caring for a severely disabled person.

- *Enhanced disability premium* – For disabled children and adults receiving the highest rate of Disability Living Allowance care component.

- *Bereavement premium* – For claimants aged 55–60 on expiry of an award of Bereavement Allowance.

(See **6.6–6.16** above for further details of qualifying conditions for premiums.)

Once the claimant's applicable amount has been established it will be offset against the claimant's income, in the same way as for Income Support (see **6.23** above).

Income   9.21

All the income that a claimant has will be assessed as with all means-tested benefits (see **CHAPTER 2**) but generally the following will be taken into account:

- *Earnings* – This is net earned income or net profit from self-employment.

- *Other income* – This may include income from sources such as other State benefits, periodical payments from trust funds, payments from occupational pensions etc.

- *Maintenance payments* – This includes voluntary maintenance payments, or maintenance payments under a court order, or maintenance payments paid in consequence of a child support liability order.

- *Tariff income from capital* – This is a weekly assumed income from capital as prescribed by the State. Any interest that a claimant receives on his capital will not be deemed to be income.

Disregarded income   9.22

There is some scope for elements of income to be disregarded. Where the claimant is a lone parent the first £25 of his earned income will be disregarded. Where the claimant attracts a carer premium or disability premium the first

£20 of his earned income will be disregarded. If the claimant is a member of a couple the first £10 of the joint earned income will be disregarded, regardless of whether one or both members of the couple are working. In all other cases only the first £5 of the claimant's earned income will be disregarded. (For full details of all other disregarded earned income see *SI 1987 No 1971, Sch 3* and *SI 1992 No 1814, Sch 3.*)

Childcare costs   9.23

Some parents who are working may be entitled to a disregard of up to £175 per week for childcare costs for one child under the age of 15 (16 if the child is either registered blind or in receipt of Disability Living Allowance), or £300 per week childcare costs for two or more children under the age of 15 (16 if the child is either registered blind or in receipt of Disability Living Allowance). The childcare disregard from earned income will be applied for childcare costs paid to an authorised provider of childcare or registered childminder where either the claimant is a lone parent, or the claimant is one of a couple and both members of the couple are working or one member is working and the other parent is disabled.

Where the claimant's earnings are insufficient to benefit from the total eligible childcare charges (when added to actual earnings disregards), any excess eligible childcare costs which cannot be deducted from the claimant's earnings should be disregarded from any award of Working Tax Credit (WTC).

EXAMPLE

A lone parent has an earned income of £80 per week and pays £60 per week eligible childcare costs. From his earned income he will have a £25 disregard (see **9.22** above), leaving only £55. The first £55 of childcare costs will be deducted, leaving him with an earned income of nil; the remaining £5 will be deducted from his WTC award.

Disregard for those working for more than 30 hours   9.24

The 30-hour disregard of £14.90 will be added to the claimant's earnings disregard where the claimant works for 30 hours or more and either attracts:

- the 30-hour disregard in the assessment of WTC (see **CHAPTER 8 TAX CREDITS**);

- the family premium;

- the disability premium or higher pensioner premium; or

- the claimant's partner is working for more than 16 hours or attracts the disability premium or higher pensioner premium.

Where the claimant's earnings are insufficient to benefit from the additional 30-hour disregard (when added to actual earnings disregards and eligible childcare disregard from earnings) the 30-hour disregard should be applied to any award of WTC.

Other income   9.25

There is also scope in the regulations for other income to be disregarded in respect of items such as Attendance Allowance, Disability Living Allowance which are disregarded in full, and income from boarders, or student loans etc which are disregarded in part. (For a full list of sums disregarded see *SI 1987 No 1971, Sch 4* and *SI 1992 No 1814, Sch 4.*)

Maintenance   9.26

The first £15 per week of any maintenance payment paid in respect of a dependent child or children will be disregarded. Maintenance that is paid to a former spouse/partner will not attract a maintenance disregard.

Capital   9.27

If the claimant and partner jointly have savings, investments or capital of £16,000 or more, there will be no entitlement to HB or CTB.

In all cases, there will be a disregard of some of the capital of the claimant and partner to the value of £6,000. (*SI 1987 No 1971, Reg 37, Sch 5; SI 1992 No 1814, Reg 28, Sch 5.*)

All the capital of the claimant and partner will be assessed in line with all other means-tested benefits. Tariff income is applied in respect of any capital over the threshold of £6,000. This tariff income will be assessed at £1 per week for every £250 (or part) by which the claimant's capital exceeds £6,000 for those under 60, and at £1 per week for every £500 for those 60 or over (see **CHAPTER 2**).

For instance, a claimant and partner under the age of 60 have savings, capital and investments to the value of £8,800. The first £6,000 will be ignored and the remaining £2,800 will attract a tariff income of £12 per week – this amount will be added to the claimant's weekly income for the assessment of entitlement to HB and CTB.

Disregarded capital 9.28

Certain types of capital can be totally disregarded so they do not come into the calculation at all, and the fact that the claimant owns all or any of them will not affect his entitlement to HB and CTB. These are listed in full in *SI 1987 No 1971, Sch 5* and *SI 1992 No 1814* (see further **CHAPTER 2**).

Capital taken into account 9.29

If the capital does not fall within any of the disregards set out in the schedules contained in the above regulations, the next question is whether it is of such a nature that it has to be taken into account.

Capital includes all assets of any kind owned by the claimant and will thus include money saved in the home, bank or building society accounts, premium bonds, stocks and shares, unit trusts, items of value such as paintings, stamp collections etc. Also included will be items such as debts or other courses in action which have a market value and can be sold, even though they may not be payable until some future date (see **CHAPTER 2**).

The final calculation 9.30

The final part of the calculation involves comparing income with the applicable amount.

If the assessed income is *the same as or less* than the applicable amount then the claimant will be entitled to 100% of his eligible rent by way of HB, subject to any non-dependant deductions (see **9.31** below). Claimants on Income Support, income-based Jobseekers Allowance or the guarantee credit of Pension Credit qualify for maximum HB under this rule.

If the assessed income is *greater* than the applicable amount, the claimant may still be entitled to some HB at a reduced rate.

The amount is established by offsetting the applicable amount against the assessed income of the claimant and his family to find the difference between these two amounts.

Any excess income that remains after this offsetting will be subject to the application of a 65% taper to that excess.

Once 65% of the claimant's excess income is established, this will be the amount that will be deducted from the claimant's eligible rent for HB.

The amount of eligible rent that remains following this deduction will be the amount of HB payable, subject to any non-dependant deductions (see **9.31** below).

Non-dependants 9.31

If there are any non-dependants living in a claimant's home, i e non-tenants over the age of 18 (e g children, relatives or friends) (see **CHAPTER 3 CLAIMING FOR THE FAMILY** for a full definition of non-dependants), then there will be deductions from any award of HB in respect of these non-dependants at the following rates (*SI 1987 No 1971, Reg 63*).

Non-dependants with gross incomes of:

Income	*Amount deducted from HB award*
£338.00 or more	£47.75
£271.00 to £337.99	£43.50
£204.00 to £270.99	£38.20
£157.00 to £203.99	£23.35
£106.00 to £156.99	£17.00
£106.00 or less	£7.40
In receipt of IS, Pension Credit or income-based JSA and age 25 or over or aged 18 and not working	£7.40

Note: This rule also applies to Income Support, guarantee credit of Pension Credit and income-based Jobseekers Allowance where housing costs are being claimed.

If a claimant has not given details and proof of a non-dependant's gross income, the HB department will apply the highest possible non-dependant deduction. Therefore, it is in the claimant's interest to give all details of income of non-dependants.

If a claimant is registered blind or receives Attendance Allowance or the care component of Disability Living Allowance then no non-dependant deductions will be made.

EXAMPLE

Barbara and Peter are a couple with a maximum eligible rent of £60. Peter is aged 63 and is in receipt of Disability Living Allowance higher rate mobility component and an occupational pension of around £128 per month. He is working 18 hours per week and has a net income of £110 per week and WTC of £58.38 per week. ➡

Barbara is aged 58 and receives Carer's Allowance of £46.95 per week as she cares for her mother, who is severely disabled and receiving high rate Attendance Allowance and lives with them – the mother's income is guarantee credit of Pension Credit.

If Barbara is the person who claims HB, the couple will attract the 30-hour disregard as her partner is disabled and this disregard can be applied if the claimant's partner works for more than 16 hours. If Peter were to claim this benefit, he would not attract the disregard as the claimant would have to be working for more than 30 hours.

HB will be calculated as follows.

Applicable amount		*Income*	
Personal allowance	£174.05	Peter's income	£110.00
Carer premium	£26.35	*less* disregard	£20.00
		less 30-hour disregard	£14.90
		Occupational pension	£29.46
		Carer's Allowance	£46.95
		DLA mobility (disregarded)	£00.00
		WTC	£58.38
Total	**£200.40**	**Total**	**£209.89**

Difference = £9.49 × 65% = £6.16.

Rent of £60 less £6.16 = HB entitlement of £53.84 per week.

However, as Barbara's mother is living with them, a non-dependant deduction will be applied to this entitlement. This will be £7.40 as the mother is over the age of 25 and in receipt of Guarantee Credit.

HB entitlement of £53.84 less non-dependant deduction £7.40 = £46.44 HB award per week.

Housing Benefit in special circumstances   9.32

Claimants that can be treated as 'occupying' the property during short periods when they are not.

Payments of Housing Benefit on
two properties   9.33

To qualify for HB under the special circumstances rule, the claimant must:

- make an application asking for a 'regulation 5' consideration;
- have a liability to pay rent which he cannot avoid;
- intend to return to the property within the specified period.

In addition:

- the property must not be sub-let;
- if the claimant is absent the property must not be occupied by another person.

Where the claimant has vacated his property and does not intend to return to it through fear of violence from a person who was formerly a member of the family, and the claimant has a liability to make payments in respect of that property which are unavoidable, he would qualify for benefit in respect of that vacated property for a period of up to 28 days after leaving (*SI 1987 No 1971, Reg 5(7)(a)*).

Where a claimant has a liability to pay rent on his current property and a liability in respect of a new property, but is not able to move into that new property because there is a necessary delay in order to adapt the new property to meet the disablement needs of the claimant or a member of his family, then benefit can be paid on both properties for an overlapping period of four benefit weeks immediately preceding the date on which the claimant moves (*SI 1987 No 1971, Reg 5(5)(d) and (e)*).

Where a claimant is temporarily absent from his home because of domestic violence, and has been rehoused temporarily by the housing authority, but is still liable to make payments on his previous property and intends to return there, benefit can continue to be paid for up to 52 weeks in respect of both liabilities.

Where a claimant has moved into a new property and for some reason still has a liability to accommodate rent on his old property, and the duplication of liability is unavoidable, he may be entitled to HB on both properties for a period not exceeding four weeks.

Where a claimant who is not currently in receipt of HB has a liability for rent on a new property, but is not able to move into that property and the delay is necessary because the claimant was waiting for the outcome of a Social Fund application and the claimant has a child under the age of five or would qualify for a disability premium, pensioner premium, disabled child premium or severe disability premium, or the claimant was in hospital or in residential care, and it is reasonable that he has a liability to pay rent before moving into the property, he may be awarded HB in respect of the new rent liability for a period not exceeding four weeks.

In all cases, an application for such payments should be made by the claimant in writing and the authority should ensure that they have made sufficient enquiries in order to give their full consideration to each individual application, as these payments demand specific requirements of the claimant or a member of his family, i e that the move at the appropriate time was unavoidable or that a previous liability was unavoidable.

Other temporary absences   9.34

Where a claimant is temporarily absent from his home with good cause, e g through fear of domestic violence or because he is in hospital etc, he can continue to receive benefit in respect of his rent liability provided he intends to return to his property. In such cases benefit can continue to be paid for up to 52 weeks of absence provided his absence is unlikely to exceed 52 weeks. (Note that in these cases benefit is only paid in respect of the property from which the claimant is temporarily absent, and not in respect of the property where the claimant has gone to stay temporarily.)

If the claimant is temporarily absent from his home and intends to return within 13 weeks, payments can continue for up to 13 weeks of absence. This will apply, for example, if the claimant goes away on holiday or to visit relatives (*SI 1987 No 1971, Reg 5(8)*).

Other overlapping provisions   9.35

Where a claimant has left his home through fear of domestic violence and does not intend to return, but has a liability to make payments which is unavoidable, he may receive benefit in respect of that liability for a period of up to four weeks.

Prisoners in remand or bail hostels pending conviction will qualify for HB during their period of absence, provided their absence is unlikely to exceed 52 weeks. They will qualify for benefit for up to 52 weeks during their period of absence. Prisoners who have been convicted will only qualify for HB where their period of absence is not likely to exceed 13 weeks (however, any time spent on remand prior to conviction will count towards this).

Housing Benefit for people in residential care 9.36

There are two categories of claimants who are treated quite differently under this rule.

Where a claimant goes into residential care for reasons *other than it being on a trial basis* he can receive HB for up to 52 weeks during his period of absence from his home. HB can only be paid in these circumstances where the claimant intends to return home within 52 weeks and his home is not occupied by another person or sub-let.

Where a person goes into residential care on a *trial basis* he can receive HB for up to 13 weeks during his period of absence from his home. HB can only be paid in these circumstances where the claimant intends to return home if the residential accommodation does not meet his needs within 13 weeks and his home is not occupied by another person or sub-let.

In both cases, HB can be paid if the claimant intends to return home within the specified period, being that of either 52 or 13 weeks.

Once the claimant makes a decision not to return home his HB will cease from the date on which he made that decision.

Any temporary periods of absence commence from the first Monday following the absence and the absence must be continuous. Consequently, if the claimant returns to his home for a period exceeding 24 hours then the period of absence will start to run again (*R v Penwith District Council Housing Benefit Review, ex p Burt (1990) 22 HLR 292*).

Backdated claims 9.37

HB claims can be backdated for a period of up to 52 weeks. For backdated claims to be considered a claimant will have to show continuous good cause for not having claimed at an earlier date where backdated benefit is requested. This means that the claimant must have a very good reason for not having claimed when he should have done so, and a very good reason for not having claimed until he actually did.

In such cases, it is imperative that great care is taken in deciding from what date good cause can be established.

For instance, if the claimant has requested that his claim be backdated from 1 February 2006 to 1 March 2005 (the date on which his last award of benefit expired) and he has stated that he was not able to make an earlier claim because he was very ill, then consideration must be given to the date on which the claimant became so ill that it prevented him from making a claim. So if, in fact, he became ill at the end of August and his doctor supports this evidence, then consideration should be given to backdating the claim to August.

However, that claimant must also demonstrate that his 'good cause' has been continuous from August until the date of his application in February 2006. His claim cannot be backdated to March as his 'good cause' only started in August.

Good cause may be that the claimant was too ill (mentally or physically) to make a claim, the claimant was not aware that a partner had not made a claim, the claimant was left to understand that another organisation would register a claim for him, e g the Citizens Advice Bureau, Welfare Rights, solicitor etc.

The most common good cause is where the authority failed to advise the claimant in his HB application form that an application form can be submitted to the authority without proof of income or proof of rent, provided that the further information is provided within a specified period, i e 28 days or any longer period which is agreed with the department. In such cases the claimant must have good cause for not providing the evidence or information when requested.

A further reason for delayed claim is where the claimant has been in receipt of Income Support and for some reason the Income Support ceases. In most cases the claimant says that he advised the Income Support department and thought that the department would advise the authority. This does not accommodate the good cause rule as when the claimant signs the declaration contained within the HB form, he is stating that he will notify the authority of any changes in his circumstances – if he only notifies the DWP then he has failed to comply with the HB rules.

In respect of good cause readers are directed to Social Security Commissioners' decisions which examine the definition of good cause. In *R(S)3/79*, Commissioner Monroe stated that ordinary people cannot be expected to know what the law is or that they ought to enquire about it. He warned that it was a 'dangerous over-simplification' to assume that ignorance of rights cannot amount to good cause so a further inquiry must be made to determine whether the claimant's ignorance was reasonable in all the circumstances. In *R(G)3/83*, it was stated that claimants who could not reasonably have been expected to be aware that there was anything to enquire about, or whose failure to assert their rights was due to mistaken belief reasonably held, may escape disqualification as such circumstances may amount to good cause.

Extended payments 9.38

Under *regulation 62A* of the *Housing Benefit (General) Regulations 1987*, a claimant will be eligible for an extended payment of HB where the Secretary of

State has certified to the HB department that the claimant was entitled to Income Support or income-based Jobseekers Allowance or Training Allowance for a continuous period of at least 26 weeks and that entitlement has ceased in consequence of the claimant having taken up employment or increased his income in that employment, which is expected to last for five weeks or more (in either an employed capacity or self-employed capacity).

There is no scope whatsoever in the regulations for the HB department to determine whether the claimant has satisfied this condition of entitlement to the extended payment.

Schedule 5A(2) of the regulations specifically states that:

> 'The conditions prescribed in this paragraph are that the Secretary of State has certified to the appropriate authority'.

In other words, if the DWP does not confirm to the authority that the claimant has been in receipt of the relevant benefit for the prescribed period of time, then the HB department cannot make any award of extended payment to the claimant.

The question as to whether the claimant satisfies the qualifying conditions of entitlement to the benefit, or for the qualifying benefit period, is a question which must be determined by the Secretary of State. Consequently, the DWP must determine any question arising in relation to this matter.

Provided the claimant has made the application to the HB department within four weeks of ceasing to be entitled to the relevant benefit because he has started work either in a self-employed capacity or an employed capacity, the claimant will be entitled to continue to receive HB at the rate which he was receiving when in receipt of Income Support for a continuous period of 28 days. This extended payment will be paid whether the claimant is earning £200 per week or £2,000 per week. However, there is no scope for any late claim outside of the allocated four-week period.

When a claimant starts work he must do the following:

- make a claim for an extended payment within four weeks of coming off benefit, either to the jobcentre, DWP or HB office;

- he must also, within 14 days, submit a standard new HB claim to the authority, which will commence at the end of the extended payment period;

- if the claimant has not been in receipt of Income Support or income-based Jobseekers Allowance *continuously* for at least six months, he will not qualify for the extended payment;

- if the claimant has taken a temporary job which will not be expected to last for more than five weeks, he will not qualify for the extended payment.

How to claim 9.39

Claims should be made by completion of a standard HB claim form, which can be obtained from the local authority in the area where the claimant lives. Claim forms will be dated at the time of issue and a date for the required return of the form will also be identified on the claim form. Benefit will be paid from the Monday following the date of issue of the form, provided the form is completed and returned to the HB department with all required evidence and information by the date so prescribed.

On making an initial claim, claimants will be required to provide evidence of their and their partner's National Insurance numbers (e g a letter from HMRC or the DWP), identity (e g birth certificate, passport etc) and proof of residence (e g a recent utility bill etc), along with evidence of any income and capital that the claimant or partner has and proof of any rent liability. This evidence must be by way of original documents (not photocopies).

Payments of HB can be paid either to the claimant or directly to the landlord and in most cases these payments will be made four-weekly in arrears.

HB claims should be dealt with within 14 days of the local authority having received all relevant information or as soon thereafter as possible. In the event of delays in claims being processed, the HB department can make a payment on account if a claimant requests this.

These payments on account will be assessed on what is called an indicative rent level which is usually at a figure lower than the actual rent (*SI 1987 No 1971, Reg 91*).

Challenging decisions 9.40

Once benefit has been assessed, the claimant will be sent a notification of benefit entitlement, but this will not generally include any reasons for the decision. If the claimant requires written reasons for the decision, he must write to the HB department requesting them.

If the claimant is not happy with a decision made by the authority in respect of his assessment of benefit, he can request a revision, but must do so in writing to the authority within one month of the issue of the notification of entitlement. Any time taken by the authority in issuing written reasons will be added to the one-month time limit where written reasons have been requested (see **CHAPTER 4 CLAIMS, DECISIONS AND APPEALS**).

In applying for a revision, the claimant must first decide which of the several elements of the decision he would like revised. The authority is only required to take account of issues raised in the revision request.

The assessment of rent 9.41

In this case, the claimant does not have any right of appeal directly to the rent officer. However, if he writes directly to the HB department saying that he is not happy with the assessment of rent, the HB department is obliged to request that the rent officer reviews his determination, enclosing with their request a copy of the claimant's letter. The rent officer will then usually visit the claimant's home to view the property to assist in a re-assessment. It is important to remember that upon review a rent can be either increased, decreased or remain the same.

The assessment of income or capital 9.42

The claimant should write to the HB department stating that he feels that the assessment of his income or capital is incorrect. The HB department will carry out a revision of the assessment of income and/or capital and notify the claimant of the outcome. Where the DWP has determined a claimant's entitlement to Pension Credit and made an award, the local authority is then bound by the DWP decision on the amount of capital the claimant possesses.

The assessment of applicable amount 9.43

Where there is a mistake in the allocation of the applicable amount, this is usually due to computer error, the wrong age of a member of the claimant's family being input into the computer, or wrong information about the claimant's disability benefits being input into a computer etc. The HB department will carry out a re-assessment and notify the claimant of the outcome of this reconsideration.

Changes in circumstances 9.44

Where the claimant's circumstances change he must request a revision of his benefit award as soon as the change of circumstances takes place, otherwise an overpayment will arise for which the claimant will be responsible to repay. A claimant might wish to ask the authority to review its decision to require a repayment of benefit relating to changes in circumstances.

Where the claimant is not happy with the outcome of a revision (with the exception of a rent officer's review) the claimant can appeal against that decision to an independent tribunal, but must do so in writing within one month of the decision being issued to him – see **CHAPTER 4**.

Common problems   9.45

1. The claimant has made a claim for HB for the first time, and provided all the information and evidence requested, but six weeks later benefit has not been assessed and the landlord is threatening eviction.

Where, after having provided all the necessary information to the authority, a claim has not been dealt with after the expiry of 14 days, the claimant can request 'a payment on account'. The authority must make a payment on account in these circumstances, but such payments are usually less than the actual payment due. The payment will be based on an average rent for that type of property in the area.

Once full entitlement to benefit is established, the claimant will be reimbursed with any shortfall of benefit entitlement for the period covered by the payment on account.

2. The claimant has been refused benefit because he has been deemed to have a tenancy agreement which has been created to take advantage of the benefits system.

In this situation a number of factors will be taken into account. The most important ones are as follows:

- *Rent* – Has the tenant paid rent for the property for eight weeks prior to claiming HB? If he has, then he cannot be deemed to have created his liability to take advantage of HB. If he has not, the reasons for the creation of the tenancy must be closely examined.

- *Reasons for the tenancy* – Was the tenant living in the property before his liability for rent was created? If he was, then why has he started being charged rent now? For instance, the landlord could have previously been working and has now stopped and thus needs the extra income to top up his own income; or the claimant has previously provided services for the landlord which he is not, for whatever reason, able to carry out any longer. In circumstances such as these a legitimate creation of a rent liability may be established.

  If, on the other hand, the tenant was previously working, receiving a low wage and could not afford rent out of his wage, then claims Income

213

Support or income-based Jobseekers Allowance, which alerts him to the possibility of claiming HB, then the creation of a rent liability at this point would clearly suggest contrivance.

If the tenant has only just moved into the property, then his reasons for moving must be established. If a claimant can show that his reasons for moving into a property were purely to accommodate his housing need then a legitimate creation of a rent liability may be established.

If, on the other hand, the claimant was adequately housed before moving into the property then contrivance may again be established, in particular where the new tenancy is created by the landlord and tenant who have a family or friendly relationship.

If the tenant feels that he does have a genuine tenancy agreement, then he should consider appealing against any decision not to award HB.

Council Tax Benefit 9.46

The rules relating to CTB are exactly the same as those for HB, apart from the liability to pay rent being replaced by a liability to pay council tax.

CTB can be claimed by people who have a low income and have a liability to pay council tax. It can be claimed whether or not a claimant is in full-time work. It can also be paid in addition to other benefits, like pensions and or occupational pensions.

The local authority always pays CTB and claims must be made to the local authority and not the DWP, even if a claimant is in receipt of Income Support. Where a person has a council tax liability and a rent liability, both HB and CTB can be claimed using the same application form.

A person cannot claim CTB if he has savings and/or capital of more than £16,000 (unless he has been awarded guarantee credit). CTB will be assessed from the first Monday after a claim is received at the benefits department of the local authority.

CTB claims should be dealt with within 14 days of the local authority having received all relevant information or as soon thereafter as possible.

The maximum CTB that can be awarded is 100% of the council tax liability. Claimants may qualify for additional help with excess council tax liability by way of a discretionary housing payment (see **9.48**).

If the only people liable to council tax are in receipt of Income Support, guarantee credit of Pension Credit or income-based Jobseekers Allowance they will get 100% CTB (less any non-dependant deductions).

Where the liable persons are not claiming Income Support, guarantee credit or income-based Jobseekers Allowance, but have a low income and less than £16,000 capital, they may be able to claim a rebate.

CTB is worked out in exactly the same way as HB with the exception of a 20% taper of excess income and the non-dependant deductions being as follows.

Non-dependant deductions	
Non-dependants with gross incomes of	**Amount deducted from CTB award**
£338.00 or more	£6.95
£271.00 to £337.99	£5.80
£157.00 to £270.99	£4.60
£157.00 or less	£2.30
In receipt of IS, PC or income-based JSA and aged 25 or over	£2.30

EXAMPLE

So in the example at **9.31** above (for HB) Barbara and Peter's HB was established, but if we apply to this case a council tax liability of £12.60 per week CTB will be calculated as follows.

Applicable amount		*Income*	
Personal allowance	£174.05	Peter's income	£110.00
Carer premium	£26.35	*less* disregard	£20.00
		less 30-hour disregard	£14.90
		Occupational pension	£29.46
		Carer's Allowance	£46.95
		DLA mobility (disregarded)	£00.00
		WTC	£58.38
Total	**£200.40**	**Total**	**£209.89**

Difference = £9.49 × 20% = £1.89.

Council tax liability of £12.60 less £1.89 = CTB entitlement of £10.71 per week. ➤

However, as Barbara's mother is living with them, a non-dependant deduction will be applied to this entitlement – this amount is £2.30 as the mother is over the age of 25 and in receipt of Pension Credit.

CTB entitlement of £10.71 less non-dependant deduction £2.30 = £8.41 CTB award per week.

Second adult rebates 9.47

There is also another benefit which can be applied for under the benefit scheme where there are two liable people who are not partners. A claimant may be better off claiming a second adult rebate. This is particularly helpful where a claimant is a single person who has a non-dependant in the property.

If the second adult is receiving Income Support or income-based Jobseekers Allowance, then he will get a 25% rebate.

If the second adult has an income of less than £157.00 per week, then he will get a 15% rebate.

If the second adult has an income of £157.00–£203.99 per week, then he will get a 7.5% rebate.

EXAMPLE

Council tax £500.00 per year = £9.59 per week (500 divided by 365 × 7).

The claimant is aged 75 and receives a pension of £84.25 plus an occupational pension of £50.00 per week. Her grandson lives with her – he is 27 and earns £160.00 per week gross.

Applicable amount		Income	
Personal allowance	£131.95	Retirement pension	£84.25
		Occupational pension	£50.00
Total	£131.95	Total	£134.25

Difference: £2.30 less 20% taper = £0.46. ➡

Weekly benefit award of £9.13 per week (£9.59 less £0.46 = £9.13) less non-dependant of deduction £4.60 per week.

Benefit award = £4.53 per week.

Second adult rebate

This will be calculated on a 7.5% discount as the grandson's income is less than £203.99 per week.

Council tax £500.00

Weekly £9.59

7.5% (maximum rebate) £0.72

If this amount is greater than the previous calculation then the claimant should take the option to apply for this second adult rebate as opposed to the initial benefit for herself.

Obviously in this case the claimant is better off receiving CTB in her own right rather than being considered for the second adult rebate.

Checklist

Claim specification	Details
Basic entitlement conditions	Claimant must have a rent liability and/or a council tax liability. Claimant and partner must have less than £16,000 in savings and capital and be habitually resident in the UK. Entitlement is wholly subject to a means test of the family unit.
Dependant additions	Additions for a dependent partner, dependent children and provisions for disregarding some income are included in any assessment of entitlement to this benefit.
Where to claim	Claims must be made a prescribed Housing/Council Tax Benefit claim form obtainable from the local authority where the claimant lives.

Claim specification	Details
How difficult is the claim form to complete?	Quite difficult, requiring factual information about the claimant and family and comprehensive details regarding income, capital and extremely detailed information relating to rent liability. The claimant will also have to provide proof of all income, capital and rent with this claim. This is a long form requiring approximately 60 minutes for completion.
Changes of circumstances that need to be notified	If the claimant has any changes in his circumstances at all, including people moving into or out of his home, changes in hours of work, changes in income and capital, going into or out of hospital, changes in disability etc. If the claimant changes address and if the claimant or partner claims any other benefit.
Frequency of periodic reviews	Benefit is awarded indefinitely, although reviews are usually carried out at least once a year, and frequently every 26 weeks or so.
Time limits for reviews and appeals	Applications must be made in writing within one month of the date that the decision under review/appeal was issued.
Benefit reductions	Benefit entitlement may be reduced if the claimant's partner goes into hospital and is an in-patient for more than 52 weeks.
Other linked benefits	Can be claimed in addition to any other Social Security benefit or source of income. Also gives rise to possible entitlement to Social Fund payments for funeral expenses only.
Attracting a NICs credit	No.
Taxable	No.

Discretionary housing payments 9.48

(*Discretionary Financial Assistance Regulations 2001 (SI 2001 No 1167); Child Support, Pensions and Social Security Act 2000, ss 69, 70*).

Discretionary housing payments (DHPs) were introduced in July 2001 and are administered by the local authority, but do not form part of the HB scheme. This means that any department of the local authority may administer such payments.

Each local authority has been provided with a capped budget funded in part by central government. Full details are contained in the *Discretionary Housing Payments (Grants) Order 2001 (SI 2001 No 2340)*.

An authority cannot retain any unspent government contribution towards DHPs.

Local authorities are not permitted to make any DHP awards which will exceed their overall spending limit in any financial year. Therefore, any authority with insufficient funding left in its budget to make a DHP award would have to refuse the award on the basis of its having no funds available to make the award.

Who can claim? 9.49

To be eligible to claim a DHP the claimant must be entitled to:

* HB to qualify for a DHP to help with his rent; or

* CTB to qualify for a DHP to help with council tax liability.

In addition:

* the claimant must be able to demonstrate that he *needs* the financial assistance of a DHP payment (this can only realistically be demonstrated by the provision of a financial statement showing the income and expenditure of the claimant);

* DHPs provide further financial assistance to those qualifying for HB and CTB where the benefit awarded is not sufficient to accommodate the claimant's housing costs.

For example, DHPs may be applied where a person can show that he cannot meet his full rent or council tax liability. Reasons for this may include one of the following:

* the rent officer has restricted the claimant's rent;

* a non-dependant deduction has been applied to the claimant's award of benefit;

- the claimant is having to pay child support payments, or incurs additional expenditure because of a disability, travel to work expenses or accommodating the essential needs of children etc.

Discretionary hardship payments cannot be made if the need for financial assistance arises because the claimant has to meet the costs of ineligible services (such as fuel, water rates, meals etc), or where the need arises because the claimant has a reduced income because of a suspension or penalty having been imposed on any other Social Security benefit.

For example, the claimant's rent is £80 per week – £10 of this is for water rates and fuel, leaving £70 eligible for HB. However, the rent officer restricts the rent for HB to £60 per week.

The claimant may apply for a DHP for the £10 per week restriction. If, after the assessment of income, the claimant has to make a further contribution of, say, £25 towards his rent, he may make an application for a DHP to the value of £35 per week (i e the £10 shortfall in actual rent, plus his £25 contribution).

Any award will be based on the claimant's ability to pay this £35 out of his income. If it is established that the claimant could afford to pay say £23, he may be awarded the shortfall of £12 so that he can afford his rent and is not at risk of losing his home.

Length of award   9.50

An award can only be made from the date of application. The length of any award of DHP will be entirely at the discretion of the local authority. Considering each case on its own merit may help. For instance, if the claimant has short-term problems that may be resolved within six weeks, then a short-term award of six weeks will be sufficient. In other cases the need may be for a longer term.

Notifications   9.51

The local authority may show the DHP award on the HB and/or CTB notification, but it must be shown quite separately from the HB/CTB award and the local authority must show a clear audit trail of all DHP awards.

If the award of DHP is shown on the HB/CTB notification it must:

- make clear that these are DHP payments;
- provide information on how they are to be paid; and

- provide information on the claimant's right to request a review (*SI 2001 No 1167, Reg 6(3)*). (These appeal rights are very different from the HB/CTB appeal rights.)

Changes of circumstances   9.52

The authority must also advise the claimant of his duty to notify the local authority of a change of circumstances, and the manner in which this should be done (i e whether this must be in writing or by telephone etc). This information should be contained in every leaflet, letter, notification of award or other document that is sent to the claimant.

Challenging decisions   9.53

There is no right of appeal to the tribunals in respect of DHP disputes, but the local authority must make provisions for reviews internally. An officer who did not deal with the initial application should carry out the review and outcomes must be notified in writing to the claimant, giving reasons for the decision (*SI 2001 No 1167, Reg 8(2)*).

Stopping payments   9.54

If the authority wishes to stop a DHP during an award period (without a change of circumstances) they can do so in cases where:

- the award was made because the claimant provided false or misleading information or failed to disclose information in his application for the DHP; or

- the award was made in consequence of an official error.

In either case the authority can seek recovery of any DHP incorrectly awarded (*SI 2001 No 1167, Reg 8(1)*).

Recovery   9.55

Recovery cannot be made from any ongoing entitlement to HB/CTB or any other Social Security benefit.

Recovery should be made by way of an arrangement for repayment by the claimant, or by recovery of a civil debt in the county court.

Effect on other Social Security benefits 9.56

Any DHP award should be disregarded in the assessment of income for all means-tested and non means-tested benefit entitlement (*Social Security Amendment (Discretionary Housing Payments) Regulations 2001 (SI 2001 No 2333)*).

How to claim 9.57

The claimant must make a claim for a DHP to the local authority, but how such claims are accepted is totally at the discretion of each local authority. In most cases, claims will be required in writing.

Example letter 9.58

Example letter of application for a DHP

To Housing Benefit/local authority Discretionary Housing Payments Department

Date:

Dear Sirs,

I/We [name of tenant/s]

of [address]

NI number [....] (claimant)   [....] (partner)

wish to register a claim for a discretionary housing payment to help with my rent/council tax. I do get Housing Benefit/Council Tax Benefit, but still have to make a contribution towards my rent/council tax liability that would otherwise be eligible for benefit.

The reason that I have to make a contribution to my rent/council tax is that [.....]

and the reason that I cannot afford to make this contribution towards my rent/council tax is [....].

I attach for your reference details of my income and expenditure and would ask for your earliest consideration of this application.

Yours sincerely

Signed [.....] (claimant)   Signed [.....] (partner)

---

10   Home Renovation Grants

Introduction   10.1

Home renovation grants are administered by the local authority and provide
financial assistance to people on low incomes who need help with the cost of
renovating or repairing their home, adapting their home for a disabled person,
or insulating and draught-proofing their home. The assessment of entitlement
in most cases will be dependent on a means test, which is similar to that
applied for the assessment of entitlement to Housing Benefit.

Grants available   10.2

The system of grants to improve or repair housing changed radically from July
2003. Until then, there were five main types of grant assistance:

- renovation grants;

- common parts grants;

- disabled facilities grants;

- Houses in Multiple Occupation grants;

- group repair grants; and

- minor works grants.

These were paid under the *Housing Grants, Construction and Regeneration Act 1996*
and regulations made under it. The new grants system is set up under the same
1996 Act. Guidance is to be found in the Office of the Deputy Prime Minister
(ODPM) *Housing Renewal Guidance 2002*. The ODPM also publishes a series of
leaflets setting out the assistance available.

Under the new regulatory order local authorities have a general power to help
with improving living conditions. This can include adaptation or improvement
of living conditions by means of grants, loans, materials or any other form of
assistance. The local authority can only exercise this general power if it has a
published policy setting out the type of assistance it is willing to provide and in
what circumstances. Advisors should seek a copy of the policy adopted by the
local authority for the area they are advising about. The previous system of
grants, with the exception of the mandatory disabled facilities grant, was
abolished from 18 July 2003.

Disabled facilities grants 10.3

These mandatory grants are designed to assist with meeting the cost of adapting a property for the needs of a disabled person.

Eligibility – the applicant must be one of the following:

- an owner occupier;

- a private tenant;

- a landlord with a disabled tenant;

- a local authority tenant;

- a housing association tenant; or

- an occupier of some types of mobile homes.

For these purposes, someone will be treated as disabled if:

- his sight, hearing or speech is substantially impaired;

- he has a mental disorder or impairment of any kind;

- he is physically substantially disabled by illness, injury or impairment, present since birth or otherwise; or

- he is registered (or could be registered) as disabled with the Social Services department.

Grants can be awarded for the following works:

- facilitating a disabled applicant's access to and from the dwelling;

- making the dwelling safe for the disabled occupant and others residing with him;

- facilitating a disabled occupant's access to a room used or usable as the principal family room;

- facilitating a disabled occupant's access to, or providing, a room used or usable for sleeping in;

- facilitating a disabled occupant's access to, or providing, a room in which there is a lavatory, bath or shower and wash basin, or facilitating the use of any of these;

- facilitating the preparation and cooking of food by the disabled occupant;

- improving the heating system to meet the disabled occupant's needs, or providing a suitable heating system;

- facilitating a disabled occupant's use of a source of power, light or heat; and

- facilitating access and movement around the home to enable the disabled occupant to care for someone dependant on him who also lives there.

The means test   10.4

Disabled facilities grants are means-tested. The test is applied to the disabled person and any partner, whether or not he is the person applying for the grant. For example, if an adult disabled person lives with his parents, the test of resources would be applied to the disabled son, even if the application was made by his parents. If the disabled person is a child or young person, then the test is applied to the parent or adult with responsibility for his care.

The means test is very similar to that for Housing Benefit, but with the following differences:

- there are no non-dependent deductions;

- there is an extra premium – known as the housing allowance – to reflect housing costs. This is £56.40;

- there is a variable disabled child premium ranging from £1,610 for families with a disabled child or young person, to £32.70 for lone parents with a disabled child or young person with at least one child under 1;

- where the applicant is on Income Support, income-based Jobseekers Allowance or Pension Credit, his applicable amount is deemed to be £1 and all income and capital are disregarded, giving a zero contribution;

- £15 is disregarded from the earnings of disabled people and carers;

- there is no upper capital limit. The first £6,000 of capital is disregarded and tariff income is applied to any capital above this level;

- there is a staged taper system for income above the applicable amount.

Calculating the contribution   10.5

The purpose of the means test is to assess how much the applicant can afford to contribute to the cost of works. This is done by calculating the value of a notional loan that could be afforded using a proportion of the 'excess income' over the applicable amount. If there is no 'excess income' then the contribution is zero. Owner occupiers are expected to be able to take out a loan over ten years, while tenants are assumed to repay any loan over five years. The higher the income is over the applicable amount, the greater will be the proportion of that income assumed to be available to pay a loan.

The calculation process 10.6

- **Capital**

  The capital of the disabled person and any partner are aggregated. Some capital is disregarded (see rules for Housing Benefit). The value of the property to which the grant application relates is always disregarded. Tariff income of £1 per £250 of capital over £6,000 is added to the income figure, or £1 per £500 for people over 60.

- **Income**

  Average earnings and other income are assessed over the preceding twelve months, or a shorter period if that produces a more accurate figure. Disregards are as for Housing Benefit.

- **Applicable amount**

  This represents the assumed level of needs and is based on Housing Benefit figures, with the addition of the housing allowance and variable disabled child premium (see **10.4**).

- **Calculation of excess income**

  This is the amount by which income exceeds the applicable amount.

- **Working out the contribution**

  Excess income is applied to up to four bands and multiplied by a specified 'loan factor' (see below). These figures are usually uprated annually.

Loan generation factors 10.7

			Owner occupiers	Tenants
Band 1	first £47.95	**Factor**	19.97	11.21
Band 2	£47.96–£95.90		38.73	22.41
Band 3	£95.91–£191.80		154.93	89.66
Band 4	£191.81 plus		387.33	224.15

The aggregate of the amounts produced from bands 1–4 is the value of the notional loan the applicant could be expected to contribute to the cost of works.

EXAMPLE

An applicant who is a tenant, with excess income of £100, would calculate his contribution as follows:

Band 1	47.95 x 11.21	= 537.51
Band 2	47.95 x 22.41	= 1,074.55
Band 3	4.10 x 89.66	= 367.60
Applicant's contribution		**= 1,979.66**

Further grants   10.8

If an applicant had to make a contribution to a previous grant given for the same dwelling, within the last ten years (owner occupiers) or five years (tenants), then the amount of that contribution is deducted from any assessed contribution on any further grant application. This offsetting only applies if the earlier works were carried out to the local authority's satisfaction. In a case where the assessed contribution on the earlier works was actually higher than the cost of the works (leading to a 'nil grant approval'), then the actual cost of the earlier work can be deducted from the assessed contribution for the subsequent application.

How to claim   10.9

Disabled facilities grants are administered by local housing authorities, which should provide an application form. The completed application must be accompanied by a certificate confirming that the disabled occupant will continue to live in the property for at least five years after the completion of the works. A shorter period can be approved for health or other special reasons.

The maximum amount payable as a mandatory disabled facilities grant is £25,000 in England and £30,000 in Wales. Local authorities have discretion to pay above this figure for mandatory items, if the total costs exceeds the maximum. There is no upper limit to the discretionary element of a grant.

Approval process 10.10

The authority must be satisfied that the work proposed is both necessary and appropriate for the needs of the disabled person, and also that it is reasonable and practicable in relation to the property. The housing authority must consult the Social Services department in relation to the 'necessary and appropriate' part of the test. This is commonly assessed by the occupational therapy section of the Social Services department. The authority is required to make a decision within six months of the formal application being submitted to it.

If approved, the work should normally be completed within one year by one of the contractors submitting an estimate. The authority does have a discretion to approve a grant, but specify that it will not be paid for up to twelve months from the date of approval. If the disabled applicant's circumstances change between approval and the completion of the work, the authority has discretion to reconsider the grant approval.

Discretionary assistance with housing repairs, adaptations and improvements 10.11

The *Regulatory Reform* (*Housing Assistance*) (*England and Wales*) *Order 2002* (*SI 2002 No 1860*) introduced a wide discretionary power to provide financial and other assistance for repairs, adaptations and improvements, with some constraints. Under the order, local authorities have power to set their own conditions for assistance, including as to whether to apply a means test and the circumstances in which any assistance would have to be repaid. Assistance may be provided as a grant, a loan, labour or materials, advice or any combination of these. The power may be used for:

- acquiring accommodation;
- adapting, improving or repairing accommodation;
- demolishing accommodation; or
- replacing accommodation that has been demolished.

Local authorities have power to take a charge over property. Assistance can be given to owner occupier, tenants or landlords.

The new scheme extends the powers of local authorities to give loans in addition to, or instead of, grants. Government guidance recognises that loans would not be appropriate where there is hardship, or where the applicant has no or negative equity in the property. The order also requires:

- authorities to have regard to the applicant's ability to pay before making any condition about repayment or the making of a contribution;

- full terms and conditions attached to any assistance must be set out in writing, and authorities must be satisfied that applicants are aware of these;

- authorities to make, publish and act in accordance with a policy relating to housing renewal activities. This must set out how the authority proposes to use its powers; and

- applicants to provide full details of their financial circumstances and supporting evidence of all matters relating to their application for assistance, including to prove that conditions have been met after approval has been given.

Guidance for the exercise of this new discretionary power is issued by the ODPM. This makes clear that a policy of providing no assistance at all would not be acceptable.

Energy efficiency grants   10.12

The Warm Front Grants Scheme provides help towards improvements in insulation, room heating and water heating. It is available to disabled people and families with children who receive a qualifying benefit. Warm Front provides a maximum grant of £1,500 for installing insulation and improving heating systems. Those eligible are:

- householders with a child under 16 or who are pregnant, who are receiving Income Support, income-based Jobseekers Allowance, Housing Benefit or Council Tax Benefit;

- householders receiving one of the following:

  o Working or Child Tax Credit with an income below £15,050 per annum;

  o Income Support, Housing Benefit or Council Tax Benefit, including the disability premium;

  o Attendance Allowance or Disability Living Allowance;

  o Industrial Injuries Constant Attendance Allowance; or

  o War Disablement Pension, including mobility supplement or constant attendance allowance.

People over 60 on Pension Credit, Housing Benefit or Council Tax Benefit may be eligible for the more generous Warm Front Plus Grant. This provides up to £2,500 in grant aid.

The scheme is administered by Eaga Partnership. For information telephone: 0800 316 6011; or visit www.eaga.co.uk. Applications can be made online.

11 Assessment of Means in Community Care

Introduction   11.1

Where a disabled person needs assistance with his care either at home or by way of a place in a nursing or residential care home, the responsibility for the provision of care services and accommodation rests with Social Services and the provision of any nursing services rests with the NHS Trust in the area where the disabled person usually lives.

Social Services have an obligation to carry out a care assessment of any individual requesting this service, and although there is a duty to provide any care or accommodation service that the claimant is found to be in need of, Social Services may charge. The assessment of any charges will entail the means testing of the applicant. However, since April 2002, charges cannot be made of an individual in a nursing home for 'nursing care', as this is now funded through the Primary Care Trust, based on an assessment of the level of need for care from a registered nurse.

Domiciliary care   11.2

Where Social Services have established that a person needs non-residential community care, either in his own home or day care within the community, it may make a reasonable charge for those services. However, each Social Services department will have its own charging policy, based closely on the guidelines set out in the Government's 'Fairer Charging' policy.

The Social Services charging policy is based on a discretionary power under *section 17* of the *Health and Social Services and Social Security Adjudications Act 1983*, which states that an authority providing a service to which this section applies may recover such charge (if any) as they consider reasonable. However, *section 17(3)* further states that the authority shall not require a person to pay more for a service that it is reasonably practicable for him to pay.

Social Services cannot, however, charge for services provided under *section 117* of the *Mental Health Act 1983*, or *section 2* of the *Chronically Sick and Disabled Persons Act 1970*, or for services provided by the NHS, including nursing care in the home (*Health and Social Care Act 2001 (HSCA 2001), s 49*).

A means test of a person's ability to pay for domiciliary care (which is usually provided to the claimant in his own home) will be required. The procedure for this should be set out in the authority's charging policy. If, however, the applicant does not provide sufficient information for the processing of the means test, he can be held liable to pay for the cost of care in full.

In carrying out a means test, the authority may only take into consideration the income and capital of the disabled person who needs the care ('the service user') and not the income of any other member of his family.

All the income of a service user will be taken into consideration with the exception of Disability Living Allowance mobility component and any payment being received from the Independent Living (1993) Fund. This means that any income that a service user has, such as Income Support, retirement pensions, Disability Living Allowance care component, Attendance Allowance and Incapacity Benefit etc may be taken into consideration, depending on the policy of the particular local authority.

Furthermore, any income which is managed by another person (for example, under a trust arrangement or a power of attorney) that belongs to the service user will also be taken into consideration.

Once the income of the service user has been established, the authority must give consideration to the service user's living expenses, for example food, clothing, heating, laundry, housing costs, telephone, prescription charges or any other expense which is reasonably incurred in consequence of the person's disability.

The authority, in consideration of the service user's overall financial position, should not impose a charge that is not reasonably practicable for the service user to pay. If the service user cannot pay any or all of the charge for the services that he has been assessed as liable to pay, the authority does have an overall discretion to waive or reduce charges in any particular case.

The effect of non-payment 11.3

Where a service user refuses to pay any charge imposed by the assessment, the authority may pursue the debt through recovery procedures including, if necessary, through the magistrates' court, or the small claims system in the county court. However, the authority should not withdraw any service provision, as the assessment of the service user's need for care is quite separate from the decision to charge for services.

Assessment of means in residential care 11.4

Where a person enters residential or nursing home care, funding for assistance with the cost of care (but not nursing care – as from 8 April 2002, charges cannot be made for this) may be available from Social Services. The Social Security system no longer directly contributes to the costs of residential care. Any access to financial assistance with the cost of residential care will be subject to a means test.

Income Support or Pension Credit in residential care   11.5

Capital   11.6

Where an applicant is in temporary residential/nursing home care, the capital limit for claiming Income Support is £16,000 with a tariff income applied to all savings above £6,000 as is the case for all other benefit claimants. However, a claimant who is in residential care on a permanent basis, or who is in care on a trial basis (with a view to accepting a permanent placement) will have the first £10,000 disregarded; and the tariff income will only be applied to savings over £10,000 up to the capital limit of £16,000 (*Income Support (General) Regulations 1987 (SI 1987 No 1967), Regs 45, 53(1)–(6)*). (See **CHAPTER 6 INCOME SUPPORT**.) For the Guarantee Credit or Pension Credit, the same rules apply in respect of tariff income on capital over £6,000 or £10,000, but with no upper capital limit (see **CHAPTER 25 PENSION CREDIT**).

Who is assessed?   11.7

A claimant will always be treated as a member of his normal 'family unit' (see **CHAPTER 3 CLAIMING FOR THE FAMILY**) where he is in temporary residential/nursing home care. Therefore, the assessment of any means will apply to the claimant and any partner and other family members (see **CHAPTER 2 ASSESSMENT OF MEANS**). Where a claimant is in permanent residential/ nursing home care he will be treated as a single claimant and therefore the assessment of means will be applied only to his income.

Registered independent homes   11.8

Since April 2003, all claimants have their entitlement to means-tested benefits (Income Support or Pension Credit) while in residential care calculated in the normal way. There are no longer any special rules or additional payments.

If the claimant in temporary residential care has a partner who is not in residential care, then Income Support or Pension Credit will be calculated by giving each member of the couple their own personal allowances and premiums etc (*SI 1987 No 1967, Reg 7(9)*).

The couple's income will be assessed jointly for Income Support and Pension Credit, and their capital will be assessed as joint capital.

233

Once a claimant's stay in residential care becomes permanent the couple will be assessed for Income Support or Pension Credit separately. If the person in care is claiming any State benefit (State Retirement Pension, Incapacity Benefit, Severe Disablement Allowance etc) which includes a dependant addition for a partner, this dependant's addition will be treated as income belonging to the partner.

EXAMPLE

A claimant aged 66 is in residential care and his income is a State Retirement Pension of £134.75 per week, £50.50 of which is a dependant addition for his wife. He is also getting £100 per week occupational pension. His wife, who has no actual income of her own, will be treated as having the amount of adult dependant addition of £50.50, so that her husband's pension is deemed to be £84.25.

Their assessed income will be.

Claimant		*Wife*	
Retirement pension	£84.25	Dependant addition	£50.50
Occupational pension	£100.00		
Total	**£184.25**	**Total**	**£50.50**

Once a person in care is either in permanent care or in care on a trial basis with a view to permanency, capital belonging to a couple jointly will be divided between the two and 50% of the capital allocated to each partner for the assessment of Income Support or Pension Credit. Furthermore, because the stay in residential care has become permanent, the claimant in care will be allowed £16,000 for Income Support purposes, £10,000 of which will be disregarded before applying the tariff income.

Local authority-owned care homes   11.9

In local authority homes, Income Support and Pension Credit are calculated in the ordinary way.

Social Services' contribution towards costs   11.10

Capital   11.11

Whether the claimant is in temporary or permanent care, any capital belonging to the claimant and his partner will be divided equally between the partners from the day the claimant enters residential care. The capital limit for the person in care in England will be £21,000, of which £12,750 will be disregarded before applying the tariff income – this rule applies whether the claimant is in temporary or permanent care. The 2005/06 figures for Wales are £21,000 and £14,750 respectively – the revised figures for 2006/07 were not available at the time of writing.

In *R v Sefton Metropolitan Borough Council, ex p Help the Aged and Blanchard (1997) 1 CCLR 57*, it was found that, even where a claimant's savings had reduced to below £16,000 (the upper limit at the time), Social Services were not bound to make contributions to the funding of residential care costs where a claimant (namely Charlotte Blanchard) had been self-funding in care but had never had an assessment of needs carried out by the Social Services department.

In consideration of this case, we now see a greater requirement for every person entering into care, whether self-funding or not, to request an assessment of needs by Social Services prior to entering the residential/nursing care home.

The authority does not have to carry out a charging assessment for the first eight weeks of the claimant being in care – it can charge whatever it considers to be reasonable during this period. If the claimant is deemed to be a 'less dependent' resident then Social Services can ignore the whole charging assessment if they consider it to be reasonable in the circumstances.

Furthermore, the authority must disregard the value of a claimant's home for the first three months of being in permanent care, and thereafter must give the person in care a choice of either:

- allowing the local authority to place a charge on his property which will defer any requirement to make contributions while in care; or

- making contributions towards his care cost.

Income   11.12

Only the income of the person in care will be assessed – so a partner's income cannot be taken into account. The claimant should always be left with £19.60 per week to accommodate his own personal expenses following an assessment. So in effect, if the claimant's partner who is not in residential care is the person who is claiming Income Support or Pension Credit for the couple during a period of temporary care, then the Income Support which is paid to the partner cannot be taken into account in the assessment of the claimant's income.

The following rules apply:

- any payment of Attendance Allowance or Disability Living Allowance will only be disregarded where the claimant is in temporary residential care. If the stay in care is permanent then this income will be counted in full, although the benefit is likely to stop after four weeks of local authority funding, in any event;

- any element of Income Support or Pension Credit to accommodate mortgage interest or home improvement loans interest will be disregarded;

- any payment which the claimant is making towards his housing costs will be disregarded while the claimant is in temporary care;

- all other income that the claimant has will be taken into account in the assessment of income (including Income Support if this is paid to the claimant);

- £5.05 (£7.50 for couples) is disregarded from Savings Credit or other savings income from people aged 65 or over.

The value of the claimant's home   11.13

The value of a claimant's home will only be disregarded where the claimant is a temporary resident (and his stay is not likely to exceed 52 weeks) and he intends to return home or is selling his property with the intention of purchasing a more suitable property. However, Social Services do have a discretion (unlike for Income Support) to disregard the value of any property which is occupied by a third party where they consider it would be reasonable to disregard the value of those premises.

Where the claimant is in permanent care, the value of his interest in the home is taken into account after three months. If after the first three months the value is more than £20,500, the claimant can still receive funding from Social Services provided he consents to the local authority registering a charge on his property to enable them to recover excess funding at a later date when the property is sold (*HSCA 2001, s 54*).

This rule is different from the Income Support ruling on property; the value of the claimant's property will be ignored, provided that he is making reasonable efforts to dispose of the property. When he does sell the property, Income Support payments will stop. The claimant will not have to pay back the amount of Income Support he has been paid while the house has been up for sale.

How residential care affects other benefit entitlement   11.14

When a claimant goes into residential care the following benefits will be affected.

Disability Living Allowance and Attendance Allowance   11.15

Where Social Services assist the claimant with his cost of residential care (in an independent home), he will no longer qualify for these benefits after 28 days of being in care. This rule will also apply to those people receiving benefit who are in NHS funded hospital care as an in-patient for more than 28 days.

If, however, the claimant is in independent residential/nursing home care and is not provided with financial assistance from Social Services, then he can continue to receive these benefits as long as he continues to satisfy the qualifying conditions of entitlement to them. Additionally, a claimant who is an in-patient in a privately funded hospital may also retain full entitlement to these benefits.

Shorter periods of less than 28 days are aggregated if they are less than 28 days apart. So, if someone goes into a residential home, funded by social services, for a two-week period, and then returns to residential care within 28 days of returning home, the second period in the home would be counted as part of the earlier period when counting the 28 days. The day someone goes into residential care or hospital, and day he comes out, are both treated as days 'at home'.

Housing Benefit   11.16

Where a claimant is temporarily absent from his home with good cause, i e because he is in hospital etc, he can continue to receive benefit in respect of his rent liability, provided he intends to return to his property. In such cases benefit can continue to be paid for up to 52 weeks of absence.

Housing Benefit can be paid in respect of the claimant's own home when he is in temporary residential/nursing home care. Where a claimant has a partner who is not is residential care, Housing Benefit will continue to be paid for the person occupying the home. However, where the claimant has no partner or both members of a couple are in residential care the rules are quite different.

There are two categories of claimants who are treated quite differently under this rule. Where a claimant goes into residential care other than on a trial basis he can receive Housing Benefit for up to 52 weeks during his period of absence from home.

Housing Benefit can only be paid in these circumstances where the claimant intends to return home within 52 weeks and his home is not occupied by another person or sub-let.

237

Where a person goes into residential care on a trial basis he can receive Housing Benefit for up to 13 weeks during his period of absence from his home.

Housing Benefit can only be paid in these circumstances where the claimant intends to return home if the residential accommodation does not meet his needs within 13 weeks and his home is not occupied by another person or sub-let.

In both cases, Housing Benefit can be paid if the claimant intends to return home within the specified period, of either 52 or 13 weeks.

Once the claimant makes a decision not to return home his Housing Benefit will cease from the date on which he made that decision.

EXAMPLE

Mr Morris lives alone and is disabled. He goes into residential care on a trial basis to see if the home is suitable. After eight weeks he decides that he likes the home and his stay is going to be permanent – he is then made an offer of a permanent place. Because he no longer intends to return home his entitlement to Housing Benefit ceases. If he is required to give four weeks' notice to his landlord then he will have to meet his full rent liability out of his own income for the period of notice.

If, on the other hand, after eight weeks, he feels that he would probably like to remain in the home but is undecided, and his offer of a permanent place is postponed, he could hand in his notice to his landlord, with the provision that if he changes his mind he can relinquish his notice prior to the date of expiry, then Housing Benefit could be paid for the entire period of notice.

If after a trial period Mr Morris decides that he does not want to stay in the home, but is unable to go back to his own home, perhaps because he is deemed not to be capable of caring for himself, then his period of absence for the purpose of entitlement to Housing Benefit will then be extended to 52 weeks. This is relevant because the conditions are that the 'claimant must intend to return home' and it is the claimant's intentions that are most important, even where the case is that, in practical terms, it is unlikely that the claimant will achieve that intention.

Any temporary periods of absence commence from the first Monday following the absence, and the absence must be continuous. Consequently, if the claimant returns to his home for a period exceeding 24 hours then the period of absence will start to run again (*R v Penwith District Council Housing Benefit Review, ex p Burt (1990) 22 HLR 292*).

Where the claimant is in temporary residential care, but has a partner living in the property, then the partner can continue to receive Housing Benefit. However, after 52 weeks of the partner being in residential care or hospital, any award of Housing Benefit may be reduced in so far that a couple's personal allowance will be reduced to that of a single person. This could give rise to the taper for the assessment of Housing Benefit to bring about a lesser award of Housing Benefit for the claimant (see **CHAPTER 9 HOUSING BENEFIT, COUNCIL TAX BENEFIT AND DISCRETIONARY HOUSING PAYMENTS**).

Where the claimant's partner is in permanent residential care, the claimant will be treated as a single claimant and Housing Benefit will be assessed based on the claimant's income. The partner who is in care will not form any part of the claimant's assessment for Housing Benefit.

Council Tax Benefit   11.17

If the claimant is only in temporary care then the same rules as for Housing Benefit will apply to Council Tax Benefit.

If the claimant has left his own home unoccupied and is not claiming Council Tax Benefit and he is in temporary care, then he will be awarded a 50% discount on his council tax liability during his stay in residential/nursing home care.

If the claimant is in permanent residential care and his home is unoccupied, he will be exempt from paying council tax, if his main and sole place of residence is a residential/nursing care home.

If the person in permanent care has a partner who is living in the accommodation, the partner will be able to claim a single householder's council tax discount of 25% (provided that the partner is the only adult living in the property). The partner will also be able to claim Council Tax Benefit, which will be subject to a means test based on the partner's income and capital only.

12 National Health Service Benefits

Introduction   12.1

Most services available under the NHS, such as care from a doctor or hospital care, are free at the point of delivery. However, service charges may be payable for the following NHS services:

- NHS prescriptions;
- NHS dental treatment;
- NHS sight tests, glasses and contact lenses; and
- NHS travel costs to and from hospital for treatment.

Help with these costs may be available depending on an individual's personal disability or age, or help may be available to those with low incomes based on a means test or to those in receipt of relevant prescribed Social Security benefits.

Who can claim?   12.2

Free treatment will be available for NHS charges where the claimant is in receipt of and can prove receipt of certain means-tested benefits. Proof may be provided by way of a benefit payment book or by production of a benefit award letter showing the applicant's name and National Insurance number (these will be cross checked with the Department of Work and Pensions (DWP) – where a person is found not to be in receipt of the relevant benefit at the date of signing the exemption declaration a fine of £100 may be imposed or the applicant may be prosecuted). People in receipt of tax credits should receive confirmation of their entitlement to NHS benefits from the Prescription Pricing Authority. The persons exempt will be those who are members of the claimant's family for the purpose of the assessment of entitlement to the means-tested benefit (see **CHAPTER 3 CLAIMING FOR THE FAMILY**). Exemptions apply to the following:

- all those in receipt of Income Support;
- all those in receipt of the guarantee credit of Pension Credit;
- all those in receipt of income-based Jobseekers Allowance; and

- some people in receipt of tax credits. This will include those on:

  ○ Child Tax Credit only, with incomes below £15,050 per annum;

  ○ Child Tax Credit and Working Tax Credit, with incomes below £15,050; and

  ○ Working Tax Credit with disability element, with incomes below £15,050.

NHS prescriptions 12.3

Most people have to pay for prescriptions. The charge set by Parliament each year in April will be applied to the number of items on a prescription, rather than one charge per prescription. The charge for 2005/06 is £6.50 per item, so if an applicant has three items on a prescription, he will have a charge to pay of £19.50.

Patients who may require a number of prescriptions in a given period may benefit from applying for a prescription prepayment certificate. This will be of benefit where the applicant needs more than five items in four months or more than 14 items in twelve months, in which case a four or twelve-month prescription prepayment certificate will save money. However, the prepayment certificate must be purchased in advance using application Form FP95, although this can be started from up to seven days before the date that the application is received by the health authority.

People exempt from prescription charges 12.4

The following are exempt from prescription charges:

- a claimant or partner who *is in receipt* of a relevant benefit (see **12.2** above);

- children under 16 or aged 16–18 in full-time education;

- persons aged 60 and over;

- women who hold a maternity medical exemption certificate (during pregnancy and for twelve months following the birth of a child – application Form FW8 available from GPs);

- persons holding an exemption certificate (application Form FP92A) because they are suffering from one of the following conditions:

  ○ epilepsy where continuous anti-convulsive therapy is required;

  ○ myxoedema – where thyroid hormone is required;

○ a permanent fistula – requiring an appliance or continuous surgical dressing;

○ diabetes – except where treatment is by diet alone;

○ hypoparathyroidism;

○ Addison's disease and other forms of hypoadrenalism.

Refunds of payments for those exempt 12.5

People who have applied for an exemption certificate, or are waiting for an assessment of entitlement to a relevant benefit at the time they need the prescription, will initially have to pay for the prescription, but should request an FP57 receipt. If they are then awarded the exemption or benefit they will be able to claim a refund of the prescription charges on production of that receipt.

There is no provision for a reduction in charges for prescriptions for a claimant with a low income.

NHS dental treatment 12.6

Most people have to pay for NHS dental charges. However, certain services provided by a dentist under the NHS scheme (but not private) are free regardless of the claimant's income or circumstances.

These services are:

• repairs to dentures;

• stopping bleeding after extraction;

• calling an NHS dentist to his surgery in an emergency; and

• home visits by an NHS dentist if necessary.

A dentist cannot charge for these services – he can only charge for normal treatment as he would in normal hours of practice.

Claimants exempt from NHS dental charges 12.7

The exemption is based on the applicant's circumstances at the start of any treatment, so if a person is exempt because he is under 18 when the treatment starts, but the following week he is 19 and his treatment is due to span six weeks, he will remain exempt throughout his course of treatment.

The following are exempt:

- children and young people under the age of 18;

- young people age 18–19 in full-time education;

- women who are pregnant or who have had a baby in the twelve months prior to the date of treatment;

- claimants and partners who are in receipt of a relevant benefit (see **12.2** above).

Claimants who may qualify for reduced NHS dental charges   12.8

Claimants who are on a low income may qualify for exemption from dental charges or reduced dental charges, but the claimant must submit an application form to his local DWP office or dentist. The claim form is Form HC1. On submitting the application form the claimant will be issued with a certificate HC2 (providing total exemption from charges) or HC3 (providing reduced charges for treatment). These certificates will show the maximum amount that a claimant will be liable to pay during a period of treatment. On production of these certificates the dentist will not charge the claimant any more than the assessed payment for services available under the NHS. (For the assessment of means see **12.13** et seq below.)

The HC2 or HC3 certificate will identify all persons by name who qualify for the reduced charge services. Therefore, if a claimant obtains a HC3 certificate for himself and his wife, both members of the couple will be identified as being eligible for reduced cost treatment.

NHS sight tests, glasses and contact lenses   12.9

A person normally has to pay for a sight test. However, persons who fall into the following groups are exempt:

- children and young people under the age of 16;

- young people aged 16–19 in full-time education;

- people over the age of 60;

- claimants and partners who are in receipt of a relevant benefit (see **12.2** above);

- people who are diagnosed diabetic, or as having glaucoma, or aged 40 or over and their child, brother, sister or parent has been diagnosed as having glaucoma;

- people who are referred for a test by a hospital eye department.

Claimants who may qualify for reduced charge sight tests

12.10

Claimants who are on a low income may qualify for exemption from sight test charges or reduced sight test charges. The claimant should submit an application form to his local DWP office or optician. The required claim form is HC1. On submitting the application form the claimant will be issued with a certificate HC2 (providing total exemption from charges) or HC3 (providing reduced charges for treatment). These certificates will show the maximum amount that a claimant will be liable to pay during a period of treatment. On production of these certificates the optician will not charge the claimant any more than the assessed payment for services available under the NHS. (For the assessment of means see **12.13** et seq below.)

The HC2 or HC3 certificate will identify all persons by name who qualify for the reduced charge services. So if a claimant obtains a HC3 certificate for himself and his wife, both members of the couple will be identified as being eligible for reduced cost treatment.

If the applicant requires spectacles or contact lenses once an eye test is carried out, he will be issued with a voucher (graded A–H depending on the applicant's clinical requirements) to the value of the full standard NHS charges for his clinical requirement if he is exempt from paying for his sight test charges and he is:

- a child or young person under the age of 16;
- a young person aged 16–19 in full-time education;
- a person in receipt of a relevant benefit (see **12.2** above); or
- a holder of an HC2 certificate.

If the applicant is a holder of an HC3 certificate he will receive a reduced value voucher for NHS spectacles or contact lenses.

These vouchers may be used in payment or part payment for the spectacles or contact lenses. The vouchers provided do not in any way restrict the applicant from purchasing any type of frame or lenses that he prefers. If an applicant on Income Support is issued with a voucher to the value of £48.80 for single vision lenses grade B and the applicant prefers frames and grade B lenses costing £69.00, the applicant will simply have to make up the difference in the cost (i e pay the shortfall of £20.20).

NHS travel costs to and from hospital for treatment

12.11

Applicants will be entitled to help with travel costs provided through the hospital travel cost scheme where:

- they are receiving NHS treatment under the care of a hospital consultant; or

- they are attending a hospital or centre to receive disablement services relating to artificial limbs, wheelchair provision or facilities, articles or appliances to be used in caring for a severely disabled person; and

- they or their partner or a member of their family unit (see **CHAPTER 3**) are in receipt of a relevant benefit; or

- they hold a current HC2 certificate.

If the patient needs an escort for the journey to the hospital or centre for medical reasons, or because the patient is a child under the age of 16, the travel cost of the escort can also be claimed.

Holders of the HC3 certificate may also receive financial assistance towards the cost of travel. The amount they will be expected to contribute will be detailed on the HC3 certificate.

What travel costs can be paid? 12.12

The following travel costs can be claimed:

- public transport fares;

- the estimated cost of fuel for private transport (but not exceeding the public transport cost);

- any contribution the patient may have to pay for the transport service to organisations like Dial a Ride or a local disabled or aged group community transport scheme; and

- taxi fares, but only where there is no other means by which the patient could reasonably travel.

The hospital in which the patient is being treated, or which has referred the patient, will be responsible for the reimbursement of any travel expenses – these can usually be claimed on the day the claimant attends the hospital.

Also note that Income Support, Pension Credit guarantee credit and income-based Jobseekers Allowance recipients may qualify for assistance with travel costs for attending or visiting a member of their family unit in hospital from the Social Fund as an alternative (not additional) source of funding (see **CHAPTER 13 THE SOCIAL FUND**).

Assessment of means for the low income scheme 12.13

This applies to HC2 and HC3 certificates.

The capital limit for claiming help with NHS charges is £8,000 for those aged under 60 and £12,000 for those aged 60 and over.

The assessment of means under this scheme is the same as for the assessment of the applicable amount for Income Support (see **CHAPTER 6 INCOME SUP-PORT**). It provides for personal allowances for the claimant or member of a couple, amounts for dependent children based on their ages, premiums, with the exception that a person who has been incapable of work for at least 28 weeks will qualify for a disability premium (unlike Income Support which requires a period of incapacity of 52 weeks) – a higher pensioner premium will be applied to all applicants over the age of 60.

Additionally, housing costs to the value of actual interest payments and capital repayments (or endowment premiums) which were incurred to purchase a house or to carry out essential home improvements will be allowed.

Any rent liability (excluding fuel charges etc) which is not covered by Housing Benefit will be allowed, provided this is not paid to a close relative living in the same house as the applicant.

The applicant will then have his allowable expenses offset against his income.

The assessment of income is the same as for Income Support, including provisions for disregarding certain incomes in whole or in part (see **CHAPTER 2 ASSESSMENT OF MEANS**).

Deducting the allowable expenses from the claimant's assessable income will produce an excess income.

EXAMPLE

A couple are both aged 55 with no dependent children. They have an endowment mortgage of £300 per month and the husband is in receipt of Incapacity Benefit of £70.05 following a period of sickness of 30 weeks. He also receives Industrial Injuries Benefit of £25.42 and he has a small works occupational pension of £19.60 per week. His wife works part time and earns £100 net per week. The husband also receives Disability Living Allowance mobility component highest rate and care component lowest rate.

Their assessment will be carried out as follows. ➡

Applicable amount		Income	
Couple's personal allowance	£90.10	Husband's Incapacity Benefit	70.05
Couple's disability premium	£34.95	Industrial Injuries Benefit	£25.42
Housing cost	£69.04	Wife's wages	£100.00
		less disregard	£10.00
			£19.60
		Husband's works pension	
		DLA (disregarded)	£0.00
Total	**£194.09**	**Total**	**£205.07**

The difference between these amounts = £10.98 per week which is excess income.

Amount payable   12.14

The amount of help awarded is based on multiples of the excess income as follows:

- NHS dental treatment – up to three times the excess income towards each course of dental treatment;

- NHS sight tests – up to the excess income towards sight test;

- NHS vouchers for glasses and contact lenses – the voucher will be reduced by twice the excess income;

- NHS travel costs to and from hospital for treatment – up to the excess income towards the travel costs in any one week.

In the example in **12.13** above, the couple will receive a HC3 certificate saying that their contributions towards the costs of NHS services will be as follows:

- NHS dental treatment – £32.94 (3 × excess income of £10.98);

- NHS sight tests – £10.98 (1 × excess income of £10.98);

- NHS vouchers for glasses and contact lenses – the voucher will be reduced by £21.96 (2 × excess income);

- NHS travel costs to and from hospital for treatment – £10.98 (1 × excess income in any one week).

How to claim 12.15

Claim forms HC1 can be obtained from any office of the DWP, any NHS hospital, GP or dentist surgery, or by telephoning the Social Security Health Benefits Division: telephone 0191 203 5555. Claims should be sent in the prepaid envelope provided with the claim form to the Health Benefits Division, Sandyford House, Archbold Terrace, Jesmond, Newcastle Upon Tyne, NE2 1DB. The claimant will be required to provide evidence of all his income, capital and housing costs.

Common problems 12.16

There are no particular problems arising from this scheme other than the fact that it is one of the most unknown and under-publicised forms of assistance which is available to all members of the public. Financial assistance under the low income scheme has for many years been the most under-claimed available benefit in the Social Security system.

Checklist 12.17

Claim specification	Details
Basic entitlement conditions	Claimant and partner must have capital of less than £8,000 if under 60 and £12,000 if 60 or over and entitlement is dependent on a full comprehensive means test.
Dependant additions	N/A.
Where to claim	The means test HC1 form is available at the DWP, doctors' surgeries, hospitals and dentists and should be sent to Health Benefits Division, Sandyford House, Archbold Terrace, Jesmond, Newcastle Upon Tyne, NE2 1DB.
How difficult is the claim form to complete?	Requires detailed information relating to income, capital and housing costs and evidence of this. Based on factual information requiring 40 minutes or so for completion.
Changes of circumstances that need to be notified	Any change of address.

Claim specification	Details
Frequency of periodic reviews	Certificates are valid for six months from date of issue; the claimant should re-apply no more than four weeks before a certificate is due to expire.
Time limits for reviews and appeals	N/A.
Premiums attracted for IS, HB and CTB	No underlying entitlement.
Other linked benefits	N/A.
Attracting a NICs credit	No.
Taxable	No.

13   The Social Fund

Introduction 13.1

The Social Fund is made up of cash-limited budgets provided to each local Department for Work and Pensions (DWP) office for the purpose of assisting those who have low incomes to meet with expenses which cannot usually be budgeted for in the claimant's day-to-day expenditure.

The Social Fund is made up of two parts – the discretionary Social Fund scheme and the regulated Social Fund scheme. Access to both schemes requires the claimant to be in receipt of specific means-tested benefits in order to qualify.

Discretionary Social Fund payments include the following:

- Community Care Grants – to assist a person to remain in or establish himself in the community. These grants do not have to be repaid;

- budgeting loans – to assist with essential costs which could not easily have been budgeted for by a claimant in receipt of a means-tested benefit. These are interest-free loans and are normally repaid by deducting a weekly amount from the claimant's benefit;

- crisis loans – these are emergency loans which can be claimed by those in crisis. They are interest-free loans and are normally repaid by deductions from the claimant's benefit.

Regulated Social Fund payments include:

- Sure Start Maternity Grants (see **CHAPTER 20 PARENTHOOD BENEFITS**);

- Social Fund funeral expenses payments; and

- cold weather payments.

Discretionary Social Fund payments 13.2

The Social Fund has a strictly limited budget and payments are discretionary. The rules are only concerned with eligibility and how the discretion is to be exercised. Many payments from the fund are made in the form of loans, which will be recovered in instalments from a claimant's weekly benefit.

Discretionary Social Fund awards are made up of two parts:

- Community Care Grants, which do not have to be paid back; and

- loans, which will be recovered from a claimant's weekly benefit in instalments.

Community Care Grants   13.3

To claim a Community Care Grant a claimant must normally be in receipt of Income Support, Pension Credit or income-based Jobseekers Allowance. The only exception to this rule is for those who:

- are or have been living in institutional or residential care within six weeks of the date of making the claim for a Community Care Grant; and

- are likely to be awarded Income Support or income-based Jobseekers Allowance when they leave.

When assessing a claim for a Community Care Grant, capital of £1,000 (or £2,000 if the claimant or his partner is aged over 60) will be disregarded. If the claimant's capital exceeds this figure any award will be reduced pound for pound by the excess.

A claimant must require a Community Care Grant of at least £30 for his application to be considered unless he is applying for travelling expenses, or living expenses for a prisoner home on leave – in such cases a smaller amount can be awarded.

A Community Care Grant will only be made in the following circumstances:

- to help the claimant or a member of his family re-establish himself in the community following a stay in institutional or residential care, e g in local authority care, custody or a detention centre, a nursing home, a resettlement or rehabilitation centre, a hostel, hospital etc;

- to help a claimant or a member of his family to remain in the community rather than enter institutional or residential care. This could include improving living conditions, moving into more suitable accommodation, or moving to obtain support for setting up home in cases where the claimant would otherwise be homeless;

- to ease exceptional pressures on the claimant or a member of his family. This could be following a breakdown of a relationship where a person has to move, or where the claimant or a member of his family has been subjected to harassment or victimisation and is obliged to move home as the only way of resolving the matter.

  Applications in all cases should only be for essential items such as clothing, a cooker, beds, bedding, floor covering, curtains, pots and pans, crockery, table and chairs etc. Other items such as a fridge will not be considered to be essential items unless there are specific reasons why such items should be considered as essential, e g a member of the family has to take medication, which has to be stored in a fridge;

- where particular items need to be purchased to accommodate the needs of a disabled person living in the house;

- where minor structural repairs are needed to keep a home safe and habitable for children;

- to allow a claimant or his partner to care for a prisoner or young offender on home leave;

- to help a claimant or a member of his family with travelling expenses in certain circumstances, e g attending a relative's funeral, visiting a close relative who is ill or in hospital, visiting a child pending a court decision.

Because funds for Community Care Grants are limited the DWP will usually give priority to certain groups of people such as the elderly, the disabled, the mentally ill, ex-offenders, families under stress, young people leaving care, etc. This list is to be used as a guide only and should not deter a claimant from making an application. The most important thing is to always give the reasons why a claimant's circumstances should be treated as high priority.

Loans   13.4

There are two types of Social Fund loans:

- budgeting loans; and
- crisis loans.

Budgeting loans   13.5

A claimant must be in receipt of Income Support, Pension Credit or income-based Jobseekers Allowance for a continuous period of at least 26 weeks prior to the date of the claim, and the loan must be required to meet intermittent expenses which would be difficult to budget for.

The loan must be for at least £100 and is subject to the same capital restrictions as the Community Care Grant (see **13.3** above). The claimant or his partner must not be involved in a trade dispute and the loan must not exceed an amount which the claimant is likely to be able to repay.

These loans are only available for expenses falling under one of the following prescribed headings:

- furniture and household equipment;

- clothing and footwear;

- rent in advance or removal costs to help secure a home for the claimant and his family;

- improvement, security and maintenance of the home;

- travelling expenses;

- expenses associated with re-entering or seeking work; or

- hire purchase or other debts, which have been incurred by the claimant in meeting the costs of the above categories.

The procedure for claiming budgeting loans has become much simpler under the new scheme as the claimant does not have to state exactly why he needs any particular item. The claim form no longer takes into account any need of the claimant or a member of his family due to disability, because a 'weighting' criteria will be applied, based on the length of time that a claimant has been in receipt of benefit and the number of people who are members of the claimant's family.

Amount payable 13.6

The personal circumstances of the claimant will be allocated a weighting, which will depend on the period for which the claimant has been in receipt of Income Support, Pension Credit or income-based Jobseekers Allowance and the number of members of the claimant's family.

A claimant who has been in receipt of benefit for 26 weeks will be awarded weighting, which will have a cash value attached (this being the maximum budgeting loan available to the claimant). From April 2006, the maximum budgeting loan will be determined using three rates – once for single people, once for couples without children, and once for families with children. The actual amounts will vary with demand on the loans budget.

A claimant who has been in receipt of benefit for three years will be awarded weighting of 1.5 times the minimum period of 26 weeks. Therefore, the longer the claimant has been in receipt of benefit, the greater the maximum budgeting loan available to him (subject to the overall maximum amount of budgeting loan which can be awarded at any one time, i e £1,500) (*Social Fund Guidance Direction 52*).

The weighting applied to family size will start at a single claimant, who will have the minimum weighting for family size applied. If the claimant has a partner, the weighting will increase by one third and any dependent children will add a further one third (per child) to the weighting (*Social Fund Guidance Direction 52*).

There is a maximum budgeting loan attached to each weighting. These are set annually and are under the remit of district budgets.

The applicant will receive a maximum budgeting loan within the range set by the specified weighting, or the amount that he has actually requested (whichever is the smaller) (less any deductions applied in consequence of his capital exceeding the prescribed amount of £1,00 or £2,000).

If, once any deduction has been applied, the claimant's entitlement is nil, a wider criteria may be applied. The wider criteria looks at whether the claimant is in receipt of a secondary benefit and the period of award of that benefit, whether the claimant has other people in his household (non-dependants) in receipt of a qualifying benefit, whether the claimant is pregnant or whether the claimant or his family were in receipt of Working Families Tax Credit, Working Tax Credit or Housing or Council Tax Benefit in the period before his receipt of Income Support or income-based Jobseekers Allowance (*Social Fund Guidance Direction 52*).

Repayment 13.7

No budgeting loan can be awarded exceeding the amount that the claimant is able to repay (*Social Fund Guidance Direction 11*) and all loans will be deemed to be repayable within a period of 78 weeks. This maximum repayment period is to be increased.

The repayment requirements are as follows – if there is no evidence of existing budgeting loan commitments he will be offered a choice of:

- a reduced loan repayable at the standard rate of 12% of the Income Support or Jobseekers Allowance applicable amount (less housing costs);

- the full amount requested repayable at a rate of up to 25% of the Income Support or Jobseekers Allowance applicable amount (less housing costs);

- the maximum loan that can be repaid at a rate of 25% of the Income Support or Jobseekers Allowance applicable amount (less housing costs) over a period of 78 weeks; or

- an amount that can be repaid within 78 weeks when combining the proposed new loan with an existing Social Fund debt (including other budgeting loans and crisis loans that the claimant might have) which can be repaid at a rate of 25% of the Income Support or Jobseekers Allowance applicable amount (less housing costs).

If none of these repayment arrangements are possible, then no budgeting loan award can be made (*Social Fund Guidance, paras 6754, 6756 and Directions 5, 11*).

Crisis loans   13.8

These are to meet the immediate short-term needs of a claimant and his family emergencies and will only be awarded if a loan is the only means by which serious damage or risk to the health and safety of the claimant or a member of his family can be prevented. This could apply when a claimant is waiting for a first payment of benefit and he has no money for food and/or heating or other essential needs. They are sometimes referred to within the DWP as an 'alignment crisis loan' even though this phrase does not appear in the Social Fund Guidance Directions, so it may be helpful to refer to it in this way when making a claim. Further examples of when it would be reasonable to argue that there is a serious threat to the health and safety of the claimant and members of his family are where a claimant has lost his Giro or had it stolen, or has been a victim of a burglary which has been reported to the police and has no money to provide his family with essential needs.

Amount payable   13.9

The amount payable for a crisis loan in respect of living expenses will be 75% of the personal allowances for the claimant and his partner, plus £45.58 for each dependent child. The amount payable for items of a capital nature, e g furniture, will be the reasonable cost of replacement.

Paying back Social Fund loans   13.10

The general rule is that a claimant should be able to pay back the sum loaned over a period of 78 weeks (although in exceptional circumstances this could be extended to 104 weeks). The DWP does, however, have the authority to deduct benefit of up to 25% of a claimant's applicable amount (excluding housing costs). If deductions are fixed at this level a review can be requested if severe financial hardship to the claimant and his family would result.

When making an application for benefit deductions to be reduced a claimant will be asked to provide details of his weekly expenditure.

If a claimant has an outstanding loan from the Social Fund which is being deducted from his benefit and he ceases to be in receipt of Income Support, Pension Credit or income-based Jobseekers Allowance then the DWP is entitled to make deductions from the following benefits in order to recover the loan:

* Retirement Pension;

- Jobseekers Allowance, both contributory and income-based;

- Incapacity Benefit;

- Severe Disablement Allowance;

- Carer's Allowance;

- Widows' Benefit (not lump sum widows payment);

- Disablement Benefit, Reduced Earnings Allowance, Industrial Death Benefit;

- War Pensions;

- Maternity Allowance.

Social Fund loans cannot be recovered from Child Benefit, Statutory Sick Pay, Statutory Maternity Pay, Disability Living Allowance, Attendance Allowance, and Council Tax Benefit or Housing Benefit.

A loan can legally be recovered from:

- the claimant;

- the claimant's partner;

- a liable relative if the claimant's benefit has ceased due to receipt of maintenance payments;

- a sponsor if the loan has been claimed because the sponsor has stopped maintaining the claimant.

Regulated Social Fund payments   13.11

This covers such items as Social Fund cold weather payments which are automatically assessed by the Benefits Agency in periods of extreme cold weather.

Regulated Social Fund payments are payments which a claimant is legally entitled to receive, provided he satisfies the eligibility rules. Such payments are not discretionary and the claimant has a right to request a review or appeal to an appeal tribunal against any decision made on his claim – the decision being made by a decision maker rather than a Social Fund officer.

Sure Start Maternity Grant   13.12

This can be claimed where the claimant or a member of the claimant's family is expecting a baby or, within the last three months, has given birth or adopted a child under the age of twelve months (see **CHAPTER 20**). In the case of *Francis* *v Secretary of State for Work & Pensions* [2005] EWCA Civ 1303, the Court of Appeal ruled that the carer of a child under a residence order has the same entitlement to a Sure Start Maternity Grant as adoptive and birth parents.

Funeral expenses payment 13.13

This can be claimed where the claimant or a member of his family takes responsibility for the cost of a funeral where no other person could have taken primary responsibility for the cost of the funeral. The claimant does not have to be a relative of the deceased. Where the claimant is a close friend of the deceased no payment will be made if the deceased had a close relative who is not a benefit claimant.

The claimant will qualify if he is in receipt of Income Support, Pension Credit, income-based Jobseekers Allowance, Council Tax Benefit or Housing Benefit at the date of the claim.

The payments for funeral expenses will cover the cost of:

- an ordinary coffin or urn;

- the undertakers' fees inclusive of collection and transport of the coffin up to a maximum of £500;

- essential documentation;

- the cost of digging the grave or cremation;

- up to £25 for flowers from the claimant; and

- reasonable travelling expenses for one return visit inside the UK in connection with the arrangements or attendance at the funeral.

The rules relating to Social Fund payments for funeral expenses provide that where a deceased person, who has no partner but did leave surviving relatives, i e a parent, son or daughter aged 16 or over at the date of death, who are not in receipt of Income Support, then no funeral payment can be made from the Social Fund to any person who may claim it. The reason for this is that the deceased's next of kin would reasonably take responsibility for the funeral arrangements and payments.

Claims for funeral expenses must be made within three months of the date of the funeral and the DWP will recover any payments made in respect of funeral expenses from any monies in the deceased's estate.

Capital **13.14**

The rules relating to capital limits for funeral payments have changed; all capital of the claimant will be ignored.

Challenging decisions **13.15**

Decisions are made by Social Fund officers (SFOs) and there is no right of appeal against their decision, except in respect of funereal and maternity grants. However, there is provision for decisions to be reviewed.

A claimant will receive written notification of the decision and if he is dissatisfied he should write to the DWP within 28 days of the date of the decision, requesting a review and giving reasons for his request.

The procedure for review is set out in *sections 64* to *66* of the *Social Security Contributions and Benefits Act 1992* and the *Social Fund Directions*. These provide that a decision can be reviewed if based on a mistake of law or ignorance of or mistake as to some material fact, or if circumstances have changed since the decision.

If the SFO decides not to revise the decision in the claimant's favour he must give the claimant an opportunity to attend an interview, accompanied by a friend or representative if he wishes, where the reasons for the decision will be explained and the claimant will be given the chance to make further representations. An agreed written record of the interview must be made.

If following the interview (or the claimant fails to attend) the SFO still considers the original decision to be correct, he must pass the papers to another SFO not below the rank of higher executive officer who must consider all the circumstances again and then notify the claimant of his decision.

14 Child Support Assessments

Introduction 14.1

Although Child Support assessments are not Social Security or State benefits, the assessment of Child Support maintenance payments for dependent children of a family is governed by Social Security regulations under the *Child Support Act 1991 (CSA 1991)*, the *Social Security Act 1998*, the *Welfare Reform and Pensions Act 1999* and the *Child Support, Pensions and Social Security Act 2000*.

Furthermore, where a claimant is claiming income-based Jobseekers Allowance or Income Support, there is a mandatory requirement to co-operate with the Child Support Agency (CSA) in providing all the information that is reasonably known and available to them for the purpose of an assessment of Child Support liability in respect of any children living with a claimant, for whom he is claiming benefit, where both the natural or adoptive parents of a child do not live in the same family unit.

New system from March 2003 14.2

The main changes under the 'Children First Scheme' were to be introduced after the April 2002 Budget and are as set out below. They were introduced for new cases from March 2003.

There is no maintenance assessment of needs or assessment of ability to pay for things like housing costs.

Assessments will, in most cases, be applied on a standard liability based on the absent parent's assessed net income. The standard liability will be:

* 15% of the absent parent's net income where the absent parent is responsible for one child;

* 20% of the absent parent's net income where the absent parent is responsible for two children;

* 25% of the absent parent's net income where the absent parent is responsible for three or more children.

These assessments look at the absent parent's responsibility for children. Where, for example, the absent parent has one child with a former partner and another child living with him, the 20% assessment will be applied. The outcome of this 20% assessment will be divided and attributed equally to all children for whom he is responsible.

So, for example, the absent parent has one child living with him and one child who is living with the parent with care. He has a net income of £315 per week:

£315 × 20% = £63 available for maintenance which is attributable to two children.

£63 divided by 2 = £31.50. Therefore the Child Support liability for the child with the parent with care would be £31.50 per week.

These changes will affect only those who register an application after the date of implementation. People receiving Child Support payments under the new system who are on Income Support or income-based Jobseekers Allowance will have £10 of the maintenance disregarded per week.

Those who currently have a Child Support liability will be gradually phased in. So far, due to computer problems, the CSA has not been able to start transferring 'old' cases to the new child support formula. There is currently no date for this process to start. In these cases, should a new assessment result in an increased liability, there will be transitional protection to ensure that the previous liability is not increased by more than £5 per week (this being based on what the assessment would have been under the old rules).

(For more details see *Tolley's Social Security and State Benefits Looseleaf*.)

Previous system – a brief guide 14.3

Since April 1993, the CSA has been responsible for ensuring that new claimants and current recipients of Income Support, and income-based Job-seekers Allowance who are responsible for bringing up children on their own, i e one parent families, pursue Child Support maintenance payments in respect of their children.

Parents with care are required to provide as much information about the absent parent as possible, including name, date of birth, place of work, last known address, physical description etc.

Should the parent with care fail to disclose such information then he will be asked to attend an interview with a CSA official. Under *section 46* of the *CSA 1991*, if a parent with care fails to co-operate without good cause he can be penalised by having his award of benefit reduced for a period of 18 months. For the first six months any award of benefit will be reduced by 20% of the personal allowance for a single person over the age of 25 and for a further twelve months by ten per cent of the personal allowance. However, before this penalty is imposed the claimant will be given six weeks to reconsider his refusal to co-operate.

If a parent with care establishes good cause for his failure to disclose information, for example because of fear of violence, or because he simply does not know, the benefit restrictions should not be imposed. If they are, the parent with care has a right of appeal (see **CHAPTER 4 CLAIMS, DECISIONS AND APPEALS**).

A parent with care who is not in receipt of any of the above benefits can ask the CSA to make a Child Support assessment if he has no existing court order for child support.

When the parent with care has provided all the relevant information to the CSA, the CSA will send a maintenance enquiry form to the absent parent requiring him to provide details of his finances to enable a maintenance assessment to be made. This information must be provided within 14 days of the request. Should the absent parent fail to respond or only partially respond then the CSA will make an interim order against him of one-and-a-half times the maintenance requirement. This amount will probably be substantially more than he will ultimately be required to pay.

However, where the absent parent responds by completing the Child Support assessment form within four weeks of issue, the date of liability will be deferred for eight weeks from the date that the maintenance enquiry was issued.

Once the CSA has obtained all the required information a maintenance assessment will be made in accordance with a set formula, and the absent parent will be notified of the amount he has to pay. If he disagrees with the assessment he also has a right of appeal to the Appeals Service (see **CHAPTER 4**).

Where a court has made a 'clean break' order on or after April 1993 and the parent with care is in receipt of one of the relevant benefits the CSA still has power to make an enforceable assessment of Child Support maintenance.

Where a court has made a clean break order *prior* to April 1993, provisions will be made in the exempt income assessment to take into account these and a 'broad brush' approach will be adopted as follows.

Where property or capital have been transferred it will be assumed that each partner in any case would be entitled to half each of the value of the transfer. For example, if an absent parent transferred his property valued at £50,000 to the parent with care and there was an outstanding mortgage of £30,000 then it will be assumed that the absent parent had given up equity of £10,000.

No allowance will be given where the amount transferred was less than £5,000. Transfers greater than this will be divided into bands to provide a weekly exempt income.

Band	Exempt income rate
£5,000 to £9,999	£20
£10,000 to £24,999	£40
£25,000	£60

The maintenance assessment will be reviewed every two years, although there are provisions for earlier reviews where there has been a change in circumstances either relating to the parent with care or the absent parent, such as a reduction or increase in income, the birth of another child, or either parent separating from a partner or having a partner come to live with them.

The Child Support maintenance calculation 14.4

(*Child Support (Maintenance Assessments and Special Cases) Regulations 1992 (SI 1992 No 1815)*).

If the absent parent is in receipt of Income Support or income-based Jobseekers Allowance he will only have to contribute ten per cent of his personal allowance per week in Child Support and no further calculation will be required. If he is receiving Income Support or income-based Jobseekers Allowance and in addition he attracts a disability premium or is treated as being responsible for a child, or has shared care of the child where the child stays with him overnight, he will not be required to make any payment of Child Support under the Child Support 'special cases'.

The maintenance calculation will be based predominantly on the current Income Support rates and will be made up of the following elements.

The maintenance requirement 14.5

This is the amount which covers the day-to-day expenses of keeping the qualifying children. It is made up of:

* Income Support personal allowances for each qualifying child;
* any family premium;

- if the child is aged under 16, an adult personal allowance; and

- if the parent with care does not have a partner, the lone parent premium.

Note: The amount paid in respect of the person with care will be reduced by 25% where all the children are aged at least eleven, and 50% where all the children are aged at least 14. Where all the children are aged at least 16 there will be no amount payable in respect of the parent with care.

After these amounts have been added together then any Child Benefit (but not the single parent addition) must be deducted, leaving a total maintenance requirement.

EXAMPLE – WHERE ONLY ABSENT PARENT IS WORKING

Sarah, who is claiming Income Support, is now a single parent with two dependent children, aged nine and ten. She separated from her husband eight years ago and has no arrangement for maintenance payments from her husband as he has a new family to support. Her maintenance requirement will be as follows.

Child allowance aged 10	£45.58	
Child allowance aged 9	£45.58	
Family premium	£16.25	
Adult allowance	£57.45	
Sub total	**£164.86**	
less basic Child Benefit	£29.15	
Total	**£135.71**	= the maintenance requirement

Exempt income 14.6

The next step is to assess both the parents' exempt income. Where a parent with care is in receipt of Income Support it is not necessary to carry out a calculation of his exempt income as he is treated as having no income.

Exempt income is the amount that each parent needs to meet his expenses before maintenance is calculated. It is made up of:

- Income Support personal allowance for a single person aged over 25 (regardless of the actual age of the parent involved);

- any premiums for which the parent would qualify if he were to claim Income Support;

- any child allowances for the parent's own children;

- any family premium attributable to the parent's own child; if an absent parent has a new partner living with him who is working and has a child from his own relationship, only one half of any child personal allowance, disabled child premium or family premium will be taken into account for that child;

- housing costs, which will be allowed in full, taking into account all the family requirements;

- amounts attributable to clean break orders made prior to April 1993, based on the 'broad brush' approach (see **14.3** above); and

- an allowance of £0.10 per mile in respect of travel to work exceeding 150 miles per week. For example, where an absent parent travels 250 miles per week to and from work he will be allocated an exempt amount of £10 per week (£0.10 per mile for 100 miles).

EXAMPLE

Sarah was divorced from Andrew and Andrew now has a new wife, who has three children from her previous marriage, twins aged five and a child aged nine. Andrew and his wife have one child of their own aged one. They have housing costs of £90 per week and a council tax liability of £10.19 per week.

When Andrew and Sarah were divorced prior to April 1993 he transferred the matrimonial property which was valued at £50,000 but had an outstanding mortgage of £34,000. Taking this into account Andrew will be presumed to have given up equity of £8,000.

Andrew is now working and has an assessable income of £320 per week, but travels 200 miles to and from work per week. His wife is receiving maintenance from her former partner of £50 per week and Child Benefit for all four children of £52.55 per week.

➤

Andrew's personal allowance	£57.45	
Child addition	£45.58	(only 50% if wife was working)
Family premium	£16.25	(only 50% if wife was working)
Housing costs	£90.00	
Travel to work @ 10p per mile	£5.00	
Lost equity	£20.00	
Total exempt income	**£234.28**	
Net income	320.00	
less exempt income	£234.28	
Total assessable excess income	**£85.72**	

50% excess income = £42.86. As this amount does not exceed the maintenance requirement, this will be the amount that Andrew will be assessed as being liable to pay in child support maintenance, subject to two further cross checks of affordability (see **14.7** below).

If 50% of the excess income were more than the maintenance requirement, an additional calculation for extra maintenance would have to be considered.

Test of affordability 14.7

The next stage is to calculate the absent parent's protected income to ensure that the absent parent will not be left in a worse position financially than he would be if he were receiving Income Support.

EXAMPLE

Andrew is working and earning £320 per week after tax, National Insurance and 50% of his pension contributions have been deducted. His wife is receiving £50 per week maintenance from her former husband and £52.55 Child Benefit. When carrying out the exempt income calculation, however, only Andrew's income will be taken into account. ➡

Andrew's total income is £320 so that after deducting his exempt income of £234.28 he is left with a total assessable income for maintenance payments of £85.72 (see example in **14.6** above).

Note: He will, however, not be required to pay more than 30% of his net income in any circumstances, so if his maintenance requirement was more than £96 per week (30% of £320) his maintenance liability could not exceed this amount.

Furthermore, cross checks will be made to ensure that the absent parent can actually afford to meet the proposed liability. This assessment entails cross checking with the income and expenditure of the absent parent's new family in a protected income calculation.

As stated above this is to ensure that making the maintenance payment of £42.86 would not leave him worse off than he would be if he was in receipt of benefit. The protected income calculation will include requirements for Andrew's new family and is based on Income Support rates, taking into account that the family would qualify for 100% Council Tax Benefit if they were in receipt of Income Support. They will also be given an extra standard fixed addition of £30 per week to bring them above the Income Support rates.

The protected income calculation is as follows.

Andrew's requirements

Couple's personal allowance	£90.10
Child aged 1	£45.58
Child aged 5	£45.58
Child aged 5	£45.58
Child aged 9	£45.58
Family premium	£16.25
Housing costs	£90.00
Council Tax	£10.19
Standard addition	£30.00
Total	**£418.86**

At this point all the income from the family will be taken into account, i e Andrew's income of £320 plus Child Benefit of £52.55 plus maintenance received by his wife of £50, giving a total income of £422.55. ➧

The protected income of £418.86 is then deducted from the total income of £422.55 leaving a difference of £3.69. There is finally an additional allowance of 15% of this difference (i e £0.55) to be added to the protected income thereby increasing the protected income to £419.41.

The difference between the total income of £422.55 and the protected income of £419.41 is £3.14. As this amount is insufficient to pay Andrew's assessed Child Support liability of £42.86 per week, Andrew will only be held liable to pay this reduced amount in Child Support.

Self-employed cases   14.8

In cases where it is difficult for a self-employed person to provide full details of his income, a provisional order would be made for the absent parent to pay £30 per week (the average self-employed assessment completed by the agency to date). This will be adjusted back to the start of liability at a time when the full assessment has been completed. There will, however, be provisions for this £30 to be reduced if the absent parent can show that it would cause him severe hardship.

Such provisional assessment can be retrospectively reassessed back to the date of provisional liability once the CSA receives all the required information and evidence to carry out an accurate assessment.

15   Child Benefit

Introduction

Child Benefit is available to every individual who is responsible for a dependent child, regardless of the claimant's income or capital. This benefit is paid for each child who is:

- under the age of 16;

- aged 16–19 and in full-time further education up to A level, NVQ level 3 or equivalent (full-time education = twelve or more hours supervised study per week);

- is aged under 18 and who does not work or is not on a training scheme and registered at the careers office for work or work-based training for young people; or

- aged under 19 and on an unwaged training scheme.

Who can claim?

15.2

(Child Benefit (General) Regulations 2003 (SI 2003 No 493), Regs 30, 31).

To qualify for Child Benefit the claimant must:

- be present in Great Britain; and

- be ordinarily resident in Great Britain.

If the claimant remains ordinarily resident in Great Britain, and his absence is unlikely to exceed 52 weeks, Child Benefit continues to be paid during:

- the first eight weeks of a temporary absence; or

- the first twelve weeks of any period when he is temporarily absent from Great Britain if the absence, and any extension of that absence, is in connection with treatment for an illness or disability of the claimant, partner, dependent child or other relative, or the death of one of those people.

Claimants from abroad must also fall within one of the following categories:

- he or a member of his family must be a citizen of Great Britain or of one of the other members of the European Union or of Norway, Iceland or Liechtenstein;

- he or a member of his family must be lawfully working in Great Britain and be a citizen of Algeria, Morocco, Slovenia, Tunisia or San Marino;

- he must be a citizen of a country which has a reciprocal arrangement with Great Britain regarding residence;

- he must have leave to remain in Great Britain without any limitation on such leave;

- he must have been given exceptional leave to enter Great Britain by the Home Office.

The child   15.3

The child must live in the same house as the claimant in 'a settled course of daily living'. So where the child only lives with one parent for a couple of days per week and lives with his other parent for the remainder of the week, he will be treated as living with the parent where he is most settled and spends most of his time.

However, the case may arise where a child lives with one parent for one week and the other parent the next week, or lives with one parent during term time and the other parent during the school holidays.

Only one parent may receive Child Benefit for a child at any one time and in this situation both parents would qualify for Child Benefit for the time that the child spends with them. If both parents claimed Child Benefit, entitlement would have to be decided under the priority rules.

Rules of priority   15.4

A claim made by a claimant with whom the child is living will take priority over any other claims, for example, by someone contributing to the child's maintenance. The following rules apply:

- a claimant with an existing entitlement takes priority over anyone else's claim for up to four weeks; this, in effect, means that if Child Benefit is in payment the status quo will be maintained for up to four weeks while the later claim is investigated;

- if a husband and wife are residing together and both make a claim, the wife's claim will take priority. If they are living apart then the spouse with whom the child is actually living will have priority;

- if a wife leaves her husband with the children, for whom she has previously been receiving Child Benefit, he will not be able to claim the Child Benefit for 56 days – he and his wife will be deemed to be still living together for the first 91 days and so she will be deemed to still be living with the children, and absences of up to 56 days are ignored;

- in the case of an unmarried couple living together, the mother takes priority;

- where the child is not a child of a couple, the parent of the child will take priority over any other claimant. 'Parent' includes a step-parent, a person holding a court residence order and an adoptive parent;

- if the child is not living with a parent, the person who does have the child living with them will take priority because the second rule of priority will apply.

If none of rules outlined in the list above applies, benefit is paid to the person claiming Child Benefit.

If there is a disagreement between eligible persons HMRC will decide to whom Child Benefit should be paid, and on doing so it may look at who takes the primary responsibility for the child, particularly in cases where the child is living with both applicants for an equal amount of time.

Factors taken into account include the provision for the health, well-being and education of the child by reference to which applicant makes provision for taking the child to the doctor/dentist/hospital and at what address the child is registered for school and for his medical records etc.

Basic rules 15.5

(*Social Security Contributions and Benefits Act 1992, s 142*).

A 'child', for the purpose of Child Benefit, must be present in Great Britain (although he can be temporarily abroad) and must be either:

- a person under 16;

- a person under 19 receiving full-time secondary or further education in a recognised educational establishment or under such other arrangement as may be approved by the Secretary of State. From April 2006 this can also be extended beyond 19 to enable the young person to complete their educational course;

- a person aged 16 or 17 who has ceased education but is not receiving Income Support and who is registered for employment or youth training but who is neither actually employed for more than 24 hours a week nor actually attending a youth training scheme; or

- a person under 19 who is on unwaged work-based training. In England this includes the Entry to Employment or Programme Led Pathways schemes, and in Wales the Skill Build and Foundation Modern Apprenticeship schemes.

Interruptions to education of any length due to illness or disability, and absences of up to six months for some other good reason, can be disregarded.

Child Benefit will cease to be payable if the child starts work or a youth training course, or goes on to advanced or higher education, or if the child claims another earnings replacement Social Security benefit in his own right, i e Income Support, Incapacity Benefit, Severe Disablement Allowance etc.

Child Benefit during temporary absences   15.6

Child Benefit may continue to be paid to a claimant during a period of temporary absence of up to 56 days (eight weeks) in any 16-week period.

Children in hospital   15.7

Child Benefit will not be affected where the child is in hospital for a period of up to twelve weeks. After twelve weeks, if the child is still in hospital, a parent may continue to receive Child Benefit until the child has been in hospital for up to 20 weeks, but entitlement to this extended period of Child Benefit will only be secured where the claimant is regularly visiting the child in hospital and occasionally spending money on the child by taking him gifts, toys, magazines, drinks etc.

Children abroad   15.8

If the claimant is going abroad he can get Child Benefit if the absence abroad is for a temporary period unlikely to exceed eight weeks. If the child goes abroad temporarily (and the claimant remains in Great Britain) the claimant can continue to receive Child Benefit for up to twelve weeks, but this may be extended where the reason for the child being abroad is to:

- receive full-time education in an European Economic Area country;

- take part in an education exchange visit with the written approval of the school or college which the child attended in Great Britain; or

- receive medical treatment for an illness, which began before the child left Great Britain.

Children in legal custody or in local authority care 15.9

If the child is taken into legal custody or local authority care, payment of Child Benefit will cease after eight weeks (i e 56 days). However, if the child spends time with the claimant while subject to a care order, benefit will be payable for any week that the child lives with the claimant for periods as follows:

- throughout the week ('week' being Monday to Sunday);

- for part of a day ('day' being midnight to midnight) in that week plus the following six days;

- for a full day in that week plus the previous six days; or

- regularly for at least one whole day each week (which in reality means at least two consecutive nights since a day runs from midnight to midnight).

However, payment will not be made under the list above if the claimant is receiving a boarding-out allowance from the local authority (this is usually paid to foster parents).

Amount payable 15.10

Child Benefit is paid at three rates, which are (for 2006/07):

- a higher rate for the first child of the family of £17.45 per week;

- a lower rate for each subsequent child of £11.70 per week; and

- a third rate for lone parents eligible since April 1998, who receive £17.55 per week for the eldest or only child.

How to claim 15.11

Claims for Child Benefit cannot usually be backdated for more than one month, so it is important to ensure that a claim is made as soon as possible.

The claim is made on Form CH2. These forms are issued to all parents who have given birth in Great Britain (in the new baby Bounty Pack issued by midwives and the hospital), or can be obtained from the local DWP office, HMRC enquiry office or by contacting the Child Benefit centre on 0845 302 1444. Claims can also be made online at www.hmrc.gov.uk. Each claim will require the child's birth or adoption certificate and confirmation of the claimant's National Insurance number. The form must be sent to the Child Benefit Centre in Newcastle. No claim can be made before the child is born but must be made within six months of the birth.

In addition, a separate claim must be made for each child, i e a claim for the first child does not include a claim for any other child born later.

Challenging decisions   15.12

Once benefit has been assessed, the claimant will be sent a full written decision in respect of the claim. If a claimant is not happy with the decision for whatever reason, he will need to ask that the decision be reviewed. Applications for review must be made in writing and delivered to the decision maker within one month of the date of the original decision having been issued.

The decision maker will look at the claim again and take into account any new information that the claimant has raised in his application for review. The decision maker will then issue a further decision, and if the claimant is not happy with that decision, he may, in certain circumstances, appeal to the Appeals Service, but must do so within one month of the date of issue of the most recent decision (see **CHAPTER 4 CLAIMS, DECISIONS AND APPEALS**).

Checklist   15.13

Claim specification	*Details*
Basic entitlement conditions	The claimant must be responsible for a child who is living with him who is aged under 16 or aged 16–19 and in full-time education, or aged 16–18 who has left school and is registered with the careers service for youth training or employment. The child must not be absent from the claimant's household other than for prescribed periods of temporary absence.
Dependant additions	None.
Where to claim	Any local DWP or HMRC office or the Child Benefits Centre, Washington, Newcastle Upon Tyne.
How difficult is the claim form to complete?	This is a very easy form to complete requiring very limited factual information and approximately ten minutes for completion.

Claim specification	Details
Changes of circumstances that need to be notified	If in any circumstances the child is absent from the claimant's home for more than eight weeks, if the child is in hospital for more than twelve weeks, or if the claimant is abroad for more than eight weeks. Additionally, any change of address should be notified to the Child Benefit office.
Frequency of periodic reviews	There is no specific requirement for a review. However, reviews may be carried out at any time if requested by the claimant, or if HMRC believes that there is a question outstanding regarding the claimant's entitlement.
Time limits for reviews and appeals	Applications for reviews and appeals should be made within one month of any decision being notified to the claimant.
Premiums attracted for HB and CTB	Family premium.
Other linked benefits	This benefit may be claimed in addition to any other Social Security benefit, but will be counted in full as income for the purpose of any assessment of entitlement to Housing or Council Tax Benefit (but is ignored in the assessment of tax credits and IS and JSA).
Attracting a NICs credit	No (but may give rise to home responsibilities protection if required in the assessment of State pension entitlement).
Taxable	No.

16 Contributory Jobseekers Allowance

(Jobseekers Allowance Regulations 1996 (SI 1996 No 207)).

Introduction   16.1

There are two elements of Jobseekers Allowance (JSA), namely:

- *Income-based Jobseekers Allowance* – For those people who are unemployed but available for and seeking work, and either do not or no longer qualify for contributory JSA or need to claim additional benefit because they have dependants and/or housing costs. This benefit is subject to a full and comprehensive means test, but can be paid for as long as a claimant satisfies all the qualifying conditions of entitlement (see **CHAPTER 7 INCOME-BASED JOBSEEKERS ALLOWANCE**).

- *Contributory Jobseekers Allowance* – Where entitlement is conditional upon a claimant having paid sufficient National Insurance contributions (NICs) prior to becoming unemployed. This benefit is not, however, the subject of a detailed means test and is payable for up to 168 days (six months).

Basic rules   16.2

Contributory JSA is a contributory benefit for those who have paid sufficient NICs in the two years prior to the date of claim. This benefit is available for claimants who are no longer working, or are working part time for less than 16 hours per week.

Overlapping benefits rule   16.3

Because contributory JSA is what is known as an earnings replacement benefit it cannot be paid in addition to a benefit paid for a similar purpose. These benefits are as follows:

- Incapacity Benefit*;
- Severe Disablement Allowance*;
- Maternity Allowance*;
- Carer's Allowance*;
- Retirement Pension*;
- Widowed Parent's Allowance; and

- Bereavement Allowance.

These benefits are known as overlapping benefits. Where a claim is made for contributory JSA and one of the prescribed overlapping benefits is already in payment, the claimant will be awarded whichever benefit will attract the greatest amount of income for the claimant (*Social Security (Overlapping Benefits) Regulations 1979 (SI 1979 No 597), Reg 6, Sch 1*).

If the claimant's partner is in receipt of one of these overlapping benefits and is claiming an additional amount for a dependent partner (who has now claimed contributory JSA), the partner's benefit will be reduced by the amount that was in payment for the dependent partner. (The benefits that include a dependant addition are marked *.)

Contributory JSA is not technically a means-tested benefit. However, the award of this benefit will be reduced where a claimant has income from employment or self-employment and where a claimant is in receipt of an occupational pension above a certain limited amount. The claimant's capital, income from other sources and any income of a partner (with the exception of dependant additions explained in the overlapping benefit rules above) will not affect any entitlement to this benefit. However, if a partner is in receipt of an overlapping benefit any dependant addition for a partner will be removed from that entitlement.

Contributory JSA can only be paid in respect of the claimant – there are no provisions for additional amounts to be claimed in respect of dependent partners, children or housing costs. There is, however, provision for a claimant to claim income-based JSA in addition to contributory JSA in order to accommodate any needs of dependants (see **CHAPTER 7**).

Who can claim?   16.4

A claimant must:

- be under retirement age;

- be present in Great Britain;

- have made sufficient NICs in the two years prior to the date of claiming;

- either not be working in remunerative employment or working for less than 16 hours per week;

- be available for employment;

- actively seeking employment; and

- have entered into a jobseekers agreement.

Age of the claimant 16.5

A claimant must be under State retirement age to claim contributory JSA. The claimant's age will also affect the amount of benefit that can be awarded to him, regardless of whether all other conditions of entitlement are met. There are three rates of payment: a lower rate for claimants aged under 18, a slightly higher payment for claimants aged 18 but under 25 and a higher rate of payment for those aged 25 and over (see **CHAPTER 1 INTRODUCTORY MATERIALS** for current benefit rates).

Contribution conditions 16.6

Claimants will have to satisfy two contribution conditions in order to qualify for contributory JSA. The requirements mean that the claimant must have paid or been credited with sufficient NICs in the two complete tax years prior to the benefit year in which a claim is made. (Tax years run from 6 April to 5 April each year and benefit years run from the first Sunday in January to the first Saturday in January of the following year.) (*Social Security Contributions and Benefits Act 1992, s 21; Jobseekers Act 1995, s 2*).

For example:

- a claimant who makes an application for contributory JSA in December 2005 will have had to satisfy the contribution conditions for the tax years 2002/03 and 2003/04 (as the benefit year in which contributory JSA is claimed started on the first Sunday in January 2005 and ended on the first Saturday in January 2006);

- a claimant who makes an application for contributory JSA in June 2004 will have had to satisfy the contribution conditions for the tax years 2001/02 and 2002/03 (as the benefit year in which contributory JSA is claimed started on the first Sunday in January 2004 and ended on the first Saturday in January 2005).

First contribution condition 16.7

The claimant must have actually paid, in one of the relevant years, Class 1 NICs with an earnings factor of at least 25 times the lower earnings limit:

- the lower earnings limit in 2002/03 was £75 × 25 = earnings factor of £1,875;

- the lower earnings limit in 2003/04 was £77 × 25 = earnings factor of £1,925;

- the lower earnings limit in 2004/05 was £79 × 25 = earnings factor of £1,975;

- the lower earnings limit in 2005/06 was £82 × 25 = earnings factor of £2,050;

- the lower earnings limit in 2006/07 of £84 x 25 = earnings factor of £2,100.

Second contribution condition 16.8

The claimant must also have paid or been credited with, in one of the relevant years, Class 1 NICs with an earnings factor of at least 50 times the lower earnings limit:

- the lower earnings limit in 2002/03 was £75 × 50 = earnings factor of £3,750;

- the lower earnings limit in 2003/04 was £77 × 50 = earnings factor of £3,850;

- the lower earnings limit in 2004/05 was £79 × 50 = earnings factor of £3,950;

- the lower earnings limit in 2005/06 was £82 × 50 = earnings factor of £4,100;

- the lower earnings limit in 2006/07 of £84 x 50 = earnings factor of £4,200.

These rules do not actually mean that the claimant will have had to have worked and paid Class 1 NICs for at least 25 or 50 weeks in the relevant year – the requirement is that he must have worked and paid Class 1 NICs on at least the relevant earnings factor in the relevant year.

A claimant can be credited with Class 1 NICs for each whole week that he satisfied the qualifying rules for claiming JSA, Incapacity Benefit, Statutory Sick Pay, Carer's Allowance, Statutory Maternity Pay. He can also be credited if he was in receipt of Disabled Person's Tax Credit or Working Families Tax Credit or Working Tax Credit and has earnings below the lower earnings limit, and additionally where he spends part of the week on jury service.

Remunerative employment 16.9

A claimant will not be entitled to contributory JSA if he is in remunerative employment, which results in his working on average for 16 hours or more per week. Remunerative employment is defined as work of 16 hours or more per week, which is done in realistic expectation of payment.

Therefore, if a claimant works for 16 hours or more on average and at the time of doing so he expects to be paid for that work, but is subsequently not paid, he will still be treated as being in remunerative work for that period and will not be entitled to JSA. This may apply where the claimant is self-employed and works to secure contracts, which he does not actually secure, or where he undertakes work and is not paid by the person engaging his services. Alternatively, it may apply where a claimant has worked for a friend or relative or employer who implied that the claimant would be paid for his work, but subsequently does not pay him.

This rule will not apply where the claimant is working for a voluntary or charitable organisation as a volunteer, where he is reimbursed for 'out of pocket expenses' such as travel etc, the reason being that the work was undertaken as a volunteer with no expectation of payment.

Available for employment 16.10

If claiming JSA for the first time following a period of employment, or following the completion of specific training or education, a claimant may only be required to make himself available to undertake work of a similar nature to his previous job or occupation and/or work that he is suitably qualified to do. This is called a 'permitted period' and the length of the period can vary between one and 13 weeks.

The permitted period will be agreed between the claimant and the Employment Service officer, and the time allowed will be specific to the claimant in question, but will take into consideration the likelihood of the claimant securing employment in that field (*SI 1996 No 207, Reg 16*).

However, in all other cases claimants must satisfy the very strict rules of making themselves available for work.

This requirement involves a claimant being able to take up an available job immediately should one become available. There are, however, some exceptions to this rule, in particular where a claimant is unable to start work immediately because of caring responsibilities, i e a single parent needing to make provision for the care of dependent children or a person caring for a disabled person who needs to make provisions for someone else to care for the disabled person, or if the claimant is working voluntarily for a charitable organisation. In these circumstances the claimant would have to be available to start work at 48 hours' notice.

Additionally, the claimant must be available and prepared to work for at least 40 hours per week, but must be prepared to accept employment of less than 40 hours per week. However, unless provision is made in the claimant's jobseekers agreement, the claimant can refuse any offer of employment of less than 24 hours per week (*SI 1996 No 207, Reg 72(5A)(b)*).

The requirement of availability must be satisfied for each individual week of claiming benefit; there are some exceptions to this rule, however, where a claimant will be treated for a short period as being available for work in a week that he is not. These are quite prescribed circumstances (see **CHAPTER 7**) (*SI 1996 No 207, Regs 53–55*).

Actively seeking work 16.11

A claimant will be required to demonstrate that he has taken steps to find employment and/or improve his prospects of finding employment during each week that he is claiming benefit. This may include:

- making applications for employment (oral or written);

- attending the jobcentre or other recruitment agency to see if any suitable jobs are being advertised;

- registering with an employment agency, either in person or by registration on the Internet;

- looking for job vacancies in newspapers, magazines or employers' vacancy bulletins;

- securing assistance with the preparation of a CV; or

- attending a job club.

A claimant will be required to show that he has complied with the requirements to take 'steps' (which means that a claimant must show that he has taken at least two steps) to find or increase his prospects of securing employment each week.

Claimants may also be required to change the steps, or increase the steps that they are taking to find employment, where after a period of time the steps that they have been taking have proved to be unsuccessful.

Written jobseekers agreement 16.12

The agreement will set out the steps that a claimant agrees to take to find work or to increase his prospects of finding work.

Payment of benefit will require a jobseekers agreement to be signed by both the claimant and an officer of Jobcentre Plus. However, the Jobcentre Plus officer will not sign the agreement unless he is satisfied that the contents will satisfy the requirement of availability and actively seeking work. If there is a disagreement in the proposed agreement, either party can refer it to the Secretary of State for a decision as to whether the agreement should be effective.

The Secretary of State should make a decision within 14 days, giving such directions as he feels appropriate. Any such directions will be binding. If the claimant disagrees with the decision or directions then he will be able to appeal to the appeal tribunal (see **CHAPTER 4 CLAIMS, DECISIONS AND APPEALS**).

After the agreement has been signed, it may subsequently be changed to take into account any changes in the claimant's circumstances or changes in the job market. (See **CHAPTER 7** for further details.)

Suspensions of benefit   16.13

If JSA is not awarded because the Jobcentre Plus officer is making further enquiries into the claimant's entitlement to the benefit, under the direction of the Secretary of State, he may suspend any entitlement to JSA pending the outcome of that enquiry.

Benefit can be suspended where:

- the claimant has lost his job through misconduct or has left his employment without good cause or fails to make himself available for work. Benefit can be suspended for a period of between seven days and 26 weeks; or

- the claimant has failed to attend or complete a training scheme or employment programme. Benefit will be suspended for a fixed period of two weeks (or four for persistent offenders).

Amount payable   16.14

The assessment of entitlement to contributory JSA will be based on the claimant being allocated a set rate of payment. The amount will depend on the claimant's age. The rates for 2006/07 are:

- £34.60 per week for claimants aged under 18;

- £45.50 per week for claimants aged 18–24;

- £57.45 per week for claimants aged 25 and over.

There are no dependant additions payable but these may be claimed through income-based JSA (see **CHAPTER 7**).

The claimant's set rate of payment will be reduced where the claimant receives income from earnings (either employed or self-employed earnings).

The net earned income that the claimant receives will attract an earnings disregard of £5 and benefit entitlement will be reduced by any amount by which the claimant's income exceeds £5. For the assessment of net earned income see **CHAPTER 2 ASSESSMENT OF MEANS**.

Additionally, the claimant's set rate of payment will be reduced if the claimant is in receipt of an occupational pension which exceeds £50 per week. The amount of the reduction will be the amount by which the occupational pension exceeds £50. So, if the claimant receives an occupational pension of £246 per month, equating to £56.62 per week (£246 × 12 divided by 365 × 7 = £56.62), his entitlement to contributory JSA will be reduced by £6.62 per week.

EXAMPLE ASSESSMENT

Timothy is married with one dependent child. He has recently been made redundant, but he does have an occupational pension from the army of £246 per month and he also works as a bar man for six hours per week earning £30 per week.

His wife is working and earns £20,000 per annum. The couple have savings of £12,000.

Contributory JSA will be assessed as follows.

Prescribed JSA amount		*Income*		
Claimant aged over 25	£57.45	Timothy's earnings	£30.00	
		less disregard	£5.00	
		Assessable earnings		£25.00
		Occupational pension	£56.62	
		less disregard	£50.00	
		Assessable pension		£6.62
Total	**£57.45**	**Total**		**£31.62**

The award of contributory JSA to which Timothy will be entitled will be £25.83 per week, i e standard allowance of £57.45 less assessable income ➡

> £31.62 = £25.83 per week contributory JSA. This can be paid for up to
> 168 days in any benefit year.

If a claimant does not qualify for any monetary award of contributory JSA because his means do not allow, he should continue to 'sign on' (and will be required to satisfy all the qualifying conditions of entitlement to contributory JSA) in order to ensure that he continues to receive Class 1 National Insurance credits.

Job Grant   16.16

From October 2004 the previously available 'back to work bonus' was abolished, and replaced by a new Job Grant.

Job Grant is aimed at helping people who have been in receipt of Income Support, Jobseekers Allowance, Severe Disablement Allowance or Incapacity Benefit for six months or more when they leave benefit to start full-time work. Claimants receiving benefit for six months or more may be eligible for a payment of £100 (£250 for lone parents and couples with children), and four weeks' additional assistance with rent or mortgage interest. Claims should be made to Jobcentre Plus, on leaflets JSP1 or WK1. These grants are payable under the *Employment and Training Act 1973, section 2.*

How to claim   16.17

Before claiming JSA a claimant must either attend his local jobcentre to make an appointment to go along and 'sign on' for JSA, or telephone Jobcentre Plus to make an appointment to sign on. (See **7.23** above for further details of how to claim.)

Payments of contributory JSA will generally be paid fortnightly in arrears directly into the claimant's bank account. However, a claimant may request that benefit be paid by way of a benefit payment book or benefit smart card, and in such circumstances payments of this benefit will be made fortnightly. No benefit will be paid in respect of the first three days of unemployment, unless the claimant was receiving an alternative earnings replacement benefit immediately before claiming JSA.

Challenging decisions   16.18

Once benefit has been assessed, the claimant will be sent a full written decision in respect of the claim. If a claimant is not happy with the decision for whatever reason, he will need to ask that the decision be reviewed. Such applications for review must be made in writing and delivered to the decision maker within one month of the date of the notification of the original decision.

The decision maker will look at the claim again and take into account any new information that the claimant has raised in his application for review. The decision maker will then issue a further decision, and if the claimant is not happy with that decision, he may, in certain circumstances, appeal to the Appeals Service, but must do so within one month of the date of issue of the most recent decision (see **CHAPTER 4**).

Common problems   16.19

1. The claimant does not sign on at his due date and his benefit is immediately withdrawn.

The claimant may request a review of this decision, but will have to show good cause for not having signed on – having forgotten will not satisfy the requirement of good cause. However, if the reasons were due to unforeseen circumstances such as adverse weather conditions disrupting public transport, or a domestic emergency arising, or the reason was due to the claimant being ill, then benefit may be reinstated.

Applications for reviews must be made in writing and should include any reasons or information relevant to the circumstances (see **CHAPTER 4**).

The claimant should also make a new benefit claim immediately in order that benefit can be reinstated at the earliest possible date. If his request for a review is refused, he would have lost further entitlement to benefit while awaiting the outcome of his application for review.

If the claimant does not apply for a review then, on reclaiming benefit, he may have any entitlement to JSA suspended for a period of up to 26 weeks. This is because by not signing on when he should have, the claimant could be deemed to have failed to make himself available for work.

2. The claimant claims contributory JSA in December and although he has been working for the last two years, he does not satisfy the contribution conditions at the time of making the claim.

The claimant cannot qualify for contributory JSA if he does not satisfy the contribution conditions. However, he may well satisfy the contribution conditions in the next benefit year as this will look at contributions falling to be paid or credited a year later.

Therefore, in circumstances such as these, the claimant could reapply for contributory JSA after the first Sunday in January (which is the start of the new benefit year).

Checklist

Claim specification	Details
Basic entitlement conditions	Claimant must not be working, or working for less than 16 hours per week, and must satisfy the NIC conditions by having paid and been credited with Class 1 NICs in the two years prior to claiming. Claimant must be resident in the UK. Claimant must be available for and actively seeking full-time work and be required to enter into a jobseekers contract. Entitlement is not means-tested but will be reduced if the claimant is earning and/or in receipt of a pension of more than £50 per week.
Dependant additions	None (but income-based JSA could be claimed).
Where to claim	Claims must be made on a prescribed JSA application form obtainable from the local jobcentre. A claimant must also attend an initial jobseekers interview and enter into a written jobseekers agreement which is contractually binding.
How difficult is the claim form to complete?	The form is quite simple, requiring factual information about the claimant. The claimant will also have to provide proof of all earned income and pension with this claim and evidence of his last payment details. This is a short form requiring approximately 30 minutes for completion. The claimant will also be required to state what he intends to do to find work and how he will do this. This is often quite difficult as whatever the claimant says he will do, he must do, otherwise his benefit entitlement could be suspended.

Claim specification	Details
Changes of circumstances that need to be notified	Any changes in the claimant's circumstances at all, including changes in hours of work, changes in pension, going into or out of hospital, going on holiday, changes in disability etc, change of address, whether the claimant claims or receives any other benefits. The claimant must also notify of any changes that he wishes to make to his jobseekers agreement and these must be agreed with Jobcentre Plus before they are implemented.
Frequency of periodic reviews	Reviews can be carried out at any time. However, most claimants will be required to sign on every two weeks, and in effect this requirement produces a fortnightly review. The claimant will have a more detailed review carried out every 13 weeks by attending a restart interview.
Time limits for reviews and appeals	Applications must be made within one month of the date that the decision under review/appeal was issued.
Benefit reductions	Benefit entitlement is reduced if the claimant goes into hospital and his period of sickness is likely to exceed two weeks. He will no longer qualify for this benefit and will have to claim Income Support as an alternative. Benefit will be withdrawn in most cases if the claimant is not available for work in any benefit payment week. If the jobseekers agreement is not complied with the claimant will have benefit entitlement suspended for a fixed period.
Other linked benefits	Can be claimed in addition to income-based JSA, Industrial Injuries Benefit, Housing Benefit and Council Tax Benefit. This benefit does not give any linking entitlement to Social Fund payments and NHS benefits.
Attracting a NICs credit	Yes.
Taxable	Yes.

17 Incapacity Benefit and Statutory Sick Pay

Incapacity Benefit 17.1

Incapacity Benefit is available to those who are incapable of work because of some specific disease or illness and do not qualify for Statutory Sick Pay (SSP) from their employer (see **17.22** et seq below).

Because Incapacity Benefit is what is known as an earnings replacement benefit it cannot be paid in addition to a benefit paid for a similar purpose. These benefits are prescribed as follows:

- contributory Jobseekers Allowance*;

- Severe Disablement Allowance*;

- Maternity Allowance*;

- Carer's Allowance*;

- Retirement Pension*;

- Widowed Parent's Allowance; and

- Bereavement Allowance.

These benefits are known as overlapping benefits. Where a claim is made for Incapacity Benefit and one of the prescribed overlapping benefits is already in payment, the claimant will be awarded whichever benefit will attract the greatest amount of income for the claimant (*Social Security (Overlapping Benefits) Regulations 1979 (SI 1997 No 597), Reg 6, Sch 1*).

If the claimant's partner is in receipt of one of these overlapping benefits and is claiming an additional amount for a dependent partner (who has now claimed Incapacity Benefit), the partner's benefit will be reduced by the amount that was in payment for the dependent partner (the benefits that include a dependant addition are marked *).

Amount payable 17.2

It is paid at three rates which (for 2006/07) are:

- a lower rate of £59.20 for the first 28 weeks of sickness;

- a higher rate of £70.05 for the next 24 weeks of sickness, bringing the sickness period to 52 weeks;

- a long-term rate of £78.50 for those who are sick for more than 52 weeks.

However, where a claimant is in receipt of the highest rate of Disability Living Allowance care component (see **CHAPTER 23 DISABILITY LIVING ALLOW-ANCE**) or is terminally ill (and expected to die within 28 weeks), he will be awarded the long-term Incapacity Benefit after 28 weeks of sickness rather than have to wait for the full 52 weeks to benefit from this increase.

After the first 28 weeks of payment this benefit becomes taxable. This will not, however, apply to those who were in receipt of the old Invalidity Benefit (i e those who have been in continuous receipt of Incapacity Benefit since prior to 13 April 1995).

Where the claimant became incapacitated prior to the age of retirement and then reaches the age of retirement, the benefit will be payable at the following rates for those over retirement age:

- for short-term claimants, i e less than 28 weeks, £75.35 per week with an adult dependant increase of £45.15 per week; and

- a long-term rate of £78.50 per week with an adult dependant increase of £46.95 per week.

Where the claimant has a partner he can claim an adult dependant allowance of £36.60 per week for short-term Incapacity Benefit claimants, and £46.95 per week for long-term Incapacity Benefit claimants, along with additions for dependent children of £5.60 for the first child and £11.35 for each subsequent child per week, which is payable to both short-term and long-term claimants. A child addition will not be paid if the claimant's partner earns more than £175 per week – this sum increases by £23 for each additional child after the first child.

Claims for child additions can no longer be made after April 2003, when they were replaced by the Child Tax Credit.

If the adult dependant earns any money during the period of the benefit award which exceeds the amount of benefit payable for the adult dependant then no adult dependant addition can be paid.

If the claimant undertakes any work while claiming Incapacity Benefit he will be deemed to be capable of work.

Permitted work 17.3

For many years there have been some limited circumstances where it has been acceptable for someone to do a limited amount of work, while still being 'incapable of work'. These have been based on an assessment of the work as 'therapeutic'. The new 'permitted work' rules replaced the old system of 'therapeutic work' from April 2002, and remove the need for medical certification. The intention is for the new system to work as a 'stepping stone into work'.

There are three categories of permitted work:

- *Permitted work lower limit* – People can earn up to £20 per week in any kind of work with no time limit.

- *Supported permitted work* – Certain people can earn up to £81 per week in certain supported work with no time limit. The DWP must be informed in writing of the work before it ends, and work must be supervised by a public or local authority or voluntary organisation, or be under medical supervision.

- *Permitted work higher limit* – People can earn up to £81 per week in any kind of work of less than 16 hours per week for a 26-week period. This can be extended by another 26 weeks if this could improve capacity for full-time work. The DWP must be notified within 42 days of the work starting. For the period to be extended there must be evidence that the work is likely to improve their capacity to take on full-time work.

There is a further addition to benefit in cases where the claimant became incapable of work before he reached the age of 35. In these circumstances he will qualify for an extra payment of £16.50 per week. Where the claimant became incapable of work between the ages of 35 and 45 he will qualify for an extra weekly payment of £8.25 per week.

Where the claimant has become incapacitated after reaching the age of 45 there will be no additional payment.

Basic rules 17.4

Who can claim? 17.5

Benefit payment is based on the claimant having made sufficient National Insurance contributions (NICs) over a two-year period prior to claiming this benefit. However, claimants who have not satisfied the contribution conditions, but satisfy the personal capability test (see **17.11** and **17.12** below) may qualify for Income Support on the grounds of being incapable of work (see **CHAPTER 6 INCOME SUPPORT**).

Contribution conditions   17.6

Claimants must satisfy two contribution conditions in order to qualify for Incapacity Benefit. The requirements are that the claimant must have paid or been credited with sufficient Class 1 or Class 2 NICs in any two complete tax years prior to the benefit year in which a claim is made, but must have paid contributions in one of the three benefit years preceding the date of claim. (Tax years run from 6 April to 5 April each year and benefit years run from the first Sunday in January to the first Saturday in January of the following year.) (*Social Security Contributions and Benefits Act 1992, s 21.*)

First contribution condition   17.7

The claimant must have actually paid in any one year, within the three years prior to the date of claim, Class 1 or Class 2 NICs with an earnings factor of at least 25 times the lower earnings limit:

- the lower earnings limit in 2001/02 was £72 × 25 = earnings factor of £1,800;

- the lower earnings limit in 2002/03 was £75 × 25 = earnings factor of £1,875;

- the lower earnings limit in 2003/04 was £77 × 25 = earnings factor of £1,925;

- the lower earnings limit in 2004/05 was £79 × 25 = earnings factor of £1,975;

- the lower earnings limit in 2005/06 was £82 × 25 = earnings factor of £2,050;

- the lower earnings limit in 2006/07 of £84 x 25 = earnings factor of £2,100.

Second contribution condition   17.8

The claimant must also have paid or been credited with, in the two years before the date of claim, NICs with an earnings factor of at least 50 times the lower earnings limit. (See **16.8** above.)

Evidence of incapacity   17.9

The first 28 weeks of incapacity will be based on the claimant's inability to do his own job, provided that he has worked for at least 16 hours per week for at least eight weeks in the 21 weeks prior to the date of his claim. In all other cases (and in cases such as these after 28 weeks) the claimant's incapacity will be subject to a personal capability assessment. Therefore, there will be two tests:

- the own occupation test;

- the personal capability assessment (a medical examination carried out for and on behalf of the Secretary of State).

The following rules apply:

- a claimant can be self-certificated for the first seven days of incapacity;

- where the own occupation test applies, the claimant must obtain a certificate of sickness from his own general practitioner;

- where the personal capability assessment applies but the assessment has not been carried out, the claimant's general practitioner will be asked to complete a new prescribed form confirming the claimant's incapacity and stating that the claimant should either refrain from work for an unlimited period of time or for a period of not more than two weeks;

- where the claimant has been found fit for work within the previous 26 weeks, he must show that his condition has deteriorated or that he is now suffering from a new medical condition.

Assessment of incapacity   **17.10**

The assessment for incapacity for the personal capability assessment may be carried out in any of the following ways:

- a questionnaire completed by the claimant – if the claimant fails to complete this without good cause he will be deemed to be fit for work (Form IB50);

- additional information requested by the Secretary of State, for example a medical report from the claimant's general practitioner (Form MED 4); or

- a medical examination by an appointed doctor – if the claimant fails to attend without good cause he will be deemed to be fit for work.

A claimant will be automatically treated as incapable and will not be subject to further testing where:

- he is receiving the highest rate of Disability Living Allowance care component;

- he is registered blind;

- he is suffering from paraplegia, tetraplegia, persistent vegetative state, or dementia;

- he is certified as suffering from a number of prescribed conditions, i e severe learning difficulties, muscle wasting, inflammatory polyarthritis, severe mental illness, or progressive impairment of cardio-respiratory function;

- he is an in-patient in hospital or is under observation as a carrier or has been in contact with an infectious or contagious disease;

- he is receiving regular dialysis, chemotherapy or radiotherapy (but only on the days when he receives this treatment); or

- she is an expectant mother who is not getting Statutory Maternity Pay (SMP) six weeks before the expected date of confinement and two weeks after the birth, or any time during the pregnancy where working would cause a serious risk to the health of the mother or baby.

Personal capability assessment 17.11

A claimant must be suffering from a specific medical condition which affects his ability to perform various functions.

Where the claimant is unable to perform any function he will score the number of points allocated to that function. To qualify for benefit he must score:

- 15 points for physical functions;

- 10 points for mental functions; or

- 15 points for a combination of the two.

However, where the claimant has both a mental and physical incapacity, any points awarded for mental incapacity which amount to five or less will not count, but any points which amount to six or more will be rounded up to nine.

So if the claimant is awarded twelve points on the physical test and four on the mental incapacity test, he will fail his personal capability assessment as only the twelve points for physical incapacity will count.

But if the claimant scores seven points on the physical incapacity test and six points on the mental incapacity test he will be awarded 15 points and will be passed on the personal capability assessment (i e 6 points [rounded up to 9] + 7 = 16 points).

There are two assessments of the claimant's ability to walk, one being to walk on the flat and one being to walk up and down stairs. However, points awarded for these two similar functions cannot be joined together; only the highest scoring points will count in the assessment of the physical test.

The capability for work test, however, will require more information from the claimant than previously required in order to establish whether the claimant would benefit from retraining with a view to increasing his employment prospects.

On receipt of the personal capability assessment application from the claimant, the Secretary of State may call upon the claimant to attend a work-focused interview with a personal adviser, which he must attend (otherwise benefit can be suspended). At the work-focused interview the claimant will be given advice, information and encouragement to look to areas where he might find employment.

The assessment itself   17.12

The personal capability assessment looks at the following functions which the claimant is able to carry out, or is restricted in being able to carry out. Such assessments can be carried out as frequently as is directed by the Secretary of State, but in most cases assessments are carried out at least every two years:

- *Walking* – Points of between 0–15 can be awarded where the claimant cannot walk at all or is only able to walk short distances because of physical disability. In *CIB/3013/97* it was held that a tribunal must take into account not only the point in distance at which the claimant stops walking because of severe discomfort but also the point at which the onset of severe discomfort occurs.

- *Stairs* – Points of between 0–15 can be awarded where the claimant cannot walk up and down stairs at all or is only able to do so with difficulty because of physical disability. *CIB/15804/96* holds that in order to qualify for three points for only being able to walk up and down a flight of twelve stairs 'one step at a time', it is sufficient that the claimant has this problem either while going up or going down; it does not have to apply both while going up and coming down.

  (Points are only awarded for the higher of the 'walking' and 'stairs' categories.)

- *Vision* – Points of between 0–15 can be awarded where the claimant cannot see or is severely visually impaired. *CSIB/13/96* confirms that defective vision can be counted not only under vision but also under any other activities such as going up and down the stairs, so a claimant could, if appropriate, score points under both activities. This seems sensible, as of course a claimant with a bad back can score under any number of different descriptions and there seems to be no reason why vision should be treated any differently.

- *Sitting* – Points of between 0–15 can be awarded where the claimant cannot sit comfortably at all without having to keep moving from the chair, or is only able to sit for a short period of time because of physical disability. *CSIB/38/96* confirms that it is only if the sitting itself causes discomfort that points can be scored; any discomfort which already exists must be discounted. *CSIB/12/96* underlines that the test must relate to an upright chair with a back but no arms and the test for all the sitting descriptors except the first is whether the claimant is suffering discomfort from sitting which after time becomes so uncomfortable that he has to leave the chair.

- *Bending and kneeling* – Points of between 0–15 can be awarded where the claimant cannot bend to touch his knees and straighten up again without severe pain or is restricted in the ability to bend and kneel because of physical disability. *CSIB/38/96* holds that if assistance is required to straighten up from bending the descriptor will be met. *CSIB/12/96* held that where the claimant had been advised by her physiotherapist not to bend and lift things, if there was a real risk which would deter a reasonable person from bending then it might be legitimate to say that the claimant is unable to bend.

- *Manual dexterity* – Points of between 0–15 can be awarded where the claimant has great difficulty in using his hands because of physical disability. *CSIS/17/96* confirms that the use of a pen or pencil must be considered in the light of reasonableness and regularity, and the fact that a claimant completed his claim form himself does not necessarily mean that he must be taken as being able to use a pen or pencil. If the time taken to complete the form was sufficiently long or if the claimant needed to take breaks then he might satisfy the test notwithstanding the fact that he could write to some extent. In *CIB/16237/96* Commissioner Rice confirmed that the words 'cannot use a pen or pencil' mean being unable to physically write with either the left or the right hand, i e whichever is the claimant's dominant hand. If a claimant is ambidextrous or has had to change hands due to injury or disease, he will not satisfy the test so long as he has sufficient use of one hand to write reasonably clearly and at a reasonable speed.

- *Continence* – Points of between 0–15 can be awarded where the claimant suffers from bowel or bladder incontinence at least once per week or less frequently where incontinence is unpredictable. *CSIB/38/96* confirms that it is only if there is some degree of urgency which the exercise of the claimant's will cannot postpone that a claimant can be said to have no voluntary control over his bladder, and any control which is assisted by medication must be ignored. If the claimant does have some degree of voluntary control then the extent to which he actually loses control, either by frequency or actual incontinence, must be considered. In

CIB/14332/96 Commissioner Goodman dealt in detail with the meaning of 'loses control of bowels' and indicated that this can in some cases include the situation where, although the claimant has never actually soiled himself, he would do so unless he were able to get to a nearby lavatory very quickly.

- *Physical activities* – Points are also awarded for the physical activities of:

  - standing;

  - rising from sitting;

  - lifting and carrying;

  - reaching;

  - speech;

  - hearing; and

  - remaining conscious.

- *Mental health* – Points of between 1–2 can be awarded where the claimant suffers from mental incapacity, but this descriptor covers all mental health problems from depression, poor concentration and anxiety to severe learning and communication difficulties.

- *Incapacity test for mental health* – New provisions have been introduced whereby if a claimant identifies a mental health problem on his IB50, the DWP will automatically send a Form IB113–DLS to the claimant's general practitioner which will ask for further details of the claimant's mental health. Following the completion of this form the DWP-appointed doctor would carry out a full mental health assessment in any medical assessment for the capability for work test.

Disqualification   17.13

A claimant will be disqualified for up to six weeks where:

- he has become incapable through his own misconduct;

- he fails to attend treatment which might improve his condition;

- he fails to refrain from behaviour which inhibits his recovery;

- he moves house without leaving a new address.

How to claim 17.14

Claims for Incapacity Benefit should be made directly to the claimant's local DWP office, where he will be required initially to complete a claim Form SC1. This should be accompanied by a certificate of sickness from the claimant's general practitioner.

No payment of benefit will be made for the first three days of incapacity; thereafter he will qualify for the short-term award of benefit for a period for 364 days before falling into entitlement to the long-term benefit payment.

Periods of incapacity which are separated by eight weeks or less will be linked together to give continuous claims status. However, each period would continue to have the three initial days of waiting before falling into benefit payment on the fourth day of incapacity.

Challenging decisions 17.15

Once benefit has been assessed, the claimant will be sent a full written decision in respect of the claim accompanied by the assessment of points allocated for any personal capability assessment which has been carried out. If a claimant is not happy with the decision for whatever reason, he will need to ask that the decision be reviewed. Applications for revision must be made in writing and delivered to the decision maker within one month of the date of the original decision having been issued.

The decision maker will look at the claim again and take into account any new information that the claimant has raised in his application for review. The decision maker will then issue a further decision, and if the claimant is not happy with that decision, he may, in certain circumstances, appeal to the Appeals Service, but must do so within one month of the date of issue of the most recent decision (see **CHAPTER 4 CLAIMS, DECISIONS AND APPEALS**).

Common problems 17.16

1. The claimant is refused benefit following the first submission of his completed IB50.

Frequently, new claimants incorrectly complete their initial application form of self-assessment because of a failure to understand the full meaning of the questions put before them.

If the claimant's doctor has advised him to refrain from work in consequence of a disability or illness the claimant should always look to challenge any refusal of entitlement. However, in challenging decisions it is important that the claimant seek advice and assistance with regard to the requirements of the personal capability assessment.

Advice may be obtained from any Citizens Advice Bureau, Welfare Rights Office, trade union, and many other local advisory groups in the claimant's locality. Advice can also be obtained from Community Legal Service Direct on 0845 345 4 345. Contact details can be found on the Community Legal Service website (www.clsdirect.org.uk).

2. The claimant is refused benefit following a review of his entitlement after a further medical examination has been carried out.

If a claimant is not happy with the outcome of a decision he may apply for a revision, but where the claimant has been refused benefit following a medical assessment, applications for revision are rarely successful without the claimant providing substantial further medical evidence that would bring the medical report on which the decision was based into question.

In the majority of cases the claimant will have to appeal to an appeal tribunal (see **CHAPTER 4**). It is, however, important to note that any appeal hearing can only consider the claimant's circumstances and health as it was on the date the original decision to refuse benefit was made. There can be no consideration of the claimant's condition or deterioration in the time he is waiting for the appeal hearing.

Statutory Sick Pay 17.17

Who can claim? 17.18

To qualify, the claimant must be in employment, must be under 65 (whether the claimant is a man or a woman) and must be earning more than £84 per week gross (for 2006/07).

It is not payable while there is a stoppage of work due to a trade dispute at the claimant's place of work, nor is it payable while the claimant is entitled to SMP or Maternity Allowance.

To be eligible for payment the claimant must have been incapable of work because of illness or injury for four consecutive days (including Sundays and days on which the claimant would not normally work). This period is called a 'period of incapacity for work'. Absences of less than four consecutive days do not count, and so if the claimant is off work ill on Monday, back at work on

Tuesday, off Wednesday and Thursday and back on Friday there is no period of incapacity for work. If, however, he is off work continuously from Monday to Thursday then he will be eligible.

When he will first be entitled to receive a payment, however, depends on which of those days count as 'qualifying days', that is days when the claimant would normally be required to work. This is because SSP is only payable to a claimant for days when he would normally be required to work – qualifying days – and is not made for the first three qualifying days of absence ('waiting days').

Amount payable 17.19

There is now one set rate of SSP, being £70.05 per week for 2006/07 (some employment contracts have more favourable sick pay schemes).

'Earnings' means the average of the claimant's gross pay over a period of eight weeks immediately before the beginning of the period of entitlement, whether those earnings are representative or not. In other words, it is the average of the claimant's actual earnings over the eight weeks prior to the claim, even if the claimant usually earned more or less than this. During those eight weeks payments of maternity pay or SSP, or weeks when no payment at all was made, will all count.

Unlike most other benefits, SSP is paid to the claimant by his employer rather than by the DWP.

If, however, the employer does not or will not pay SSP, the claimant can request that HMRC makes a decision about his SSP entitlement. He does this by registering a claim SSP14 with the NI contributions office of HMRC. The address can be obtained from any local HMRC office. Any decision made by HMRC will be binding on the employer.

Ceasing payment 17.20

Once payment has commenced it will continue until whichever of the following first occurs:

- the claimant's period of incapacity for work comes to an end;

- the claimant's contract of employment ends, although if an employer dismisses solely or mainly for the purpose of avoiding payment of SSP he will continue to be liable to pay;

- the claimant has been incapable of work for 28 weeks – this does not have to be a continuous period as any two periods of incapacity for work (i e four or more consecutive days of illness) which are separated by not more than eight weeks are treated as one single period;

- the claimant is disqualified because of pregnancy;

- the third anniversary of the beginning of the period of entitlement – because the periods of absence do not have to be continuous, and because absences from the same employment with less than eight weeks between them are linked together it is, in theory, possible for entitlement to stretch over more than three years, for example one week off sick, seven weeks back at work, another week off sick, seven weeks back at work etc; or

- the claimant goes outside an EU country.

Once the 28 weeks' entitlement to SSP has been exhausted, it will not be possible to claim SSP again until at least eight weeks after the end of that period of incapacity, i e until the claimant has been back at work again for eight weeks.

How to claim   17.21

Notification of absence   17.22

The claim is, of course, made to the employer, who cannot insist upon the claim being made on a special form.

Notice of absence should, however, be given in writing unless there is agreement to the contrary and if given by letter will be deemed to have been given on the day it was posted.

The claimant must notify the employer of his absence through sickness within seven days of his first day of incapacity, or earlier if there is an agreement to that effect, but an employer cannot require notification to be given before the end of the first qualifying day.

If there is good cause for delay a late claim must be accepted unless the delay is longer than 91 days from the first day of absence.

Checklist   17.23

Claim specification	Details (*Incapacity Benefit*)
Basic entitlement conditions	Claimant must be certified as being incapable of work by a doctor following the first seven days of sickness. He will have to undergo a personal capability assessment which will be subject to a medical examination carried out by a DWP doctor. The claimant must have paid or been credited with sufficient NICs in the three years before the year of claim. The claimant must be under the age of 65.
Dependant additions	Dependent partner addition payable where partner's income is not more than the amount of the dependant addition for any partner.
Where to claim	Claim forms can be obtained from any local DWP office.
How difficult is the claim form to complete	Quite simple, requiring only factual information. This is a short form requiring approximately 20 minutes for completion.
Changes of circumstances that need to be notified	If the claimant recovers or his medical condition improves. If the claimant's income details change, or the income details of the claimant's partner. If the claimant changes address. If the claimant claims any other contributory benefit. If the claimant wishes to do any part-time work while claiming benefit.
Frequency of periodic reviews	Reviews can be carried out at any time, there is no specific requirement for a fixed-term review.
Time limits for reviews and appeals	Applications must be made within one month of the date that the decision under review/appeal was issued.
Premiums attracted for IS, HB and CTB	Where the long-term higher rate benefit is in payment the claimant will qualify for a disability premium or higher pensioner premium (if over 60).
Other linked benefits	Can be claimed in addition to Income Support, Housing Benefit and Council Tax Benefit.

Claim specification	Details (*Incapacity Benefit*)
Attracting a NICs credit	Yes.
Taxable	Yes after the first 28 weeks (but not if the claimant has been in continuous receipt since prior to 13 April 1995).

18   Industrial Disablement Benefit

Introduction   18.1

Industrial Injuries Disablement Benefit is a non-contributory weekly benefit payable to claimants suffering loss of faculty as a result of an industrial accident or specified disease contracted while engaged in certain employment. It is not taxable.

This means that provided a person is in employment when he suffers an injury or disease he can qualify regardless of how long he has been in that employment or whether he has paid any National Insurance contributions (NICs). Therefore, in theory, a claimant could start work for a new employer and suffer an injury on the first morning of employment – this injury would be a qualifying injury for the purpose of claiming this benefit.

Basic rules   18.2

Who can claim?   18.3

The claimant must be an employee (i e an employed earner, not a self-employed person) and must have either suffered injury by accident in the course of his employment, or contracted a disease or illness as a result of his employment *and* be suffering continuing symptoms as a result of the accident or disease.

The claimant must establish either:

*   that he has suffered personal injury as the result of an accident in the course of his employment; or

*   that he has contracted one of a list of specified diseases or illnesses in the course of his employment, which must be one of the employments listed in *Schedule 1* to the *Social Security (Industrial Injuries) (Prescribed Diseases) Regulations 1985 (SI 1985 No 967)*.

This schedule prescribes certain types of diseases that may qualify for this benefit and the type of occupation that the claimant would have to be engaged in when he contracts the disease. (A full list of these diseases and occupations can be found in *Tolley's Social Security and State Benefits Looseleaf*.)

For example, noise-induced deafness will only entitle the claimant to benefit if it was contracted while the claimant was working in one of the occupations listed (e g using a chain saw in forestry work) and not if it was contracted while, say, the claimant was working as a long-distance lorry driver.

Industrial Disablement Benefit can be claimed whether or not the claimant has returned to work because it is not means-tested and simply depends on the claimant having a disability; it will therefore continue to be paid even if the claimant goes back to work.

If the claimant remains incapable of work it can be paid in addition to Incapacity Benefit, or can be paid in addition to contributory Jobseekers Allowance if the claimant is not working but is found to be capable of some work.

It is payable from three months (90 days) after the accident or the onset of the disease. If a claim is made later it can be backdated for three months.

For example, a claimant had an accident at work in 1975 and damaged his back and has been troubled ever since, but was not aware of this benefit or did not think that he could claim it because he has continued to work (which is commonly the case). Now he has severe arthritis (which is a direct result of that accident). He could claim Industrial Injuries Benefit, but will not be able to recover the benefit that he could have reasonably claimed since 1975. He will only be able to claim this benefit from three months prior to the date of his application.

How benefit is calculated 18.4

The benefit works on the basis that a normal person is to be regarded as 100% fit and the degree of disablement is then assessed in percentage terms. Certain injuries have fixed percentages of disablement attached to them.

For example, loss of a hand and a foot is equivalent to 100% disablement, loss of an arm through the shoulder joint is equivalent to 90% disablement, loss of a thumb, 30%, loss of a whole index finger, 14%, or the loss of an index finger tip with no bone damage, 5%, and so on (*Social Security (General Benefit) Regulations 1982 (SI 1982 No 1408), Sch 2*).

Most injuries, however, such as broken arms or legs, head injuries, back strains etc do not have a fixed percentage value but are instead assessed by a regional medical officer who will carry out an examination of the claimant and determine what he considers to be the correct percentage of disablement.

The amount payable then depends upon the degree of disablement, based on the 'loss of faculty'; so, for example, an assessment of 100% will result in a payment of £127.10 per week, 80% will be £101.68 per week, 40% will be £50.84 per week and so on. (Lower weekly payments are made if the claimant is under 18 and has no dependants.) (See **CHAPTER 1 INTRODUCTORY MATERIALS** for full rates.)

If the claimant has been assessed and then subsequently suffers a further non-industrial injury, the result will depend on whether the original assessment was more or less than 14%. If less, the subsequent injury is ignored altogether – if more, then the two injuries are assessed together and then the value of the second injury is deducted.

For example, if the claimant has an industrial accident and loses two fingers, he will be assessed at 20% disabled; if he then has a non-industrial accident and loses two more fingers on the same hand, the loss of four fingers would normally be assessed at 50%. As the loss of two fingers is specified at only 20%, this is deducted from the total of 50% leaving 30%. Therefore, the claimant's entitlement to benefit will be assessed as 20% and the additional 30% disablement will not qualify for benefit.

Similarly, if the claimant has been assessed as 20% disabled following a back injury, and then falls in the street, injuring his back further, he may well be extremely disabled and assessed as 40% disabled, but his additional disability will not be attributable to an industrial accident. Therefore, his assessment for the purpose of benefit entitlement will remain at 20%.

Amount payable   18.5

If the assessment is more than 20% it will be rounded either up or down to the nearest multiple of 10% (so 23% will be rounded down to 20% while 27% will be rounded up to 30%) and multiples of 5% will be rounded upwards. Any assessment between 14% and 19% will be rounded up to 20%.

If the assessment is less than 14% then the claimant will not receive any payment unless:

- he first became entitled to disablement benefit before 1 October 1986, before which date an assessment of only 1% was sufficient to receive a payment. So, if as the result of an accident in 1985 a claimant received an award of 8% and has continued to qualify ever since, he will carry on receiving payment; or

- the claimant is suffering from pneumoconiosis, byssinosis or diffuse mesothelioma when only 1% disability is required for payment to be made.

How to qualify 18.6

The claimant must first establish that at the time the disability commenced he was employed as an 'employed earner', i e a person 'gainfully employed in Great Britain either under a contract of service or in an office including elective office with emoluments chargeable to income tax under Schedule E'.

He does not, however, have to satisfy any conditions as to how many NICs he has paid, so if, for example, he is unfortunate enough to have an accident on his first day at work he will be eligible.

The benefit is not available to the self-employed, nor to people on employment training or youth training (although the DWP administers a similar scheme for those on a government approved training scheme).

Next he must establish:

- *either* personal injury resulting from an industrial accident arising out of and in the course of his employment; *or*

- that he is suffering from a prescribed industrial disease; *and*

- that as a result he has suffered loss of faculty, either physical or mental; *and*

- that as a result of that loss of faculty he is disabled.

How to claim 18.7

A claim for a declaration of industrial accident should be made on Form BI 95, obtainable from the DWP.

However, such a claim does not constitute a claim for benefit; a separate claim for Disablement Benefit must be made on the appropriate claim Form BI 100A, again obtainable from the DWP. The claimant will be required to undergo a medical examination.

The *Social Security (Claims and Payments) Regulations 1979 (SI 1979 No 628), Regulations 24, 25, Sch 4* prescribe the minimum information required in a claim:

- full name and address and occupation of the injured person;

- date and time of accident (e g at 11.50 am on 15 July 1999);

- place where the accident happened (e g shop name on Market Street, Wigan);

- cause and nature of injury (e g fell over a box and suffered severe sprain to right ankle); and

- name, address and occupation of the person to whom the injury was reported (e g John Smith, store manager at shop, Market Street, Wigan).

Where a claimant has suffered more than one industrial injury, he must make a separate claim for each injury as soon as possible after the injury occurs. If the claimant is a professional footballer, for instance, he will need to make a claim in respect of each injury he sustains (this could easily be many in number).

Should a claimant's injury deteriorate once an assessment has been made, for instance, if arthritis develops etc, the medical board's assessment can be reviewed at any time under what is known as the 'unforeseen aggravation' procedure.

This is particularly useful if a claimant has been assessed as disabled, awarded benefit, but then fully recovers, but later in life he has a reoccurrence of the effects of the injury.

Length of award 18.8

There are two types of disablement benefit award: provisional and final.

A provisional award will run for a fixed period, usually six or twelve months, after which there will be a further medical examination to review the situation at that time.

Provisional awards are made in the sort of case where a definite prognosis cannot yet be made, such as a back injury with possible disc involvement; the medical situation would be unlikely to remain the same but it might be impossible to predict how things would develop, in that it could get better or worse. Alternatively, the claimant could be waiting for an operation, the outcome of which is uncertain.

A provisional award could, therefore, give an automatic power to review the position after a fixed period of time has elapsed. Quite often in difficult cases a series of provisional awards might be made over several years while the degree of disablement is monitored.

Alternatively, in a clearer, more obvious case, a final award could be made immediately. This could be either for a fixed period, say of two years, for a straightforward whiplash neck injury where a full recovery was likely within that time; or the award could be for an indefinite period in a situation where there was clearly going to be no significant change in the claimant's condition, for example the loss of a leg or an arm.

Disqualification 18.9

The same grounds for disqualification from disablement benefit apply as to Incapacity Benefit (see **CHAPTER 17 INCAPACITY BENEFIT AND STATUTORY SICK PAY**) except that a claimant cannot be disqualified for behaving in a manner likely to retard his recovery.

Challenging decisions 18.10

Once benefit has been assessed, the claimant will be sent a full written decision in respect of the claim. If a claimant is not happy with the decision for whatever reason, he will need to ask that the decision be reviewed. Such applications for review must be made in writing and delivered to the decision maker within one month of the date of the original decision having been issued.

The decision maker will look at the claim again and take into account any new information that the claimant has raised in his application for review. The decision maker will then issue a further decision and if the claimant is not happy with that decision, he may, in certain circumstances, appeal to the Appeals Service, but must do so within on month of the date of issue of the most recent decision (see **CHAPTER 4 CLAIMS, DECISIONS AND APPEALS**).

Common problems 18.11

1. The claimant had an injury at work many years ago, and the employer has not retained any information relating to that accident so the claimant cannot prove that he had an accident at work.

The benefit authority is only required to obtain evidence relating to an injury from the claimant's employer. If this is not available, for whatever reasons, it is the responsibility of the claimant to provide evidence that the injury occurred on that date at his place of work. This evidence may be obtained by a witness statement from any person who actually witnessed the accident or by verifying the accident by any other means available, which may be persuasive in showing that 'on the balance of probability' the accident did occur at work. For instance, if the claimant had to go to hospital or to his doctor, the fact that he had an accident at work will be noted on the hospital medical records. The injury can then be cross-checked against the claimant's statement, occupation and nature of employment, resulting in very persuasive evidence that an accident did actually occur.

2. The claimant has had an assessment of disablement and is not happy with the percentage allocated.

For instance, the claimant has developed arthritis resulting from the injury and has been deemed to be 40% disabled, but only with 10% being allocated to the injury, the remaining 30% being classed as constitutional (inherent in the nature of a person) and not resulting from the industrial accident.

Unfortunately, the older a claimant is, the more likely this type of outcome to an assessment. It is up to the claimant to prove otherwise, which is very difficult to do without obtaining an independent medical opinion. The independent opinion should address the extent of percentage of disablement the claimant would have in the circumstances where he had not suffered the industrial injury. This type of opinion can only usually be obtained from a consultant who, in the majority of cases, will charge the claimant for his professional services.

Claimants should be aware that most trade unions have funds to assist in the cost of obtaining such medical opinions for their members. Additionally, Legal Services Commission funding may also be available for the claimant who requires this evidence for an appeal. However, entitlement to such funding will depend on a means test of the claimant's ability to pay for legal services.

Checklist   18.12

Claim specification	Details
Basic entitlement conditions	Claimant must have suffered an injury or disease during the course of his employment (in paid employment for an employer). He must continue to suffer from a disablement for more than 90 days as a result of the injury.
Dependant additions	None.
Where to claim	Any local DWP office.
How difficult is the claim form to complete?	Quite simple, requiring only factual information. This is a short form requiring approximately 20 minutes for completion.
Changes of circumstances that need to be notified	If the claimant is no longer suffering from the disablement that benefit is paid in respect of. If the claimant changes address.
Frequency of periodic reviews	Reviews can be carried out at any time and there is no specific requirement for a fixed-term review other than as directed by the period over which the assessment is made and this will be prescribed.

Claim specification	Details
Time limits for reviews and appeals	Applications must be made within one month of the date that the decision under review/appeal was issued.
Premiums attracted for IS, HB and CTB	None.
Other linked benefits	Can be claimed in addition to any other means-tested or non-means-tested benefit; can also be claimed regardless of whether or not the claimant is working.
Attracting a NICs credit	No.
Taxable	No.

19 Carer's Allowance

(Social Security (Invalid Care Allowance) Regulations 1976 (SI 1976 No 409)).

Introduction

19.1

Carer's Allowance (CA) is a non means-tested benefit that is paid to someone who cares for a severely disabled person. This benefit can be paid regardless of whether the claimant has previously paid National Insurance Contributions (NICs) or not. Until April 2003 it was called Invalid Care Allowance.

Overlapping benefits rule

19.2

Because CA is what is known as an earnings replacement benefit it cannot be paid in addition to a benefit paid for a similar purpose – these benefits are prescribed as follows:

- Incapacity Benefit*;

- Severe Disablement Allowance*;

- Maternity Allowance*;

- Retirement Pension*;

- Widowed Parent's Allowance;

- Bereavement Allowance.

These benefits are known as overlapping benefits – where a claim is made for CA and one of the prescribed overlapping benefits is already in payment, the claimant will be awarded whichever benefit will attract the greatest amount of income for the claimant *(Social Security (Overlapping Benefits) Regulations 1979 (SI 1979 No 597), Reg 6, Sch 1)*.

If the claimant's partner is in receipt of one of these overlapping benefits and is claiming an additional amount for a dependent partner (who has now claimed CA), the claimant's benefit will be reduced by the amount that was in payment for the dependent partner (the benefits that include a dependant addition are marked *).

CA is available for people who spend 35 hours per week or more caring for a disabled person who is in receipt of the Attendance Allowance (see **CHAPTER 24 ATTENDANCE ALLOWANCE**) or Disability Living Allowance (see **CHAPTER 23 DISABILITY LIVING ALLOWANCE**) care component paid at the middle or higher rate. The claimant does not have to be living with the disabled person to qualify for CA, so it can be claimed by relatives, friends or neighbours of the disabled person.

If a disabled person has more than one carer, only one of those carers can claim the benefit. If the carer is caring for two qualifying disabled people, the claimant can only claim CA for one of those disabled people.

The claimant must be aged 16 or over at the date of claiming CA. Until October 2002 there was an upper age limit of 65 for claiming CA. Previously, someone still receiving CA on reaching 65 could then continue to receive it, even if he was no longer caring for a disabled person. It continued as a sort of non-contributory retirement pension for those without entitlement to a pension. Since October 2002, however, anyone making a claim after age 65 has to meet the normal caring conditions of entitlement and continue to do so.

In practice, this removal of the upper age limit will mainly benefit those without entitlement to a retirement pension, and those eligible for Income Support or the Pension Credit. Entitlement to CA, even if it is not received due to the overlapping benefit rules, still gives entitlement to the carer premium of £26.35 per week.

CA is not means-tested. However, if the claimant earns more than £84 per week he will not qualify for this benefit, as he will be deemed to be 'gainfully employed' and as such excluded from entitlement.

If a claimant is in receipt of one of the above overlapping benefits, he should still make a claim for CA, as by doing this he will attract an additional carer's premium which will increase any entitlement to Income Support, income-based Jobseekers Allowance, Pension Credit, Housing Benefit or Council Tax Benefit that the claimant might have.

Who can claim? 19.3

(Social Security Contributions and Benefits Act 1992, s 70).

At the date of claiming CA, and for each week of entitlement thereafter, the claimant must:

- be ordinarily resident in Great Britain, and must have been present in Great Britain for 26 weeks in the last twelve months (though short periods of absence of up to four weeks will not count) *(SI 1976 No 409, Reg 9)*;

- be aged over 16 *(SI 1976 No 409, Reg 11)*;

- not be in full-time education – full-time education is where the claimant is receiving at least 21 hours per week supervised study (meal breaks and unsupervised study do not count) (*SI 1976 No 409, Reg 5*);

- not be gainfully employed – the claimant will be deemed to be gainfully employed where he is working and earning £84 or more per week after deduction of tax, NICs and 50% of any pension contributions; and any care costs that the claimant pays to another person (who is not a close relative of the claimant or disabled person) to look after the disabled person or a child of the claimant who is under the age of 16, to the value of up to 50% of the claimant's net earnings (*SI 1976 No 409, Reg 8; Social Security Benefits (Computation of Earnings) Regulations 1996 (SI 1996 No 2745), Sch 3*);

- regularly and substantially care for another person for 35 hours or more per week (time spent preparing for the disabled person to visit or cleaning up after the disabled person will count towards the 35 hours) (*SI 1976 No 409, Reg 4*); and

- the person being cared for must be receiving Disability Living Allowance care component middle or higher rate, or Attendance Allowance (either rate) or constant Attendance Allowance (*SI 1976 No 409, Reg 3*).

Amount payable   19.4

The amount payable is £46.95 per week for the claimant, plus an increase of £28.05 for a partner living with the claimant, plus £5.75 for the first child and £11.35 for each additional child living with the claimant. Increases for dependent children cannot be claimed after April 2003 when they were replaced by Child Tax Credit.

The increase for the claimant's partner is payable in respect of the spouse of the claimant, or any adult residing with the claimant, who is looking after a child for whom the claimant is receiving or entitled to receive Child Benefit.

The increase for the claimant's partner will only be paid if the claimant is residing with that person and the partner, if working, is earning less than the amount of the increase. If the partner is in receipt of certain other benefits in his own right, such as Incapacity Benefit, Maternity Allowance, contributory Jobseekers Allowance, State retirement pension or Severe Disablement Allowance, the increase will be reduced pound for pound by the amount of any such award of benefit (*Social Security Benefits (Dependency) Regulations 1977 (SI 1977 No 343), Sch 2(6)*).

If the partner earns more than £175 a week, the child increase will be lost in respect of the first child. For each extra £23 earned by the partner one more child increase will be lost (*SI 1977 No 343, Sch 2(2B)*).

Ceasing payment   19.5

Payment of CA will cease if:

•   the disabled person's receipt of Attendance Allowance, Disability Living Allowance or constant Attendance Allowance stops;

•   the disabled person has been in hospital for four weeks (twelve weeks if he is under 16);

•   the claimant is no longer regularly and substantially caring for the disabled person for 35 hours or more per week. However, the carer will be entitled to some time off simply for a rest, or to enable the disabled person to go into hospital. In effect the rule is that if the carer has only temporarily ceased to satisfy the 35-hour requirement and:

    O   he has satisfied it for at least 14 weeks out of the preceding six months; and

    O   he would have done so for at least 22 weeks out of the preceding six months but for the fact that he or the invalid were in hospital or a similar institution,

    then he will still be entitled to the benefit (*SI 1976 No 409, Reg 4*).

The basic benefit is taxable, as is any partner increase, but the child increase is not.

CA is an earnings replacement benefit, so is taxable but provides the claimant with Class 1 NIC credits.

How to claim   19.6

Claims should be made by completion of a claim Form DS 700, which can be obtained from any local DWP office. The completed form should be sent to the CA Unit, Palatine House, Lancaster Road, Preston, Lancashire PR1 1NS.

Claims for CA can be backdated for up to three months before the date of claim, provided that the claimant can show that he has satisfied all the qualifying conditions of entitlement to this benefit throughout the backdated period.

Payments of CA will generally be paid directly into the claimant's bank account four weekly in arrears. However, a claimant may request that benefit be paid by way of a benefit payment book, and in such circumstances payments of this benefit will be paid weekly or fortnightly.

Challenging decisions 19.7

Once benefit has been assessed, the claimant will be sent a full written decision in respect of the claim. If a claimant is not happy with the decision for whatever reason, he will need to ask that the decision be revised. Such applications for revision must be made in writing and delivered to the decision maker within one month of the date of the original decision having been issued.

The decision maker will look at the claim again and take into account any new information that the claimant has raised in his application for revision. The decision maker will then issue a further decision, and if the claimant is not happy with that decision, he may appeal to the Appeals Service, but must do so within one month of the date of issue of the most recent decision (see CHAPTER 4 CLAIMS, DECISIONS AND APPEALS).

Common problems 19.8

1. The claimant is caring for a disabled person who has only recently applied for Attendance Allowance, which has not yet been awarded.

Where a claimant is caring for a disabled person whose claim for Attendance Allowance or Disability Living Allowance has not yet been determined, he should register his claim for CA in the absence of the decision relating to the disabled person's benefit. If the claim is registered, any decision will be deferred until after the qualifying disability benefit has been determined. However, the claimant's application for CA will be considered from the date of receipt of that claim by the CA Unit, which will ensure that the claimant does not lose any entitlement to benefit because he is awaiting the outcome of another application for benefit.

2. The carer is concerned that the disabled person may suffer a reduction in benefit entitlement if the claimant registers a claim for CA.

Where a disabled person is in receipt of Income Support, Housing Benefit or Council Tax Benefit *and* the disabled person lives alone (i e there are no other people living in the disabled person's home who are over the age of 18), the disabled person would qualify for a severe disability premium to be included in his assessment of entitlement to these means-tested benefits. If, however, the carer claims CA to care for the disabled person, the disabled person will lose any entitlement to the severe disability premium.

This would affect the disabled person's entitlement to Income Support and may affect entitlement to Housing Benefit and Council Tax Benefit if, by losing the severe disability premium, the claimant is no longer entitled to Income Support (see **CHAPTER 9 HOUSING BENEFIT, COUNCIL TAX BENEFIT AND DISCRETIONARY HOUSING PAYMENTS** for example).

If the disabled person does not live alone, or is not in receipt of Income Support, Housing Benefit or Council Tax Benefit, then the carer's claim for CA will not affect the disabled person's entitlement to State benefits at all.

Checklist   19.9

Claim specification	Details
Basic entitlement conditions	Claimant must be spending 35 hours per week caring for a disabled person who is in receipt of Attendance Allowance or the middle rate care component of DLA. The claimant must be aged 16 or over and must not have an earned income of more than £82 per week.
Dependant additions	Dependent partner addition payable where partner's income is not more than £28.05 per week.
Where to claim	CA Unit, Preston (see **19.6** above). Claim forms can also be obtained from any local DWP office.
How difficult is the claim form to complete?	Quite simple, requiring only factual information. This is a short form requiring approximately 20 minutes for completion.
Changes of circumstances that need to be notified	The claimant stops caring for the disabled person. The claimant's earned income details change, or the income details of the claimant's partner. The claimant changes address. The claimant claims any other contributory benefit.
Frequency of periodic reviews	Reviews can be carried out at any time, there is no specific requirement for a fixed-term review.
Time limits for reviews and appeals	Applications must be made within one month of the date that the decision under review/appeal was issued.
Premiums attracted for IS, HB and CTB	Carer premium.

315

Claim specification	Details
Other linked benefits	Can be claimed in addition to Income Support, Housing Benefit, Council Tax Benefit, Industrial Injuries Benefit, Child Benefit and Disability Living Allowance.
Attracting a NICs credit	Yes.
Taxable	Yes (but a dependent child increase is not).

20   Parenthood Benefits

Introduction   20.1

There are five forms of parenthood benefits available to parents:

- *Statutory Maternity Pay* – For those taking maternity leave from employment, which is payable by the claimant's employer.

- *Statutory Adoption Pay* – For those taking adoption leave from employment, which is payable by the claimant's employer.

- *Statutory Paternity Pay* – For those taking paternity leave from employment, which is payable by the claimant's employer.

- *State Maternity Benefit* – Payable by the Secretary of State for those who have been working and earning at least £30 per week, but for some reason do not qualify for Statutory Maternity Pay (i e those who have been employed for less than 26 weeks or self-employed people etc).

- *Sure Start Maternity Grants* – Payable to individuals expecting a baby who are in receipt of certain means-tested benefits.

Statutory Maternity Pay   20.2

A claimant who satisfies the qualifying conditions will be entitled to Statutory Maternity Pay (SMP) regardless of whether or not she intends to return to work after the birth of her child. SMP is paid by the claimant's employer in a similar way to Statutory Sick Pay (SSP) (see **CHAPTER 17 INCAPACITY BENEFIT AND STATUTORY SICK PAY**).

Basic rules   20.3

An expectant mother will qualify for SMP where she:

- has been continuously employed by the same employer for at least 26 weeks up to and including the first day of the 15th week before the expected date of confinement (the 'qualifying week');

- is still pregnant by the eleventh week before the expected date of confinement or has already given birth by then;

- has given her employer at least 21 days' notice of her intention to take maternity leave and has notified her employer of her expected date of confinement;

- earns on average more than £84 (in 2006/07) per week gross; and

- does not undertake any work during the period of payment of SMP.

The claimant must satisfy all of these conditions in order to be paid SMP. If the expectant mother does not satisfy the above requirements she may qualify for State Maternity Allowance instead (see **20.8** et seq below).

Additionally, if the claimant is in legal custody or goes outside the European Community at any time during the first week of the maternity pay period there will be no entitlement to SMP.

'Continuous employment' includes absences from work because of:

- sickness or injury of less than 26 weeks;

- pregnancy; and

- lay-off, or a trade dispute which does not involve the claimant having days on strike.

Continuous employment will also apply to a transfer of employment on a sale or take-over of the employer's business, or a period between unfair dismissal and reinstatement.

'Confinement' means labour resulting in the birth of a living child (if the labour is extremely premature) or labour after 28 weeks of pregnancy resulting in the birth of a child whether alive or dead. If a woman goes into labour on one day and gives birth on the next, the second day is the day of confinement.

Amount payable 20.4

SMP is paid for 26 weeks in total and is paid at two rates, depending on the claimant's normal average earnings prior to the period of maternity leave.

The higher rate is 90% of the claimant's average gross weekly earnings for six weeks, followed by £108.85 (in 2006/07) per week for the next 20 weeks.

The lower rate is paid for the entire SMP payment period where 90% of the claimant's average earnings are less than the standard SMP payment of £108.85. In these cases, the standard SMP of £108.85 will be paid for 26 weeks.

Average earnings 20.5

If the claimant is paid weekly, the average gross weekly earnings are arrived at by averaging the gross wages actually paid for the eight weeks prior to the qualifying week; or if paid monthly, by multiplying the last two payments before the end of the qualifying week by six and dividing the result by 52.

SMP is paid by an employer for a maximum period of 26 weeks (the maternity pay period) to a claimant who is pregnant or who has recently given birth.

Like SSP, it is paid by the employer rather than by HMRC.

Length of award 20.6

As indicated, SMP can be paid for up to 26 weeks, commencing at any time after the start of the eleventh week before the expected date of confinement.

The earliest date from which payment can commence is the start of eleventh week before the expected date of confinement, or – if the claimant stops work later than that – the week after she stops work.

As long as she stops work between the eleventh and sixth week before the expected date of confinement she will receive her full 26 weeks' entitlement.

However, if the claimant continues to work after the sixth week before the expected date of confinement, she will lose entitlement to the lower rate of SMP for each week she works. For example, if the claimant stops work four weeks before the expected date of confinement, she will receive six weeks' SMP at the higher 90% rate and 18 weeks at the standard rate, giving only 22 weeks' entitlement to SMP.

The latest time to stop work and still receive full entitlement will, therefore, be the last day of the seventh week before the expected date of confinement. Payment will then commence on the first day of the sixth week and continue until the first day of the eleventh week after the week of confinement.

Payment will cease after 26 weeks (or such lesser period for which the claimant is entitled in the event of a late claim) has elapsed or until one of the following occurs:

- the claimant dies;
- the claimant is taken into legal custody;
- the claimant goes outside the European Community; or
- the claimant goes to work for another employer after the birth. If she works for another employer before the birth, however, her entitlement is unaffected.

If the claimant works for her usual employer during her maternity pay period she will not receive SMP for any week in which she works.

The maternity pay period will always be a maximum of 26 weeks; it will simply start and end earlier if the birth is premature. If the claimant is still incapable of work when the period expires she should claim SSP or Incapacity Benefit (see **CHAPTER 17**).

If the pregnancy results in a miscarriage, i e death of the foetus in the first 24 weeks of pregnancy, SSP or Incapacity Benefit will be payable instead of SMP.

If the pregnancy results in a stillbirth, i e death of the foetus after 24 weeks of pregnancy, SMP is payable in full, commencing the week after the stillbirth.

The right to SMP is quite separate from the right to return to the same job after the birth. The claimant will be entitled to full SMP regardless of whether she intends to return to work after the birth of the baby.

How to claim 20.7

The claimant should, if possible, give at least 21 days' notice of her intention to take maternity leave. This can be any time between the qualifying week and the sixth week before her expected date of confinement.

The notice should preferably be in writing, and if given late, the claimant will have to provide a reason for the delay. If the employer refuses to accept the reason the claimant can refer the matter to HMRC, and thereafter either party has a right of appeal to the Appeals Service (see **CHAPTER 4 CLAIMS, DECISIONS AND APPEALS**).

The claimant must also supply the employer with medical evidence, usually on a maternity certificate from her doctor or midwife, to confirm the expected date of confinement.

Payment will be made by the employer in the same way as if he were paying wages, and all normal deductions such as tax and National Insurance contributions (NICs) should be made.

The employer will subsequently obtain full reimbursement (in practice by withholding NICs which he would otherwise pay to HMRC).

If the employer simply fails or refuses to pay, or becomes insolvent, the claimant should apply to HMRC for payment to be made by them.

State Maternity Allowance 20.8

State Maternity Allowance (SMA) is a benefit for expectant mothers who have either paid sufficient NICs, or who have been working and earning on average at least £30 per week immediately prior to the maternity leave period.

This benefit, therefore, accommodates those claimants who work for an employer but do not earn £84 (in 2006/07) per week, those who have only recently started work and those who are self-employed when taking maternity leave.

Basic rules 20.9

An expectant mother will qualify for SMA where she:

- has paid Class 1 or Class 2 NICs for at least 26 weeks in the 52-week period up to and including the first day of the 15th week before the expected date of confinement (the qualifying week); and

- is still pregnant by the eleventh week before the expected date of confinement or has already given birth by then; and

- has been employed or self-employed for at least 26 weeks in the period of 66 weeks prior to the expected date of confinement (the 26 weeks in work does not need to be continuous, nor does the work need to have been for the same employer); or

- has been earning on average more than £30 per week for 13 consecutive weeks in the 66 weeks prior to the expected date of confinement; and

- does not undertake any work during the period of payment of SMA.

Amount payable 20.10

SMA is paid for 26 weeks in total and is paid at two rates, depending on the claimant's normal average earnings prior to the period of maternity leave.

The standard rate of £108.85 (in 2006/07) per week will be paid where the claimant has satisfied the contribution condition, either by way of payment of Class 1 or Class 2 NICs.

The lower rate is paid where a claimant earns at least £30 per week, but does not satisfy the contribution condition. The lower rate is 90% of the claimant's average earnings prior to taking maternity leave, up to a maximum of the standard rate of payment of £108.85 per week. In these cases the lower SMA will be paid for 26 weeks.

For example, if the claimant has been working and her average earnings are £50 per week, her SMA will be paid at 90% of this amount, i e £45 per week for 26 weeks.

Average earnings 20.11

When assessing the claimant's average earnings for the lower rate SMA, the assessment will be based on the earnings of the claimant during 13 consecutive weeks in the period of 66 weeks before the expected date of confinement. This assessment must be over a continuous period of 13 weeks, but the claimant can chose which 13-week period is taken into account for the assessment of her average weekly earnings.

Overlapping benefits rule 20.12

Because SMA is what is known as an earnings replacement benefit it cannot be paid in addition to a benefit paid for a similar purpose. These benefits are prescribed as follows:

- Incapacity Benefit*;

- Severe Disablement Allowance*;

- income-based Jobseekers Allowance;

- Carer's Allowance*;

- Retirement Pension*;

- Widowed Parent's Allowance; and

- Bereavement Allowance.

These benefits are known as overlapping benefits. Where a claim is made for SMA and one of the prescribed overlapping benefits is already in payment, the claimant will be awarded whichever benefit will attract the greatest amount of income (*Social Security (Overlapping Benefits) Regulations 1979 (SI 1979 No 597), Reg 6 and Sch 1*).

If the claimant's partner is in receipt of one of these overlapping benefits and is claiming an additional amount for a dependent partner (who has now claimed SMA) the partner's benefit will be reduced by the amount that was in payment for the dependent partner (the benefits that include a dependant addition are marked *).

Length of award 20.13

SMA is payable for 26 weeks (the 'Maternity Allowance period'), the earliest starting date for payment being the beginning of the eleventh week before the expected date of confinement. The rules for calculating the Maternity Allowance period and for premature births are the same as for SMP (see **20.6** above).

How to claim 20.14

If the claimant is employed but does not qualify for SMP she should obtain Form SMP1 from her employers and send it to her local DWP together with a certificate from her doctor or midwife confirming the expected date of confinement. If she is not employed, the claimant should claim between the qualifying week (15th) and the eleventh week before her expected date of confinement.

Sure Start Maternity Grants 20.15

Sure Start Maternity Grants are available to claimants who have a low income and are expecting a baby within eleven weeks or have given birth to a child or have adopted a child under the age of twelve months within the last three months.

Sure Start Maternity Grants are administered by the Social Fund of the claimant's local DWP office, but are only available to those parents or expectant parents who are in receipt of certain means-tested benefits.

Basic rules 20.16

At the date of claim, the claimant or her partner must be in receipt of one of the following means-tested benefits:

- Income Support;
- income-based Jobseekers Allowance; or
- Child Tax Credit at more than the rate of the family element.

The claimant must also obtain from her midwife, health visitor or doctor a signed certificate confirming that she has received advice and information relating to her health needs as an expectant mother and/or the health needs and general welfare of the baby.

If the claim is from an expectant mother, she must provide a certificate confirming her expected date of confinement. If the baby has already been born, she will have to produce the baby's birth certificate, or confirmation of the baby's date of birth if the birth certificate is already in the possession of some other benefit department (e g with Child Benefit, Income Support etc).

If the baby has been adopted, the mother will have to produce the baby's date of birth and the adoption papers or parental order (these should be the original documents and not photocopies). A person caring for a baby under a residence order is eligible to claim, even if no adoption is being considered.

The claim should be made on a Form SF100 Sure Start, which can be obtained from the claimant's local DWP office.

Amount payable 20.17

The Sure Start Maternity Grant is a one-off lump sum payment of £500 per child. The grant is intended for maternity needs and for the cost of providing essential equipment for a baby, such as clothes, a cot and pram etc. Furthermore, new rules have been introduced to ignore any capital that the claimant might have when assessing entitlement to a maternity fund grant.

How to claim 20.18

The claimant must complete Form SF100 Sure Start from her local DWP. The claim must be made on or after the 29th week of pregnancy but within three months following the birth of the child.

If a child is adopted the claim must be made within twelve months of the child's date of birth, but within three months of the date of the adoption.

New paternity and adoption benefits 20.19

From April 2003, two new employer administered benefits were introduced giving adoptive parents and fathers the right to paid time off work around the time of the adoption or birth of their child.

Parents of children due to be born, or placed for adoption, on or after 6 April 2003 may be entitled to:

- 26 weeks' paid adoption leave;
- two weeks' paid paternity leave (adoption);
- two weeks' paid paternity leave (birth).

The new rights apply to people earning above the lower earnings limit (£84 per week from April 2006) who have worked for the same employer for 26 weeks by either the 26th week of the pregnancy, or by the time of the notification of the adoption.

Statutory Adoption Pay (SAP) can be claimed by either the adoptive mother or father if the couple are married, and the parent who does not claim SAP will be able to claim Statutory Paternity Pay.

Statutory Paternity Pay (SPP) – either for birth or adoption – can also be claimed by the partner of the biological mother or adoptive parent, and for this purpose 'partner' includes a same sex partner (*Paternity and Adoption Leave Regulations 2002 (SI 2002 No 2788)*).

Statutory Adoption Pay   20.20

In order to qualify for SAP, an adoptive parent must:

- be adopting a child under UK law up to 18 years of age, from within the UK or overseas;

- have worked for the same employer for 26 weeks by the week in which he was notified of a match with a child for adoption;

- have earned at least the lower earnings limit in the eight weeks leading up to notification of the adoption match; and

- have stopped working for his employer.

An employee wanting to take adoption leave must give his employer notice of intention to take leave within a week of receiving notification of the adoption match. The notice must include a matching certificate provided by the adoption agency, as well as the date the employee wants leave to start. The employee must give 28 days' notice of when he wants SAP to begin, or give notice as soon as is reasonably practicable (*Social Security Contributions and Benefits Act 1992, s 171ZL*). The notice should confirm that the employee has chosen to be paid SAP rather than SPP (adoption).

SAP can be paid from the date of placement, or up to 14 days before the placement is due to begin. If the adoption placement breaks down and the child is returned to the adoption agency, the child dies, or the adoption does not take place after the adoption pay period has already begun, SAP will end after eight weeks.

Amount payable   20.21

SAP is paid for 26 weeks at £108.85 per week, or 90% of average earnings, whichever is lowest.

Statutory Paternity Pay (adoption)   20.22

In order for an employee to be eligible for SPP (adoption) he must:

- fulfil the same employment and earnings conditions as for SAP above;

- be taking leave from work to care for an adoptive child, or to support an adoptive parent;

- still be employed by the same employer when the child is placed for adoption.

An employee wanting to take paternity leave (adoption) must give his employer notice of intention to take leave within a week of receiving the notification of the adoption match. In order to claim SPP (adoption), he must give the employer 28 days' notice of the date SPP is expected to begin, or give as much notice as reasonably practicable. Notice must be in writing, must include evidence of the relationship with the other adoptive parent, and confirmation that the adoptive parent has chosen to be paid SPP (adoption) rather than SAP. The notice must include the date of notification and placement for adoption and the period the employee wishes the SPP to be paid.

SPP can only be paid from the actual date of the adoption placement. If the child is not placed by the day SPP is due to start, the employee must notify the employer that he wishes the SPP to start from a different date. SPP can only be claimed for leave completed within 56 days of the placement for adoption.

Amount payable 20.23

SPP is paid for a maximum of two weeks at £108.85 per week, or 90% of average earnings if this is less. SPP has to be paid for whole weeks and if two weeks are taken they must be together.

Statutory Paternity Pay (birth) 20.24

The employment and earnings conditions for SPP (birth) are broadly the same as those for SMP (see above). The employee must:

- be taking leave from work to care for his child or to support the birth mother;

- have worked for the same employer for 26 weeks by the 15th week before the expected date of confinement (known as the qualifying week). If a baby is born early the employee will qualify if the conditions would have been met had the baby not been premature;

- have earned at the least the lower earnings limit (£82 per week) in the eight weeks leading up to the end of the qualifying week; and

- still be employed by the same employer by the time of the birth.

Someone wishing to take SPP (birth) must give notice of his intention to his employer by the qualifying week. He must give 28 days' notice of the date SPP is to start, or as much notice as is reasonably practicable. Notice must include the expected date of birth (or the actual date if relevant), a statement of the employee's relationship with the mother or child, and the period he wishes the SPP to be paid.

SPP can only be paid from when the baby is born. If the baby is not born by the time the SPP is due to start, the employee must notify the employer that he wishes the SPP to start on a different date. SPP must be paid within 56 days of the birth, unless the baby is premature, in which case SPP may be claimed any time from the birth to 56 days after the expected date of birth. If a baby is stillborn after the 24th week of pregnancy, SPP is still payable and the qualifying week will be the eight weeks leading up to the actual birth.

Amount payable   20.25

SPP is paid for a maximum of two weeks at £108.85 per week, or 90% of average earnings if this is less. SPP has to be paid for whole weeks and if two weeks are taken they must be together.

Dismissal and payment   20.26

If an employee had worked for an employer for at least eight weeks and the contract was terminated in order to avoid paying SPP or SAP, the employee will still be treated as fulfilling the qualifying conditions.

SAP and SPP cannot be paid in any week in which the person is entitled to SSP. Employers are reimbursed SAP and SPP in the same manner as SMP. The rules for challenging decisions on SAP and SPP is the same as for SMP and SSP.

Challenging decisions   20.27

Once benefit has been assessed, the claimant will be sent a full written decision in respect of the claim. If a claimant is not happy with the decision for whatever reason, he will need to ask that the decision be reviewed. Applications for review must be made in writing and delivered to the decision maker within one month of the date of the original decision having been issued.

The decision maker will look at the claim again and take into account any new information that the claimant has raised in his application for review. The decision maker will then issue a further decision and if the claimant is not happy with that decision, he may, in certain circumstances, appeal to the Appeals Service, but must do so within one month of the date of issue of the most recent decision. (See **CHAPTER 4**.)

Checklist

Claim specification	Details
Basic entitlement conditions	Claimant must be expecting a baby in the next eleven weeks and have been working for at least 26 weeks during the 66 weeks prior to the date the baby is due. The claimant must not be working at all during the period of payment of this benefit.
Dependant additions	Dependent partner addition payable with Maternity Allowance where partner's income is not more than £36.60 per week. There are no additions for dependent children.
Where to claim	Claim Forms MA1 can be obtained from any local DWP office.
How difficult is the claim form to complete?	Quite simple, requiring only factual information. This must be completed and returned to the DWP with a Mat B1 (certificate from midwife confirming pregnancy and due date) on or after the 14th week before the baby is due. This is a short form requiring approximately 15 minutes for completion.
Changes of circumstances that need to be notified	If the claimant leaves the country, is detained in custody, returns to or undertakes any paid work, or the income details of the claimant's partner change. If the claimant changes address, if the claimant claims any other contributory benefit.
Frequency of periodic reviews	Paid only for 26 weeks, but review can take place if necessary at any time.
Time limits for reviews and appeals	Applications must be made within one month of the date that the decision under review/appeal was issued.
Premiums attracted for IS, HB and CTB	None.
Other linked benefits	Can be claimed in addition to any means-tested benefit, i e Income Support, Housing Benefit and Council Tax Benefit, but cannot be awarded in addition to any earnings replacement benefit.

Claim specification	Details
Attracting a NICs credit	Yes.
Taxable	Yes.

21 Retirement Pensions

Introduction 21.1

Retirement pensions become payable once a claimant reaches State retirement age – presently this is 60 for a woman and 65 for a man. The retirement age is to be equalised at 65 for both men and women over a ten-year period starting in April 2010 (*Social Security Act 1986; Pensions Act 1995; Welfare Reform and Pensions Act 1999; Child Support, Pensions and Social Security Act 2000*).

Overlapping benefits rule 21.2

Because State Retirement Pension (SRP) is what is known as an earnings replacement benefit it cannot be paid in addition to a benefit paid for a similar purpose. These benefits are as follows:

- income-based Jobseekers Allowance;

- Incapacity Benefit*;

- Severe Disablement Allowance*;

- Maternity Allowance*;

- Carer's Allowance*;

- Widowed Parent's Allowance; and

- Bereavement Allowance.

These benefits are known as overlapping benefits. Where a claim is made for SRP and one of the prescribed overlapping benefits is already in payment, the claimant will be awarded whichever benefit will attract the greatest amount of income (*Social Security (Overlapping Benefits) Regulations 1979 (SI 1979 No 597), Reg 6, Sch 1*).

If the claimant's partner is in receipt of one of these overlapping benefits and is claiming an additional amount for a dependent partner (who has now claimed SRP), the partner's benefit will be reduced by the amount that was in payment for the dependent partner (the benefits which include a dependant addition are marked *).

Basic rules 21.3

SRP is divided mainly into three categories:

- Category A, payable on the claimant's contribution record;

- Category B, payable on a spouse's contribution record; and

- Category D which is non-contributory but only payable to those aged over 80.

A claimant does not have to retire upon reaching State retirement age and has the option to carry on working if he wishes.

Category A and B SRP may be deferred for five years in return for which the claimant will become entitled to a higher rate of pension. At 2006/07 rates, this amounts to an additional:

- £8.76 per week with one year's deferment; or

- £17.53 per week with two year's deferment, increasing to £43.82 per week with five year's deferment.

Category A retirement pensions 21.4

The amount payable (for 2006/07) is:

- claimant: £84.25;

- adult dependant: £50.50;

- child dependant: £11.35 (not claimable after April 2003).

Payment of a full retirement pension is dependent on the claimant having satisfied two contribution conditions prior to the date of claiming his pension.

First condition 21.5

The claimant must have actually paid Class 1, 2 or 3 National Insurance contributions (NICs) of at least 52 times the weekly lower earnings limit in a tax year since 1978, or Class 1 of at least 50 times the lower earnings limit in a tax year between 1975 and 1978; or have paid at least 50 flat rate NICs in a tax year before 1975.

Where the claimant was receiving Invalidity Allowance (i e long-term higher rate Incapacity Benefit or Severe Disablement Allowance), on attaining State retirement pension age he will also be treated as having satisfied the first contribution condition.

Second condition **21.6**

The claimant must show that his contribution record shows that he has fulfilled the minimum number of NICs (which may have been paid or credited or a combination of the two) during the qualifying tax years in his working life. (For the extensive details of requirements see *Tolley's Social Security and State Benefits Looseleaf, Chapter 21.*)

If, at any time, the claimant is not sure whether he may qualify for a full SRP or wishes to establish exactly what is needed by way of contribution payments prior to his retiring, he can obtain a detailed pension forecast at any time by writing to the Retirement Pensions Forecast Agency at the Pensions and Overseas Directorate, Tyneview Park, Whitely Road, Newcastle Upon Tyne NE98 1BA.

When a claimant is aged 80 or over he will receive a further addition of 25p per week.

In addition to the basic SRP, a claimant may qualify for a graduated pension and an additional pension based on SERPS and/or a higher pension where retirement pension has been deferred.

All retirement pension recipients will receive a £10 Christmas bonus.

Category B retirement pension for married women **21.7**

This is payable to married women whose husbands have satisfied both the Category A contribution conditions and both members of the couple have reached retirement age.

In cases where the husband has been receiving an adult dependant increase with payment of Category A retirement pension, any Category B retirement pension for a married woman will replace that dependant addition.

The reaction of most claimants to this rule is to say that there is little point in claiming. However, as retirement pension is taxable it could prove to be beneficial for tax purposes as each member of the couple would be allocated individual tax allowances.

In addition to this, the claimant will receive a further 25p when aged 80 or over plus a higher pension where retirement pension has been deferred.

All retirement pension recipients will receive a £10 Christmas bonus.

Category B retirement pension for widows and widowers   21.8

This is payable to those widows whose late spouse satisfied the contribution conditions or whose spouse died as a result of an industrial injury or disease, provided that the widow was aged 60 or over when he died. Those widows who had not reached retirement age at the date of their spouse's death will receive a Bereavement Pension (see **CHAPTER 22 BEREAVEMENT BENEFITS**).

The amount payable (for 2006/07) is:

- claimant: £84.25;

- child dependant: £11.35 (not claimable after April 2003).

A claimant aged 80 or over will receive a further addition of 25p per week. In addition to this, a claimant may qualify for a higher award based on the spouse's graduated pension, and an additional pension based on the late spouse's entitlement to SERPS, and/or a higher pension where retirement pension has been deferred.

All retirement pension recipients will receive a £10 Christmas bonus.

Payments will not cease if the widow remarries or starts to live with a partner as man and wife after attaining retirement age.

Category D retirement pension   21.9

This can be claimed by pensioners who are aged 80 or over and who are ordinary residents of the UK and who are not entitled to any other retirement pension which is less than the current rate of this pension.

The amount payable (for 2006/07) is:

- claimant: £50.50.

In addition to this the claimant will receive an extra 25p per week because he is aged over 80 and a Christmas bonus of £10.

How to claim   21.10

Retirement pensions must be claimed on attaining State retirement age and in cases where no claim has been made, the claimant will be treated as having 'deferred' his retirement.

Claimants will normally be invited to claim retirement pension several months prior to attaining retirement age. It is only by responding to this invitation that a claimant will generate the process for the registering of his claim in time for it to come into payment on the date of his reaching retirement age.

The claims can be made at any DWP office and the claim process is very straightforward, with no assessment of means required. However, claims can take several months because of the requirement for checking contribution conditions.

Challenging decisions   21.11

Once benefit has been assessed, the claimant will be sent a full written decision in respect of the claim. If a claimant is not happy with the decision for whatever reason, he will need to ask that the decision be reviewed. Applications for review must be made in writing and delivered to the decision maker within one month of the date of the original decision having been issued.

The decision maker will look at the claim again and take into account any new information that the claimant has raised in his application for review. The decision maker will then issue a further decision, and if the claimant is not happy with that decision, he may appeal to the Appeals Service, but must do so within one month of the date of issue of the most recent decision. (See **CHAPTER 4 CLAIMS, DECISIONS AND APPEALS**.)

Common problems   21.12

1. The claimant reaches retirement age and has expected that his pension will come through automatically, but this has not happened. The most common reason for this is that the claimant has not responded to the invitation to claim issued several months earlier.

The claimant should immediately telephone his local DWP office to advise them that he has not received his pension – whether the claim has been registered or not can be established within minutes. If the claim has not been registered he must ask for a claim form, this will be issued for his completion.

The claim will ask from what date the claimant wants his pension to be paid. He can ask for it to be paid from the date of his having attained retirement age. However, this benefit cannot be backdated for more than three months.

For example, if the claimant attained the age of retirement on 10 May 2005 and claims his pension on 29 July 2005 he will be paid his pension from the date of his retirement.

If, however, he claims on 10 October 2005 he will only be paid from 10 August 2005 (three months prior to the date of claim).

Checklist

Claim specification	Details
Basic entitlement conditions	Claimant must have attained State retirement age and satisfied all required contribution conditions prior to retiring.
Dependant additions	Dependant partner addition payable where partner's income is not more than £57.45 per week.
Where to claim	Claim forms can be obtained from any local DWP office.
How difficult is the claim form to complete?	Quite simple, requiring only factual information. This is a short form requiring approximately 20 minutes for completion.
Changes of circumstances that need to be notified	If the claimant changes address, if the claimant claims any other contributory benefit.
Frequency of periodic reviews	Reviews can be carried out at any time, there is no specific requirement for a fixed-term review.
Time limits for reviews and appeals	Applications must be made within one month of the date that the decision under review/appeal was issued.
Premiums attracted for HB and CTB	Pensioner premium or enhanced pensioner premium, or higher pensioner premium (dependent on age and disability).
Other linked benefits	Can be claimed in addition to Pension Credit, Housing Benefit, Council Tax Benefit, Industrial Injuries Benefit, Disability Living Allowance or Attendance Allowance.
Attracting a NICs credit	No.
Taxable	Yes.

22   Bereavement Benefits

Introduction   22.1

The *Welfare Reform and Pensions Act 1999* made provision for new benefits to give support in bereavement to be introduced in April 2001. The changes affected both widows and widowers, who are now treated equally. The changes only affected those claimants who registered a claim following the date of implementation. Those claimants already in receipt of, or who had claimed, Widow's Pension or Widowed Mother's Allowance before April 2001 were not affected by the changes.

There are three bereavement benefits which can be claimed by an applicant whose spouse has died. Entitlement to the bereavement benefits, in most cases, is dependent on the deceased spouse having paid sufficient National Insurance contributions (NICs) prior to the date of death. (Contributions made by the widow or widower will not count.)

Basic rules affecting all
bereavement benefits   22.2

The applicant for the bereavement benefit must have been legally married to the deceased at the date of death. However, benefit will not be payable where:

- the claimant was divorced from the late spouse;

- the claimant is living with someone else as man and wife;

- the claimant has remarried; or

- the claimant is in prison or being held in legal custody.

The three benefits are:

- bereavement payments – replacing the previous widow's lump sum payment;

- Widowed Parent's Allowance – replacing the Widowed Mother's Allowance; and

- Bereavement Allowance – replacing Widow's Pension.

Bereavement payments 22.3

Bereavement payments are a tax-free lump sum payment of £2,000, which an applicant may apply for following the death of a spouse. This benefit can only be claimed where:

- the deceased was not entitled to retirement pension at the date of death; or

- the applicant was under the State retirement pension age at the date of the spouse's death, and

the deceased must have paid sufficient NICs prior to his death, or his death must have been caused by his employment.

Widowed Parent's Allowance 22.4

Widowed Parent's Allowance is a taxable benefit, which includes a basic allowance for the applicant, additions for each dependent child (if claimed prior to April 2003) (see **CHAPTER 3 CLAIMING FOR THE FAMILY**) and any qualifying entitlement to additional State Earnings Related Pension (SERPS) that the deceased may have had. Payments will be equivalent to those previously paid under the Widowed Mother's Allowance scheme. These rates are set out at **22.7** below.

The applicant must be:

- in receipt of or entitled to Child Benefit in respect of any dependent child; or

- expecting a child of the late husband, with whom she was living at the date of his death. (This includes any pregnancy as a result of artificial insemination or in vitro fertilisation as long as the widow was living with her late husband at the date of his death.)

The deceased spouse must have made sufficient NICs prior to death.

This benefit will be available to widows and widowers equally, and will also be available to widowers whose wife died prior to its introduction.

Bereavement Allowance 22.5

Bereavement Allowance is a taxable benefit which includes a basic allowance for the applicant equivalent to the allowance paid under the previous Widow's

Pension entitlement. The Bereavement Allowance does not include any additional SERPS pension that the applicant's late spouse or civil partner may have accrued prior to the date of death.

This benefit is only payable for 52 weeks following the date of death of a spouse or civil partner, whereas previous Widows Pension payments were not time limited.

The following conditions apply:

- the applicant's spouse or civil partner must have paid sufficient NICs prior to his date of death, or the spouse or civil partner's cause of death must have been in consequence of his employment;

- the applicant must be over the age of 45 at the date of death of the spouse or civil partner; and

- the applicant must not be entitled to Widowed Parent's Allowance.

Applicants who are aged 55 or over when widowed will receive the full bereavement allowance (equivalent to the previous Widow's Pension – see rates in **22.8** below).

Applicants who are aged between 45 and 54 when widowed will receive the rate of Bereavement Allowance reduced by 7% for every year by which their age falls below 55.

For example, a person becoming a widow at the age of 52 will have any Bereavement Allowance reduced by 21%; a person becoming a widow at the age of 45 will have any Bereavement Allowance reduced by 70%.

If the applicant receives the full rate of Bereavement Allowance following the death of a spouse or civil partner (i e the applicant is aged 55 or over at the date of death of the spouse or civil partner), on attaining retirement age he will inherit any additional SERPS pension from the deceased. If the applicant only receives a reduced payment of Bereavement Allowance, he will not qualify for the full rate of inherited SERPS on reaching retirement age. (From 6 October 2002 inherited SERPS will be reduced from 100% to 50% in all cases where an applicant is bereaved and claims Bereavement Allowance after this date.)

Rates 22.6

Rates of Widowed Parent's Allowance from April 2006 22.7

Widowed Parent's Allowance	£84.25
Allowance for first child	£5.65
Allowance for each additional child (child additions only paid if claimed prior to April 2003)	£11.35

Bereavement Allowance 22.8

Age when became widowed	*Reduction*	*Rate of payment*
55 or over	0%	£84.25
54	7%	£78.35
53	14%	£72.46
52	21%	£66.56
51	28%	£60.66
50	35%	£54.76
49	42%	£48.87
48	49%	£42.97
47	56%	£37.07
46	63%	£31.17
45	70%	£25.28

Overlapping benefits rule 22.9

Because Widowed Parent's Allowance and Bereavement Allowance are what are known as earnings replacement benefits they cannot be paid in addition to a benefit paid for a similar purpose. These benefits are prescribed as follows:

- contributory Jobseekers Allowance;

- Incapacity Benefit;

- Severe Disablement Allowance;

- Maternity Allowance;

- Carer's Allowance;

- Retirement Pension;

- Widowed Parent's Allowance.

These benefits are known as overlapping benefits. Where a claim is made for contributory Jobseekers Allowance and one of the prescribed overlapping benefits is already in payment, the claimant will be awarded whichever benefit will attract the greatest amount of income (*Social Security (Overlapping Benefits) Regulations 1979 (SI 1979 No 597), Reg 6, Sch 1*).

Additional help with other linked benefits   22.10

The first £10 of any entitlement to Widowed Parent's Allowance will be ignored in the assessment of any entitlement to Income Support.

The first £15 of any entitlement to all bereavement benefits will be ignored in the assessment of any entitlement to Housing Benefit and Council Tax Benefit.

If the applicant is aged 55 or over when the new bereavement benefit begins and is widowed within the five years following the introduction of the new bereavement benefits, he will be able to claim Income Support, as an alternative to having to meet the requirement of Jobseekers Allowance. (This is because the Bereavement Allowance is only actually paid for 52 weeks following the date of death, therefore most applicants will have to claim an alternative benefit like Income Support or Jobseekers Allowance when payments of bereavement benefit cease.)

Additionally, such applicants will be awarded an extra premium in the assessment of any entitlement to a means-tested benefit (like Income Support, Jobseekers Allowance, Housing Benefit or Council Tax Benefit etc) to the value of £26.80 as soon as payments of Bereavement Allowance cease at the end the 52 weeks' award of this benefit, provided that a claim is made within eight weeks of the Bereavement Allowance ceasing.

How to claim   22.11

Claims for the bereavement benefits should be made to the local DWP where the claimant lives within three months of the date of death of the spouse or civil partner. Claims can be made later, but claimants will lose out on benefit entitlement as these benefits can only be backdated for three months. Applicants will be required to provide an original full death certificate of their late spouse or civil partner. There is also a Pensions Info-Line providing information and impartial advice regarding all pensions and benefits in bereavement: telephone 0845 731 32 33. The advice line can arrange to send a claim form out to the applicant for completion.

Challenging decisions   22.12

Once benefit has been assessed, the claimant will be sent a full written decision in respect of the claim. If a claimant is not happy with the decision for whatever reason, he will need to ask that the decision be revised. Applications for review must be made in writing and delivered to the decision maker within one month of the date of the original decision having been issued.

The decision maker will look at the claim again and take into account any new information that the claimant has raised in his application for revision. The decision maker will then issue a further decision, and if the claimant is not happy with that decision, he may appeal to the Appeals Service, but must do so within one month of the date of issue of the most recent decision (see **CHAPTER 4 CLAIMS, DECISIONS AND APPEALS**).

Checklist   22.13

Claim specification	*Details*
Basic entitlement conditions	The applicant must have been legally married to the deceased, or have been in a registered civil partnership at the date of death, but must not be divorced from his late spouse (or the civil partnership must not have been dissolved), living with someone else as a couple, remarried or be in prison or being held in legal custody. In most cases the late spouse or civil partner must have paid sufficient NICs or have died as the result of an accident at work.
Dependant additions	Only with Widowed Parent's Allowance if claimed prior to April 2003.
Where to claim	Claimant's local DWP.
How difficult is the claim form to complete?	Very simple factual claim forms requiring only 20 minutes or so to complete.

Claim specification	Details
Changes of circumstances that need to be notified	If the claimant remarries, or lives with a partner as a couple, or is held in custody or prison.
Frequency of periodic reviews	No specific requirement but may be reviewed at any time.
Time limits for reviews and appeals	One month from date of issue of any decision.
Premiums attracted for IS, HB and CTB	Bereavement premium.
Other linked benefits	Can be claimed in addition to Income Support, income-based Jobseekers Allowance, Housing Benefit, Council Tax Benefit, Tax Credits, Disability Living Allowance, Attendance Allowance and Industrial Injuries Benefit.
Attracting a NICs credit	Yes.
Taxable	Yes.

23 Disability Living Allowance

Introduction

23.1

Disability Living Allowance (DLA) is a non means-tested, non-contributory, non-taxable benefit and provides a weekly fixed sum for the purpose of assisting a claimant to accommodate his disabled needs. There is no requirement for the assessment of any claimant's income, capital or National Insurance contributions. Furthermore, this benefit can be paid to a claimant regardless of whether he is working or not.

This benefit is only available to claimants who are under the age of 65 at the date of making the initial application, although awards of this benefit can continue to be paid to claimants who are aged 65 or over (for benefits for the over 65s see **CHAPTER 24 ATTENDANCE ALLOWANCE**).

There are two components to DLA:

- *Care component* – This is for help a claimant needs in his home in tending to his personal care requirements or in ensuring that he is supervised to prevent danger to himself or others. However, any requirement for help or supervision must be in consequence of the claimant suffering from a physical or mental disablement. Claimants must also have needed the help or supervision for at least three months and be likely to continue needing that help or supervision for a further six months.

- *Mobility component* – This is for help which a claimant needs outdoors because of mobility problems or because he needs to be supervised outdoors to prevent danger to himself or others. Any mobility problems or requirement for supervision must be in consequence of the claimant suffering from a physical or mental disablement. Claimants must also have needed the help or supervision for at least three months and be likely to continue needing that help or supervision for a further six months.

Disability Living Allowance care component

23.2

DLA care component is a fixed-rate benefit payable to claimants aged under 65 at the date of claim who, because of physical or mental disablement, need help with their daily personal needs or supervision to prevent danger to their health or safety.

It is paid at three different rates which are (for 2006/07):

- highest rate: £62.25 per week;
- middle rate: £41.65 per week;
- lowest rate: £16.50 per week.

Basic rules   23.3

The claimant must be resident in Great Britain and aged 65 or under and living in a private dwelling or in self-funded private residential or nursing home care (i e this benefit is not available for those in NHS or Social Services funded care).

The qualifying conditions   23.4

DLA care component will be payable to a claimant aged 65 or under at date of claim who is so severely disabled, either physically or mentally, and one of the following conditions applies:

(*a*)   He requires attention with his bodily functions for a significant portion of the day, whether during one single period or a number of periods.

For instance, this may occur where the claimant who has arthritis needs help to get up, wash and dress himself and is then perhaps able to cope until bedtime, when the need for help is repeated.

(*b*)   He is aged 16 or over and could not prepare a cooked meal for himself if he had the ingredients.

For instance, where the claimant, in preparing a meal for one person, cannot peel and chop vegetables, or has difficulty using the cooker or holding pans and draining hot pans etc. This difficulty may arise for claimants who have arthritis in their hands, or are visually impaired, or suffer from some mental incapacity. Additionally, where a claimant suffers from visual or mental impairment, choosing appropriate foods, reading and or understanding instructions, sell by dates, use by dates etc may all be factors of relevance.

If either of the conditions in (*a*) or (*b*) above is satisfied the claimant would qualify for the lowest rate of £16.50 per week.

(*c*)   He requires attention with his bodily functions frequently throughout the day.

For instance, where a claimant needs help by way of physical attention or prompting in washing and dressing etc in the morning, then needs help

344

during the day, perhaps in getting around the house, toileting, rising from sitting, eating etc, this may satisfy the test of frequency throughout the day.

(*d*)   He requires continual supervision throughout the day to avoid substantial danger to himself or others.

This may be required where a person has a tendency to fall and hurt themselves, or where a person suffers from fits which come on with no warning, or whose behavioural problems are unpredictable and severe etc.

(*e*)   He requires prolonged or repeated attention in connection with his bodily functions during the night.

The requirement here is for attention that is prolonged. This has been defined by Commissioners as meaning periods of more than 20 minutes. However, regardless of how long a claimant needs attention during the night, there is also alternatively a requirement for the attention to be repeated, i e the claimant must need attention on at least two occasions during the night.

(*f*)   He requires another person to be awake for a prolonged period or at frequent intervals during the night to avoid substantial danger to himself or others.

This involves the need for the claimant to be checked on during the night. It is of significant relevance to a claimant who may be prone to having epileptic fits during the night or to claimants who self harm, or who may wander during the night.

(*g*)   He is undergoing renal dialysis on a kidney machine for two or more sessions per week, the dialysis being of a type which requires, or the claimant in fact requiring, the attendance or supervision of another person (this will include a claimant undergoing dialysis in hospital, provided no member of the staff is assisting or supervising him).

If any of the above conditions in (*c*)–(*g*) are satisfied the claimant will receive the middle rate of £41.65 per week.

(*h*)   The claimant is terminally ill.

(*j*)   He satisfies one of the day tests *and* one of the night tests, i e satisfies (*c*) or (*d*) together with (*e*) or (*f*).

If either (*h*) or (*j*) above is satisfied the claimant will receive the highest rate of £62.25 per week.

The normal upper age for claiming is 65. There is no lower age limit so that the benefit can be awarded to a child or even a baby, although a claimant under 16 cannot qualify by using the main meal test in (*b*) above; he will have to satisfy one or more of the other tests and in addition he will also have to show:

- that he needs attention or supervision 'substantially in excess of the normal requirements of a child of his age'; or

- that he needs substantial attention or supervision 'which younger persons in normal physical or mental health would not have'.

'Severely disabled'   23.5

This must relate to a physical or mental illness or condition which can be medically defined and diagnosed. It does not cover general anti-social or aggressive behaviour, which is not the result of a mental illness.

'Attention'   23.6

This is active assistance or personal service that is reasonably required to enable the claimant to cope with his disability. (It is important to note that a claimant need only show that attention is 'reasonably required' regardless of whether or not the claimant actually receives that service.)

'Bodily functions'   23.7

This involves those activities such as dressing, washing, eating, toileting, reading, communicating etc which a person normally does for himself. However, domestic chores, such as shopping and housework, are not included.

Supervision test   23.8

Supervision is passive and means someone being with the claimant and ready to intervene if necessary, but not actually intervening except in emergencies. However, it may overlap or merge with attention; for example, a claimant who is unsteady on his feet may require supervision while moving about and attention if he actually stumbles or falls. The object of supervision is to avoid substantial danger which may or may not in fact arise, so supervision may be precautionary and anticipatory, yet never result in intervention, or may be ancillary to and part of active assistance given on specific occasions to the claimant.

The danger must be 'substantial', i e real not fanciful, but the test does involve looking to the future as well as to the past, i e just because it has not happened yet does not mean it never will. Even if the risk is remote it could still be substantial, particularly if the consequences are likely to be serious. For example, if the claimant enjoys cooking but has arthritis in the hands which makes it difficult for him to lift heavy pans it could be argued that there is a substantial danger of scalding or burning.

There are four elements necessary in order to satisfy the continual supervision test:

- the claimant's medical condition must be such that it gives rise to a substantial danger either to himself or to someone else;

- the substantial danger must not be too remote a possibility;

- there must be a need for supervision by somebody else to ensure that the claimant avoids the substantial danger; and

- the supervision must be continual.

It is reasonable to expect the claimant to take precautions himself to avoid the risk, unless of course the risk is unpredictable or the claimant is incapable of appreciating the danger.

Disability Living Allowance mobility component

23.9

This is a weekly benefit payable to claimants aged between three and 65 who, because of disability, cannot walk or can hardly walk, or who are deaf and blind or require guidance or supervision while walking.

It is paid at two different rates which are (for 2006/07):

- higher rate: £43.45 per week;
- lower rate: £16.50 per week.

The claimant must be a resident in Great Britain and aged between five and 65 and:

- physically disabled so that he is unable to walk or virtually unable to walk;
- has no feet;
- the exertion of walking is a danger to his health;
- deaf and blind;
- he is severely mentally impaired and has severe behavioural problems so that he is a danger to himself or others;
- is mentally or physically disabled; and

- require guidance or supervision while walking outdoors in unfamiliar surroundings (lower rate).

The qualifying conditions   23.10

Higher rate   23.11

Difficulty in walking   23.12

Legislation prescribes that, to qualify for the higher rate mobility component, a claimant's difficulty in walking must be a result of a physical rather than a psychological cause. In *R(M)1/88*, the Court of Appeal emphasised that the inability to walk is not itself the physical disablement; there must be some physical disablement such that he is unable to walk. Therefore, the mere fact that a claimant is in a wheelchair does not establish entitlement; the reason why he is in a wheelchair has to be investigated. This was re-emphasised by two recent decisions of a Tribunal of Commissioners – *CDLA/2879/2004* and *CDLA/2899/2004*. These held that pain, dizziness or other symptoms are not features of the claimant's physical condition as a whole unless they have a physical cause. However, where there are both physical and mental factors, then the higher rate mobility component may be awarded where the physical disorder is a material cause of the mobility problems.

Most cases will be clear-cut, for example, a claimant who cannot walk because of a spinal injury will qualify whereas an agoraphobic will not, although he may be eligible for the lower rate.

Other cases will not, however, be so straightforward. In *R(M)1/88*, the tribunal's decision to disallow the claim because the claimant's inability to walk was due to hysteria was upheld by the Court of Appeal. However, subsequent psychiatric evidence suggested that the claimant's hysteria was due to pain which resulted from the original injury and subsequent operative treatment.

That opinion gave a physical cause to the hysteria and accordingly a later claim was successful.

As the Court of Appeal said: 'where hysteria is caused by a physical condition (for example, pain due to some spinal condition) the inability to walk may itself be caused by the same physical condition'.

The requirement that a person is unable to walk or hardly able to walk will generally fall into four groups:

(a)   the claimant cannot walk at all – this would generally apply to claimants who are wheelchair-bound because of a physical disablement;

(b) the claimant was born without feet or is a double amputee – cases of this nature are considered to automatically pass the test of entitlement;

(c) the claimant is virtually unable to walk – this heading is the one which gives rise to the majority of claims, and to most difficulties;

(d) the exertion required to walk would constitute a danger to life or would be likely to lead to a serious deterioration in health.

The test which must be satisfied for (c) above is that the claimant is virtually unable to walk, i e can hardly walk or has practically no mobility; it does not simply mean that the claimant's ability to walk is limited, e g that he is confined to the estate where he lives or is unable to walk such a distance as would enable him to carry on a normal life – the lack of mobility must be more than that.

The phrase 'virtually unable to walk' means 'unable to walk to any appreciable extent or practically unable to walk'.

It is therefore a question of degree and each case has to be considered on its own facts. It will always be necessary to look at the four factors to determine whether the claimant's 'ability to walk out of doors' is so limited, as regards the:

- distance over which; or
- the speed at which; or
- the length of time for which; or
- the manner in which,

the claimant can make progress on foot without severe discomfort (including such breathlessness that he is virtually unable to walk).

All four aspects must be considered, no single one of them being decisive. Since distance is only one of the aspects, and there is no set distance laid down in the regulations, the fact that the claimant may perhaps be able to walk 75 to 100 yards will not necessarily mean he will fail the test.

For example, if the claimant has to stop every few yards to rest and regain his breath and so takes 15 minutes to walk a very short distance, the 'manner' of his walking may mean he satisfies the test.

Any walking which is accompanied by severe pain or discomfort (including breathlessness) does not count. So, in simple terms, if the claimant can actually walk 60 yards, but for the final 20 of those yards suffers severe pain or discomfort, those 20 yards must be ignored and he is to be treated as only being able to walk 40 yards.

The ability to walk must be judged out of doors, on the flat, on a reasonably level surface. The test is ability to walk, not ability to climb, and so the fact that the claimant has difficulty walking up hills is irrelevant. Particular problems relating to the area where the claimant lives, e g broken pavements, rough ground, steep slopes etc must also be disregarded.

The test in (d) above includes a condition which might be induced or precipitated by walking, and it must then be established that on a balance of probabilities the exertion involved in walking would involve a danger to life or lead to a serious deterioration in health. The expression does not extend to conditions or symptoms which might intervene during the course of walking without there being any connection or relationship to or with walking or being precipitated by the exertion of walking.

There is no authority on what exactly constitutes a 'serious' deterioration in health; clearly it does not need to be life threatening, as this is specifically covered by 'danger to life' but presumably severe pain or discomfort would qualify, as would cases where the effort of walking on one day, would bring about a situation where the claimant then had to rest for several days in consequence of that action.

Deaf and blind   23.13

The claimant does not have to be totally deaf and totally blind – the degree of deafness required is generally taken as being equivalent to not being able to hear a question from about one metre distance and blindness does not have to be total, but must be equivalent to a 100% disablement assessment, i e the claimant will satisfy this test if he can just about distinguish light and shade.

A claimant who is either deaf or blind would not qualify under this heading, although he may be able to claim the lower rate, as might a claimant with restricted vision.

Mental impairment   23.14

Under the regulations a person is to be treated as being severely mentally impaired if he suffers from a state of arrested development or incomplete physical development of the brain, which results in severe impairment of intelligence and social functioning. It therefore seems clear that only those with a congenital problem will satisfy this test and not those who suffer brain damage in an accident.

In addition to being severely mentally impaired the claimant must have severe behavioural problems, i e he must exhibit disruptive behaviour which:

• is extreme;

- regularly requires another person to intervene and physically restrain him to prevent injury to himself or another or damage to property; and

- is so unpredictable that he requires another person to be present and to watch over him whenever he is awake.

Lower rate 23.15

The lower rate will be paid if the claimant can walk but is so severely disabled physically or mentally that he requires guidance or supervision from another person most of the time to make sure he is safe, e g because he has no road sense or he would otherwise be unable to find his way around even in places familiar to him or because he is unsteady on his feet.

This condition will have to have been in existence for at least three months prior to the date of claim and must be likely to last for at least a further six months after the claim, so that a merely temporary disablement will not suffice.

However, unlike the higher rate, to qualify for the lower rate the cause of the disability could be psychological. It does not have to be physical, and so an agoraphobic could qualify, or a claimant suffering from a mental health problem or severe learning difficulty. A claimant who has poor vision or who is deaf might also qualify if it could be shown that he reasonably required help to get around safely.

Long-term disability requirement 23.16

In view of the fact that at least nine months' disability is required (three months prior to the date of claim and six months after) the benefit is clearly only intended to be payable to the long-term disabled, so that a claimant with a temporary mobility problem such as a broken leg would not be covered.

The only exception to this is in respect of the terminally ill (i e those suffering from a progressive disease who are expected to die within six months) who do not have to satisfy either the three-month or the six-month test. They will be eligible immediately if the claim is made specifically on the basis that the claimant is terminally ill, but such claimants must still satisfy one or more of the qualifying tests (e g unable to walk, virtually unable to walk, deaf and blind etc).

How to claim 23.17

Claims should be made by completing a DLA claim pack which can be obtained from any DWP or by calling the DLA helpline on (lo call) 08457 123456 – this line is open from 8.00 am to 6.00 pm on weekdays.

Claim forms will be dated at the time of issue and a date for the required return of the form will also be identified on the claim form. Benefit will be paid from the date of issue of the form, provided the form is completed and returned to the claimant's local regional Disability Benefits Centre by the date so prescribed.

The claim is primarily a self-assessment and will need to be backed up with medical evidence. The claimant will be required to give details of his general practitioner and any hospital specialist he attends – information may be sought from either of these by the Disability Benefits Centre for the purpose of the assessment of this claim, but more frequently the Disability Benefits Centre will appoint a medical examining practitioner for the purpose of carrying out an independent medical examination of the claimant in his own home.

Although the appointed doctor is trained in carrying out the medical assessment of the claimant for the purposes of the assessment of entitlement to DLA, such assessments have been the subject of many appeals. For this reason a claimant should, where possible, try to obtain his own letter of support for his claim for DLA from his own general practitioner, which should, if possible, be enclosed with the application form when returning it to the Disability Benefits Centre. Other useful supporting evidence may include letters of support from the claimant's social worker, community psychiatric nurse, consultant or health visitor etc.

The assessment of DLA claims can take from several weeks to several months. However, once entitlement has been established payments will be made from the Monday following the date of the issue of the claim form. Payments of DLA will generally be paid directly into the claimant's bank account. However, a claimant may request that benefit be paid by way of a benefit payment book or benefit smart card, and in such circumstances payments of this benefit will be paid weekly or fortnightly.

Challenging decisions   23.18

Once benefit has been assessed, the claimant will be sent a written decision in respect of the claim. If a claimant is not happy with the decision for whatever reason, he will need to ask that the decision be revised. Applications for revision must be made in writing and delivered to the decision maker within one month of the date of the original decision having been issued.

If the claim has been refused based on the medical assessment carried out by the appointed examiner, the claimant will have to obtain supporting medical evidence to substantiate his needs for care or mobility from a suitably qualified person, i e his general practitioner, consultant, social worker etc.

The decision maker will look at the claim again and take into account any new information that the claimant has raised in his application for revision. The decision maker will then issue a further decision, and if the claimant is not happy with that decision, he may appeal to the Appeals Service, but must do so within one month of the date of issue of the most recent decision (see **CHAPTER 4 CLAIMS, DECISIONS AND APPEALS**).

Common problems 23.19

1. The claimant has claimed DLA and his general practitioner has been sent a form of enquiry about the claimant's needs for care or mobility, and based on this information his claim has been refused.

This is a common problem due to the fact that doctors are asked about the claimant's ability to perform certain tasks in the home or his ability to walk etc.

Many patients who visit the doctor do not go on to tell the doctor about the personal difficulties they encounter in consequence of their disability, for the simple reason that there is little or nothing that the doctor can do about it.

There is little that can be done to resolve this matter. However, if the claimant makes his GP aware of the fact that he has registered a claim for DLA and the reasons why, the doctor would be better equipped to deal with any enquiries made of him.

Alternatively, if an unfavourable doctor's report has been obtained, the claimant could request a copy of the report and go and discuss its contents with his doctor, who may be in a position to provide a more favourable slant on the report once all the facts are known to him.

2. The claimant is simply unable to complete the extensive claim form.

If a claimant finds that he is overwhelmed by the claim form or is unable to complete it, the claimant may contact a number of sources to assist him. There are, of course, many sources of advice agency help in certain areas but the level of services provided throughout the country varies.

There is also a telephone advisory service provided by the Disability Benefits Centre and their contact telephone numbers are always included in additional information that the claimant receives with the form. However, obtaining telephone assistance with completing the claim form often proves quite difficult for claimants who are disabled, as such assistance does involve the claimant being on the telephone and responding to questions for several hours.

Checklist

Claim specification	Details
Basic entitlement conditions	Claimant must be aged under 65 and physically or mentally disabled and need help with personal care or supervision, and/or has difficulty in walking or needs supervision while walking out doors. Claimant must be resident in the UK, and any help or supervision that is needed must be needed for at least three months before entitlement can commence and a further six months after date of claim.
Dependant additions	None.
Where to claim	Regional Disability Centre: telephone 08457 123456. Claim forms can also be obtained from any local DWP office.
How difficult is the claim form to complete?	This is one of the most difficult benefit claim forms in the Social Security system. The claim form is in three parts comprising of 48 pages for the purpose of a self-assessment. This claim form will require approximately two hours for completion.
Changes of circumstances that need to be notified	If the claimant goes into hospital or care for more than four weeks, if the claimant's disability improves or worsens and if the claimant changes address.
Frequency of periodic reviews	Reviews can be carried out at any time. Awards are usually made for a fixed period, but if the claimant's condition is unlikely to improve an award can be made for an indefinite period.
Time limits for reviews and appeals	Applications must be made within one month of the date that the decision under review/appeal was issued.
Premiums attracted for IS, PC, HB and CTB	Disability premium, disabled child premium, enhanced disability premium for a child, severe disability premium and higher pensioner premium.

Claim specification	Details
Other linked benefits	Carer may be able to claim Carer's Allowance. High rate mobility component will attract car tax exemption, disabled persons parking badge entitlement, and can be traded for a Motability car if period of award is three years or more.
Attracting a NICs credit	No.
Taxable	No.

24 Attendance Allowance

Introduction

24.1

Attendance Allowance is a non means-tested, non-contributory, non-taxable benefit and provides a weekly fixed sum for the purpose of assisting an elderly claimant to accommodate disabled needs. There is no requirement for the assessment of any claimant's income, capital or National Insurance contributions. Furthermore, this benefit can be paid to a claimant regardless of whether he is working or not.

Attendance Allowance entitlement requires that a claimant is over the age of 65 at the date of claim, and because of physical or mental disablement that he needs help with his daily personal needs or supervision to prevent danger to his health and/or safety.

It is paid at two different rates which are (for 2006/07):

- higher rate: £62.25 per week;

- lower rate: £41.65 per week.

It is available where disability begins at or after age 65 years, or before that age but where the claim is not made until after age 65 years.

The claimant must be ordinarily resident in Great Britain and must either be a British national or not subject to immigration control. No payment can be made while the claimant is an in-patient in a NHS hospital or is in local authority residential accommodation, the idea being that claimants should not be entitled to payment for care needs when those needs are already being met by the State or a local authority. (However, the first 28 days of being in hospital or care do not count.)

Attendance Allowance is payable at two rates, the lower rate being for those who need attention or supervision either by day or by night and the higher rate being for those who need attention or supervision both day and night or are terminally ill (i e expected to die within six months).

There is a six-month qualifying period and the disability must be expected to last for a further six months at least. So twelve months of disability is required, which would rule out someone temporarily incapacitated by a broken leg or some other short-term illness. However, these periods do not apply if a claimant is terminally ill, in which case payment can be made immediately.

Once awarded it will continue to be paid irrespective of age for as long as the qualifying criteria continue to be satisfied. The higher rate may provide a passport to certain other benefits.

The benefit can be awarded either for a fixed period or for an indefinite period. Obviously, if the claimant's condition is expected to improve, either naturally or because of treatment, e g a hip replacement operation, a fixed-term award will be appropriate, whereas if the condition is never likely to improve an indefinite period award will be made.

Lower rate   24.2

The lower rate is for those who either need attention in connection with their bodily functions frequently throughout the day, or who require continual supervision throughout the day in order to avoid substantial danger.

Attention   24.3

It is attention which is reasonably required that counts, not that which is actually provided, so that a person struggling to cope on his own without help could qualify. Quite often elderly people will try their best to cope with everyday living on their own, without help which they might well require, out of a sense of independence and pride, and also perhaps out of fear that if they are seen to be in need of help they may be forced out of their home and into residential care.

It is therefore important to look beyond the stated needs, which may well be understated, and to consider what help is actually required. It is also essential to discount whatever help is in fact being given by relatives or neighbours, and to consider instead how the claimant would cope if left entirely to his own devices. A claimant will often say that he does not do something because his partner or relative does it for him; it is then necessary to consider whether the claimant could do it for himself if the carer was not there.

Bodily functions   24.4

This has a restricted meaning, being limited to things like dressing, washing, bathing, toileting, reading, communicating, getting around the house etc – activities such as shopping or housework are not included.

Seeing and hearing are bodily functions, so that assistance with dressing in the case of a blind or partially sighted claimant would count as attention, as would guidance when walking out of doors; dealing with correspondence could also be relevant, as could physically helping such a claimant to prepare a meal provided it was reasonable for the claimant to prepare a meal himself –

357

although cooking is not a bodily function the seeing and lifting required in order to cook a meal are, and could count towards the total attention needs.

If the needs are concentrated at the beginning and end of the day then the test will not be satisfied as there must be a need for attention 'frequently throughout the day', i e on several occasions during the day.

Helping out of bed, dressing, helping in or out of a bath or shower, washing, toileting, shaving, organising and giving medication, cutting up food, lifting a cup to the mouth, physically helping up from a chair or up the stairs, physically supporting when walking, undressing, helping into bed, would all count as attention in connection with bodily functions.

If the claimant is able to carry out these functions, but in consequence of mental disablement he needs constant prompting to do them, this will also count.

Help with housework, e g vacuuming, washing clothes, ironing, washing up dishes, cooking meals, do not qualify, and neither does shopping.

A useful test of whether an activity counts as a bodily function is to ask whether it can be done in the absence of the claimant; if it cannot then it could well count. If it can, then it undoubtedly will not count.

Communication in the form of interpreting for a deaf claimant by means of sign language could also count as attention in connection with bodily functions, *a fortiori* if the claimant also had difficulty with speech as a result of the hearing loss (many profoundly deaf people being unable to speak). Carrying on a conversation by means of sign language between two people fluent in that language probably would not count, whereas interpreting to a stranger, e g in a shop, would.

Supervision 24.5

'Continual' is different from 'continuous' and would include the situation where the claimant could safely be left alone for short periods.

It must, however, be necessary for the claimant to be supervised for most of the day rather than just on specific occasions or when carrying out particular activities, therefore supervision at bath times or when taking medication would not in itself be sufficient.

Supervision is different from attention in that supervision means keeping an eye on someone and being ready to intervene if the need arises, whereas attention is actually intervening and assisting.

It is not essential that the danger be eliminated by the supervision, i e by being ready at all times to catch someone in danger of falling as this would be virtually impossible, it is sufficient that the supervision reduces the risk of harm.

The most likely candidates to qualify under this head are those who are mentally confused, suffer from grand mal epilepsy or are liable to fall possibly due to dizzy spells or physical frailty.

In respect of falls and epileptic fits, it may be relevant to determine whether these are predictable or not. If they are predictable, i e the claimant gets some warning before they occur, then there may not be a need for supervision as the claimant can take the necessary action himself to prevent harm, e g sitting down, taking medication etc.

Normally petit mal epilepsy will not of itself give rise to a supervision need, as this does not involve unconsciousness or falls, but simply means that the person 'goes off into a world of his own' or goes blank, possibly only for a few seconds at a time. Grand mal, on the other hand, involves actual loss of consciousness and fits with risk of injury either from the fall itself (e g head injury) or from the fit (e g swallowing the tongue).

According to one recent Commissioner's decision, choosing to live alone is an indication that supervision is not needed – this, however, seems somewhat contentious, as many older people will try to maintain their independence for as long as possible by living alone in their own home even when they have a struggle to manage.

Higher rate   24.6

The higher rate is payable if the claimant requires either attention or supervision not only during the day but also during the night. Night is not defined in the regulations but basically covers the period after the household has closed down and gone to bed.

Night time needs might involve rearranging bedclothes, turning the claimant, assisting with medication, helping the claimant to the toilet, changing nightclothes (e g if incontinent). The rule relating to night supervision is somewhat different from the day in that it requires someone to be awake frequently or for prolonged periods to watch over the claimant. The risk of a severe asthma attack or epileptic fit, or the risk of a mentally confused person wandering off, could count.

How to claim 24.7

The claim pack includes a lengthy self-assessment questionnaire and there is space for the claimant's doctor or carer to add his comments. Although medical evidence in support of the claim is not essential, and the Secretary of State can decide straightforward claims on the questionnaire alone, it can obviously be helpful, and sometimes save time, if supporting medical evidence is submitted. The Secretary of State can always request medical evidence if he feels it necessary to do so, either from the claimant's own general practitioner or from a DWP doctor (an examining medical practitioner) who will visit the claimant at his home to carry out an examination and assessment of the claimant's needs.

Claims should be made by completion of an Attendance Allowance claim pack which can be obtained from any DWP, or by calling the Disability Benefits Centre helpline – telephone number (lo call) 08457 123456 (open from 8.00 am to 6.00 pm on weekdays).

Claim forms will be dated at the time of issue and a date for the required return of the form will also be identified on the claim form. Benefit will be paid from the date of issue of the form, provided the form is completed and returned to the claimant's local regional Disability Benefits Centre by the date prescribed.

The claim is primarily a self-assessment and will need to be backed up with medical evidence. The claimant will be required to give details of his general practitioner and any hospital specialist he attends. Information may be sought from either of these by the Disability Benefits Centre for the purpose of the assessment of this claim, but more frequently the Disability Benefits Centre will appoint a medical examining practitioner for the purpose of carrying out an independent medical examination of the claimant in his own home.

Although the appointed doctor is trained in carrying out the medical assessment of the claimant for the purposes of the assessment of entitlement to Attendance Allowance, such assessments have been the subject of many appeals. For this reason, a claimant should, where possible, try to obtain his own letter of support for his claim for Attendance Allowance from his own GP, which should, if possible, be enclosed with the application form when returning it to the Disability Benefits Centre. Other useful supporting evidence may include letters of support from the claimant's social worker, community psychiatric nurse, consultant or health visitor etc.

The assessment of Attendance Allowance claims can take from several weeks to several months. However, once entitlement has been established payments will be made from the Monday following the date of the issue of the claim form. Payments of Attendance Allowance will generally be paid directly into the claimant's bank account. However a claimant may request that benefit be paid by way of a benefit payment book, and in such circumstances payments of this benefit will be paid weekly or fortnightly.

Challenging decisions 24.8

Once benefit has been assessed, the claimant will be sent a written decision in respect of the claim. If a claimant is not happy with the decision for whatever reason, he will need to ask that the decision be revised. Applications for revision must be made in writing and delivered to the decision maker within one month of the date of the original decision having been issued.

If the claim has been refused based on the medical assessment carried out by the appointed examiner, the claimant will have to obtain supporting medical evidence to substantiate his needs for care or mobility from a suitably qualified person, i e his general practitioner, consultant, social worker etc.

The decision maker will look at the claim again and take into account any new information that the claimant has raised in his application for revision. The decision maker will then issue a further decision, and if the claimant is not happy with that decision, he may appeal to the Appeals Service, but must do so within one month of the date of issue of the most recent decision (see **CHAPTER 4 CLAIMS, DECISIONS AND APPEALS**).

Common problems 24.9

1. The claimant has claimed Attendance Allowance and was visited by a DWP visiting medical officer for the purpose of assessing the claimant's needs for care. Based on the medical report obtained his claim has been refused.

This is a common problem due to the fact that a claimant who is examined in his own home by a person in authority may well play down the effect that the disability has on his ability to cope alone (due to fear that he might lose his independence), and often the fact that the claimant does not really see himself as actually needing help because it is already being provided.

For this reason, claimants should always consider having someone with them (preferably a carer) when a visiting doctor examines them.

A claimant who is faced with an unfavourable medical report should request a copy of that report and carefully consider its contents. He should then select any elements of the report that he is not happy with and request a review of the determination (see **CHAPTER 4**). However, where benefit has been refused based on medical opinion, the claimant will need supporting evidence from a suitably qualified person, i e a doctor, social worker, health visitor etc.

Additionally, the claimant might give practical examples of what has happened when care or supervision has not been provided, for instance if the claimant has fallen, if he is forgetful and has left the cooker on or the bath running, if he has not been able to get to the toilet quickly enough etc.

2. The claimant has been examined by a visiting medical doctor who was very helpful and indicated that the claimant clearly needed help, but benefit is still refused.

This is a very common scenario and is of particular relevance where the claimant has played down his own needs for care in his application form. There are generally two common reasons for this, being:

- the claimant is concerned that he might be seen to be incapable of living independently and fears being 'put in a home'; and/or

- the claimant has learned to cope with his disability.

Most elderly claimants do not realise that the Attendance Allowance unit cannot contact Social Services with details of a claimant's need for care without the prior written consent of the claimant. Furthermore, Social Services will only look at providing residential care for a person who wants it, and then only as a last resort. Indeed, Social Services very actively support all applications for Attendance Allowance for and on behalf of their service users.

The claimant having learned to 'cope' with his disability is not one who should be disqualified from assistance under the Attendance Allowance scheme.

The true test of disability is to compare the claimant with a person of the same sex, race and age who does not have the claimant's disability in order to establish whether the care or supervision that the claimant 'reasonably requires' substantially exceeds that of the non-disabled person.

One of the most helpful items of evidence in an appeal or review would be the claimant's copy of any community care plan or community care assessment that has been carried out by Social Services.

Therefore, if the claimant reasonably requires assistance or supervision from another person, whether this is provided or not, he should request that his application be revised and if necessary appealed against (see **CHAPTER 4**).

Checklist

Claim specification	Details
Basic entitlement conditions	Claimant must be aged 65 or over and physically or mentally disabled and need help with personal care or supervision. Claimant must be resident in the UK, and any help or supervision that is needed must be needed for at least six months before entitlement can commence and a further six months after date of claim.
Dependant additions	None.
Where to claim	Regional Disability Centre: telephone 08457 123456. Claim forms can also be obtained from any local DWP office.
How difficult is the claim form to complete?	This is one of the most difficult benefit claim forms in the Social Security system. The claim form is in three parts comprising of 42 pages for the purpose of a self-assessment. This claim form will require approximately two hours for completion.
Changes of circumstances that need to be notified	If the claimant goes into hospital or care for more than four weeks, if the claimant's disability improves or worsens and if the claimant changes address.
Frequency of periodic reviews	Reviews can be carried out at any time, awards are usually made for a fixed period, but if the claimant's condition is unlikely to improve an award can be made for an indefinite period.
Time limits for reviews and appeals	Applications must be made within one month of the date that the decision under review/appeal was issued.
Premiums attracted for IS, PC, HB and CTB	Higher pensioner premium and severe disability premium.
Other linked benefits	Carer's Allowance for carer.
Attracting a NICs credit	No.
Taxable	No.

25　Pension Credit

(State Pension Credit Act 2002; State Pension Credit Regulations 2002 (SI 2002 No 1792)).

Introduction 25.1

Pension Credit (PC) was introduced from October 2003 and replaced Income Support for people over 60, which was also sometimes known as Minimum Income Guarantee. The new credit also provides a 'top-up' for people with modest incomes, from pensions or other sources, over the level of the basic State retirement pension. This is to answer the criticism, long voiced by pensioners' groups, that there was no point in having made modest provision for retirement – by an occupational or personal pension – since it was just deducted from entitlement to Income Support, Housing Benefit and other means-tested provision. This was always a valid point and the savings credit goes some way to addressing this issue.

The credit is administered by the Pension Service, part of the Department for Work and Pensions (DWP).

Key changes 25.2

Although many of the rules are the same as for Income Support for people over 60, the following are the key features:

- the savings credit provides a 'reward' for making private provision for retirement;

- there is no longer a limit on paid work of 16 hours per week;

- there is no upper capital limit;

- the rate of income assumed from capital is £1 per week for each £500, instead of £250 as previously; and

- benefit is paid usually for five years without the need for a reclaim.

Who can claim? 25.3

Guarantee credit 25.4

Someone is eligible for the guarantee credit if he:

- is aged 60 or over;

- is present and habitually resident in Great Britain;
- has an income below the 'appropriate minimum guarantee'; and
- is not subject to immigration control.

Savings credit   25.5

Someone is eligible for the savings credit if he:

- is 65 or over (or has a partner who is);
- is present and habitually resident in Great Britain;
- is not subject to immigration control; and
- has a qualifying income over the savings credit threshold, but not too high to produce an award.

The 'qualifying income' is all the income taken into account for the guarantee credit, other than Working Tax Credit, Incapacity Benefit, contribution-based Jobseekers Allowance, Severe Disablement Allowance, Maternity Allowance and maintenance payments received.

Entitlement to Pension Credit is linked to the minimum age at which a woman can qualify for retirement pension, which is currently 60. This will rise to 65 between 2010 and 2020. The claimant or partner must be 65 or over to claim the savings credit.

PC only provides for the claimant and his partner. No allowances are made for any dependent children, who are provided for via Child Tax Credit.

Calculating the guarantee credit   25.6

The amount of guarantee credit depends on whether the claimant is single, or part of a couple, and whether he has severe disabilities, caring responsibilities or eligible housing costs. The rules about income and capital are very similar to those which apply to Income Support and Housing Benefit (see **CHAPTER 2 ASSESSMENT OF MEANS, CHAPTER 6 INCOME SUPPORT** and **CHAPTER 9 HOUSING BENEFIT, COUNCIL TAX BENEFIT AND DISCRETIONARY HOUSING PAYMENTS**).

The maximum guarantee credit is referred to as the appropriate minimum guarantee and is made up of two parts:

- standard minimum guarantee; and
- if applicable, additional amounts.

The standard minimum guarantee is £114.05 per week for a single person and £174.05 per week for a couple (married or unmarried, same or opposite sex). If there are no additional needs then this is the figure that someone's weekly income should be brought up to. The amounts for additional needs are closely related to the system of premiums and housing costs applying to Income Support.

Severe disability 25.7

Single	Couple
£46.75	£93.50

To qualify as a single person, the claimant must be receiving Attendance Allowance or the middle or highest rate care component of Disability Living Allowance. There must be no one receiving Carer's Allowance for him and there must be no adult non-dependants living with him. For a couple to qualify, both must be receiving the appropriate disability benefit, in addition to the other conditions.

Carer 25.8

Single	Couple
£26.35	£26.35 (for each partner qualifying)

The claimant or partner must have claimed Carer's Allowance for caring for a disabled person. The addition remains payable even if the Carer's Allowance is not actually paid, due to receipt of another higher benefit, such as retirement pension.

Housing costs 25.9

Owner occupiers are able to obtain assistance with some housing costs, mainly associated with mortgages and other secured loans. These rules are virtually the same as apply to Income Support and are probably the most complex area of means-tested benefits. For further detail, refer to **CHAPTER 6**. Those housing costs that are eligible include payments of interest on mortgages and other loans for house purchase, or for certain repairs or improvements, or for some service charges. To be eligible, the claimant or his partner must be liable for the charges. If he shares the costs with someone who is liable, he can be treated as liable for his proportionate share. Where someone else is liable, is not paying and the costs have to be met in order for the claimant to stay living in the property, then he can be treated as liable. This could apply to a mortgage in one party's sole name, where that person leaves following a relationship break-down, leaving the non-liable partner in the property.

The following issues should be borne in mind in relation to housing costs:

- additional borrowing taken out while the claimant was on Income Support, income-based Jobseekers Allowance or PC is not usually eligible for benefit. The main exception to this applies to loans to buy a home more suited to the needs of a disabled person;

- loans are usually only eligible up to a total of £100,000;

- interest charges are met at the DWP standard rate of interest;

- deductions will be made where there are other adults (non-dependants) living in the claimant's household (other than commercial boarders);

- unlike Income Support, housing costs are paid for PC from the start of the claim.

Transitional amount   25.10

People transferring to PC from Income Support or income-based Jobseekers Allowance in October 2003 received an additional allowance if their entitlement to PC would be less than their previous entitlement to Income Support or income-based Jobseekers Allowance.

The amount of the guarantee credit is calculated by subtracting income from the appropriate minimum guarantee.

Calculating income and capital   25.11

Unlike other means-tested benefits, PC has no upper capital limit beyond which there is no entitlement. Instead, a level of notional income from capital is assumed where capital exceeds £6,000 (£10,000 for people in care homes). The rate of 'tariff income' assumed is £1 per week for each £500 above the threshold. Capital includes most assets that are available to the claimant. The main exceptions are:

- the home normally lived in;

- a former home that the claimant is trying to dispose of, or is still lived in by his spouse/partner or other elderly or disabled relative;

- the surrender value of life insurance or endowment policies;

- personal injury compensation whether or not it has been placed in a trust fund.

Capital that someone has deliberately deprived himself of in order to make a benefit claim is added back into the calculation. This does not apply, however, where capital has been used to pay off debts, or to purchase goods or services where this was reasonable in the circumstances.

Most income is taken into account in full for PC. The most common disregards are:

- *Fully disregarded* – Attendance Allowance, Disability Living Allowance, Housing Benefit, Council Tax Benefit, Child Tax Credit, Child Benefit, child support maintenance (spousal maintenance is included, however).

- *£20 disregarded* – From earnings for carers, lone parents and some disabled claimants. Otherwise £10 is disregarded from the earnings of a couple and £5 from a single claimant.

- *£10 disregarded* – From Widowed Parent's Allowance, War Disablement and War Widow's Pensions.

Calculating the savings credit   25.12

This part of the credit applies to claimants with 'qualifying income' over the *savings credit threshold* (this is the level of the standard rate of retirement pension). This is £84.25 for single people and £134.75 for couples. Qualifying income over this threshold, up to the level of the appropriate minimum guarantee, is eligible for the savings credit.

The amount of savings credit is subject to a *maximum savings credit* of £17.88 for single people and £23.58 for couples. The amount of the savings credit is calculated at 60% of the qualifying income over the threshold, up to the rate of the appropriate minimum guarantee.

Where claimants have total income above the level of the guarantee, 40% of this figure is calculated, and deducted from the savings credit so far calculated.

The amount of the savings credit calculated is paid in addition to the guarantee credit.

EXAMPLE

Mr and Mrs A are both over 65. They have a total weekly income of £154.75, made up of £134.75 retirement pension and £20.00 personal pension. Their standard minimum guarantee is £174.05. Their total➡

---

income is £19.30 less than this so they receive guarantee credit of £19.30. They have qualifying income of £20.00 over the savings credit threshold. They are, therefore, entitled to savings credit of 60% of this, namely £12.00. Their total PC entitlement is £31.30.

If the same couple had a personal pension of £50.00 instead of £20.00, their total income would be £184.75. This is higher than the standard minimum guarantee for a couple (£174.05), so they would not receive any guarantee credit. Their qualifying income between the threshold of £134.75 and the level of the appropriate minimum guarantee is £39.30, 60% of which produces a figure of the maximum savings credit of £23.58. However, they have income over the appropriate minimum guarantee of £9.70. Therefore, 40% of this figure (£3.88) has to be deducted from the maximum savings credit, producing an actual savings credit entitlement of £19.70.

Claims and backdating   25.13

People on Income Support immediately before the introduction of PC in October 2003 were treated as having made a claim for PC. They did not have to do anything. All other potential claimants have to make a claim in writing, over the telephone, or in person. If a claim is made over the telephone then a pre-completed form is sent out for the claimant to sign and return.

Claims for PC may be backdated by twelve months, so long as the claimant qualified during that period.

Challenging decisions   25.14

The rules on decisions and appeals for PC are the same as for all other Social Security benefits.

Assessed income periods   25.15

Claimants are normally required to notify the Pension Service of any changes in their income or capital that may affect their benefit. However, certain types of income – known collectively as 'retirement provision' – can be treated as remaining the same for an 'assessed income period' of up to five years. This only applies if both the claimant and any partner are over 65, and applies to income from a retirement pension (other than the state retirement pension), from an annuity and from capital. The retirement provision will be assumed to increase in line with either the contractual terms, or with the Social Security uprating. If the retirement provision decreases during the period then this can be notified and the amount of PC adjusted. Where an assessed income period is notified to the claimant, there is no obligation to notify changes in retirement provision during that period.

People in residential care or nursing homes and hospitals
25.16

PC works in the normal way for people in residential care or nursing homes. However, if the claimant or partner is permanently resident in a care home then they no longer count as a couple. In addition, the lower capital limit, below which no tariff income is assumed from capital, rises to £10,000 from £6,000. If one of a couple is only temporarily in a care home, they still count as a couple if they have not been apart substantially more than 52 weeks.

For people in hospital, there is no effect on the amount of the savings credit. The guarantee credit, however, is reduced after a partner stays in hospital for 52 weeks. After this period, the patient is no longer treated as being part of a couple.

Checklist
25.17

Claim specification	Details
Basic entitlement conditions	Claimant must be at least 60. Any partner may be younger than this. For the savings credit the minimum age is 65. There is no upper capital limit and any capital below £6,000 is disregarded. The claimant must be habitually resident in the UK. Entitlement is wholly subject to a means test of the family unit.
Dependant additions	Additions for a dependent partner and homeowner housing costs are included in any assessment of entitlement to this benefit.
Where to claim	Claims must be made using a prescribed PC application form obtainable from local DWP. Alternatively claims may be made by telephone to 0800 991234

Claim specification	Details
How difficult is the claim form to complete?	Quite simple, requiring factual information about the claimant and family and comprehensive details regarding income and capital. The claimant will also have to provide proof of all income and capital with this claim. This is a long form requiring approximately 30–40 minutes for completion. This can be carried out by a Pensions Service adviser over the telephone.
Changes of circumstances that need to be notified	Any changes in the claimant's circumstances at all, including people moving into or out of his home, changes in hours of work, going into or out of hospital, changes in disability etc. Any changes of address and if the claimant or partner claims or receives any other benefits or sources of income or capital. Some changes of income or capital – known as retirement provision – do not have to be disclosed between claim reviews.
Frequency of periodic reviews	The intention is that claims should be renewed every five years.
Time limits for reviews and appeals	Applications must be made within one month of the date that the decision under review/appeal was issued.
Benefit reductions	Benefit entitlement is reduced if the claimant or partner goes into hospital and is an in-patient for more than 52 weeks. Benefit will be withdrawn in most cases if the claimant or partner goes abroad for more than 28 days.
Other linked benefits	Can be claimed in addition to Housing Benefit and Council Tax Benefit. Otherwise this benefit is paid as a top-up to any other Social Security benefit. Also gives rise to possible entitlement to Social Fund payments and NHS benefits, such as free prescriptions, dental treatment, sight tests etc and free school meals for children of school age.
Attracting a NICs credit	No.
Taxable	No.

Index

[all references are to paragraph number]

A

Actively seeking work
contributory jobseekers
  allowance, and,   16.11
income-based jobseekers
  allowance, and,   7.5

Additional family element
child tax credits, and,   8.13

Additions for dependants
amounts
  2001/02,   1.13
  2002/03,   1.12
  2003/04,   1.11
  2004/05,   1.10
  2005/06,   1.9
  2006/07,   1.7–1.8
backdating, and,   4.38

Adoption pay
amounts
  generally,   20.21
  2001/02,   1.13
  2002/03,   1.12
  2003/04,   1.11
  2004/05,   1.10
  2005/06,   1.9
  2006/07,   1.7–1.8
backdating, and,   4.38
challenging decisions,   20.27
checklist,   20.28
dismissal, and,   20.26

Adoption pay – *contd*
eligibility,   20.20
introduction,   20.19

Affordability
child support assessments,
  and,   14.7

Age of claimant
contributory jobseekers
  allowance, and,   16.5

Annual review
tax credits, and,   8.19–8.20

Appeals
adjournment,   4.31
applications,   4.25
benefits,   4.11
Commissioner, to,   4.35–4.36
composition of tribunal,   4.26
Court of Appeal, to,   4.37
decisions of tribunals,   4.32–4.34
introduction,   4.23
leave to appeal,   4.35
medical examination,   4.27
oral hearings,   4.29–4.31
physical examinations,   4.28
postponement,   4.31
procedures,   4.30
record of hearing,   4.33
setting aside decisions,   4.34
tax credits,   4.10
time limits,   4.24

Applicable amount
disabled facilities grants,
  and,   10.6
housing benefit, and
  challenging decisions,   9.43
  introduction,   9.18
  personal allowances,   9.19
  premiums,   9.20
income support, and
  housing costs,   6.18
  introduction,   6.4
  personal allowances,   6.5
  premiums,   6.6–6.17

Assessment of incapacity
content,   17.12
generally,   17.10
personal capability,   17.12

Assessment of means
community care, in
  and see below
  generally,   11.1–11.17
disabled facilities grants,
  and,   10.4
general,   2.2
introduction,   2.1
means-tested benefits, for
  and see below
  generally,   2.3–2.34
National Health Service
  benefits, and
  amount payable,   12.14
  claims,   12.15
  common problems,   12.16
  generally,   12.13
tax credits, for,   2.35

**Assessment of means
  (community care)**
attendance allowance,   11.15
capital
  income support,   11.6

**Assessment of means (community
  care)** – *contd*
capital – *contd*
  social services'
    contribution,   11.11
council tax benefit,   11.17
disability living allowance,   11.15
domiciliary care,   11.2
effect of non-payment,   11.3
housing benefit,   11.16
income
  income support,   11.6
  social services'
    contribution,   11.11
income support
  capital,   11.6
  local authority-owned
    care homes,   11.9
  person assessed,   11.7
  registered independent
    homes,   11.8
  introduction,   11.1
pension credit
  capital,   11.6
  local authority-owned
    care homes,   11.9
  person assessed,   11.7
  registered independent
    homes,   11.8
  introduction,   11.1
residential care
  effect on other benefits,   11.14–11.17
  income support,   11.5–11.9
  introduction,   11.4
  pension credit,   11.5–11.9
  social services'
    contribution,   11.10–11.12
  value of claimants home,   11.13

Assessment of means (community care) – *contd*
social services'
    contribution
    capital, 11.11
    income, 11.12
value of claimants home, 11.13

Assessment of means (means-tested benefits)
capital
    disregarded sums, 2.12
    generally, 2.10
    nature requiring to be
      taken into account,
      of, 2.13–2.16
    notional sums, 2.16
    ownership, 2.14
    tariff income, 2.11
    valuation, 2.15
childminders, and, 2.27
child's income, 2.29
council tax benefit, 2.8
disregarded sums
    capital, 2.12
    child's income, 2.29
    earned income, 2.28
    other income, 2.33
employed earnings
    generally, 2.18
    net income, 2.21
housing benefit, 2.7
income
    disregarded sums, 2.28–2.29
    employed earnings, 2.18
    introduction, 2.17
    non-dependants' income, 2.34
    notional sums, 2.31
    other sums, 2.30

Assessment of means (means-tested benefits) – *contd*
income – *contd*
    self-employed earnings, 2.19–2.27
    treated as capital, 2.32
income-based jobseekers
    allowance, 2.5
income support, 2.4
introduction, 2.3
net income, 2.21
non-dependants' income, 2.34
notional capital, 2.16
notional income, 2.31
other income
    disregarded sums, 2.33
    generally, 2.30
    period of assessment, 2.20
partnerships, and, 2.27
pension credit, 2.9
period
    employed earnings, 2.18
    net income, 2.21–2.22
    other income, 2.20
    self-employed income, 2.19
self-employed income
    business expenses, 2.23
    childminders, and, 2.27
    drawings, 2.24
    generally, 2.19
    national insurance
      contributions, 2.25
    net income, 2.22–2.25
    net profit, 2.26
    partnerships, and, 2.27
    tax payments, 2.25
state pension credit, 2.9
tariff income, 2.11

Attendance allowance
amounts
2001/02,	1.13
2002/03,	1.12
2003/04,	1.11
2004/05,	1.10
2005/06,	1.9
2006/07,	1.7–1.8
'attention',	24.3
'bodily functions',	24.4
challenging decisions,	24.8
checklist,	24.10

claims
generally,	24.7
introduction,	4.1
common problems,	24.9
higher rate,	24.6
introduction,	24.1
lower rate,	24.2–24.5
residential care, and,	11.15
supervision,	24.5

Available for employment
contributory jobseekers allowance, and,	16.10
income-based jobseekers allowance, and,	7.4

B

Back to work bonus
income-based jobseekers allowance, and,	7.22

Backdating benefits
administrative,	4.39
automatic,	4.38
discretionary,	4.41
generally,	4.38
housing benefit, and,	9.37
pension credit, and,	25.13
special rules,	4.40

Basic element
working tax credits, and,	8.10

Benefit rates
2001/02,	1.13
2002/03,	1.12
2003/04,	1.11
2004/05,	1.10
2005/06,	1.9
2006/07,	1.7–1.8

Bereavement benefits
additional help,	22.10

amounts
generally,	22.6–22.8
2001/02,	1.13
2002/03,	1.12
2003/04,	1.11
2004/05,	1.10
2005/06,	1.9
2006/07,	1.7–1.8
basic rules,	22.2

bereavement allowance
amount payable,	22.8
generally,	22.5
bereavement payments,	22.3
carer's allowance, and,	19.2
challenging decisions,	22.12
checklist,	22.13

claims
generally,	22.11
introduction,	4.1
incapacity benefit, and,	17.1
introduction,	22.1
lump sum,	22.3
overlapping benefits rule,	22.9
retirement pension, and,	21.2
state maternity allowance, and,	20.12
types,	22.2

widow's parent's allowance
amount payable,	22.7

Bereavement benefits – *contd*
  widow's parent's allowance – *contd*
    generally,   22.4
Bereavement premium
  housing benefit, and,   9.20
  income support, and,   6.16
Budgeting loans
  amount payable,   13.6
  generally,   13.5
  repayment,   13.7

C

Capital
  disabled facilities grants,
    and,   10.6
  funeral expenses payment,
    and,   13.14
  housing benefit, and
    challenging decisions,   9.42
    disregard sums,   9.28
    introduction,   9.27
    taken into account,   9.29
  income-based jobseekers
    allowance, and,   7.20
  income support, and
    disregarded sums,   6.21
    generally,   6.20
    taken into account,   6.22
  means-tested benefits, and
    disregarded sums,   2.12
    generally,   2.10
    nature requiring to be
      taken into account,
      of,   2.13–2.16
    notional sums,   2.16
    ownership,   2.14
    tariff income,   2.11
    valuation,   2.15
  pension credit, and,   25.11
  residential care, and
    income support,   11.6

Capital – *contd*
  residential care, and – *contd*
    social services'
      contribution,   11.11
Care component
  amount payable,   23.2
  'attention',   23.6
  basic rules,   23.3
  'bodily functions',   23.7
  generally,   23.2
  introduction,   23.1
  qualifying conditions,   23.4–23.8
  'severely disabled',   23.5
  supervision test,   23.8
Carer's allowance
  amounts
    generally,   19.4
    2001/02,   1.13
    2002/03,   1.12
    2003/04,   1.11
    2004/05,   1.10
    2005/06,   1.9
    2006/07,   1.7–1.8
  backdating, and,   4.38
  bereavement benefits, and,   22.9
  cessation,   19.5
  challenging decisions,   19.7
  checklist,   19.9
  claimants,   19.3
  claims
    generally,   19.6
    introduction,   4.1
  common problems,   19.8
  incapacity benefit, and,   17.1
  introduction,   19.1
  overlapping benefits rule,   19.2
  retirement pension, and,   21.2
  state maternity allowance,
    and,   20.12

Carer's premium
housing benefit, and,   9.20
income support, and,   6.15

Challenging decisions
appeals
adjournment,   4.31
applications,   4.25
benefits,   4.11
Commissioner, to,   4.35–4.36
composition of tribunal,   4.26
Court of Appeal, to,   4.37
decisions of tribunals,   4.32–
                                        4.34
introduction,   4.23
leave to appeal,   4.35
medical examination,   4.27
oral hearings,   4.29–4.31
physical examinations,   4.28
postponement,   4.31
procedures,   4.30
record of hearing,   4.33
setting aside decisions,   4.34
tax credits,   4.10
time limits,   4.24
attendance allowance, and, 24.8
benefits,   4.11–4.22
bereavement benefits, and, 22.12
carer's allowance, and,   19.7
child benefit, and,   15.12
contributory jobseekers
allowance, and,   16.18
disability living allowance,
and,   23.18
discretionary housing
payments, and,   9.53
housing benefit, and
assessment of applicable
amount,   9.43
assessment of capital,   9.42
assessment of income,   9.42

Challenging decisions – *contd*
housing benefit, and – *contd*
assessment of rent,   9.41
change in circumstances,   9.44
introduction,   9.40
incapacity benefit, and,   17.15
income-based jobseekers
allowance, and,   7.24
income support, and,   6.32
industrial disablement
benefit, and,   18.10
parenthood benefits, and,   20.27
pension credit, and,   25.14
retirement pension, and,   21.11
Social Fund, and,   13.15
tax credits, and
generally,   8.19–8.20
introduction,   4.10

Change of circumstances
decisions, and,   4.8
discretionary housing
payments, and,   9.52
housing benefit, and
challenging decisions,   9.44
overpayment,   5.17
tax credits, and,   8.17

Child benefit
amounts
generally,   15.10
2001/02,   1.13
2002/03,   1.12
2003/04,   1.11
2004/05,   1.10
2005/06,   1.9
2006/07,   1.7–1.8
appeals, and,   4.23
backdating, and,   4.38
challenging decisions,   15.12
checklist,   15.13
'child',   15.5

Child benefit – *contd*
children abroad, 15.8
claimants
'child', 15.3
introduction, 15.2
persons abroad, 15.2
priority rules, 15.4
claims, and
generally, 15.11
introduction, 4.1
hospitalised children, 15.7
imprisoned children, 15.9
introduction, 15.1
local authority care, 15.9
persons abroad, 15.2
priority rules, 15.4
prisoners, 15.9
temporary absences, 15.6

Child support assessments
'Children First Scheme', 14.2
introduction, 14.1
maintenance calculation
affordability test, 14.7
exempt income, 14.6
introduction, 14.4
maintenance
requirement, 14.5
new system, 14.2
old system, 14.3
self-employed, 14.8

Child tax credit
administration
challenging decisions, 8.26
decisions, 8.25
payment, 8.24
transitional
arrangements, 8.27
amounts
2003/04, 1.11

Child tax credit – *contd*
amounts – *contd*
2004/05, 1.10
2005/06, 1.9
2006/07, 1.7–1.8
annual review, 8.19–8.20
appeal rights, 4.10
assessment of means, 2.35
calculation
apply taper, 8.17
assess income, 8.16
compare income to
threshold, 8.17
maximum credit for
relevant period, 8.15
challenging decisions, 8.26
change of circumstances, 8.17
checklist, 8.28
claims
generally, 4.4
introduction, 4.1
decisions
generally, 8.25
introduction, 4.6
elements, 8.13
eligibility, 8.12
end of year reconciliations, 8.18
generally, 8.11
income, 8.16
introduction, 8.1
legislation, 8.2
maximum amount
calculation, 8.15
generally, 8.13
overpayments, and
interest, 5.27
introduction, 5.24
mid-year reductions, 5.25
recovery methods, 5.26
payment, 8.24

Child tax credit – *contd*
primary legislation, 8.2
'reconciliation', 8.19
renewal, 8.21
review, 8.19–8.20
secondary legislation, 8.2
taper, 8.17
threshold, 8.17
timetable, 8.22
transitional arrangements, 8.27
Childcare costs
assessment, 3.17
housing benefit, and, 9.23
introduction, 3.16
Childcare element
working tax credits, and, 8.10
Childminders
means-tested benefits, and, 2.27
Children
cohabitation, and, 3.10
Child's income
means-tested benefits, and, 2.29
Civil partners
claims for the family, and, 3.3
Claimants
carer's allowance, and, 19.3
child benefit, and
'child', 15.3
introduction, 15.2
persons abroad, 15.2
priority rules, 15.4
contributory jobseekers
allowance, and
actively seeking work, 16.11
age, 16.5
available for
employment, 16.10
contribution conditions, 16.6–16.8
introduction, 16.4

Claimants – *contd*
contributory jobseekers allowance, and
– *contd*
remunerative
employment, 16.9
written agreement, 16.12
discretionary housing
payments, and, 9.49
housing benefit, and, 9.10
incapacity benefit, and, 17.5
income-based jobseekers
allowance, and, 7.3
income support, and, 6.3
industrial disablement
benefit, and, 18.3
National Health Service
benefits, and, 12.2
pension credit, and
guarantee credit, 25.4
savings credit, 25.5
statutory sick pay, and, 17.18
Claims
attendance allowance, and, 24.7
benefits, 4.3
bereavement benefits,
and,, 22.11
carer's allowance, and, 19.6
child benefit, and, 15.11
claimant unable to act, 4.5
contributory jobseekers
allowance, and, 16.17
disability living allowance,
and, 23.17
disabled facilities grants,
and, 10.9
discretionary housing
payments, and, 9.57–9.58
housing benefit, and, 9.39
incapacity benefit, and, 17.14

Claims – *contd*
income-based jobseekers
  allowance, and,   7.23
income support, and,   6.31
industrial disablement
  benefit, and,   18.7
introduction,   4.1
pension credit, and,   25.13
retirement pension, and,   21.10
statutory sick pay, and,   17.21–
     17.22
tax credits,   4.4
wrong benefit, for,   4.3

Claims for the family
childcare costs
  assessment,   3.17
  introduction,   3.16
civil partners,   3.3
cohabitation
  children,   3.10
  cohabitation,   3.5
  dependent children,   3.12–3.15
  excluded situations,   3.16
  financial arrangements,   3.8
  introduction,   3.4
  members of same
    household,   3.6
  public repute,   3.11
  sexual relationship,   3.9
  stable relationship,   3.7
dependent children
  introduction,   3.12
  membership of the
    household,   3.15
  'normally living' with
    claimant,   3.13
  'usually' live with
    claimant,   3.14
family unit
  civil partners,   3.3

Claims for the family – *contd*
family unit – *contd*
  introduction,   3.2
  married couples,   3.3
  unmarried couples,   3.4–3.16
introduction,   3.1
married couples,   3.3
unmarried couples
  children,   3.10
  cohabitation,   3.5
  dependent children,   3.12–3.15
  excluded situations,   3.16
  financial arrangements,   3.8
  introduction,   3.4
  members of same
    household,   3.6
  public repute,   3.11
  sexual relationship,   3.9
  stable relationship,   3.7

Cohabitation
children,   3.10
cohabitation,   3.5
dependent children
  introduction,   3.12
  membership of the
    household,   3.15
  'normally living' with
    claimant,   3.13
  'usually' live with
    claimant,   3.14
excluded situations,   3.16
financial arrangements,   3.8
introduction,   3.4
members of same
  household,   3.6
public repute,   3.11
sexual relationship,   3.9
stable relationship,   3.7

Cold weather payments
Social Fund, and,   13.1

Common parts
generally, 10.2

Community care
attendance allowance, 11.15
capital
  income support, 11.6
  social services'
    contribution, 11.11
council tax benefit, 11.17
disability living allowance, 11.15
domiciliary care, 11.2
effect of non-payment, 11.3
housing benefit, 11.16
income
  income support, 11.6
  social services'
    contribution, 11.11
income support
  capital, 11.6
  local authority-owned
    care homes, 11.9
  person assessed, 11.7
  registered independent
    homes, 11.8
introduction, 11.1
pension credit
  capital, 11.6
  local authority-owned
    care homes, 11.9
  person assessed, 11.7
  registered independent
    homes, 11.8
  introduction, 11.1
residential care
  effect on other benefits, 11.14–11.17
  income support, 11.5–11.9
  introduction, 11.4
  pension credit, 11.5–11.9

Community care – *contd*
residential care – *contd*
  social services'
    contribution, 11.10–11.12
  value of claimants home, 11.13
social services'
  contribution
    capital, 11.11
    income, 11.12
  value of claimants home, 11.13

Community care grants
Social Fund, and, 13.3

Contact lenses
National Health Service
  benefits, and 12.9

Contribution conditions
contributory jobseekers
  allowance, and, 16.6–16.8
incapacity benefit, and, 17.6–17.8

Contributory jobseekers allowance
actively seeking work, 16.11
age of claimant, 16.5
amounts
  generally, 16.14
  reductions, 16.15
  2001/02, 1.13
  2002/03, 1.12
  2003/04, 1.11
  2004/05, 1.10
  2005/06, 1.9
  2006/07, 1.7–1.8
appeals, and, 4.23
available for employment, 16.10
basic rules, 16.2
bereavement benefits, and, 22.9
challenging decisions, 16.18
checklist, 16.20

Contributory jobseekers allowance – *contd*

claimants

  actively seeking work,   16.11

  age,   16.5

  available for

    employment,   16.10

  contribution conditions,   16.6–16.8

  introduction,   16.4

  remunerative

    employment,   16.9

  written agreement,   16.12

claims

  generally,   16.17

  introduction,   4.1

common problems,   16.19

contribution conditions,   16.6–16.8

earned income,   16.15

incapacity benefit, and,   17.1

introduction,   16.1

Job Grant,   16.16

meaning,   16.1

overlapping benefits rule,   16.3

reduction,   16.15

remunerative employment,   16.9

suspension,   16.13

written agreement,   16.12

Council tax benefit

amounts

  2001/02,   1.13

  2002/03,   1.12

  2003/04,   1.11

  2004/05,   1.10

  2005/06,   1.9

  2006/07,   1.7–1.8

appeals, and,   4.23

assessment of means, and,   2.8

checklist,   9.47

Council tax benefit – *contd*

  claims, and,   4.1

  generally,   9.46

  membership of the

    household, and,   3.15

  residential care, and,   11.17

  second adult rebates,   9.47

Crisis loans

amount payable,   13.9

generally,   13.8

repayment,   13.10

D

Decisions

appeals

  adjournment,   4.31

  applications,   4.25

  benefits,   4.11

  Commissioner, to,   4.35–4.36

  composition of tribunal,   4.26

  Court of Appeal, to,   4.37

  decisions of tribunals,   4.32–4.34

  introduction,   4.23

  leave to appeal,   4.35

  medical examination,   4.27

  oral hearings,   4.29–4.31

  physical examinations,   4.28

  postponement,   4.31

  procedures,   4.30

  record of hearing,   4.33

  setting aside decisions,   4.34

  tax credits,   4.10

  time limits,   4.24

backdating benefits

  administrative,   4.39

  automatic,   4.38

  discretionary,   4.41

  generally,   4.38

  special rules,   4.40

Decisions – *contd*
challenges to
  benefits,   4.11–4.22
  tax credits,   4.10
change of circumstances,   4.8
generally,   4.6
HMRC, and,   4.10
interplay of benefits,   4.7
introduction,   4.1
revision of decisions
  introduction,   4.15
  late applications,   4.17
  subject to time
    limitations,   4.16
  that are revieaable at any
    time,   4.18
Secretary of State, by
  evidence,   4.14
  general,   4.11
  information,   4.14
  introduction,   4.12
  revisions,   4.15–4.18
  supersessions,   4.19
  suspension of benefit,   4.13
supersessions,   4.19
suspension of benefit
  failure to attend medical
    examination,   4.21
  generally,   4.20
  introduction,   4.13
  payment of suspended
    benefit,   4.22
tax credits
  appeal rights,   4.10
  generally,   8.25
  introduction,   4.6

Dental treatment
exempt persons,   12.7
introduction,   12.6
reduced charges,   12.8

Dependants' additions
amounts
  2001/02,   1.13
  2002/03,   1.12
  2003/04,   1.11
  2004/05,   1.10
  2005/06,   1.9
  2006/07,   1.7–1.8
backdating, and,   4.38

Dependent children
introduction,   3.12
membership of the
  household,   3.15
'normally living' with
  claimant,   3.13
'usually' live with claimant, 3.14

Disability element
working tax credits, and,   8.10

**Disability living
  allowance**
amounts
  2001/02,   1.13
  2002/03,   1.12
  2003/04,   1.11
  2004/05,   1.10
  2005/06,   1.9
  2006/07,   1.7–1.8
'attention',   23.6
'bodily functions',   23.7
care component
  amount payable,   23.2
  'attention',   23.6
  basic rules,   23.3
  'bodily functions',   23.7
  generally,   23.2
  introduction,   23.1
  qualifying conditions,   23.4–
                               23.8
  'severely disabled',   23.5
  supervision test,   23.8

Disability living allowance – *contd*
challenging decisions, 23.18
checklist, 23.20
claims
  generally, 23.17
  introduction, 4.1
common problems, 23.19
deaf and blind, 23.13
difficulty in walking, 23.12
introduction, 23.1
long-term disability
  requirement, 23.16
mental impairment, 23.14
mobility component
  deaf and blind, 23.13
  difficulty in walking, 23.12
  generally, 23.9
  higher rate, 23.11–23.14
  introduction, 23.1
  long-term disability
    requirement, 23.16
  lower rate, 23.15
  mental impairment, 23.14
  qualifying conditions, 23.10–23.15
residential care, and, 11.15
'severely disabled', 23.5
supervision test, 23.8
Disability premium
housing benefit, and, 9.20
income support, and
  enhanced, 6.13
  general, 6.12
  severe, 6.14
Disabled child element
child tax credits, and, 8.13
Disabled child premium
housing benefit, and, 9.20
income support, and, 6.8

Disabled facilities grants
applicable amount, 10.6
approval process, 10.10
calculation of contribution
  introduction, 10.5
  loan generation factors, 10.7
  procedure, 10.6
capital, 10.6
claims, 10.9
eligibility, 10.3
further grants, 10.8
generally, 10.3
housing allowance, 10.4
income, 10.6
means test, 10.4
premiums, 10.4
relevant works, 10.3
**Discretionary financial
assistance**
repairs, adaptations and
  improvements, 10.11
**Discretionary housing
payments (DHP)**
challenging decisions, 9.53
change of circumstances, 9.52
claimants, 9.49
claims, 9.57–9.58
duration, 9.50
effect on other benefits, 9.56
introduction, 9.48
notifications, 9.51
recovery, 9.55
termination, 9.54
Disqualification
incapacity benefit, and, 17.13
industrial disablement
  benefit, and, 18.9
Disregarded capital
housing benefit, and, 9.28
means-tested benefits, and, 2.12

Disregarded income
housing benefit, and,   9.22
means-tested benefits, and
    child's income,   2.29
    earned income,   2.28
    other income,   2.33
Domiciliary care
residential care, and,   11.2

E

Earnings
contributory jobseekers
    allowance, and,   16.15
employed
    generally,   2.18
    net income,   2.21
income support, and,   6.19
means-tested benefits, and
    generally,   2.18
    net income,   2.21
self-employed
    business expenses,   2.23
    childminders, and,   2.27
    drawings,   2.24
    generally,   2.19
    national insurance
       contributions,   2.25
    net income,   2.22–2.25
    net profit,   2.26
    partnerships, and,   2.27
    tax payments,   2.25
statutory sick pay, and,   17.19
Employment option
New Deal, and,   7.10
**End of year
    reconciliations**
tax credits, and,   8.18
Energy efficiency grants
generally,   10.12

**Enhanced disability
    premium**
housing benefit, and,   9.20
income support, and,   6.13
Environment task force
New Deal, and,   7.11
Evidence
incapacity, and,   17.9
Extended payments
housing benefit, and,   9.38
50+ element
working tax credits, and,   8.10

F

Family element
child tax credits, and,   8.13
Family premium
housing benefit, and,   9.20
income support, and,   6.6
Family unit
civil partners,   3.3
introduction,   3.2
married couples,   3.3
unmarried couples
    children,   3.10
    cohabitation,   3.5
    dependent children,   3.12–3.15
    excluded situations,   3.16
    financial arrangements,   3.8
    introduction,   3.4
    members of same
       household,   3.6
    public repute,   3.11
    sexual relationship,   3.9
    stable relationship,   3.7
Financial arrangements
cohabitation, and,   3.8
Fraud
overpayments, and
    housing benefit,   5.17

Fraud – *contd*
overpayments, and – *contd*
  payment continues too
    long,   5.4
Full-time education
housing benefit, and,   9.7
income support, and,   6.25
New Deal, and,   7.12
Funeral expenses
  payment
capital,   13.14
generally,   13.13

G

Gateway
New Deal, and,   7.9
Glasses
National Health Service
  benefits, and,   12.9
Group repair grants
generally,   10.2
Guarantee credit
calculation,   25.6
carer,   25.8
eligibility,   25.4
housing costs,   25.9
severe disability,   25.7
transitional amount,   25.10
Guardian's allowance
amounts
  2001/02,   1.13
  2002/03,   1.12
  2003/04,   1.11
  2004/05,   1.10
  2005/06,   1.9
  2006/07,   1.7–1.8
appeals, and,   4.23
backdating, and,   4.38

Guides to entitlement
carer for disabled person
  for more than 35
    hours per week,   1.20
incapable of work,   1.16
introduction,   1.14
not in work, under 60 and
  capable of work,   1.15
pensioner,   1.19
single parent not working
  more than 16 hours
    per week,   1.21
widow(er),   1.18
working more than 16
  hours per week,   1.17

H

HC2 and HC3 forms
assessment of means,   12.13
dental treatment,   12.8
sight tests,   12.10
travel costs to hospital for
  treatment,   12.11
HM Revenue and
  Customs (HMRC)
decisions, and,   4.10
Home
residential care, and,   11.13
Home renovation grants
claims, and,   4.1
disabled facilities grants
  approval process,   10.10
  calculation of
    contribution,   10.5–10.7
  claims,   10.9
  eligibility,   10.3
  further grants,   10.8
  generally,   10.3
  means test,   10.4
  relevant works,   10.3

Home renovation grants – *contd*
discretionary assistance
with repairs,
adaptations and
improvements, 10.11
energy efficiency grants, 10.12
introduction, 10.1
legislation, 10.2
types, 10.2

**Homeless persons
premium**
income-based jobseekers
allowance, and, 7.17
income support, and, 6.17

Hospitalised child
child benefit, and, 15.7

**Houses in multiple
occupation grants**
generally, 10.2

Housing allowance
disabled facilities grants,
and, 10.4

Housing benefit
see also Discretionary
housing payments
actual rent, 9.12
amounts
2001/02, 1.13
2002/03, 1.12
2003/04, 1.11
2004/05, 1.10
2005/06, 1.9
2006/07, 1.7–1.8
appeals, and, 4.23
applicable amount
challenging decisions, 9.43
introduction, 9.18
personal allowances, 9.19
premiums, 9.20

Housing benefit – *contd*
assessment of entitlement
actual rent, 9.12
introduction, 9.11
personal charges, 9.16
procedure, 9.17
rent elements table, 9.15
service charges, 9.13
support charges, 9.13
assessment of means, 2.7
backdated claims, 9.37
calculation
capital, 9.27–9.29
comparative element, 9.30
income, 9.21–9.26
introduction, 9.18
non-dependents, and, 9.31
personal allowances, 9.19
premiums, 9.20
capital
challenging decisions, 9.42
disregard sums, 9.28
introduction, 9.27
taken into account, 9.29
challenging decisions
assessment of applicable
amount, 9.43
assessment of capital, 9.42
assessment of income, 9.42
assessment of rent, 9.41
change in circumstances, 9.44
introduction, 9.40
change in circumstances
challenging decisions, 9.44
overpayments, 5.17
childcare costs, 9.23
claimants, 9.10
claims
generally, 9.39
introduction, 4.1

Housing benefit – *contd*
common problems,   9.45
comparative element,   9.30
council tax benefit, and
   and see Council tax
   benefit
   generally,   9.46–9.47
disregarded capital,   9.28
disregarded income,   9.22
eligibility,   9.10
excluded claimants
   full-time students,   9.7
   introduction,   9.4
   more than £16,000
     capital,   9.6
   no legal liability to pay
     rent,   9.5
   receipt of housing costs
     from other sources,   9.8
extended payments,   9.38
generally,   9.2
income
   challenging decisions,   9.42
   childcare costs,   9.23
   claimants working more
     than 30 hours,   9.24
   disregarded sums,   9.22
   introduction,   9.21
   maintenance,   9.26
   other income,   9.25
introduction,   9.1
maintenance,   9.26
membership of the
   household, and,   3.15
non-dependents, and,   9.31
other income,   9.25
overlapping provisions,   9.35
overpayments, and
   change of circumstances,   5.17
   fraud,   5.17

Housing benefit – *contd*
overpayments, and – *contd*
   introduction,   5.14
   offsetting,   5.16
   recovery methods,   5.18–5.23
   summary,   5.15
   types,   5.15
personal allowances,   9.19
personal charges,   9.16
premiums,   9.20
rent elements,   9.15
residential care, and
   generally,   11.16
   introduction,   9.36
service charges,   9.13
special circumstances, in
   introduction,   9.32
   overlapping provisions,   9.35
   person in residential
     care,   9.36
   temporary absences,   9.34
   two properties,   9.33
support charges   9.13
temporary absences,   9.34
two properties,   9.33
working more than 30
   hours,   9.24
Housing costs
income-based jobseekers
   allowance, and,   7.18
income support, and,   6.18

I
Imprisoned children
child benefit, and,   15.9
Incapacity benefit
amounts
   generally,   17.2
   2001/02,   1.13
   2002/03,   1.12
   2003/04,   1.11

Incapacity benefit – *contd*
  amounts – *contd*
    2004/05, — 1.10
    2005/06, — 1.9
    2006/07, — 1.7–1.8
  assessment of incapacity
    content, — 17.12
    generally, — 17.10
    personal capability, — 17.12
  backdating, and, — 4.38
  bereavement benefits, and, — 22.9
  carer's allowance, and, — 19.2
  challenging decisions, — 17.15
  checklist, — 17.17
  claimants, — 17.5
  claims
    generally, — 17.14
    introduction, — 4.1
  common problems, — 17.16
  contribution conditions, — 17.6–17.8
  disqualification, — 17.13
  evidence of incapacity, — 17.9
  incapacity
    assessment, — 17.10–17.12
    evidence, — 17.9
  introduction, — 17.1
  overlapping benefits rule, — 17.1
  permitted work, — 17.3
  retirement pension, and, — 21.2
  state maternity allowance,
    and, — 20.12

Income
  disabled facilities grants,
    and, — 10.6
  housing benefit, and
    challenging decisions, — 9.42
    childcare costs, — 9.23
    claimants working more
      than 30 hours, — 9.24

Income – *contd*
  housing benefit, and – *contd*
    disregarded sums, — 9.22
    introduction, — 9.21
    maintenance, — 9.26
    other income, — 9.25
  income-based jobseekers
    allowance, and, — 7.19
  income support, and, — 6.19
  means-tested benefits, and
    disregarded sums, — 2.28–2.29
    employed earnings, — 2.18
    introduction, — 2.17
    non-dependants' income, — 2.34
    notional sums, — 2.31
    other sums, — 2.30
    self-employed earnings, — 2.19–2.27
    treated as capital, — 2.32
  pension credit, and, — 25.11
  residential care, and
    income support, — 11.6
    social services'
      contribution, — 11.11
  tax credits, and, — 8.16

**Income-based jobseekers
  allowance**
  actively seeking work, — 7.5
  amounts
    2001/02, — 1.13
    2002/03, — 1.12
    2003/04, — 1.11
    2004/05, — 1.10
    2005/06, — 1.9
    2006/07, — 1.7–1.8
  appeals, and, — 4.23
  assessment of means, — 2.5
  available for employment, — 7.4
  back to work bonus, and, — 7.22

Income-based jobseekers allowance –
  contd
calculation
  capital,   7.20
  comparative element,   7.21
  housing costs,   7.18
  income,   7.19
  introduction,   7.14
  personal allowances,   7.15
  premiums,   7.16–7.17
capital,   7.20
challenging decisions,   7.24
checklist,   7.26
claimants,   7.3
claims
  generally,   7.23
  introduction,   4.1
common problems,   7.25
comparative element,   7.21
eligibility
  actively seeking work, 7.5
  available for
    employment,   7.4
  introduction,   7.3
  suspension of benefit, 7.7
  written jobseekers
    agreement,   7.6
homeless persons
  premium,   7.17
housing costs,   7.18
income,   7.19
introduction,   7.1
Job Grant,   7.22
meaning,   7.1
membership of the
  household, and,   3.15
nature,   7.2
New Deal
  employment option,   7.10
  environment task force, 7.11

Income-based jobseekers allowance –
  contd
New Deal – *contd*
  full-time education,   7.12
  Gateway,   7.9
  introduction,   7.8
  sanctions and penalties, 7.13
  training option,   7.12
  voluntary sector option, 7.11
personal allowances,   7.15
premiums
  generally,   7.16
  homeless persons,   7.17
retirement pension, and, 21.2
state maternity allowance,
  and,   20.12
suspension of benefit,   7.7
written jobseekers
  agreement,   7.6

Income support
amounts
  2001/02,   1.13
  2002/03,   1.12
  2003/04,   1.11
  2004/05,   1.10
  2005/06,   1.9
  2006/07,   1.7–1.8
appeals, and,   4.23
applicable amount
  housing costs,   6.18
  introduction,   6.4
  personal allowances,   6.5
  premiums,   6.6–6.17
assessment of means,   2.4
bereavement premium, 6.16
calculation
  capital,   6.20–6.22
  comparative element, 6.23
  housing costs,   6.18
  income,   6.19

Income support – *contd*
calculation – *contd*
    introduction, 6.4
    personal allowances, 6.5
    premiums, 6.6–6.17
capital
    disregarded sums, 6.21
    generally, 6.20
    taken into account, 6.22
carer's premium, 6.15
challenging decisions, 6.32
checklist, 6.34
claimants, 6.3
claims, and
    generally, 6.31
    introduction, 4.1
common problems, 6.33
comparative element, 6.23
disability premium
    enhanced, 6.13
    general, 6.12
    severe, 6.14
disabled child premium, 6.8
earnings, 6.19
excluded claimants
    full-time education, 6.25
    person in residential
      care, 6.30
    16—17 year olds, 6.26
    strikers, 6.28
    young people living at
      home in further
      education, 6.27
family premium, 6.6
full-time education, and, 6.25
homeless persons
    premium, 6.17
housing costs, 6.18
income, 6.19
introduction, 6.1

Income support – *contd*
maintenance payments, 6.19
membership of the
    household, and, 3.15
pensioner premium
    enhanced, 6.10
    general, 6.9
    higher, 6.11
person in residential care,
    and, 6.30
personal allowances, 6.5
premiums
    bereavement, 6.16
    carer's, 6.15
    disability, 6.12–6.14
    disabled child, 6.8
    family, 6.6
    homeless persons, 6.17
    introduction, 6.6
    pensioner, 6.9–6.11
residential care, and
    capital, 11.6
    local authority-owned
      care homes, 11.9
    person assessed, 11.7
    registered independent
      homes, 11.8
16—17 year olds, and, 6.26
strikers, and, 6.28
tariff income, 6.19
young people living at
    home in further
    education, and, 6.27

Income tax
amounts
    2001/02, 1.13
    2002/03, 1.12
    2003/04, 1.11
    2004/05, 1.10
    2005/06, 1.9

Income tax – *contd*
amounts – *contd*
2006/07, 1.7–1.8

Incorrect award
overpayments, and, 5.13

Industrial disablement benefit
amounts
generally, 18.5
2001/02, 1.13
2002/03, 1.12
2003/04, 1.11
2004/05, 1.10
2005/06, 1.9
2006/07, 1.7–1.8
appeals, and, 4.23
backdating, and, 4.38
calculation, 18.4
challenging decisions, 18.10
checklist, 18.12
claimants, 18.3
claims
generally, 18.7
introduction, 4.1
common problems, 18.11
disqualification, 18.9
duration, 18.8
eligibility, 18.6
introduction, 18.1
national insurance
contributions, and, 18.1

Industrial injuries benefit
appeals, and, 4.23
claims, and, 4.1

Interest
overpayment of tax credits,
and, 5.27

Invalid vehicle scheme
appeals, and, 4.23

J

Job Grant
contributory jobseekers
allowance, and, 16.16
income-based jobseekers
allowance, and, 7.22

Jobseekers allowances
amounts
2001/02, 1.13
2002/03, 1.12
2003/04, 1.11
2004/05, 1.10
2005/06, 1.9
2006/07, 1.7–1.8
appeals, and, 4.23
claims, and, 4.1
contributory
and see Contributory
jobseekers allowance
basic rules, 16.2–16.16
challenging decisions, 16.18
checklist, 16.20
claims, 16.17
common problems, 16.19
introduction, 16.1
income-based
and see Income-based
jobseekers allowance
basic rules, 7.2–7.22
challenging decisions, 7.24
checklist, 7.26
claims, 7.23
common problems, 7.25
introduction, 7.1
membership of the
household, and, 3.15

L
Loans from Social Fund
budgeting loans
  amount payable, 13.6
  generally, 13.5
  repayment, 13.7
crisis loans
  amount payable, 13.9
  generally, 13.8
  repayment, 13.10
introduction, 13.4
repayment, 13.10
Local authority care
child benefit, and, 15.9
Lone parent element
working tax credits, and, 8.10

M
Maintenance payments
housing benefit, and, 9.26
income support, and, 6.19
Married couples
claims for the family, and, 3.3
Maternity allowance
amounts
  generally, 20.10–20.11
  2001/02, 1.13
  2002/03, 1.12
  2003/04, 1.11
  2004/05, 1.10
  2005/06, 1.9
  2006/07, 1.7–1.8
backdating, and, 4.38
basic rules, 20.9
bereavement benefits, and, 22.9
carer's allowance, and, 19.2
challenging decisions, 20.27
checklist, 20.28
claims, 20.14
duration, 20.13

Maternity allowance – *contd*
earnings, 20.11
eligibility, 20.9
incapacity benefit, and, 17.1
introduction, 20.8
overlapping benefits rule, 20.12
retirement pension, and, 21.2
Maternity pay
amounts
  generally, 20.4–20.5
  2001/02, 1.13
  2002/03, 1.12
  2003/04, 1.11
  2004/05, 1.10
  2005/06, 1.9
  2006/07, 1.7–1.8
backdating, and, 4.38
basic rules, 20.3
challenging decisions, 20.27
checklist, 20.28
claims, 20.7
duration, 20.6
earnings, 20.5
eligibility, 20.3
introduction, 20.2
Maternity grant
Social Fund, and, 13.12
Means assessment
and see Assessment of
  means
disabled facilities grants,
  and, 10.4
generally, 2.2
introduction, 2.1
means-tested benefits, for, 2.3–2.34
National Health Service
  benefits, and, 12.13–12.16
tax credits, for, 2.35

Means-tested benefits
assessment
and see Assessment of
means
generally, 2.3–2.34
membership of the
household, and, 3.15
Medical examinations
appeals, and, 4.27
Minor works grants
generally, 10.2
Mobility component
deaf and blind, 23.13
difficulty in walking, 23.12
generally, 23.9
higher rate, 23.11–23.14
introduction, 23.1
long-term disability
requirement, 23.16
lower rate, 23.15
mental impairment, 23.14
qualifying conditions, 23.10–
23.15

N
**National Health Service
benefits**
assessment of means
amount payable, 12.14
claims, 12.15
common problems, 12.16
generally, 12.13
checklist, 12.17
claimants, 12.2
contact lenses, 12.9
dental treatment
exempt persons, 12.7
introduction, 12.6
reduced charges, 12.8
glasses, 12.9

National Health Service benefits –
contd
HC2 and HC3 forms
assessment of means, 12.13
dental treatment, 12.8
sight tests, 12.10
travel costs to hospital
for treatment, 12.11
introduction, 12.1
low income scheme
amount payable, 12.14
claims, 12.15
common problems, 12.16
generally, 12.13
prescriptions
exempt persons, 12.4
introduction, 12.3
refunds for exempt
persons, 12.5
sight tests
generally, 12.9
reduced charges, 12.10
travel costs to hospital for
treatment, 12.11–12.12
**National insurance
contributions**
amounts
2001/02, 1.13
2002/03, 1.12
2003/04, 1.11
2004/05, 1.10
2005/06, 1.9
2006/07, 1.7–1.8
industrial disablement
benefit, and, 18.1
Net income
means-tested benefits, and, 2.21
New Deal
employment option, 7.10
environment task force, 7.11

New Deal – *contd*
full-time education, 7.12
Gateway, 7.9
introduction, 7.8
sanctions and penalties, 7.13
training option, 7.12
voluntary sector option, 7.11
Non-dependants
housing benefit, and, 9.31
Non-dependants' income
means-tested benefits, and, 2.34
Notional capital
means-tested benefits, and, 2.16
Notional income
means-tested benefits, and, 2.31

O
Offsetting
housing benefit, and, 5.16
Oral hearings
appeals, and, 4.29–4.31
Other income
housing benefit, and, 9.25
means-tested benefits, and
disregarded sums, 2.33
generally, 2.30
period of assessment, 2.20
Overlapping benefits rule
bereavement benefits, and, 22.9
carer's allowance, and, 19.2
contributory jobseekers
allowance, and, 16.3
generally, 5.2
housing benefit, and, 9.35
incapacity benefit, and, 17.1
retirement pension, and, 21.2
state maternity allowance,
and, 20.12
Overpayments
appeals, and, 4.23

Overpayments – *contd*
housing benefit
change of circumstances, 5.17
fraud, 5.17
introduction, 5.14
offsetting, 5.16
recovery methods, 5.18–5.23
summary, 5.15
types, 5.15
incorrect award, 5.13
introduction, 5.1
overlapping benefits rules, 5.2
payment continues too
long
calculation, 5.10
capital, and, 5.11
determination, 5.12
failure to disclose, 5.6–5.8
'fraudulently or
otherwise', 5.4
introduction, 5.3
misrepresentation, 5.5
persons from whom
recovery can be
made, 5.9
tax credits
interest, 5.27
introduction, 5.24
mid-year reductions, 5.25
recovery methods, 5.26

P
Parenthood benefits
challenging decisions, 20.27
checklist, 20.28
introduction, 20.1
state maternity allowance
amount payable, 20.10–20.11
basic rules, 20.9
claims, 20.14

Parenthood benefits – *contd*
state maternity allowance – *contd*
 duration, 20.13
 earnings, 20.11
 eligibility, 20.9
 introduction, 20.8
 overlapping benefits
   rule, 20.12
statutory adoption pay
 amount payable, 20.21
 dismissal, and, 20.26
 eligibility, 20.20
 introduction, 20.19
statutory maternity pay
 amount payable, 20.4–20.5
 basic rules, 20.3
 claims, 20.7
 duration, 20.6
 earnings, 20.5
 eligibility, 20.3
 introduction, 20.2
statutory paternity pay
 adoption, 20.22–20.23
 birth, 20.24–20.25
 dismissal, and, 20.26
statutory sick pay, and, 20.26
Sure Start Maternity
   Grants
 amount payable, 20.17
 basic rules, 20.16
 claims, 20.18
 eligibility, 20.16
 introduction, 20.15
types, 20.1
Partnerships
self-employed income, and, 2.27
Paternity pay
adoption, 20.22–20.23
amounts
 generally, 20.21

Paternity pay – *contd*
amounts – *contd*
 2001/02, 1.13
 2002/03, 1.12
 2003/04, 1.11
 2004/05, 1.10
 2005/06, 1.9
 2006/07, 1.7–1.8
backdating, and, 4.38
birth, 20.24–20.25
dismissal, and, 20.26
Payment
tax credits, and, 8.24
Payments on account
appeals, and, 4.23
Pension credit
amounts
 2006/07, 1.7–1.8
assessment of means, 2.9
backdating
 generally, 25.13
 introduction, 4.38
basic rules, 25.2
capital, 25.11
challenging decisions, 25.14
checklist, 25.17
claimants
 guarantee credit, 25.4
 savings credit, 25.5
claims, 25.13
guarantee credit
 calculation, 25.6
 carer, 25.8
 eligibility, 25.4
 housing costs, 25.9
 severe disability, 25.7
 transitional amount, 25.10
income, 25.11
income periods, 25.15
introduction, 25.1

Pension credit – *contd*
residential care, and
  capital, 11.6
  generally, 25.16
  local authority-owned
    care homes, 11.9
  person assessed, 11.7
  registered independent
    homes, 11.8
  introduction, 11.1
savings credit
  calculation, 25.12
  eligibility, 25.5
Pensioner premium
enhanced, 6.10
general, 6.9
higher, 6.11
Person abroad
appeals, and, 4.23
child benefit, and, 15.2
Personal allowances
housing benefit, and, 9.19
income-based jobseekers
  allowance, and, 7.15
income support, and, 6.5
Personal charges
housing benefit, and, 9.16
Physical examinations
appeals, and, 4.28
Premiums
disabled facilities grants,
  and, 10.4
housing benefit, and, 9.20
income-based jobseekers
  allowance, and,
  generally, 7.16
  homeless persons, 7.17
income support, and
  bereavement, 6.16
  carer's, 6.15

Premiums – *contd*
income support, and – *contd*
  disability, 6.12
  disabled child, 6.8
  enhanced disability, 6.13
  enhanced pensioner, 6.10
  family, 6.6
  higher pensioner, 6.11
  homeless persons, 6.17
  introduction, 6.6
  pensioner, 6.9
  severe disability, 6.14
Prescriptions
exempt persons, 12.4
introduction, 12.3
refunds for exempt
  persons, 12.5
Priority rules
child benefit, and, 15.4
Prisoners
child benefit, and, 15.9
Public repute
cohabitation, and, 3.11

R
Rates of benefit
2001/02, 1.13
2002/03, 1.12
2003/04, 1.11
2004/05, 1.10
2005/06, 1.9
2006/07, 1.7–1.8
Reciprocal agreements
appeals, and, 4.23
Reconciliations
tax credits, and, 8.18
Recovery of payments
appeals, and, 4.23
discretionary housing
  payments, and, 9.55

Recovery of payments – *contd*
overpayments, and
  housing benefit,   5.18–5.23
payment continues too
  long,   5.9
tax credits,   5.26

Reduced earnings allowance
backdating, and,   4.38

Renewal
tax credits, and,   8.21

Renovation grants
generally,   10.2

Rent
housing benefit, and
  challenging decisions,   9.41
  generally,   9.12
  table,   9.15

Residential care
housing benefit, and,   9.36
income support, and,   6.30

Residential care (assessment of means)
attendance allowance,   11.15
capital
  income support,   11.6
  social services'
    contribution,   11.11
council tax benefit,   11.17
disability living allowance,   11.15
effect on other benefits,   11.14–11.17
housing benefit,   11.16
income
  income support,   11.6
  social services'
    contribution,   11.11
income support
  capital,   11.6

Residential care (assessment of means) – *contd*
income support – *contd*
  local authority-owned
    care homes,   11.9
  person assessed,   11.7
  registered independent
    homes,   11.8
introduction,   11.4
pension credit
  capital,   11.6
  local authority-owned
    care homes,   11.9
  person assessed,   11.7
  registered independent
    homes,   11.8
social services'
  contribution
  capital,   11.11
  income,   11.12
value of claimants home,   11.13

Retirement pension
amounts
  2001/02,   1.13
  2002/03,   1.12
  2003/04,   1.11
  2004/05,   1.10
  2005/06,   1.9
  2006/07,   1.7–1.8
backdating, and,   4.38
bereavement benefits, and,   22.9
carer's allowance, and,   19.2
categories
  A,   21.4–21.6
  B (for married women),   21.7
  B (for widows and
    widowers),   21.8
  D,   21.9
  introduction,   21.3
challenging decisions,   21.11

Retirement pension – *contd*
checklist, 21.13
claims
  generally, 21.10
  introduction, 4.1
common problems, 21.12
incapacity benefit, and, 17.1
introduction, 21.1
overlapping benefits rule, 21.2
state maternity allowance,
  and, 20.12
Review
tax credits, and, 8.19–8.20
Revision of decisions
introduction, 4.15
late applications, 4.17
subject to time limitations, 4.16
that are revieaable at any
  time, 4.18

S
Same household
cohabitation, and, 3.6
Savings credit
calculation, 25.12
eligibility, 25.5
Second adult element
working tax credits, and, 8.10
**Secretary of State's
  decisions**
evidence, 4.14
general, 4.11
information, 4.14
introduction, 4.12
revision
  introduction, 4.15
  late applications, 4.17
  subject to time
    limitations, 4.16

Secretary of State's decisions – *contd*
revision – *contd*
  that are revieaable at any
    time, 4.18
supersessions, 4.19
suspension of benefit
  failure to attend medical
    examination, 4.21
  generally, 4.20
  introduction, 4.13
  payment of suspended
    benefit, 4.22
Self-employed earnings
business expenses, 2.23
child support assessments,
  and, 14.8
childminders, and, 2.27
drawings, 2.24
generally, 2.19
national insurance
  contributions, 2.25
net income, 2.22–2.25
net profit, 2.26
partnerships, and, 2.27
tax payments, 2.25
Service charges
housing benefit, and, 9.13
Severe disability element
working tax credits, and, 8.10
**Severe disability
  premium**
housing benefit, and, 9.20
income support, and, 6.14
**Severely disabled child
  element**
child tax credits, and, 8.13
**Severe disablement
  allowance**
amounts
  2001/02, 1.13

Severe disablement allowance – *contd*
amounts – *contd*
2002/03, 1.12
2003/04, 1.11
2004/05, 1.10
2005/06, 1.9
2006/07, 1.7–1.8
bereavement benefits, and, 22.9
carer's allowance, and, 19.2
incapacity benefit, and, 17.1
retirement pension, and, 21.2
state maternity allowance,
and, 20.12

Sexual relationship
cohabitation, and, 3.9

Sick pay
amounts
generally, 17.19
2001/02, 1.13
2002/03, 1.12
2003/04, 1.11
2004/05, 1.10
2005/06, 1.9
2006/07, 1.7–1.8
cessation, 17.20
checklist, 17.23
claimants, 17.18
claims, 17.21–17.22
earnings, 17.19
eligibility, 17.18
notification of absence, 17.22
parenthood benefits, and, 20.26

Sight tests
generally, 12.9
reduced charges, 12.10

16—17 year olds
income support, and, 6.26

Social Fund
appeals, and, 4.23

Social Fund – *contd*
budgeting loans
amount payable, 13.6
generally, 13.5
repayment, 13.7
challenging decisions, 13.15
cold weather payments, 13.1
community care grants, 13.3
crisis loans
amount payable, 13.9
generally, 13.8
repayment, 13.10
discretionary payments
community care grants, 13.3
generally, 13.1
introduction, 13.2
loans, 13.4–13.9
funeral expenses payment
capital, 13.14
generally, 13.13
introduction, 13.1
loans
budgeting loans, 13.5–13.7
crisis loans, 13.8–13.9
introduction, 13.4
repayment, 13.10
maternity grant, 13.12
regulated payments
funeral expenses
payment, 13.13–13.14
generally, 13.1
introduction, 13.11
maternity grant, 13.12
Sure Start Maternity
Grant, 13.12

Social services'
contribution
residential care, and
capital, 11.11
income, 11.12

Social security rates
2001/02,   1.13
2002/03,   1.12
2003/04,   1.11
2004/05,   1.10
2005/06,   1.9
2006/07,   1.7–1.8

Stable relationship
cohabitation, and,   3.7

State maternity allowance
amounts
  generally,   20.10–20.11
  2001/02,   1.13
  2002/03,   1.12
  2003/04,   1.11
  2004/05,   1.10
  2005/06,   1.9
  2006/07,   1.7–1.8
backdating, and,   4.38
basic rules,   20.9
bereavement benefits, and,   22.9
carer's allowance, and,   19.2
challenging decisions,   20.27
checklist,   20.28
claims,   20.14
duration,   20.13
earnings,   20.11
eligibility,   20.9
incapacity benefit, and,   17.1
introduction,   20.8
overlapping benefits rule,   20.12
retirement pension, and,   21.2

State pension
amounts
  2001/02,   1.13
  2002/03,   1.12
  2003/04,   1.11
  2004/05,   1.10
  2005/06,   1.9

State pension – *contd*
amounts – *contd*
  2006/07,   1.7–1.8
backdating, and,   4.38
carer's allowance, and,   19.2
categories
  A,   21.4–21.6
  B (for married women),   21.7
  B (for widows and
    widowers),   21.8
  D,   21.9
  introduction,   21.3
challenging decisions,   21.11
checklist,   21.13
claims
  generally,   21.10
  introduction,   4.1
common problems,   21.12
incapacity benefit, and,   17.1
introduction,   21.1
overlapping benefits rule,   21.2
state maternity allowance,
  and,   20.12

State pension credit
amounts
  2006/07,   1.7–1.8
assessment of means,   2.9
backdating
  generally,   25.13
  introduction,   4.38
basic rules,   25.2
capital,   25.11
challenging decisions,   25.14
checklist,   25.17
claimants
  guarantee credit,   25.4
  savings credit,   25.5
claims,   25.13
guarantee credit
  calculation,   25.6

State pension credit – *contd*
guarantee credit – *contd*
  carer, 25.8
  eligibility, 25.4
  housing costs, 25.9
  severe disability, 25.7
  transitional amount, 25.10
 income, 25.11
 income periods, 25.15
 introduction, 25.1
 residential care, and
  capital, 11.6
  generally, 25.16
  local authority-owned
   care homes, 11.9
  person assessed, 11.7
  registered independent
   homes, 11.8
  introduction, 11.1
 savings credit
  calculation, 25.12
  eligibility, 25.5

Statutory adoption pay
 amounts
  generally, 20.21
  2001/02, 1.13
  2002/03, 1.12
  2003/04, 1.11
  2004/05, 1.10
  2005/06, 1.9
  2006/07, 1.7–1.8
 backdating, and, 4.38
 challenging decisions, 20.27
 checklist, 20.28
 dismissal, and, 20.26
 eligibility, 20.20
 introduction, 20.19

Statutory maternity pay
 amounts
  generally, 20.4–20.5

Statutory maternity pay – *contd*
 amounts – *contd*
  2001/02, 1.13
  2002/03, 1.12
  2003/04, 1.11
  2004/05, 1.10
  2005/06, 1.9
  2006/07, 1.7–1.8
 backdating, and, 4.38
 basic rules, 20.3
 challenging decisions, 20.27
 checklist, 20.28
 claims, 20.7
 duration, 20.6
 earnings, 20.5
 eligibility, 20.3
 introduction, 20.2

Statutory paternity pay
 adoption, 20.22–20.23
 amounts
  generally, 20.21
  2001/02, 1.13
  2002/03, 1.12
  2003/04, 1.11
  2004/05, 1.10
  2005/06, 1.9
  2006/07, 1.7–1.8
 backdating, and, 4.38
 birth, 20.24–20.25
 dismissal, and, 20.26

Statutory sick pay
 amounts
  generally, 17.19
  2001/02, 1.13
  2002/03, 1.12
  2003/04, 1.11
  2004/05, 1.10
  2005/06, 1.9
  2006/07, 1.7–1.8
 cessation, 17.20

Statutory sick pay – *contd*
checklist, 17.23
claimants, 17.18
claims, 17.21–17.22
earnings, 17.19
eligibility, 17.18
notification of absence, 17.22
parenthood benefits, and, 20.26
Strikers
income support, and, 6.28
Supersession
decisions, and, 4.19
Support charges
housing benefit, and, 9.13
Sure Start Maternity Grant
amount payable
generally, 20.17
2001/02, 1.13
2002/03, 1.12
2003/04, 1.11
2004/05, 1.10
2005/06, 1.9
2006/07, 1.7–1.8
backdating, and, 4.38
basic rules, 20.16
challenging decisions, 20.27
checklist, 20.28
claims, 20.18
eligibility, 20.16
introduction, 20.15
Social Fund, and, 13.12
Suspension of benefit
appeals, and, 4.23
contributory jobseekers
allowance, and, 16.13
failure to attend medical
examination, 4.21
generally, 4.20

Suspension of benefit – *contd*
income-based jobseekers
allowance, and, 7.7
introduction, 4.13
payment of suspended
benefit, 4.22
30-hour element
working tax credits, and, 8.10

T
Taper
tax credits, and, 8.17
Tariff income
income support, and, 6.19
means-tested benefits, and, 2.11
Tax credits
administration
challenging decisions, 8.26
decisions, 8.25
payment, 8.24
transitional
arrangements, 8.27
amounts
2003/04, 1.11
2004/05, 1.10
2005/06, 1.9
2006/07, 1.7–1.8
annual review, 8.19–8.20
appeal rights, 4.10
assessment of means, 2.35
calculation
apply taper, 8.17
assess income, 8.16
compare income to
threshold, 8.17
maximum credit for
relevant period, 8.15
challenging decisions, 8.26
change of circumstances, 8.17
checklist, 8.28

Tax credits – *contd*
child tax credit
  elements,   8.13
  eligibility,   8.12
  generally,   8.11
  introduction,   8.1
  maximum amount,   8.13
claims
  generally,   4.4
  introduction,   4.1
decisions
  generally,   8.25
  introduction,   4.6
end of year reconciliations,   8.18
income,   8.16
introduction,   8.1
legislation,   8.2
maximum amount for
  relevant period,   8.15
overpayments, and
  interest,   5.27
  introduction,   5.24
  mid-year reductions,   5.25
  recovery methods,   5.26
payment,   8.24
primary legislation,   8.2
'reconciliation',   8.19
renewal,   8.21
review,   8.19–8.20
secondary legislation,   8.2
taper,   8.17
threshold,   8.17
timetable,   8.22
transitional arrangements,   8.27
types,   8.2
working tax credit
  disability conditions,   8.9
  elements,   8.10
  eligibility,   8.4–8.8
  generally,   8.3

Tax credits – *contd*
working tax credit – *contd*
  introduction,   8.1
  maximum amount,   8.10
Temporary absences
child benefit, and,   15.6
housing benefit, and,   9.34
Training
New Deal, and,   7.12
Travel costs
hospital treatment, and,   12.11–12.12
Two properties
housing benefit, and,   9.33

U
Unmarried couples
children,   3.10
cohabitation,   3.5
dependent children
  introduction,   3.12
  membership of the
   household,   3.15
  'normally living' with
   claimant,   3.13
  'usually' live with
   claimant,   3.14
excluded situations,   3.16
financial arrangements,   3.8
introduction,   3.4
members of same
  household,   3.6
public repute,   3.11
sexual relationship,   3.9
stable relationship,   3.7
Up-rating
appeals, and,   4.23

V
Voluntary sector option
New Deal, and,   7.11

Index

W
Widowed parents allowance
additional help,	22.10
amount payable,	22.7
basic rules,	22.2
bereavement benefits, and,	22.9
carer's allowance, and,	19.2
challenging decisions,	22.12
checklist,	22.13
claims,	22.11
generally,	22.4
introduction,	22.1
overlapping benefits rule,	22.9
incapacity benefit, and,	17.1
retirement pension, and,	21.2
state maternity allowance, and,	20.12

Widow's benefit
backdating, and,	4.38

Working families tax credit
amounts	
2001/02,	1.13
2002/03,	1.12

Working tax credit
and see Tax credits
administration	
challenging decisions,	8.26
decisions,	8.25
payment,	8.24
transitional arrangements,	8.27
amounts	
2003/04,	1.11
2004/05,	1.10
2005/06,	1.9
2006/07,	1.7–1.8
annual review,	8.19–8.20
appeal rights,	4.10

Working tax credit – *contd*
assessment of means,	2.35
calculation	
apply taper,	8.17
assess income,	8.16
compare income to threshold,	8.17
maximum credit for relevant period,	8.15
challenging decisions,	8.26
change of circumstances,	8.17
checklist,	8.28
claims	
generally,	4.4
introduction,	4.1
decisions	
generally,	8.25
introduction,	4.6
disability conditions,	8.9
elements,	8.10
eligibility	
claimant over 25 without children,	8.7
claimant over 50,	8.8
couple with dependent child,	8.5
disabled claimant,	8.6
introduction,	8.4
lone parent with dependent child,	8.5
end of year reconciliations,	8.18
generally,	8.3
income,	8.16
introduction,	8.1
legislation,	8.2
maximum amount	
calculation,	8.15
generally,	8.10
overpayments, and	
interest,	5.27

Working tax credit – *contd*
  overpayments, and – *contd*

introduction,	5.24
mid-year reductions,	5.25
recovery methods,	5.26
payment,	8.24
primary legislation,	8.2
'reconciliation',	8.19
renewal,	8.21
review,	8.19–8.20
secondary legislation,	8.2
taper,	8.17
threshold,	8.17
timetable,	8.22

Working tax credit – *contd*

transitional arrangements,	8.27
types,	8.2

Written agreements

contributory jobseekers allowance, and,	16.12
income-based jobseekers allowance, and,	7.6

Y

Young people living at home in further education

income support, and,	6.27